WITHDRAWN

Library of Congress Catalog Card Number: 78-68691

OUR MARITIME HERITAGE:

MARITIME DEVELOPMENTS AND THEIR IMPACT ON AMERICAN LIFE

James M. Morris

University Press of America™

To Nancy

Outstanding wife, mother, and friend

PREFACE

When I first approached the study of American maritime history a number of years ago, certain weaknesses in the literature of the field became evident to me. First, no adequate coverage of maritime events was available for classroom use and for general reading and reference. Second, saltwater and freshwater maritime events were virtually always treated as separate entities. Coverage of one area was usually approached without sufficient reference to the other. Third, maritime events were seldom examined adequately within the broader panorama of the nation's total development, resulting in general neglect in most Americans' consciousness of factors touching their everyday lives. Indeed, I originally titled the manuscript "The Neglected Element."

This book was written to correct those weaknesses. It has been organized and written for classroom use either as a text or as collateral reading for American history, American civilization, or American economic history courses. It will also serve well as an introduction to a fascinating subject for anyone interested in knowing more about America's maritime past and present. Since no general survey can possibly be complete in any or all areas, I have relied heavily on others' work, and I have appended a select bibliography to each of the sixteen chapters to carry the interested reader further into the subject.

Many friends and colleagues have aided me over the past three years in completing this work. Dr.'s Phyllis A. Hall, Theodora P. Bostick, Timothy E. Morgan, and my good friend, the late William Parks, all from the Department of History, Christopher Newport College, have read all or parts of the manuscript in one or another of its various stages and have made valuable suggestions. My fellow maritime historians Alexander Crosby Brown and Dr. Clark G. Reynolds have read the entire manuscript and have challenged or corrected my facts or interpretations where justly deserved. Paul G. Zomberg, an editor friend of many years, cleaned up my prose in more places than I would like to acknowledge. Mrs. Linda Kelsey and the staffs of the Mariners Museum and Captain John Smith Libraries have been patient and helpful even when I was not. Miss Ellen Layman and Mrs. Webber Casey have been typists par excellence.

To all of these people and to my mentor, Dr. George Engberg of the University of Cincinnati, I offer my heartfelt thanks. If, after all their work, there are errors of fact, interpretation, or form in this work, the burden of fault must justly be mine.

Finally, my thanks to Nancy. The dedication page says it all.

J.M.M.

Newport News, Virginia
November, 1978

CONTENTS

The maritime unions
Shipbuilding
Flags of convenience
Soviet challenges
The Panama Canal
The Great Lakes-St. Lawrence system and the inland
  waterways
The merchant marine and national defense

CHAPTER I. COLONIAL FISHING: THE FOUNDATION IS LAID

The history and development of any nation are determined to a considerable degree by its geography. Its topography, the fertility of its soil, the amount of annual rainfall, the types and abundance of available land and sea life, the location and direction of its rivers, and its proximity to other areas are prime determinants of how a nation's people develop and shape themselves. For example, Great Britain is an island kingdom; its history of dependence on the waters that surround it for transportation and its interdependence in later years with territories beyond its borders for critical food supplies, raw materials, and markets are obvious. Again, Russia is a giant land essentially landlocked except in the distant Far East. Its rivers do not flow to the open seas, but rather to the icebound Arctic or to southern waters through territories claimed by others. This factor has moved Russia in the last four centuries to attempt to gain by various means easier access to the outside world. Its soil, its size, and its northern climate have also meant that it has had a constant struggle to feed its people adequately. As another example, the arid stretches of North Africa and the Near East impelled the peoples inhabiting this vast, relatively waterless region toward a nomadic, tribal basis of existence--until, of course, it was discovered that beneath the great oceans of sand there exist uncounted billions of barrels of precious petroleum crude. These Arabic nations now find their lives being profoundly improved or at least altered by the sedimentary deposits of millions of years of geological development.

Examples could be multiplied a hundredfold. Holland and its profitable co-existence with the sea, the comparative isolation of mountainous Switzerland, the grassy veld of South Africa, the jungled archipelago that makes up the Philippines, and the frigid wastes of Iceland are prominent illustrations of how geography can influence a nation's development. The point is clear: a nation's history is largely determined by its geography, plus the way in which its people respond to its natural resources. The wide belt of land and resources across the center of the North American continent, an expanse including the colonial areas that become the United States of America in 1791 and the lands added by westward expansion since then, plus its adjoining waters, is no exception. Indeed, to understand fully the history of the United States as it developed over almost four centuries, it is necessary to comprehend the land and the surrounding seas upon which its people have lived and worked. This comprehension is particularly necessary for understanding its crucial colonial beginnings.

GEOGRAPHIC SETTING. During the colonial period, the history of that part of North America which eventually became the United States took place upon the North Atlantic coastal waters and upon the stretch of land between the shoreline and the Appalachian Mountain range. The land con-

1

sists, first, of a coastal plain extending from the mouth of the Hudson River to the south. This long coastal plain gradually widens from the Hudson south until it reaches a width of about 200 miles in southern Georgia. This region, reclaimed from the sea by the forces of nature, is favored with soils suitable for tilling, so its people turned to agriculture in colonial times. Its economic development was advanced, too, by the presence within its confines of Delaware Bay and Chesapeake Bay, shallow estuaries that allowed for navigable waterways and provided ample harbors. Its rivers and bays served as highways of transit in and out of the soil-rich region.

North and east of the Hudson River, to as far as Cape Cod, the former outer coastal plain is submerged, allowing less land for agriculture, but not to the extent of seriously hindering the area's agricultural and commercial development, which flourished because of the proximity of the rivers and the ocean to the farming regions contained there. The northern coastal plain's greatest asset in early times was probably the Hudson River which penetrated far into the interior in an almost straight line to the north and eventually joined with the Mohawk flowing from the west. Along this vital line of rivers the Dutch built a very profitable fur trade with the Indians. Indeed, the fur trade via the rivers was carried on throughout the whole area of the piedmont, or Appalachian plateau, and the coastal plain from the Connecticut River basin in this region southward, including the Delaware, Lehigh, Schuylkill, Susquehanna, Potomac, and the James River valleys.

But from Cape Cod north, the continental plain is wholly submerged, as is most of the piedmont, leaving the shoreline of the North Atlantic at the very face of the mountains. This geographic submersion left the area that came to be called New England with little agricultural land. Furthermore, the soil was thin and unconducive to cultivation. The short and unnavigable rivers cutting through the land were broken by rapids and waterfalls, but hundreds of fine harbors existed where the ocean met the mountains. In addition, near the shoreline were forests of great magnitude that could be exploited for the building of sailing vessels. Because of these factors New England was geographically married to the sea from early colonial times.

Underneath the seas fronting the eastern coast of the North American continent there exists a wide, flat area called the Continental Shelf, a submerged extension of the coastal plain. It is like an underwater table gently sloping seaward from the shoreline to a depth of 100 fathoms (600 feet), whence it drops more suddenly to much greater depths. The bottom point of the Shelf is found at the southeast coast of Florida, where the Shelf is fairly narrow. From here it gradually becomes wider as it runs northward except for the projection of the North Carolina shoreline at Cape Hatteras. It broadens rapidly and noticeably from the New Jersey shore to the east and north to a width of 400 miles off the coast of Newfoundland. This broad shelf also contains numerous areas within it where the underwater land mass rises up from the ocean bottom to form underwater platforms called "banks" where the water is more shallow than in the surrounding area. The most notable of these subterranean plateaus off the coast of North America are the Grand Banks off Newfoundland and Georges Bank off the New England Coast.

2

This extensive undersea table was extremely important to human development on the adjoining North American land mass because all great fishing grounds are located in comparably shallow waters. The Continental Shelf was rich in sea life. The shallow waters near land and over the Continental Shelf produce organic carbon and dissolved minerals in sufficient quantity to support marine life. Furthermore, oceans in the stormy high and middle latitudes of the earth are the best generators of fish life because of the amount of aquatic life is determined by the amounts of plankton available in the water, and this, in turn, depends upon the amount of mineral salts in the water. Stormy seas produce a stirring up of the water and thus replenish the salt supply from the ocean floor. The mineral salts produce greater quantities of the valuable planktonic plant life upon which the fish feed. Third, invertibrates among sea life are found principally on hard-bottomed shoals, the sea surface which is found on the American continental shelf. Fourth, on these particular fishing grounds the use of drag nets for greater fish yields is practicable because of the smooth ocean bottom; these nets could not be used, for example, on the rocky coraline shoals of the tropics. Fifth, the Continental Shelf off New England, Nova Scotia, and Newfoundland is particularly conducive to certain types of fish life because of the cool water temperatures found there. These waters are made more habitable for those types of fish by the chilly waters of the Arctic brought down by the Labrador Current which disappears off the New England coast when met by the more powerful Gulf Stream flowing to the north and east. Cold-water fish have a temperature tolerance of 35° to 50°. Such a temperature is always available somewhere in New England and in the waters of the Maritime Province throughout the year. In the summer it is most abundant on the Nova Scotia banks and in deeper water. In the winter it is most abundant in the Gulf of Maine, off southern New England, and along the inshore fishing grounds.

With all these geographic factors present--and the Continental Shelf is clearly the key to the whole situation--a wealth of fish was discovered from Long Island to the Grand Banks during earlier centuries. Fish were everywhere in great abundance. They ate practically anything, and therefore took the baited hook, the chief method of harvesting the sea at that time. The large size of the fish thus caught made hook-fishing remunerative, since the fish were of the firm-fleshed variety. They, therefore, were well adapted for drying and salting, the only means then available for preserving them for the market and eventual consumption. New England, Nova Scotia, and Newfoundland fishing grounds, for all of these reasons of geography and animal biology, were among the very best in the world throughout pre-colonial and colonial times. Consequently, these waters became objects of concern, exploitation, and conflict among European nations from the early 16th century on; and they subsequently emerged as objects of concern, wealth, and conflict between England and some of its American colonies. This contention helped lead to warfare and permanent division in the late 18th century.

FISHING IN PRE-COLONIAL TIMES. Fishing in the North Atlantic waters was carried on by Europeans from at least the time of the Middle Ages. Both the Norsemen in the 9th century and the Basques from northern Spain in the 10th century sent whaling boats into the northern oceans. Centuries before the voyages of Columbus there was extensive fishing off the coast

3

of Iceland by Basques, by Bretons from France, and by Englishmen. Some
authorities argue that this fishing was not confined to Icelandic waters,
but extended to Greenland and perhaps to the Grand Banks off Newfoundland.
Exact evidence of the extent of this fishing between the 9th and the late
15th centuries cannot be found, and the details of these early ventures
are lost for all times. But the picture becomes clearer from the end of
the 15th century on, because European explorers of that period not only
visited these valuable fishing grounds off the North American coast, but
also recorded their observations faithfully. For that reason, the story
can be told with a great amount of certainty from the 15th century on, a
tale of a fishing industry that flourished for four of the most eventful
centuries in the history of Western man.

The story of the North Atlantic fishing industry in the 16th century
is primarily the chronicle of the growth of fishing off Newfoundland and
its neighboring banks by various European powers, and in particular of
the conflict there between England and France, although Portugal and Spain
were also very heavily involved for a considerable period of time.

Apparently the first Englishman to know of the Newfoundland fisheries
was the explorer John Cabot, who, on his first voyage in 1497, discovered
the large island and returned to tell the English of the rich fishing
grounds he had found nearby. The first Europeans to arrive off Newfoundland
in the 16th century for the purpose of fishing were probably the French and
the Portuguese who reached the area between 1504 and 1506. It is clear
that Norman and Breton vessels had also reached Newfoundland by 1509. By
1522, French fishermen had erected between forty and fifty houses on the
shores of Newfoundland for use during the summer fishing season. That the
English were also active in the area, however, is clear from the adventures
of Master Richard Hore who arrived off Newfoundland in 1536. After landing
and suffering famine to the point of cannibalism, and finally casting lots
to decide who should be killed so that some might live, Hore's English crew
was saved from death by the arrival of a French ship. The English promptly
took the vessel from the French and, after leaving the French crew on the
Newfoundland shore with food to await passage home by some other vessel, set
sail for England and arrived home safely. The French government was highly
incensed at this action, and King Henry VII made recompense out of his own
pocket for the misdeed.

It would appear that from this time on English vessels visited the
Newfoundland coast with great regularity. Rules regarding fishing expeditions
to the area are found in acts of Parliament in both 1540 and 1547, and existing records show also that in 1547 the English captured twenty-five French
ships with their cargoes of fish in these waters. These European fishing
boats were often of considerable size. Records show that the majority of
the French vessels sent out from La Rochelle were of fifty to eighty tons
in cargo capacity and carried a crew of eighteen to twenty-five men.

New World fisheries were destined to expand in the 16th century because
of the fact that some European nations weak in agricultural development but
having abundant supplies of cheap salt, such as Portugal, Spain, and France,
looked to the fisheries to feed their people. The fishermen's interests
were aided by the dominance of large Catholic populations in each country

who lived under Church rules proscribing the eating of meat on certain days of the week. But the development of fisheries by these West European countries, as well as by Holland, soon led to the exportation of fish to other countries, particularly to England, and thus fish became an important commodity of European trade. By the middle of the 16th century, the cod in particular was an item of tremendous importance both to those European nations exploiting it with fisheries off Newfoundland and the banks, and to those nations forced to import large quantities of fish for their own people.

Within the context of this international rivalry in fish, England's actions in the late 16th century become understandable. Gradually a shift took place during these decisive years from England's dependence upon its East Coast ports with their fishing grounds located off the coasts of Iceland, to dependence upon the West Country ports, just beginning to concentrate upon the mosre profitable Newfoundland fisheries. This change put England in a better competitive position vis-à-vis its foreign competitors such as Spain, Portugal, and France, and soon forced a decline in the Spanish and Portuguese operations. England was able to shift from importing fish to exporting the commodity, especially to the Mediterranean. In addition, English efforts to expand its market for light-salted fish from Newfoundland, especially in sending dry fish to the Mediterranean countries in exchange for salt supplies, also enabled the nation to increase its shipping and fully utilize its expanding merchant fleet. English expansion of its Newfoundland operations in the late 16th century is borne out in a letter to the chronicler Hakluyt in 1577 telling of fifty ships per year operating in the Newfoundland fishing grounds, although it would be mistaken to assume that the English were dominating the Newfoundland fisheries. As a matter of fact, in 1578 it was reported that at least 150 French vessels were off the Newfoundland coast and that the Gallic fishermen had also set up temporary posts and stations at various locations in the Gulf of St. Lawrence to dry and cure their catches.

Nevertheless, England was in the race for the North American fishing grounds in a most determined way, and it is no surprise that Sir Humphrey Gilbert in 1583 claimed Newfoundland and all the land within 200 leagues of the island (about 600 miles) in the name of the English Crown. At the end of the 16th century it was estimated that England had 200 ships in the Newfoundland fisheries and that this industry alone furnished employment for over 10,000 men and boys. But even with this expansion, by 1583 the English fishermen still furnished only one-third of the supply of fish needed in the country, fish being one of the chief elements in the people's diet. Because the Dutch had a firm hold on the fishing grounds in European waters, the English looked to America as a means of offsetting the Dutch fishing industry's dominance elsewhere, perhaps by colonies in North America. Englishmen recognized, too, that they could obtain such valuable shipbuilding commodities as pitch, tar, and masts from the colonies in America and thus could lessen their dependence on the Baltic countries.

17TH-CENTURY DEVELOPMENT. Bartholomew Gosnold in 1602 sailed to New England and attempted to make a settlement there. Although Gosnold is credited with naming Cape Cod for the great quantity of that fish caught in its vicinity, his plans for a permanent settlement fell through. Nevertheless, his adventures in the New World were published almost immediately

5

after his return to England, and Englishmen were again reminded of the wonderous fishing potential of the area. Gosnold's report argued that the fishing was even better there than off Newfoundland: ". . . the sculls [schools] of mackeral, herrings, cod, and other fish, that we daily saw as we went and came from the shore, were wonderful; and . . . were [in] but seven fathoms water, and within less than a league of the shore, when in Newfoundland they fish in forty or fifty fathoms water, and far off." Gosnold's praise of New England as being more advantageous than Newfoundland was echoed by Martin Pring, who visited the same waters in 1603, and by James Rosier's description of the voyage of George Way-mouth to the area in 1605. The blessings of the New England coast were also sung by the colonists who returned to England after Sir John Popham's abortive attempt to plant a permanent colony at the mouth of the Kennebec River in 1607. Thus by the time of the planting of the first permanent English colony in the New World in Virginia in 1607, the potential wealth of America's fisheries was well known, and, indeed, was cited by the Virginia colonists as one reason for emigrating to the new land across the sea.

The New England fisheries and those to the north attracted most of the attention of the colonists and the authorities in England. Captain John Smith, the leader of the Virginia venture, sailed to the New England coast in 1614 and, after naming both New England and Plymouth harbor, re-turned to England to issue a report in 1616. This famous report by Smith described how in the vicinity of Monhegan Island off the coast of Maine the ship's crew took 47,000 fish, which were sold upon their return to England. Smith's description of New England was glowing. He described the fertility of the soil, the abundance of timber, the various wild animals available, the small number of persons who would be needed to exploit the abundance, and also the fish:

> In March, Aprill, May, and halfe Iune, here is Cod in abundance; in May, Iune, and August, Mullet and Sturgion . . . Herring . . . the Salvuages compare their store in the Sea, to the haires of their heads . . . . In the end of August, September, October, and Nouember, you haue Cod againe, to make Cor fish, or Poore John; and each hundred [fish] is as good as two or three hundred in the Newfound Land . . . .

Smith went on to name the fish available in New England waters:

> Whales, Grampus [a whale fifteen feet in length], . . . Turbut [a large flounder of thirty to forty pounds], Sturgion, Cod, Hake, Haddock, Cole . . . , Shark, Macherell, herring, Mullet, Bas[s]e . . . , Pearch, Eels, Crabs, Lobsters, Muskles, Wilkes [a large marine snail], Oysters . . . . and Clamps [clams] . . . .

There could be no doubt of Smith's enthusiasm for New England and for nature's bounty he had discovered there, and within the next decade-and-a-half a great number of settlements were made on the New England coast for the purpose of fishing. In this the Plymouth settlement was an exception, because the Puritans came for other reasons, but even these non-fishermen colonists at Plymouth were forced to turn to the sea for food in order to survive, although they did not succeed in establish-

6

ing fishing as an industry because of their lack of skill and equipment. The fisheries were one of the more dynamic factors impelling European discovery and exploration of the New World in pre-colonial times. The fishing possibilities on the American coast, along with national and religious interests, a spirit of adventure and daring, a desire to find the wealth of the illusive Indies, and the search for the Northwest Passage, acted as a magnet to impel Europeans to turn to the New World as a part of their future development and strength and to attempt to surpass one another in their continuing contests for dominance at home and abroad.

In this competition the Portuguese and Spanish fisheries soon faded. The fishermen of both these two Iberian nations could not compete with the English, not only because of greater aggressiveness on the part of the English merchant-fisherman combination, but also because of English piracy upon their ships in Newfoundland. The Spanish, in recognition of English domination and their own inability to compete successfully, agreed by treaty in 1604 to open their home ports to English ships bringing fish into the country either from English ports or directly from the New World. By this decision, Newfoundland and New England cod in particular, for which there was much demand on the Iberian peninsula, became an important item of trade for England and a means of augmenting the wealth of the nation. Thus in the first half of the 17th century, England successfully built a commercial empire based on the lucrative Newfoundland and New England fishing activities and on its carrying trade with Spain. In this latter commercial process, as in fishing off Newfoundland, England's chief competitor was France, but this rivalry did not extend to New England proper, where the English planted their colonies far removed from French fishing expeditions.

If New England had no problem with competition from French fishing vessels, the colonists there did have a problem with developing their valuable fishing resource because of a lack of clear direction from the Crown. There was no question that New England would prove immensely valuable to England through its output of furs, grains, forests products, and fish. Its value was clearly recognized from the beginning. The question was just how these resources could best be developed for the benefit of the mother country. The fisheries, besides being very important to England for the development of its trade network, served as a training ground for its navy. Would they best be allowed to develop in relative freedom, or under the control of the Crown, in order to assure the greatest benefit to all?

The first instinct of the Crown was to grant monopoly charters so that control could rigorously be maintained. In 1620 Sir Ferdinando Gorges was granted a new charter to establish the Council of New England. This charter allowed Gorges exclusive rights to the New England fishing grounds. Gorges had insisted on the new charter because the old charter of 1606 lacked this monopoly provision and Virginia fishermen were encroaching upon "his" fishing grounds. In theory this new charter would assure to Gorges both an adequate catch and full control of the New England waters. But the delivery of the charter was delayed because of complaints of Virginia fishermen, as well as of English fishermen working

the New England waters; and, taking advantage of the delay, members of
the House of Commons introduced a bill that would have allowed freer
fishing off New England. However, Commons adjourned in 1621 before a
vote was taken on the bill, and the charter was delivered to Gorges during the ensuing recess. Nevertheless, its provisions were weakened by
a subsequent Order in Council which allowed New England and Virginia
fishing vessels to fish in each others' waters. The confused situation
continued throughout the 1620's, with Commons trying to open up the
fisheries to fishermen of other colonies and of the home country, and
the House of Lords opting for granting monopolies to favored companies.
But the charter of the Massachusetts Bay Company, issued in 1629, gave
the subjects of that colony the right to fish in adjoining waters. Thus
Gorges' monopoly was broken, and a precedent was set for the use of the
fisheries by the colonists themselves. This decision was very important
to the New England fisheries; it meant that the Crown was altering its
stance to defend the rights of the colonists to develop the fisheries
without the encumbrances of monopolies such as that held by Gorges. The
controversy and change in policy also drove most English fishermen out of
the New England fisheries to the Newfoundland area, insuring little competition for the American colonists engaged in the lucrative fishing
trade.

It must be noted that the development of the Newfoundland fisheries
was along quite another tack from that of New England. This difference
was very important to their history as time went on. The Newfoundland
fisheries were developing quite as rapidly as, or more so than, the New
England fisheries during the early 17th century; but there were significant differences between them. By 1634 the Newfoundland fisheries regularly employed more than 18,000 men and about 500 ships. But of the
persons involved, only about 500 were permanent residents, and these were
scattered all along the coast. The settlers were far outnumbered by non-
resident English fishermen. The cause of this imbalance lay in the failure
of schemes for permanent colonization such as Lord Baltimore's first colony
at Avalon which was begun with high hopes in 1621, but which never fulfilled the nobleman's dreams owing to the rigors of the northern winters
on the early colonists. These failures left the industry firmly in the
hands of the West Country fishermen instead. The causes of the failure
of colonies on Newfoundland are many and varied, but the net result was
that the development of Newfoundland and its valuable fishing industry
was left in the hands of Englishmen who went home in the winter rather
than in the hands of colonists, and control was always exercised solely
for the benefit of the persons of the home country. Accordingly, while
New England developed permanent colonies having economic fortunes of their
own and resisting English encroachments upon what they considered their
rights and privileges, the Newfoundland settlers were always small in
number and under the direct or indirect control of the Crown. Both economically and politically, New England and Newfoundland were set on di-
vergent courses early in their histories, and ended up taking different
stances regarding the mother country at the time of their full development in the late 18th century.

The Pilgrims were not fishermen by trade and did not come to
America to develop that industry, yet early in their years of settlement

they found themselves turning to the sea. In 1624 they sent a ship to England loaded with fish that they had cured with their own salt. The next year they followed with two shiploads of fish and furs. By 1628 they had established trade with the Dutch on the Hudson River in both corn and fish; and by 1630, fishing had been established also at nearby Salem. In 1633, fishing had been likewise instituted at Dorchester, Marblehead, and Scituate; and so important had the industry become to Massachusetts that in 1639 the colony's vessels engaged in fishing were exempted from taxes for a period of seven years. In 1641 the Plymouth colony built a ship for the fisheries of over forty tons, and the next year two men were given permission to build fishing stages for the curing of fish caught in nearby waters.

That New England would turn to the harvest of the nearby sea is hardly surprising, considering the wealth of sea-life found in adjoining waters. Cod in the Gulf of Maine averaged about thirty-five pounds, a good ten pounds heavier than those caught on the banks. Newfoundland cod weighed only about ten to twelve pounds and Labrador cod only three to four pounds on the average. A Salem minister in 1630, after describing the abundance of fish as "almost beyond believing," went on to portray the catch of bass as being so bountiful that the fishermen's nets "ordinarily take more than they are able to hall [sic] to land, and for want of boats and men they are constrained to let many go after they have taken them, and yet sometimes they fill two boats at a time with them...." This to say nothing of whales, mackerel, codfish, herring, turbot, sturgeon, and all types of shellfish. That same year, the first resident governor of Massachusetts, John Winthrop, reported taking with a few hooks sixty-seven cod, "some a yard and a half long and a yard in compass," in addition to other types of sea life; and a contemporary of Winthrop thanked God that the people "in the absence of bread" had "feasted themselves with fish" as Christ had done for His followers in the wilderness. In 1636 the Reverend Hugh Peter, a Salam minister, induced his flock to raise capital to build up the fishing industry there, as the people of Boston, Marblehead, Gloucester, and Manchester were doing in their towns. By 1670, Massachusetts fishermen were even intruding regularly on the Newfoundland banks.

Obviously, fishing meant much to New England by the middle of the 17th century. Since the fishermen could follow the migrations of the cod as they withdrew to the deeper waters in the spring and then returned to spawn in the gulfs and shallower waters in the fall, fishing could be pursued all year around. This all-season fishing gave New England a group of permanent consumers of other goods and gave agriculture a year-round market for its goods. Furthermore, those farmers who tilled the soil from spring to fall could find ready employment in the fisheries during slack seasons on the farm. The catches of fish, too, provided food for the fishermen's tables, in addition to providing a commodity that set New England on the road to trade. By 1641, Massachusetts alone sent 300,000 dried fish to market, and soon moved into the West Indian trade by selling its fish in return for molasses, rum, and bills of credit. The New England fisherman had the obvious advantage, moreover, of being close to his fishing grounds all year, as contrasted to the fishermen of Newfoundland, who came out from European homes during the season. With

9

all of these advantages and their application of natural talent and industry to them, New England fishermen constantly grew in number, and the prosperity of the region grew as well.

Consequently, New England fishing thrived in the latter half of the 17th century, and the New England fishermen took advantage of every opportunity that gave them superiority over their rivals. For example, the fishermen from New England solved the problem of drying fish caught on the offshore banks by sending out small ships to catch the fish and salt them down before returning. Upon their return to shore, the men would wash off the salt and dry the fish. The larger vessels coming from France or England to the North American fisheries had to anchor in the harbors and depend upon boats fishing in this limited area for their catches. Thus because of their nearness to their source of supply, the New England fishermen had the ability to fish both off shore and in the deep with no problem of preservation, an advantage not possessed by larger vessels from across the Atlantic. Furthermore, New England fishermen were most anxious to move into the Newfoundland fisheries after 1670, the very period during which the English government was trying to prevent permanent colonization there, even to the extent of burning down the homes of the settlers in the area. The English could drive the permanent settlers out of Newfoundland; they could not drive New England fishing vessels from its coasts and offshore banks. By 1675, Massachusetts alone had 665 vessels in the Newfoundland fisheries, vessels that furnished employment for more than 4,000 seamen in the trade. These vessels and their crews made an annual catch of 350,000 to 400,000 quintals in these grounds (a quintal equalled 100 fish originally, but because of size differences and spoiling, it was usually reckoned at 120 fish). It was clear to everyone that New England, led by Massachusetts, was moving into the fishing industry in a major way and taking advantage of every opportunity of fortune or hard work to establish itself in an impregnable position.

Boston in 1664 had 14,300 men engaged directly or indirectly in the fishing trade and a fleet of 1,300 fishing boats. The older towns of Massachusetts had been joined by Ipswich and Charlestown in the trade, and the Isle of Shoals alone had 1,500 fishermen. By the close of the 17th century, it was estimated, Massachusetts' exports of cod amounted to $400,000, and New England harbors shipped out an excess of ten million pounds of cured fish every year. France had seen its fishing fleets partially destroyed by wars with the English. The English fishing fleets had suffered during the Civil War and the difficulties that followed, the number of vessels dropping from about 250 vessels in 1640 or less than 100 in 1680. Spanish and Portuguese vessels had long disappeared from North American waters. American colonial vessels, and New England vessels in particular, had taken advantage of everything offered to them and had grown to preeminence in the waters off New England, Nova Scotia, and Newfoundland.

New England had gained also from an influx of fishermen from Newfoundland. By 1717, it was estimated, 1,300 fishermen had migrated to New England to take advantage of the better fishing and working conditions there. This exodus from Newfoundland caused no little consternation in the mother country since that northern fishing colony had long been envisioned as the "cradle of seamen" for England, but was becoming a "cradle"

for New England instead. Accordingly, New England shipmasters putting
in at Newfoundland were placed under bond guaranteeing they would not
take fishermen out; but apparently smuggling was very common, and the
exodus from Newfoundland continued. The result of this loss of manpower
was higher labor costs in Newfoundland and lower costs in New England, a
reality attested to by the fact that New England fish were definitely
underselling the Newfoundland products in the European markets. New
England clearly had many advantages after a century of drawing much of
its living from the sea and was surging ahead of its foreign and domestic competitors.

And yet the New England fishermen did not have a clear field in the
fisheries by any means since French fishermen were still solidly established along the coasts and in the waters off Newfoundland and Nova
Scotia, a fact well known and deeply resented by the colonial fishermen.
At the time of the Treaty of St. Germain in 1632, Charles I of England
had relinquished all places in Canada, Acadia (Nova Scotia), and Cape
Breton Island occupied by English subjects to the King of France. Although this agreement had been repudiated by Oliver Cromwell in 1654 and
the English had subsequently retaken Acadia, by the Treaty of Breda in
1667 France was awarded Acadia again. This French ownership of Acadia
had been confirmed by the Treaty of London in 1686, wherein the American
possessions of both France and England had been assented to, but the territorial limits of the individual possessions had not been defined and
frequent clashes continued. Whatever the exact legal claims of the French
to parts of the American coast, the presence of the French fishermen was
resented by the New England fishermen, who wanted the French expelled from
America entirely, particularly since the French were now claiming exclusive right to the fisheries of Nova Scotia and Cape Breton, indeed to all
territory east of the Kennebec River. The New England fishermen charged
also that the French were exacting tribute from their vessels off the
coast of Acadia and were inciting the Indians against them.

It was with a great deal of enthusiasm, then, that the colonists
joined with the mother country during King William's War (the War of the
League of Augsburg, 1689-97) in attempting to drive the French from Acadia.
Sir William Phips led a successful expedition against Acadia, but, much to
the consternation of the fishermen, all captured French territories in the
New World were returned to the French by the Treaty of Ryswick in 1697.
The New England fishermen were back where they had started, with the French
firmly established on "their" fishing grounds. During the years following
the war, the French fishing fleet in the northern waters reached a total
of 400 to 500 vessels, all armed and determined to resist any New England
challenges to its fishing rights.

18TH-CENTURY EXPANSION. When war broke out again between France and
England in 1702, the colonists were again most willing to seize the French
claims if possible in this Queen Anne's War (the War of the Spanish Succession, 1702-13). In 1710, the New Englanders equipped armed vessels entirely on their own and twice attempted the conquest of Nova Scotia (Acadia).
Finally, with 1,500 men and a fleet of thirty transport vessels, they
joined with English forces and took the valuable French possession. But at
the Treaty of Utrecht in 1713, the American colonists were again doomed to
a settlement of frustration. Acadia was ceded to England, and the French

were excluded from fishing within thirty leagues of the coast from Sable
Island to the southwest; but the French were allowed to keep Cape Breton
Island in the Gulf of St. Lawrence and all the islands at its mouth and
were allowed to land and dry their catches of fish on part of the Newfoundland coast, even though Newfoundland had been ceded to England as
part of the settlement. Although the New England fisherman now had a
monopoly off the coast of Maine and in the Bay of Fundy, as well as the
shore and bank fisheries of Nova Scotia--plus an equal chance in the other
fisheries--the French had not been excluded and were still allowed in the
valuable fishing grounds off Newfoundland. That the French had not been
effectively excluded and would take full advantage of whatever they had
preserved at Utrecht became obvious when they soon colonized Cape Breton
Island and began the 25-year project of building a strong fortress at
Louisbourg to protect their rights in the area. By 1721, the French
fishing fleet was as strong as ever, and their fishing industry in the
area was flourishing. New England's problem remained. France was firmly established in the very heart of the American fisheries.

When war broke out again, then, in 1740, the New England fishermen
were more than willing to strike at the French once again, particularly
when, at the outbreak of the war, the French made a swift capture of the
valuable trading town of Canseau (Canso) on Nova Scotia by a surprise
attack on the English garrison. The major colonial campaign of this
King George's War (the War of the Austrian Successon, 1740-48) was the
siege of the great fortress at Louisbourg on Cape Breton Island. Although the American colonies south of New England would have nothing to
do with the "mad scheme" of attempting to capture Louisbourg, the New
England colonies joined with enthusiasm as in a crusade. The eminent
Puritan preacher George Whitefield turned his sanctuary into a recruiting
station, and axes were brandished by his enthusiastic followers to illustrate how Catholic churches would be destroyed when the hated French
were driven out of Louisbourg. Fishermen, merchants, and religious enthusiasts joined in the campaign against France, and soon 4,000 volunteers had been recruited. Under the command of William Pepperell of
Maine, and aided by an English fleet of four vessels, the siege of Louisbourg was carried out in 1745. It lasted for two months and ended successfully only after the volunteers had dragged themselves and their cannon
through mud, fog, and waist-deep water to take their positions and lob
9,000 cannonballs and 600 bombs into the French works. The New England
volunteers had done the impossible and had broken the back of French
power in America. True to their religious convictions, some of the New
England volunteers went to work under the leadership of Parson Moody of
Boston and chopped to pieces all the images and the altar in the Catholic
church in Louisbourg.

These gains for the fisheries were, however, at least partially wiped
out by the ensuing Treaty of Aix-la-Chapelle of 1748, which returned Louisbourg and Cape Breton Island to France in exchange for Madras in India,
which the Crown considered more valuable to the realm. The only consola-
tion the embittered fishermen could take for their labors was that the
French were now clearly excluded from Acadia (which the English renamed
Nova Scotia). Disappointing as the Treaty of Aix-la-Chapelle was to the
New England fishermen, they were soon back at work on the fishing grounds
off their coast and off Nova Scotia and continuing to prosper. It was

not until the end of the French and Indian War (the Seven Years' War, 1756-63) that the French fishing interests were virtually excluded from the North American coasts. By the terms of the Treaty of Paris of 1763, which ended this most important and decisive fourth war between the two great European rivals in favor of England and thus assured it both European and American domination, the French lost all their territories in North America and all territory in the fishing grounds except the two small islands of Miquelon and St. Pierre south of Newfoundland. The French were still allowed to fish off Cape Breton Island, Newfoundland, and Nova Scotia; but without land bases and the means of protecting their rights in North America, the French fishing industry declined rapidly.

The New England fisheries had by the late 18th century outdistanced their English competitors and, by a series of wars between the mother country and France, had seen their major foreign competitor removed from the scene. A major industry of the sea based largely on the cod living in the cool waters off the North American coast had been born and had grown to major proportions during the 17th and 18th centuries. It provided not only a livelihood for thousands of men and boys in their schooners, shallops, and ketches as they fished the inshore waters and the great fertile banks from New England to Newfoundland, but also it provided a most important item of commerce that served as the very basis of an emerging trade network with the West Indies, Africa, and much of Europe. Boston, Gloucester, Marblehead, Salem, Brunswick, and hundreds of other towns and villages drew a substantial part of their life either directly or indirectly from the sea. The New England fishermen and the products of their labor, especially the cod with its high commercial value, were the very cornerstone of the area's prosperity and had brought New England and the other American colonies to a position of wealth and influence unrivaled by any other colonies of any other nation in the world by the latter half of the 18th century.

WHALING. But to concentrate exclusively on the valuable fishing in cod and other smaller fish and its impact on the colonies would be to overlook a second branch of the industry, which also began its period of growth during the 17th and 18th centuries, and which contributed major items of trade to the growing commercial network. This second segment of the fishing industry was whaling, which reached its height in the early 19th century, when American whalers dominated the oceans of the world, but nevertheless had its valuable beginnings in the 17th and 18th centuries. For whaling, like the cod fishery, was a major cornerstone of New England prosperity and commerce and therefore of American prosperity and development during the colonial period.

Whales were among the many species of waterlife found and recorded by the early explorers of the North American coast. In 1605, Captain George Waymouth described how the Indians killed whales near the shore with bone harpoons fastened to a rope. He reported that after a whale rose upon being struck, the Indians would shoot the mammal with arrows. The Indians probably taught the early colonists how to harass and kill the whale; contemporary accounts reveal that the Indians from Long Island to Cape Cod were considered to be very good whalemen. Furthermore, all accounts also reveal that whales were plentiful along the southern shores of New England and Long Island early in the 17th century.

It was on Long Island that the first organized system was developed for capturing whales sighted offshore. In 1644, townships there were divided into four patrols of eleven persons each, with two patrols selected at a time for the job of cutting up any whale taken. By 1650, offshore "boat expeditions" for whales had been introduced, and both Southampton and Easthampton were engaged in trading whale oil, usually to Boston or to Connecticut towns. That the trade was important enough to attract government attention for the purpose of taxation may be seen from the fact that Governor Robert Hunter, in the early 1700's, decreed that one-twentieth of all oil and bone taken had to be delivered to him in New York City. This exaction was fought all the way to the Privy Council in London by the local whalers and merchants in the person of Samuel Mulford, who journeyed to London to argue the case for the colonies. Mulford and the colonists won, and Mulford also taught a valuable lesson to the London pickpockets by sewing fish hooks into the inside of his breeches' pockets.

Massachusetts also was heavily engaged in hunting the whale in the 17th century; the colonists there were free to do so because, as in the case of other fishing, they had been granted this right as part of their original charter. In 1622, the town of Eastham voted that part of every drift whale claimed on the shore would be appropriated for the support of the ministry; and in 1688, Secretary Edward Randolph reported back to England that "New Plimouth colony have great profit by whale killing. I believe it will be one of our best returns, now [that] beaver and peltry fail us." In that same year the colony provided to whalers distinctive marks on harpoons and lances as a means of identifying a kill. Nantucket and Salem also entered into whaling late in the 17th century, along with the towns of Holmes Hole (Vineyard Haven) and Edgartown on Martha's Vineyard. Nantucket would subsequently emerge as the premier colonial whaling port in the 18th century.

Most of the whaling during this early period was either drift whaling, where a dead or foundering whale would be cut up, or else offshore whaling within sight of land. In the latter case, the dead whale would be pulled into shore by a "crab," or shore winch, and the blubber would be cut and stripped off the carcass. The blubber would then be boiled to the desired purity in large pots on the shore. The resulting oil was very valuable for the making of candles, soaps, and certain medicines, hence was suitable for both domestic and commercial use. The whale bone also was valuable as a commercial item. Indeed, the whale oil and bone formed a considerable part of the export trade of the New England merchants. Especially profitable were the spermaceti whales, whose head included a tubular "case," about two feet in diameter and about six feet deep, which served as a reservoir of pure spermaceti. Spermaceti became waxy when exposed to air and was used in making fine candles. The spermaceti candle industry was highly developed by the middle of the 18th century.

But even before the end of the 17th century, whaling was well established as an industry in New England, even if only on a small scale. The earlier process of waiting for drift whales to be cast ashore had in the main given way to boat whaling; and the products of this business, along with those of cod fishing, placed New England in a most advantageous position both in relation to the other colonies and to the markets of England and much of Europe.

The solid foundation in whaling laid in the 17th century was built upon steadily in the 18th, especially in the case of Nantucket Island off the south shore of Cape Cod. This island of less than fifty square miles could boast of only comparatively sterile soils for agriculture, so the people turned to the sea as the most attractive venture open to them. Whales were so plentiful that it was not necessary to put out far to sea to catch them. The predominantly Quaker inhabitants divided the south side of the island into four equal parts, with each part assigned to a company of six men. In the middle of each part, or division, of 3 1/2 miles, a mast or tower was erected, a contrivance for scanning the sea. From such a tower, one man would watch for the sight of a whale while the other five lived in a nearby hut awaiting their turn on watch. After a whale had been sighted, pursued, killed, and brought up to the beach, a try-works was erected on the shore; the blubber was cut up, and the process of "trying out," or boiling down the blubber, took place. At a later time, try-works were built on the decks of the vessels themselves, thus making it possible to "try-out" the blubber on board ship and then store the oil in casks below deck until the vessel returned to port.

In 1712 a Nantucket man named Christopher Hussey was blown out to sea in his boat and there made the first recorded kill of a sperm whale by a colonist. Since this venture signaled not only the possibility of greater catches away from shore, but also the presence of the valuable spermaceti whale, Nantucketers were quick to respond to this avenue of wealth. By 1730, Nantucket boasted a fleet of twenty-five vessels in whaling each of thirty-eight to fifty tons, and bringing an annual harvest of 3,700 barrels of oil, worth £3,200 in the English market. That same year, 9,200 tons of whale products arrived in England from North American ports.

Rhode Island also was in a favorable location for whaling; and in 1731, the Rhode Island assembly passed an act to encourage the catching of whales by offering bounties to Rhode Island vessels that brought their catches back to the colony. These bounties were five shillings for each barrel of whale oil and one penny for each pound of shalebone. Soon Rhode Island vessels were also sailing into deep waters in pursuit of the mammal, for their the sperm whale was most likely to be found.

But Nantucket was the hub of the whaling industry in the 18th century, so much so that the history of whaling during the century is virtually the history of Nantucket. Here whaling was a community enterprise, with coopers, sailmakers, boatbuilders, and blacksmiths all complementing the masters, steersmen, and able hands at sea in the whale fisheries. Straight Wharf was the focal point of the industry, not only for Nantucket but for all the American colonies. From Nantucket went ships to London with whale oil and bone, bringing in return cargoes of hemp, sailcloth, and other European manufactures. Gradually the Nantucket fleet of sloops grew from six vessels in 1715 to twenty-five in 1730, to fifty in 1740, and to sixty by 1748. These sloops were forty to fifty feet in length and fifteen feet in width, with a draft of six feet when fully loaded. Each carried two whaleboats for approaching the leviathans, a try-works on the deck, and a crew of thirteen men and boys. Vessels set sail in pursuit of the whale from the other Cape Cod ports too, from Wellfleet, Barnstable, and Falmouth, and from Boston, from Rhode Island, from Martha's Vineyard, and from New Bedford (then Dartmouth), which began its venture in whaling just prior to 1760, but grew to second position behind Nantucket by the time of the Revolutionary War. New Bedford's days of prominence came after the war.

Additional whaling ships sailed from still other New England towns. One expedition even set sail from Williamsburg, Virginia. These vessels, with try-works aboard and sizeable holds to store the whale oil, moved farther and farther out to sea in search of whales. By 1732, twelve American vessels had reached Davis Straits connecting Baffin Bay with the Atlantic Ocean. By 1763, American whalers had reached the African coast at Guinea; and by 1774, they were hunting the whale off the coast of Brazil.

By the mid-1770's, colonial whaling was moving to the full tide of success, with vessels sailing over the entire northern and central Atlantic regions. As with the cod fisheries, a major important colonial industry had been born and was flourishing.

The New England colonies were truly the maritime colonies. The "ripple effects" of their fishing industries were well understood and appreciated. Pork and salted-meat packing, the manufacture of biscuits, the production of ready-made clothing, the brass crafts serving ship chandlery, the making of barrels, hoops, and kettles, all of these trades had been born out of a need to supply the fishing industries. In addition, the entire colonial trade and shipbuilding network depended ultimately on the fisheries.

Despite the controls that the mother country at times imposed upon the colonial fishermen and whalers, the industries continued to flourish with little inconvenience throughout the 18th century. The Molasses Act of 1733 could have caused great hardship, since the English West Indies provided one-third of the market for colonial fish exported to the area, but it was not enforced, and the projected losses of 300,000 per year to Massachusetts alone did not materialize. Likewise, the levying of a duty in 1761 on whale oil and bone carried to England, and the requirement that it not be exported elsewhere, did not have any long-range effects, even with the additional disadvantage of British vessels receiving a bounty on whale products at the same time. The levy was soon suspended, because the English whalers could not compete with the Dutch and American vessels even with the help of discriminating legislation, and could not supply enough oil and bone to England to satisfy demands for them there. This branch of trade was, in effect, turned over to the American colonists.

Both the Navigation Act of 1764 and the Stamp Act of 1765, while potentially of great concern to the men engaged in the fisheries because of the laws' effects upon trade, were not rigidly enforced, and many possible troubles with the laws were avoided by "connivance or indulgence in the officers." Resistance to these acts centered in the merchant classes and eventually led to open resistance to the Crown; but in the 1760's they did not bring forth resistance from the fishermen and whalers as long as the new laws and regulations could be avoided and fishing and whaling could be pursued.

Both fishing and whaling continued to flourish in the decade preceding the Revolution. The early 1770's saw colonial whaling interests in their full bloom of success. While the exact numbers of ships and men engaged in whaling at the time are impossible to determine, probably at least 360 whaling vessels sailed annually and furnished employment to about 4,700 men. The annual yield from the whaleries was at least 45,000 barrels of spermaceti oil, 8,500 barrels of right whale oil, and 75,000 pounds of bone. The Nantucket whaling fleet alone consisted of at least 150 vessels, followed by Dartmouth with some 50 vessels. One report from the 1770's estimated that with the attendant shore industries dependent on whaling, the industry furnished employment for about 10,000 persons.

In cod fishing there were about 700 vessels in the industry employing about 4,000 men in 1775. In addition, it was estimated that another 350 vessels were employed in carrying fish to the markets of the world. Adding the men engaged in the extensive fishing for shad, herring, and mackerel along the New England shores brings the number of men directly employed in the total fisheries to between 9,000 and 10,000 persons. With over 1,000 vessels and up to 10,000 men engaged in the fisheries (in addition to 10,000 men in whaling) and an uncounted number indirectly engaged in servicing the vessels and men through ancillary trades, fishing was obviously a key industry in New England and in the American colonies, and policies unfavorable to the fisheries would have widespread repercussions. The telling blow to the fisheries came in February, 1775, and the Crown faced the united opposition of the fishermen and all those dependent upon them.

SUGGESTIONS FOR FURTHER READING

Ackerman, Edward A. New England's Fishing Industry. Chicago: University of Chicago Press, 1941.

Albion, Robert G. Naval and Maritime History: An Annotated Bibliography. 4th ed., rev'd. Mystic, Conn.: Marine Historical Association, Inc., 1972.

Hakluyt, Richard. The Principal Navigations, Voyages, Traffiques & Discoveries of the English Nation. 12 vols. Glasgow: James MacLehose and Sons, 1904.

Innis, Harold A. The Cod Fisheries: The History of an International Economy. New Haven: Yale University Press, 1940.

Lounsbury, Ralph G. The British Fisheries at Newfoundland, 1634-1763. New Haven: Yale University Press, 1934.

Johnson, Emory R., et al. History of Domestic and Foreign Commerce of the United States. Vol's. I and II in one volume. Washington, D.C.: Carnegie Institution, 1915.

Judah, Charles B., Jr. The North American Fisheries and British Policy to 1713. Illinois Studies in the Social Sciences, Vol. XVIII, No's. 3-4. Urbana: University of Illinois, 1933.

McFarland, Raymond. A History of the New England Fisheries. Philadelphia: University of Pennsylvania; New York: D. Appleton & Co., 1911.

Rowe, William H. The Maritime History of Maine: Three Centuries of Shipbuilding and Seafaring. New York: W.W. Norton & Co., Inc., 1948.

Stackpole, Edouard A. The Sea-Hunters: The New England Whalemen during Two Centuries, 1635-1835. New York: J.B. Lippincott Co., 1953.

Starbuck, Alexander. History of the American Whale Fishery from its Early Inception to the Year 1876. Waltham, Mass.: By the author, 1876.

Tower, Walter S. A History of the American Whale Fishery. University of Pennsylvania Series in Political Economy and Public Law, No. 20. Philadelphia: University of Pennsylvania, 1907.

CHAPTER II. COLONIAL MARITIME TRADE AND SHIPBUILDING

Fishing was not the only important maritime activity carried on in the American colonies. Building upon the demands growing out of colonial fishing ventures, enterprising colonists created two additional major industries--maritime trade and shipbuilding. Both were destined to have an important influence on American economic development long after the fishing industry had suffered a demise.

It must be borne in mind that colonies established on the western side of the Atlantic by the various European nations were not allowed to come into existence simply for the good of the colonists themselves. Caught up in a highly-spirited competition between nations on the political, religious, and economic fronts, each European state could not allow its colonies to develop without firm direction. Colonies had to work to the benefit of the mother countries or would be bad investments in money, time, and national energies. Colonies had to repay their sponsoring governments in national prestige, territorial claims, loyalty, and, perhaps above all, in gold and silver for the realm.

THE MERCANTILE SYSTEM. Financial success was to be assured by the workings of the Mercantile System. Under the accepted tenets of this complex of ideas embracing all aspects of a nation's economy, colonies were to provide raw materials, as well as be a ready market for the products of the mother country. The mother country, in turn, provided manufactured goods and the commercial protection its colonies needed. Since the colonies, according to this system, had to sell their goods to the merchants in their respective mother countries, they were selling into a closed market with little competition among the merchants for colonial products. Consequently, the prices the colonists received for their raw materials tended to be low, or at least lower than in a freely competitive market. On the other hand, since the colonists, hemmed in by the various trade laws of the founding country, generally had to buy from the latter's merchants alone and from no one else, the colonists' costs for manufactured goods tended to be high. By thus controlling the economic life of the colonies in regard to what they produced, to whom they sold, and what and from whom they bought, a monetary imbalance resulted; the value of the goods imported by the colonies was higher than the value of goods they exported. This imbalance was made up by specie (i.e., gold and silver) gained from allowable trade outside the realm. The specie thus gained was the purpose of the whole system and a major source of wealth and strength for the mother country. Of course, in return for these controls, the colonies received assurance of a market for their goods and a share of the profits of trade, and commerce to and from the colonies was reserved to the ships of the nation or its colonies as far as was practicable. This arrangement might seem strange today, but it was understood and accepted by the coloniest in the 17th and 18th centuries--as long as it worked no great hardship on them and as long as certain necessary "adjustments" or "exceptions" were allowed.

If, then, one of the primary purposes of establishing colonies was to secure profits for the mother country, how did a nation go about establishing and controlling its creations across the sea? England accomplished both through the device of chartered companies, and later by proprietary grants, through which economic, political, and administrative controls were instituted and secured. Chartered companies or proprietorships with sizeable land-grants were necessary because few individuals had sufficient capital or were in a secure enough financial position to take on the considerable risks involved in establishing a colony. Monetary return to an investor in a colony might not be forthcoming for years, and the initial and continuing outlay of cash or credit might be staggering. But whether a colony was established by a company or by an individual's being granted a vast stretch of land, and whether or not it later became a royal colony (as most English colonies did eventually), the twin principles of profit as a goal and administrative control by the government were never absent.

The London Company was established in just such a fashion by the English Crown in 1606 and was given a trade monopoly in the area it was allowed to develop. As a joint-stock company, it sent colonists and goods to the New World. Its colony at Jamestown, Virginia, established in 1607, was under the control of the Company acting for the Crown. Although the venture and therefore the Company ran onto hard times--it became a Royal Colony in 1624--the principle of control by the mother country was fully established and understood by the settlers. The Pilgrims at Plymouth, far to the north within the confines of the northern curve of Cape Cod, were also under the control of a company, the Plymouth Company (called the New England Council after 1620). The colonists in this case bought out their owners (the "adventurers" as they were called) in 1628 and went on their own. Nevertheless, they were expected to conduct their economic activities for the benefit of the Crown. The same sort of control for profit was also part and parcel of the mission of the Massachusetts Bay Company fifty miles to the north of Plymouth. The Company attempted to establish a monopoly on many items, such as furs and salt, and on the transportation of people and goods, and saw nothing contradictory in an economic dictatorship within a quasi-democratic political regime.

The Dutch, too, established colonies in the New World within the "rules" of the Mercantile System. New Netherlands was founded by the illustrious Dutch West India Company early in the 17th century, with company ownership a basic principle until 1629 when families ("patroons") were given land and control. Although private trade was eventually allowed the Dutch colonists--in company ships, of course--the same principle of mercantilistic control was maintained and accepted in the colony. New Sweden, existing on the Delaware from 1638 to 1655, when it was taken over by the Dutch, also knew the regimen of common control for the good of the colony and the mother country. Thus all along the Atlantic coast-- the birthplace of what became the English colonies and eventually the United States--a controlled economy for the benefit of the mother countries and their citizens both at home and in the New World was part of the workaday world of the colonists.

Yet within this colonial mercantile system there grew from economic necessity the embryo of a trade network that brought wealth to the colonies, tension within the British Empire, and eventually revolution and disunion. A dynamic economic system was born on the western side of the Atlantic with its own needs and demands. Trade served as the leaven of wealth, the dynamic drivewheel of the economy, and finally the spark of resistance and independence.

17TH-CENTURY BEGINNINGS IN TRADE. Although the English colonists may generally not have been allowed to trade outside the Empire, they found at an early date that their economic fortunes were well served by trade within it. New Englanders were especially quick to discover this avenue to wealth. Surplus products of New England fisheries and farms brought a fine price in other colonies along the coast or in the various West Indian colonies. Intercoastal trade began in 1636 when Thomas Mayhew of Boston and John Winthrop, the son of Governor John Winthrop of the colony, sent a small sloop to Bermuda loaded with corn and smoked pork. After a one-month voyage, the vessel returned with oranges, lemons, and potatoes--and a tidy profit. This small venture was only the beginning. In the years and decades that followed, Massachusetts fish, furs, and lumber, plus surplus grain, cattle, butter, and rum from neighboring colonies, moved in small Massachusetts vessels down the coast to the middle and southern colonies and on to the West Indies. Back and forth went the New England craft to and from small New England ports and middle colony settlements. Hugging the shore, they delivered and loaded commodities valuable to them and to their customers at home. New England fish, lumber, grain, and pork were exchanged for southern and West Indian cotton, tobacco, salt, rum, wine, and even slaves. Thus the surplus of one colony was exchanged for the surplus of another, bringing a measure of prosperity to all.

New England and northern goods were exchanged also for gold or silver coin or for bills of exchange (a written order to a person to pay a specific amount of money to the bearer of the order; a negotiable note). These coins or notes, in turn, were used to buy precious English manufactures not available in the colonies. By the 1640's, New England trade, centered particularly in Boston, was well established with the middle colonies, the West Indies, and with Virginia and Maryland, bringing with it a new and vital dimension to the colonial economy. The colonies were becoming linked to one another and to the mother country by the wooden sailing craft of New England and the men who owned and sailed them. The Dutch may have controlled the trade of New Netherlands and some of the trade of Virginia and Maryland, but the rest belonged to New England which would not let it go.

Nature may have been niggardly with New England when it came to arable farmland, and the region may not have been blessed with an extensive hinterland which could be tapped for resources, but its love affair with the sea, born of fishing, was its singular blessing; and New England knew it well. From its small sales of fish, corn, and pork in its early years, it had taken the hint of profitable commerce and made the most of it. New England could tie the colonies and their products to their necessary markets. Its vessels could bring together buyer and seller along the coast, between the mainland and the Caribbean, or between the mainland or islands and the

ports of the mother country. It lost no time in doing so. By the mid-
1640's, New England had developed its oceangoing and coastal commerce
into a profitable industry. It had made the colonies hugging the coastline part of the economy of the Atlantic world, even trading with foreign
ports where economic profits and the Crown permitted. Spanish and French
ports saw Boston sails with increasing frequency. Caribbean ports came
to depend on New England ships for their sales of tobacco, cotton, molasses, and slaves, and in the 1670's the new settlements in Carolina were
brought into the orbit of New England trade. The stern Puritan fathers
of the Massachusetts Bay Colony might well have wondered as to the effects
of the lucrative business of trade upon the souls of so many of their sons,
but there was not stopping the affairs of commerce. It had become the
most dynamic element in the New England economy. It remained so throughout
the colonial period.

One must remember that although trade grew very rapidly during the
17th century, so much so that by the end of the century Boston alone could
boast of a fleet of more than a hundred vessels, the whole system rested
on the shoulders of individuals, rather than on the efforts of large
companies. Individual tradesmen at the time relied heavily on social
acquaintances, on relatives, and on merchant contacts of long standing in
other colonial ports, in the Caribbean outlets, or in London or Bristol,
in conducting their business. Partnerships that were formed for commercial
voyages had a marked tendency to be fluid and changeable, but, of crucial
importance, the merchants came to depend most heavily on their own resources rather than on those of the London merchants, who had played such
an important part in colonial trade earlier in the century. Trade was
maturing and forming a sub-strata of New England society that maintained
and improved the commercial system through its members' rich lore of experience and contacts as the years wore on. Although decentralized and
dependent upon small units to sustain itself, the system displayed a remarkable dynamism. Boston as a port challenged Bristol as the second
greatest entrepôt in the English empire. And the merchant class challenged
the Puritan church leaders for supremacy in the life of the expanding
colony.

Natural resources, human talent, and the ability to react with zest
to an opportunity for profit and expansion pushed the commercial interests
of New England to the forefront of its consciousness. The Puritans had
indeed created in Boston and in the Bay Colony a form of a "city on a
hill" as a model for the world to follow, as the early leaders had prophesied, but the "city on a hill" overlooked a marvelous harbor bedecked
with the tall masts of ships and a waterfront filled with sights and
sounds of trade with the Atlantic colonies, the Caribbean, and Europe.
The New World as utopia was a dream very much alive, but its material
manifestations were inexorably crowding out or at least casting a pall
over its spiritual dimensions.

The middle colonies did not show the same interest in trade during
the 17th century as did New England. New Amsterdam commercialism was held
in check by the colony's land system, which granted great estates of
thousands of acres to the patroons, and by Dutch trade restrictions.
While exports of furs, cereals, barrel staves, lumber, and other commodities did take place, mostly with Europe but some with the West Indies,

the amounts were usually small. Imports, too, were limited, consisting mainly of tobacco, grain, and some fish and furs, either for the colonists' own use or for transshipment to Europe. Even when New Amsterdam was taken over by the English in 1664 and the colony became New York and part of the English commercial system, the amounts of import and export movement remained moderate throughout the remainder of the century. Whether under the Dutch or under the English, the colony had little surplus to sell and few goods it needed to buy because of its small population and because of its rather primitive state of economic development. New York had tremendous commercial potential, with a fine harbor and an extensive hinterland via the Hudson River, but it was not in a position to bring it to fruition in the 17th century.

Pennsylvania was likewise in no position to enter into commercialism in a major way in the 17th century, nor would it be until the middle of the 18th century. The few goods that were needed from outside the colony could be bought from New England coastal traders; what little it could sell could also be handled by them. Time and further economic development would change this picture, but self-sufficiency was the rule until Pennsylvania developed a more specialized economy. It then surged into the forefront in trade. The middle colonies were clearly dependent upon Boston and the New England colonies in the 17th century; the 18th century gradually saw this relationship altered.

The southern colonies of Virginia and Maryland were tobacco colonies. This specialization shaped their whole economic system. Tobacco found virtually its sole outlet in Europe, and thus direct trade with Europe, usually on English ships, became the commercial lifeline of those colonies surrounding the Chesapeake in the 17th century. The tobacco colonies exported nearly all their staples of tobacco and a few grains directly to England or to the West Indies. They received in return English manufactures and West Indian--mainly Barbadian--slaves, molasses, sugar, salt, and rum. The West Indian trade was sometimes carried on by enterprising New Englanders, but most often by English shippers or by the largest planters doing their own shipping.

This commercial network was very lucrative, and the Chesapeake colonies saw their economies more dependent on foreign commerce than any other colonies on the Atlantic coast. The forty-eight principal tributaries of the Chesapeake, which opened to trade a hinterland of 10,000 square miles, held tremendous potential. Some 1,750 miles of inland waterways were navigable for trading ships, to say nothing of more than 4,600 miles of shoreline along the Bay itself; yet the time had not yet come for major commercial development in these colonies. Tobacco dominated their economy and provided sizeable wealth via exports, and imports were available; there was no reason to develop beyond this point. The planter aristocracy was satisfied; the poorer sort would follow.

Although the Chesapeake colonies did not display the economic diversification and trend toward specialization clearly evident in New England and just beginning in the middle colonies during the 17th century, they too were vitally dependent upon the water. Without waterborne trade they would languish and die. Their jugular vein was trade; threaten it and they would be faced with ruin. Although merchants were few in the south and few ships were constructed or owned there, trade was still the sine qua non of southern economic life. These Chesapeake colonies were even more economically vulnerable than their northern counterparts, which had a greater domestic diversity by the end of the 17th century. Here, as there, trade was the difference between success and failure. Even the planter aristocracy, trying to emulate the fashions and fixtures of London on their plantations overlooking the rivers, must have sometimes paused to consider how their economic lives depended on the slender thread of trade. One-crop specialized agriculture required a market; without access to that market the growing of crops would be useless; without ships, traders, and foreign and domestic markets no access existed. The Chesapeake colonies--and other Atlantic colonies--had come far economically in the century since 1607 and the landing at Jamestown.

18TH-CENTURY TRADE PATTERNS. The maritime patterns established in the 17th century naturally carried over into the 18th, but with some alterations. Boston maintained its lead over all ports in tonnage imported and exported, and the business of collecting colonial exports in the Massachusetts trade center continued apace. Likewise, the distribution of imported foreign articles through the Boston merchants continued to thrive. Boston imported the major portion of all European goods to America and distributed them by its coasting vessels throughout the colonies. The Boston merchants drained the coastal and hinterland areas of their surplus goods and exported them to Europe and to the other colonies, receiving in return manufactures and other goods necessary for colonial existence. Edward Randolph referred to Boston as the "mart town of the West Indies" because of its continued trade with that rich Caribbean colonial area. Boston's trade increased until the fourth decade of the 18th century when the rise of shipping at other port cities cut into its virtual monopoly. Boston did not "decline," but merely could not maintain its absolute dominance of colonial trade, which was growing at an accelerating rate in all areas. It now had aggressive competitors. These competitors, elbowing their way into commerce by means of developing hinterlands from which to draw goods, broke the Boston monopoly and began the same type of commercial expansion the Bay Colony capital had experienced a century before.

One of Boston's rising competitors was nearby Newport, Rhode Island, on Narragansett Bay. By 1741 the Rhode Island city, specializing in the shipment of rum, molasses, and sugar from the island, had taken a large share of the Caribbean trade away from Boston. Its coastal vessels also increasingly made contact with merchants in the New York area. Although still dependent upon Boston for European manufactured goods, Newport came into its own in a major way as the 18th century progressed, and it became a notable participant in the workings of maritime British America.

Boston's chief competitor for commercial dominance was Philadelphia. In the early 1720's the Pennsylvania port city averaged only 116 vessels cleared per year with a carrying tonnage of 4,188 tons, but by the 1770's more than 700 vessels per year with a carrying capacity of 42,808 tons were clearing the wharves of Philadelphia. On the eve of the American Revolution, Philadelphia had inched its way past Boston to become the busiest port in North America. Boston was a close second in ship tonnage in and out of port; New York, a very poor third. The tremendous growth in Philadelphia's trade was built on the exporting of grains, lumber, tobacco, livestock, horses, and other items, especially to the Caribbean islands. Imports consisted of various manufactured goods from London and Bristol, such as hardware and clothing. But it was the grain trade that made Philadelphia the leading port in the colonies. By late in the colonial period, its flour exports were greater than all its other exports combined. Trading with the West Indies, with the European continent and the neighboring Azores and Canary Islands, with other British colonies, and with the mother country itself, the Quaker merchants built a diversified economy and provided thousands of jobs for artisans in more than a score of trades in the city.

Philadelphia ships plowed the oceans from the southern colonies to the Caribbean, on to Europe, and back again. Sometimes the vessels went to Newfoundland, then to Europe, and then returned home. Other times they went from Philadelphia to Charleston, then to England with rice, and finally home with manufactured goods. Whatever the form of the various triangles or other trade patterns the Philadelphia ships followed--or deviated from if greater profits could be made by taking advantage of a shortage of some article in Europe, in the Caribbean, or in some colonial port--the result was wealth for the city and for the neighboring colonies dependent upon its trading connections. Philadelphia, like Boston before it, had become a trading city and part of the Atlantic trading world. Pennsylvania and the other colonies it served were thus drawn into the patterns of international and colonial commerce in the 18th century and found themselves more and more dependent upon trade in every aspect of their economic lives.

New York was a poor third in the race for total tonnage in and out of port during the second century of colonial existence, but was beginning to rise to commercial prominence. In the 1740's, the city began to expand its trade with Europe by exporting the products of its hinterland, such as flour and meat, and thus initiated a steady rise in trade that would see it become the greatest port in the nation in the century following independence. Time, the development of specialized agriculture and manufacturing, the development of shipbuilding, and other factors would favor New York in the 19th century. Yet even in the 18th century it still was of major importance as a port city, seeing an excess of 56,000 ship-tons and 1,600 vessels in and out of its harbor annually on the eve of the Revolution. New York, like Boston, Newport, and Philadelphia, had become a major part of the coastal and Atlantic trading network.

Farther to the south, the Chesapeake colonies continued their dependence on the export of tobacco to the Continent as the chief feature of their trade during the 18th century. While tobacco tonnage exported at the end of the preceding century had reached twenty million pounds per year, by 1775 the amount had increased fivefold to a hundred million pounds per year. Tobacco was a sought-after item in Britain, and the Crown went out of its way to favor its importation from the American colonies. Because much of the tobacco was processed in England and then re-exported to the Continent, the Crown allowed drawbacks on import tariffs if the tobacco was re-exported within one year. The result of this policy was that by 1775, 90 percent of the tobacco imported from the southern American colonies had no tax levied on it at all. With such a favored position within the realm, southern planters continued to grow tobacco in ever-increasing amounts. With such direct demand and with the advantages of trading in tobacco with the mother country, the southern colonists were quite willing to continue to depend heavily on British ships to carry their crops to market and to return with their needed manufactured goods. Interestingly, much of this overseas trade was conducted directly from plantation wharves. The only port of any importance on the Chesapeake was Norfolk on Hampton Roads, but this was because of its specialization in the West Indian and Carolina trade for secondary items needed in the Chesapeake colonies.

Apparently many large planters in the south generally did their own buying and shipping, using the services of factors (commission merchants) in England, and also acted as shipping agents for smaller growers of tobacco in their home areas. The planters also functioned as purchasing agents and owned or chartered vessels for this purpose, for either the West Indian or the European trade. Some even extended credit to the smaller planters. As a result, a commercial agent peculiar to the tobacco colonies emerged--the planter-merchant. Indeed, almost all of the great planters of colonial Virginia and Maryland, the Byrds, the Carters, the Carrolls, and the Washingtons, also functioned as merchants.

Although tobacco and British shipping dominated the Chesapeake colonies, the area planters also engaged in a most important secondary trade with their coastal and West Indian neighbors. Such items of export as wheat, corn, pork, and flour were regularly sent to the other colonies in exchange for European manufactures, or for fish, naval stores, and wooden-ware either from the other colonies or from Britain. After 1730, vessels built on the Chesapeake began to compete with New England and West Indian vessels for the carrying of these goods. The Chesapeake colonies also conducted an extensive grain trade with the "Wine Islands" (Madeira, Cape Verde, and the Azores), and with Portugal, Spain, and Italy. Accordingly, while Virginia and Maryland continued to be dominated by tobacco and by British shipping, they were beginning to broaden their agricultural base--a process that usually proceeded rapidly when tobacco prices fell, but tended to recede when prices rose again. For the most part, the Chesapeake colonies were still building on the very narrow economic base of tobacco; that base was dependent upon intercoastal and especially trans-Atlantic trading networks. Trade was part of their life-blood. It did not dominate them as it did Boston or, increasingly, Philadelphia, but these southern colonies of Maryland and Virginia, becoming like all the colonies more and more dependent on the flow of agricultural and manufactured goods from producer to consumer, were now part of a commercial network they could neither deny nor entirely control.

26

The Carolinas, founded late in the colonial period, were the last colonies to become part of the commercial network. The late 17th century had seen virtually no trade to or from these colonies; in the 18th century, South Carolina came into its own through the port of Charleston (or Charles Town, as it was then called). Like the ports in the Chesapeake region, Charleston relied very heavily on direct trade with English cities, the ratio being 6:1 over coastal ports and 2:1 over West Indian ports. But despite its late start, the city, situated where the Ashley and Cooper Rivers meet the ocean, saw its trade grow rapidly with the exportation of forest products such as staves, hoops, shingles, pitch, and tar, and food products such as beef, pork, rice, and molasses, to England and to the West Indies. In return, Carolinians received manufactured goods, rum, and a great number of Negro slaves. The Charleston merchants also imported considerable amounts of wine from Madeira. By the end of the colonial era, Charleston was exporting more than 31,000 ship-tons of merchandise (about one-half of it to Britain) and importing almost 30,000 ship-tons (about one-third from Britain and another one-third from the Caribbean and the coastal colonies). Charleston had become the fourth busiest port in North America. Carolina's dependence on trade was fixed.

By the end of the colonial era, then, the colonies were finding wealth in traversing the coastal and Atlantic waters to sell their surpluses and to buy the surpluses of others. Trade with European ports for manufactured goods in exchange for colonial products took the larger share of their ships' cargo space, but sailing up and down the coast and out to the West Indies also constituted a considerable and vital part of their trade network. All of the colonies were involved in the coastal trade in one way or another. New Hampshire tar and turpentine went to Boston, New York, or Newport in exchange for European goods, such as woolens, glass, nails, silks, scythes, and firearms. New Jersey grain and cattle went to Philadelphia and New York to be traded for English manufactures. New York wheat was shipped to Boston or Charleston for fish, turpentine, hops, cider, flax, tin, furniture, or carriages produced in the areas of those ports or imported from Europe. Southern tobacco, rice, and naval stores were loaded upon coastal sailing vessels to be delivered to the northern ports in exchange for flour, fish, beef, clothing, ironware, and British manufactures. Sometimes these vessels made direct journeys from the southern ports to the northern; often the trade was part of the lucrative trade of the northern vessels going to and from the Caribbean.

As the coastal trade developed, as in other branches of the industry, British merchant interests disappeared from the trade, to be replaced by colonial merchants operating on their own. Most of these shippers were not producers of their own goods, but professionals in the business of trade who frequently employed their own ships. The coastal trade was falling into the hands of specialists constantly gaining expertise in their chosen line of work. By their labors the myriad products of the hinterlands were collected and distributed, not only throughout the colonies, but also to West Indian and European ports. By the effects of these merchant-traders, the products of an evolving colonial economy on the Atlantic coast were being collected and shipped throughout the Atlantic economic community. It was through the exertions of these men--and sometimes women--that the lucrative West Indian trade in particular was developed.

Since the value of goods exported to the West Indies from the American colonies usually was greater than the value of goods imported from the islands, the balance was made up in specie or in bills of exchange. Because these bills of exchange were frequently payable in London, the colonial merchant could convert them into British manufactures needed in America. The bills of exchange from the West Indian trade also facilitated payment of the debts outstanding in Europe because of the colonies' unfavorable balance of trade with the mother country and with the Continent. The profits from one branch of trade paid off the debts of the other and lubricated the whole Atlantic trading system. The coastal trade was, then, not only the means whereby the goods of the colonies were exchanged with one another and with the British colonies in the Caribbean, but also a vital factor in the colonies' trade with Europe. A dual-track and complementary trade system had developed by the eve of the Revolution, one track crossing the Atlantic at many points by many routes, the other track going up and down the Atlantic coast from Boston to Charleston and out across the blue waters of the fabled Caribbean. It was a well-developed system and an important channel of growth and prosperity for the American colonies. Colonial trade had come a long way since the early 17th century and the fledgling efforts of those days to supply the new colonists with necessary goods from London in exchange for the few products of the land available in the New World. The American colonies had 90 percent of their population drawing their living from the land in the late 18th century, but the remaining 10 percent in the cities and on the seas were engaged in economic enterprises so valuable that all would suffer if maritime trade were seriously disturbed.

As a consequence of this commercial expansion in the colonies, other benefits accrued to them. Specialized businesses appeared, the issuance of insurance began, and surplus credit from commerce was channeled into land and manufacturing enterprises. The American colonies were developing into a multi-faceted economic whole, with profit both to themselves and to the mother country. Between 1701 and 1763, Britain's trade with its American colonies increased at the phenomenal rate of 425 percent. Anglo-American trade in 1763 stood at £7,500,000, up from £760,000 only sixty years earlier. In the port towns of America, all types of ancillary industries appeared in the wake of this great commercial expansion. Shipwrights, sawyers, coopers, butchers, carpenters, bakers, and packers all served in building, maintaining, and provisioning the ships of the trade. The "ripple effects" of maritime commerce created trades and occupations important to the local economies and to the British economic world. New trades were developed to serve local needs, all tied directly or indirectly into the channels of coastal or Atlantic commerce.

SHIPBUILDING: THE 17TH CENTURY. One of the most important ancillary industries developing out of the fishing and commercial expansion of colonial times was that of shipbuilding. The shipbuilding industry, in turn, helped the development of fishing and commerce by providing at a low price the vessels necessary for those trades. The American colonists had been favored from the first by the giant stands of timber available close to the water. The availability of timber gave the impetus to the shift of much of the shipbuilding industry from northwest Europe to the English colonies in America. As fortune would have it, after about the year 1500 the rapid growth of the European states and their economic expansion resulted in increasing demands for ships. All of the European maritime countries, England, Spain, Holland, France, and Portugal, needed ships for the development of their American, West Indian, African, and East Indian trade networks. Ships were in short supply. This shortage of ships in Europe for national expansion was made more critical by the fact that, because of revolutionary changes in the internal economies of the European countries, vast stretches of forest land so necessary for shipbuilding were being converted into farm and pasture land to feed the countries' growing populations. Thus colonies that had extensive amounts of timbered land available would be in a very favorable position to develop a shipbuilding industry. It is no wonder, then, that the building of merchant ships in the American colonies was encouraged by the Crown on behalf of the proprietors and merchants whose interests coincided with that of the state. Ships were needed for the fishing, coastwise trading, and Atlantic trading industries. English colonial shipbuilders were encouraged to fill this need even though colonial enterprise in this case meant competition with shipbuilders in the home country.

Colonial shipbuilding began in New England where there was the greatest demand for vessels, a demand created by the expanding fishing and trading industries. Fishermen and tradesmen could benefit greatly by taking advantage of the lower cost of locally-built vessels. Lower cost came from the abundance of timber available to the shipwright and his assistants. Additional equipage such as cordage, sail cloth, and iron devices might have to be imported from England, but the basic hull was constructed using local woods and perhaps half a dozen men. Shipwrights had to turn to merchants for financial aid in purchasing the necessary equipment which tended to be very expensive. Because of this, a link between the shipbuilding industry--often very small in scope--and the trading industry was forged early in the 17th century.

The lower cost of colonial ships was not overlooked by British merchants, who were quite willing to order colonial-built ships for use in their trades. Consequently the New England colonists possessed an additional trade item acceptable as payment for their imports from England. By this practice an additional means of payment and another lubricant of Atlantic trade were provided. Furthermore, American-built ships were frequently sold in foreign ports upon arrival, thereby adding another method of payment to the merchants of the mother country or of a Continental power.

American-built vessels in the 17th century were generally fifty tons burden or less, a right-sized vessel for the fishing, West Indian, or intercolonial trades, although larger vessels for the Atlantic trade were constructed on demand. Indeed, American builders constructed vessels of almost any size, and of any degree of elaboration for any type of sailing, quicker and cheaper than their English counterparts. The more common vessels built in the colonies were the sloop (with a single mast and fore-and-aft sails), the schooner (two-masted, with fore-and-aft sails and a headsail, or jib) for the coastal trade, and the ship (three-masted and square-rigged) for work on the Atlantic.

Shipbuilding, then, became a part of the economic life of scores of villages and towns along the coast, especially in New England, during the 17th century. Besides the full-time builders, other village and rural tradesmen contributed their efforts toward building vessels, especially in the winter season, when agricultural work required less of their time. Carpenters, smiths, joiners, and less-skilled citizens contributed their time and energies toward the building of the ships so necessary to their economic well-being. Rope walks and sailmakers' lofts were erected near the harbors, and caulkers and braziers joined in the building of vessels with carpenters, shipwrights, other tradesment, and common laborers.

Inland from the harbors other men cut the soaring timber and "baulked" it to the rivers by teams of oxen. When not busy securing lumber products and shaping them for use in shipbuilding, the craftsmen of the colonial days also engaged in cutting and hewing masts for export directly to England--a very profitable and Crown-favored business--and in preparing shingles, boards, and barrels for the trade with European, colonial, and West Indian ports. Shipbuilding in the 17th century was part of the economic life-blood of many a New England community and served well the needs of the colonies and the empire.

Apparently very little shipbuilding took place in the ports of the middle and southern colonies in this first century of colonial life. The lesser amounts of trade and fishing in these regions, and the southern dependence on tobacco exports directly to England, undoubtedly precluded any substantial development. With the rise of these middle and southern colonies to commercial prominence in the 18th century, the shipbuilding industry also matured in these areas.

SHIPBUILDING: THE 18TH CENTURY. The shipbuilding efforts of the colonists continued to expand in the 18th century. As before, lower cost was part of the reason (finer quality was never a selling point for colonial-built vessels). Although the price of ships built in the colonies approximately doubled during the 18th century, the cost per ton was always significantly lower than for the ships built in British yards. During most of the period colonial ships cost about 3 to 4 pounds sterling per ton, whereas British-built vessels cost about 5 to 7 pounds per ton. With this cost differential as an important factor, British merchants continued to buy vessels in the colonies, often directing their agents in America to take the profits from sales of their exports and put them into the construction of a ship. The completed vessel would then be sailed to England filled with cargo, the freight being used to pay the cost of delivery. Consequently, the American shipbuilding industry with its lower costs helped the colonies, the British merchants, and the Crown in its maritime competition with other powers. By the time of the Revolution, at least one-fourth--some contend one-third--

of the more than 2,300 vessels registered in Britain were built in the American colonies. These ships saw service for British merchants all over the world.

In addition to building ships for British merchants, the colonial shipbuilder also continued to ply his trade for colonial merchants in the Atlantic and coastal trades, for merchants in the foreign-held West Indies, and for Spanish and Portuguese traders. By the second half of the 18th century, so great was the demand for American ships that many skilled journeymen and master shipbuilders emigrated from England to the colonies. This influx of skilled labor gradually led to an upgrading in the quality of colonial vessels, as improved ketches for fishing, schooners and sloops for the coastal trade, and ships and barks (square-rigged carriers with no special rig, but most were rigged as brigantines with two masts, square-rigged on the foremast, fore-and-aft on the main) for the European and West Indian trades, came off colonial shipways.

Boston retained its lead as the premier shipbuilding city in the colonies, and Massachusetts vessels dominated the shipbuilders' trade. Boston was so conscious of the importance of this industry that it passed numerous regulations to assure the high quality of Boston-built ships. Already possessing no fewer than fourteen shipyards in 1720, Boston continued to increase its shipbuilding facilities throughout the century. The whole city took pride in the construction and launching of its ships, although the Puritan divine Cotton Mather found it profane to indulge in a mock-baptism of a ship as it began its slide into the water for the first time. But shipbuilding in Boston was a major occupation, and even such "foolishness" was tolerated by the community rather than lose the business.

Yet Boston shipbuilders were beginning to experience competition in the late 18th century. Newport, Philadelphia, New York, the Chesapeake area, and other colonial towns were developing their shipbuilding by that time. Newport, with the financial backing of English and West Indian merchants, specialized in sloops for the coastal trade. New Hampshire vessels also were built for the coastal trade. Connecticut ports entered the business too, especially in the building of large ships. Pennsylvania shipyards moved into second place early in the century, and seriously challenged Boston as the century progressed.

Shipbuilding in the southern colonies remained very limited until the 1740's, largely because of the planter-merchants' preference for chartering British ships rather than building their own. But in the 1740's there occurred a sharp rise in ship construction in the Chesapeake colonies, spurred on by the planter-merchants desiring ships for their West Indian trade. By the end of the colonial period a well-developed shipbuilding industry could be found on the Chesapeake. In 1769, the Chesapeake colonies built forty-seven vessels, which represented about 12.5 percent of all tonnage built in the American colonies, more than any other region outside of New England. During the period 1763-74, at least 360 ships were built in Virginia alone. Most coastal settlements there boasted of a shipyard, although Norfolk held a substantial lead in shipbuilding over all other towns on the Chesapeake.

31

Shipbuilding represented a growing and important occupation by the end of the colonial period. Massachusetts alone turned out a hundred twenty-five vessels in 1771, followed by Rhode Island with seventy-five, New Hampshire with fifty-five, Connecticut with forty-six, Pennsylvania with twenty-one, Virginia with nineteen, Maryland with eighteen, and the other colonies trailing behind in a year that was fairly typical of the pre-Revolutionary era. Even though the building of ships was often unprofitable for the individual builder or merchant, in the larger context of colonial and imperial markets and their constant need for ships and shipping, the shipbuilding industry gradually spreading down the coast from New England to Charleston played a vital part in the transformation of the British colonies. Without it, economic progress would necessarily have been much slower.

THE IMPACT OF TRADE AND SHIPBUILDING. Many figures could be cited to illustrate the growth of trade within the colonies as part of the Atlantic economic system by the time of the American Revolution. Let a few observations suffice. The American colonies were mainly agricultural, and their imports and exports were both determined by that central fact. Manufacturing was relatively limited, partly because greater profits in most cases could be derived from agriculture and commerce. Consequently, manufactures were sorely needed, as were outlets for agricultural goods. Within this economic context, maritime commerce and its auxiliary industries derived their importance. Commerce, and commerce alone, could provide the outlets for the wide variety of surplus agricultural goods and their by-products. The southern colonies led all the others in the volume and value of their exports or agricultural products, these being chiefly tobacco, rice, indigo, and naval stores. The middle colonies, with their extensive cultivation of cereals, had led in expanding the exports of grains, flour, and biscuits, plus grain-fed animals and meat products. New England, as before, exported large quantities of fish, rum, lumber products, and ships. All of the colonies needed the markets of Europe and of the other colonies, and the manufactures of England and the rest of Europe, for their well-being.

That American colonial trade was well-distributed and extensive is illustrated by the fact that on the eve of the Revolution approximately 30 percent of gross tonnage into and out of the colonies was with Britain, 30 percent was with the West Indies, 30 percent with American colonial ports and the Bahamas, and 10 percent was with southern Europe and Africa. Furthermore, the value of American imports from Britain in 1772 was greater than Britain's entire value of exports to all parts of the world in 1704. Imports and exports between Britain and the colonies had increased 400 percent from 1700 to the outbreak of the Revolution. Commerce may not have been the very life-blood of the middle and southern colonies in such a direct way as it was of New England, with its trade in fish, rum, and other products, its shipbuilding industry, and its extensive carrying trade; but without maritime commerce, the surplus grains and foodstuffs of the middle colonies and the tobacco and other exports of the southern colonies would have rotted into waste. Overseas trade and shipbuilding never constituted the major portion of colonial occupations, but their vital function within the whole developing economic system cannot be doubted. Very few colonists were independent of the marketplace, and all would be adversely affected by any attempts to curb its workings--and the marketplace was primarily maritime as it functioned. The market place was by the late colonial period the coastal colonies, the Caribbean, and Europe. Cheap water transit made the movement of goods possible. The local market and the barter economy of the early 17th century were dead; the colonies were economically part of the world. Trade had come to occupy a central, rather than a peripheral, position in the colonial Atlantic coastal economy.

But to concentrate exclusively on the interchange of goods and the building of ships and their importance to the colonial economy would be to overlook an equally important aspect of the economic development of the American colonies. The human dimension of these spectacular changes may be more difficult to illustrate, but it represents as far-reaching a change in colonial--and later national--life as does the carrying of goods and the building of ships. A skilled trade or occupation in the American colonies was a way of economic life, rather than a set reflection of a social status. A trade or occupation could be a means of social and political ascent. Wealth could be the path to importance in colonial society, and as early as the beginning of the 18th century it was apparent that social ascent through a trade or occupation was forming a detectable pattern. Formerly unknown tradesmen, sailors, or farmers became substantial men in their communities via their success as merchants and builders. A father in turn would pass on his business and his middling position to his son, who would continue to climb the social and political ladder. As trade and commerce became leading activities in the colonial villages, some of the more successful men, by dint of hard work, became important political and social figures, perhaps being elected to the colonial Council. Such prominence could best be realized in the seafaring cities because their economic lives centered around trade and the tradesmen. Artisans and mechanics, to say nothing of sailors, looked to the merchant-tradesmen (or planter-tradesmen in the south) for leadership and success in their common undertakings of trade or of shipbuilding and outfitting. Management of the towns, cities, and colonies fell to the emerging wealthy merchants, whose function it was to guide their commercial interests.

Success as a merchant, then, meant the opportunity for further wealth, perhaps through investment in shipbuilding or land. It also provided the opportunity to exert a natural leadership in the community of commercial interests. The merchants, through their correspondence and travel, developed the economic and social connections with the market cities in the Atlantic coastal colonies, in the Caribbean, and in Europe. The interpersonal relationships among the merchants, forged over years or decades of trade, provided the cohesion that made the commercial system work. This commercial cohesion also led to social and political cohesion. Within each community and among communities there developed a provincial aristocracy of wealth, which managed the civic, economic, and cultural affairs of their limited domains. Such wealth and power might well have been resented at times by the lower classes, but no one could deny their existence.

In the 17th century, merchants such as Boston's Anthony Stoddard and John Hull emerged to help lead the Bay Colony. Newport's Nicholas Easton and Benedict Arnold both served as governors of Rhode Island. That colony also saw merchant leadership from the Cranston and Wanton families. In New York, such men as Cornelius Steenwyck, merchant king and governor, served the same function. In Philadelphia in the 17th century, William Frampton and James Claypoole assumed leadership in the city. In 18th-century Boston, John Hull's son-in-law Samuel Sewall moved into prominence and gained entrance into the company of such merchant leaders as Andrew Belcher, Thomas Amory, and Andrew Faneuil and his nephew Peter. They were joined by the Hancocks. The Lopez family of Boston was closely tied to the enterprises of Aaron Lopez in Newport. The Philadelphia merchants of the 18th century were more than adequately represented in political affairs by Edward Shippen, who served as governor, and by Samuel Powel, Charles Read, and William Allen, all merchant kings and mayors of Philadelphia. New York merchants were proud of the prominence of Samuel Bourdet and Isaac Rodrigue, and Charleston merchants saw Madam Sarah Rhett, Arthur Middleton, Jonathan Amory, and Joseph and Samuel Wragg represent their interests in local and colonial affairs. Clearly, in each trading port and in each colony supporting it, the merchant-traders' influence was considerable. Colonial merchant leadership extended far beyond their numbers.

All of these developments in trade and shipbuilding and in the rise of an important merchant class took place within the parameters of the Mercantile System as practiced by England, the cardinal principle of mercantilism being to assure wealth in the form of coin and bullion to the mother country through the creation of a favorable balance of trade with its colonies. Some production and trade were restricted (such as certain manufactured goods) in the American colonies, and some were encouraged (such as tobacco), depending on the economic needs of England. The activities of foreign merchants and shippers were generally disallowed unless the merchants and traders of the home country were unwilling or unable to develop that particular avenue of trade. Trade was designed to promote the industries, shipping, and naval power of the mother country as far as possible. This being the case, the commerce of the mother country and of its colonies was restricted, where possible, to the ships of that country, and any foreign merchant marine was excluded as a matter of basic economic and political policy.

The companies that made the first settlements in America were given exclusive trade monopolies with their colonies, and foreign trading vessels were generally excluded. Furthermore, as early as 1620 the Crown forbade the export of valuable tobacco from Virginia to any country other than England. However, during the turbulence of the Civil War in England in the 1640's, the colonists developed strong trading connections with Holland, often on Dutch ships, so that when order was restored the mother country turned to the task of bringing the American colonies under its full economic control once again.

The Navigation Act of 1651 was carefully prepared and specifically designed to re-impose English control over the trade of its colonies and thereby exclude the Dutch from this lucrative business. This commercial regulation excluded all foreign ships from carrying goods between England and its colonies, and required that foreign goods coming into England be imported only in English ships with crews having a majority of Englishmen, or else in the ships of the countries where the goods were produced. These rules, which carried a penalty of forfeiture of vessel and cargo for violation, did not give English traders a monopoly of colonial trade; English colonists had been legally considered Englishmen since 1622, and foreigners could still ship directly from their home ports to the colonies. Nevertheless, the purpose of the law was clear: England was to control and reap the benefits of trade to and from its colonies; the Dutch were to be excluded.

The Navigation Act of 1660--which became the basic navigation act for the Crown--extended the earlier law, first, by defining English ships as those in which the master and three-fourths of the crew were English; second, by forbidding any foreigner from acting as a merchant or factor in the colonies; and third, by demanding that the master of a ship give a surety bond that certain colonial products (called "enumerated") would be landed only in England or in an English colony. Enumerated items were sugar, tobacco, raw cotton, ginger, indigo, and furstic and other dye woods. Molasses, rice, and naval stores were added to the enumerated list in 1706, and copper, beaver, and other skins in 1722. This act had little effect upon the American colonies during the 17th century, since tobacco was the only export of the colonies which was enumerated in that period, and the English market for tobacco was usually very good.

The Navigation Act of 1663 added the enforcement provision that a master failing to file a bond on enumerated products would lose his cargo and vessel, and also went on to require that all non-English products being shipped to the colonies had to be shipped through England on English-built vessels with English crews (except for salt from any port and wines from Madeira and the Azores). The Act was intended to give British merchants a monopoly of exports to the colonies. But this law, like that of 1660, had little effect on the American colonies because most imports of manufactures into the colonies were made in England or purchased in England anyway. Nor was American colonial shipping or shipbuilding injured; American colonists were considered Englishmen, and American-built vessels were considered English-built. Some illegal trade in Virginia and Maryland tobacco via New Amsterdam or by transfer to Dutch ships at sea was carried on, but the amount was never great. Basically, the American colonies suffered little loss by these various trade and navigation regulations. Furthermore, intercolonial trade, growing more and more valuable, was not adversely affected by these regulations; indeed, it had protection against competition from foreign vessels.

The Navigation Act of 1673 sought to aid enforcement of the trade and navigation acts by authorizing the Customs Commissioners to appoint collectors in the colonies to grant bonds on enumerated items being landed in England or to collect a duty on enumerated items sent to another colony. The result was that for the first time intercolonial trade was subject to duties and serious restriction, but the wording of the law was so ambiguous and the machinery for enforcement was so ineffective that duties on shipments to colonial ports were frequently evaded, and colonial shipping was hardly affected. The Navigation Act of 1696, designed to improve enforcement further, fell far short of the mark, and the colonies were hardly touched by the provisions of the law through the early decades of the 18th century. American colonial trade was essentially unaffected--and, indeed, was helped in many ways--by the navigation laws and continued to grow and prosper.

Not until the enactment of the Molasses Act of 1733 was the economic well-being of the American colonies seriously endangered. This Act placed very high duties on rum, molasses, and sugar imported into the colonies from the French, Dutch, Spanish, or Danish West Indies; it was an attempt to force the colonies to buy these products in the British West Indies at a higher price. Inasmuch as colonial traders exported large quantities of fish, flour, lumber, cattle, and horses to the non-English West Indian islands in return for lower-priced and abundant sugar and molasses, the act seriously threatened an important segment of American colonial trade. This short-sighted piece of legislation would also have denied the colonists the coin and bills of exchange they needed in order to buy their needed manufactures in England. But the Molasses Act was simply ignored by the colonists, and British attempts at enforcement were no more effective than were earlier attempts to enforce the acts of 1673 and 1696. To enforce this law and all the provisions of the previous navigation acts would be to severely impinge on American colonial trade practices and important sources of wealth for the colonists. Only after 1763 was such an attempt made.

But in the meantime, colonial trade continued to prosper. The Acts of Trade and Navigation, while irritating when infrequently applied, worked no great hardship upon American colonial trade or shipbuilding, nor upon the economy of the colonies in general. The American colonists, under existing regulations, could look forward to continued and rising prosperity.

Despite the fact that the Mercantile System was designed to work to the benefit of the mother country and not to the benefit of the colonies, the American colonies by the third quarter of the 18th century, while predominantly agricultural, had become leading maritime trade and ship-building powers and part of the Atlantic trading community. The destiny of the colonists was as tied to the sea as it was to the land-mass upon which they lived. They had developed a commercial prowess unrivaled by any other area in the British Empire. Their merchant-leaders were very conscious of their power and of the place of the colonies within the British commercial system. To affect adversely the affairs of these men and the trade-conscious constituencies they represented, and to change the rules and enforcement of the British trading system under which they operated, would be to affect adversely what was perhaps the most critical segment of the economy and its leaders. England learned that lesson after 1763.

SUGGESTIONS FOR FURTHER READING

Bailyn, Bernard. The New England Merchants in the Seventeenth Century. Cambridge: Harvard University Press, 1955.

_____ and Bailyn, Lotte. Massachusetts Shipping, 1679-1714: A Statistical Study. Cambridge: Belknap Press of Harvard University Press, 1959.

Beer, George L. The Origins of the British Colonial System, 1578-1660. New York: Macmillan Company, 1908; reprint ed., Gloucester, Mass.: Peter Smith, 1958.

Bridenbaugh, Carl. Cities in the Wilderness: The First Century of Urban Life in America, 1625-1742. 2nd ed. New York: Alfred A. Knopf, 1955.

Bruchey, Stuart, ed. The Colonial Merchant: Sources and Readings. The Forces in American Economic Growth Series. New York: Harcourt, Brace & World, Inc., 1966.

Clark, William H. Ships and Sailors: The Story of Our Merchant Marine. Boston: L. C. Page & Co., 1938.

Goldenberg, Joseph. Shipbuilding in Colonial America. Newport News, Va.: The Mariners Museum, 1976.

Harper, Lawrence A. The English Navigation Laws: A Seventeenth-Century Experiment in Social Engineering. New York: Columbia University Press, 1939.

Hutchins, John G. B. The American Maritime Industries and Public Policy, 1789-1914: An Economic History. Harvard Economic Studies, Vol. LXXI. Cambridge: Harvard University Press, 1941.

Jensen, Arthur L. The Maritime Commerce of Colonial Philadelphia. Madison: State Historical Society of Wisconsin, 1963.

Johnson, Emory R., et al. History of Domestic and Foreign Commerce of the United States. Vol's I and II in one volume. Washington, D.C.: Carnegie Institution, 1922.

Middleton, Arthur P. Tobacco Coast: A Maritime History of Chesapeake Bay in the Colonial Era. Newport News, Va.: The Mariners Museum, 1953.

Pares, Richard. Yankees and Creoles: The Trade between North America and the West Indies before the American Revolution. London: Longmans, Green and Co., 1956.

Sheperd, James F. and Walton, Gary M. Shipping, Maritime Trade, and the

Economic Development of Colonial North America. Cambridge: Cambridge University Press, 1972.

The American maritime trades were prosperous and growing by the 1760's. The mother country maintained control over its American continental colonies by the Acts of Trade and Navigation dating back a full century. These various acts did not work a serious hardship either on the maritime trades or on the colonial economy. Relations between England and the colonies were amicable.

PROSPERITY UNDER MERCANTILISM. Britain encouraged specific colonial industries by paying bounties in England on naval stores, such as pitch, hemp, and tar, and by granting further protection to the colonies by placing a high tariff on supplies of these coming into the country from outside the realm. Raw silk was admitted duty free and was also given a bounty. Bounties were also awarded on lumber and lumber products, on cooperage, and on indigo. Tariffs on many colonial products being shipped into England had been completely removed by the 1760's. Pig and bar iron, lumber, wheat, flour, salt beef, and pork were in this favored category, as were rawhides and skins. Sugar from British dependencies into the American colonies bore no tariff, although foreign sugar imported did carry a duty. There had been a high tariff on foreign molasses since 1733, but, as we have seen, the law had never been enforced. Thus molasses, the basis of the very valuable West Indian trade, was secure from damaging regulation. It was a very important part of colonial maritime prosperity. Tobacco, naval stores, and sugar and sugar products also were protected by a legal monopoly in specific markets.

That these British acts controlling trade were not oppressive is illustrated by the case of tobacco. American tobacco was imported into Britain virtually without competition. Britain furnished the market for tobacco, and British bankers extended the credit needed by the American growers to plant, grow, and harvest their crops. So active was the market that between 1746 and 1771 the tobacco trade with Britain grew 400 percent. This growth, of course, was aided directly by the union of Scotland with Britain in 1707, whereby Scotland fell under the prohibition against growing tobacco in the home territories from that time forward. After 1767, the tobacco market grew 50 percent in just five years. Britain supplied the marketing centers to grade, process, and repack the tobacco for sale throughout Europe. By the 1770's probably 95 percent of the tobacco shipped into England was re-exported after processing. The American tobacco growers and the British tobacco processers had in this fashion formed a valuable alliance of interests. The processing and marketing machinery in England was vital to the tobacco growers in the colonies; the colonies were not suffering under this protective system.

The same can be said for rice and indigo production in the colonies, and of the exporting of these products to Britain as enumerated under the Acts of Trade. Rice from the lowlands of South Carolina and Georgia found its world markets through Britain, and its production was rapidly expanding in the late 18th century. Enumeration was no handicap to indigo either. Its growth was actually encouraged both by enumeration and by the bounty paid upon its importation into England. As with tobacco and rice, its prosperity and dependence on British protection and marketing systems became evident only after American independence, when the market for all three products went into precipitous decline, and then stagnation, when American growers tried to compete in the world market without British favors.

Likewise, the limits imposed by Britain on the manufactures of the colonies were not oppressive. The restrictions on the production of wool and woolen goods imposed by the Woolen Act of 1699 applied only to water exports; much of the local and colonial exchange of these goods remained untouched. The Hat Act of 1732, which forbade the exportation of colonial-made hats to Britain, had no effect upon the American hat industry which relied on manufacturing for the colonials anyway. That the British regulations on the exportation of iron products did not seriously impede the development of the colonial iron industry is illustrated by its expansion to a point where its output was greater than that of both England and Wales on the eve of the Revolution. There was not a colonial industry or area of commerce which was not experiencing expansion in the third quarter of the 18th century. Fishing; whaling; tobacco, rice, and indigo growing; iron production; naval stores; the rum, slave, and sugar and molasses triangle; the movement of goods by water or land; the grain trade; shipbuilding--all were prospering and growing by the 1760's despite, and often with the aid of, British mercantile regulations.

Wages in the American colonies were higher than anywhere else in the realm, and artisans in all trades were emigrating to the New World in the 1760's and 1770's in numbers never before witnessed. Population was doubling every twenty-five years, both from natural increase and from immigration. Evidences of prosperity in the form of new churches, schools, and comfortable houses and estates were to be seen everywhere. The American colonists were better fed, better clothed, and better sheltered than persons anywhere else in the realm, if not in the world. Use of homespun as clothing had given way to use of silks, velvets, and brocades. If the Navigation Acts were oppressive, it was not evident from either trade and manufacturing statistics or from the everyday life of some two million colonists.

The American colonists therefore had no quarrel with the Navigation Acts. They did not object to foreign ships being forbidden to carry their merchandise, because the removal of this prohibition would have harmed their own maritime trades. They did not evade the enumeration on most of their products to any great extend, particularly after 1700, because of the prosperity guaranteed within enumeration. They apparently did not object to not being able to receive non-British manufactures directly, instead of through the ports of the mother country, because the great bulk of the manufactures received in the colonies were obtained

from Britain anyway. And if they bought their silk, sailcloth, gunpowder, linen, and cordage from other sources, the colonists would lose
the valuable export bounties offered by the Crown.

Only in the case of molasses and the Molasses Act of 1733 could the
colonies be seriously harmed by British regulations, but this act, designed to force trade with the British West Indian growers, was, as we
have seen, never rigorously enforced. The colonial rum industry needed
foreign sugar and molasses, and trade with the British and foreign West
Indies was an integral part of the colonial trade network. Consequently, customs officials were willing to certify illegal French molasses
as being of British origin in West Indian ports--a process called "naturalization"--and customs officials in northern ports were quite amenable
to certifying molasses imports at lesser amounts since the duty of six-
pence per gallon would be ruinous if it were ever enforced. Thus the
Molasses Act was never a serious problem, and the Crown showed a marked
disposition to acquiesce in the systematic evasion of the law since
rigorous enforcement would have been disastrous for the colonies and
for England as well, for the shipment of sugar and molasses from the
Indies to America was an integral part of the Atlantic trading newwork.

The American colonies in the 18th century prospered under British
favors and protection as embodied in the Navigation Acts. That the Acts
were not irritants to the colonists is revealed by the fact that no colonial leaders objected to them in the decades prior to the outbreak of
hostilities between America and England in 1774. Samuel Adams, the most
prolific (and perhaps the most radical) of agitators against England,
made few attacks on the commercial system and none on the Navigation
Acts. He complained long and loudly about increased Crown revenues and
the actions of the customs officials, but not about the system. The
same was true of his cousin John Adams. Benjamin Franklin, a leading
light in the fight for independence and the most noted representative of
the colonial legislatures before the Crown in the years preceding the
Revolution, called for more open manufacturing, but never attacked the
Navigation Acts as such. John Dickinson, the agitator par excellence of
Pennsylvania, objected to the Stamp Act as a revenue measure not constitutional for America, but not to the trade regulations imposed by the
Acts. Patrick Henry did not even consider the Navigation Acts part of
the controversy, and his fellow Virginian Thomas Jefferson was quite
willing to accept the existing trade regulations. Jefferson's objections
were only to new regulations that would work to the detriment of the
colonies. In none of the resolutions passed by the various towns and
colonies in the decade prior to the war was there an attack on the commercial system, and none suggested repeal of the Navigation Acts. Even
the Declaration of Independence, designed to highlight the most glaring
defects of the British system as applied to the colonies and how they
constituted imperial tyranny, made no reference to the Acts of Trade and
Navigation.

As Oliver M. Dickerson has argued in his seminal work, The Navigation Acts and the American Revolution,

Whoever seeks to connect the Navigation Acts with the American discontent which led to the Revolution must start with the fact, proved by the acid test of war, that a century of experience under these laws had produced a colonial popula-tion that was as militantly loyal as that of England, and possibly more so. (p. 157)

This leading historian of the causes of the Revolution concludes, after sifting all of the evidence, that the Navigation Acts, rather than being a source of colonial discontent, were in reality the "most important cement of empire." The American colonies and the mother country were, indeed, one in economic mind regarding the Mercantile System and the benefits it assured for both of these integral parts of the empire. The Mercantile System as embodied in the Navigation Acts and in British prac-tices of enforcement--or in lack of rigid enforcement in the case of the Molasses Act of 1733--was not a source of irritation or even debate. As a means of regulation and protection, it was beneficial to both. The system as it had developed over a century-and-a-half of colonial experi-ence was not challenged on either side of the Atlantic. The benefits accruing to the mother country were never objected to by the American colonies; the benefits accruing to the colonies were never objected to by the Crown, Parliament, or by the British merchants. Perhaps, as some American and British writers prophesied, within half a century the com-mercial strength and population of the colonies would have matched or exceeded that of Britain, but neither the Crown nor the colonies looked upon this growth as anything other than proof that the system was working well. Had this commercial system of regulation continued on as practiced in the mid-18th century, greater prosperity would undoubtedly have been achieved. But forces were at work that doomed not only this system of regulation and protection, but also tore asunder the political ties be-tween England and its American colonies and replaced them with war be-tween the erstwhile partners in prosperity.

CHANGE OF POLICY, 1763-64. In 1763-64 the basic relationship be-tween Britain and the colonies underwent significant change. In these two crucial years, Britain began to adopt laws that added taxation for revenue to the existing Mercantile System. Edmund Burke, the great Bri-tish statesman, declared in a speech in Parliament that this was,

> . . . a new principle . . . with regard to the Colonies, by which the scheme of a regular plantation parliamentary revenue was adopted . . . . A revenue not substituted in the place of, but superadded to, a monopoly; which monopoly was enforced at the same time with ad-ditional strictness, and the enforcement put into military hands.

That this capsulization was accurate is proved by events; why the change in policy and practice took place requires explanation.

Beginning in 1689, and continuing at various intervals until 1763, Britain and France became involved in four great wars with each other. These were wars for European domination occasioned by King Louis XIV's determination to expand the area and influence of France and to break the "Hapsburg Ring" that surrounded his country. Britain stood to lose much by French domination of the Continent and was first driven into conflict in the War of the League of Augsburg (or King William's War, 1689-97). William III, the husband of Mary, King of England, and Stadholder of Orange, brought in English help to resist the attempts by Louis to take the Belgian Netherlands from the Hapsburgs, a territory too close to William's Holland to permit its conquest. Louis was driven back, but made a second attempt at expansion by arranging to place his grandson on the throne of Hapsburg Spain and thus join the Bourbon kingdom of France to that of Hapsburg Spain. This attempt resulted in the War of the Spanish Succession (or Queen Anne's War, 1702-13) in which Britain, the Netherlands, and the Hapsburg Holy Roman Empire resisted Louis' expansionism and fought him to a draw. But this war settled nothing, and thus the overall conflict for the Continent and the colonies broke out again in 1740 as the War of the Austrian Succession (or King George's War, 1740-48). France was forced to disgourge some of its colonial territories at the conclusion of this conflict, as we have seen, but the basic issue had not been settled in what had now clearly become a contest for European and colonial domination.

Thus there began in 1754 in the colonies, and in 1756 in Europe, the last of the four great wars of domination, the Seven Years' War (or the French and Indian War, 1756-63). England, with the help of its American colonies, emerged victorious from this war and was able to extract from its vanquished enemy virtually all French territories in the New World, including not only all of Canada but also the trans-Appalachian territories west of the American colonies. The British gained also East and West Florida from France's ally Spain. Britain came out of these wars, and especially from the "Great War for the Empire" between 1756 and 1763, with complete ownership and control of the lands in America from the Atlantic to the Mississippi and from Florida to Hudson's Bay. It is within the context of these wars--also very important to American colonial fishermen, as we have seen--and the new territorial gains in America resulting from them, that the change of policy beginning in 1763 must be approached.

The now-altered American colonial situation placed the Crown and Parliament in the position of being forced to redefine their policies for their American colonies. Fearful of difficulties with the Indians now released from their loyalties to the French in the newly-acquired territories--graphically illustrated by Pontiac's War in the West--and the difficulties of assuring peace for their new subjects in this broad expanse of rich land, the government decided on two measures. First, by the Proclamation Line of 1763, the area west of the crest of the Appalachians was declared to be Indian territory closed to the colonial settlers. Second, it was decided that a sizeable contingent of troops would be necessary to garrison this area to keep the Indians at peace and to keep the American colonists out.

The first of these measures, the Proclamation Line, ran directly counter to the interests of an influential group of land speculators, particularly from Virginia, North Carolina, and Pennsylvania, who had made treaties with the Indian tribes in the Ohio Valley to take over vast stretches of land, and who, accordingly, had goodly amounts of money invested in these lands now forbidden to them. Reinforcing the indignation of these speculators were the dreams and aspirations of thousands of frontier farmers who had already crossed into the Ohio Country, or who saw their future in these lands being settled as their new homes in the West. Some speculators continued to negotiate with the Indians even after the Proclamation of 1763, and the Crown did acquiesce in the inevitable and confirm certain of these treaties; but both the land speculators and the frontiersmen were still bothered by the stated inducements in the Proclamation of settling other British subjects in these areas, and by the very real fear that the territories would in fact be closed to them and permanently reserved to the Indians or to outsiders. Thus the first of these measures caused a great deal of unrest among the speculators and among the farmers all along the frontier and inclined them at least to question whether or not the Crown was still legislating in favor of the colonies. The Quebec Act of 1774, a decade later, would appear to them to be the final denial of their rights. By this act, most of this trans-Appalachian territory became part of the Province of Quebec and was thus lost to American colonial control and development. The colonial frontiersman, standing at the threshold of the unparalleled natural riches of the trans-Appalachian West and denied entry thereon, would seem to have had ample justification for questioning the motives and wisdom of those who would deny him what seemed to be his by "right" and by colonial charter.

Garrisoning of the frontier to provide security for the now-extended empire in North America would be a costly venture. It was estimated by the Crown that 7,500 troops would be needed to protect the area, requiring an annual expenditure of £300,000 to £400,000. Should not the colonials pay at least a part of this expenditure since the lands to be protected were of greater concern to them than to the mother country and since the ability of the colonies to pay was obvious? Many colonists answered in the negative and argued that the colonies could provide their own protection for the territories if needed. Yet the ill-fated Albany Plan of 1754, which had been designed to raise troops, build forts, and levy taxes to provide for colonial defense, had been scorned by the colonists in a spirit of particularism and had come to nothing. Similarly, to those colonists who objected to tax levies as a means of paying for the troops, and who would argue that requisitions from the colonies rather than taxes were the proper means of raising money, the Crown countered by declaring that during the late war with the French, requisitions had been honored when colonies were immediately menaced but had been pointedly ignored when no danger seemed near. Thus Parliament's closing of the trans-Appalachian West to the American colonists and taxing them to pay for the troops on their frontier emerged as matters of serious disagreement. Policies that seemed logical and necessary to the Crown and Parliament were seen by the colonists as a challenge to their rights and privileges as English citizens.

MERCANTILISM ALTERED. In moving toward policies that would have the colonies "pay their way" by Crown taxes after 1763, a subtle but extremely significant shift was taking place in the thinking of the mother country concerning the very purpose of imperial policy. Under British mercantilism to this point, both controls and revenue had been used to assure that the interests of the mother country would be well served, but control was the key, and taxes were secondary and only a means of achieving the goal of effective control and coordination. Yet as early as the decade 1715-25, changes had been considered which, if put into effect, would have put the emphasis on gaining greater revenues, stronger admiralty courts, stamp duties, and a molasses tax for revenue. A generation later, during the years 1753-54, Charles Townshend, as a very junior minister, had put forth the essentials of the scheme for colonial reform he would carry into effect in the 1760's. On these and other precedents, a new policy of mercantilism, which placed revenue as the primary goal, a policy of "fiscality," emerged in the decisions of 1763-64 on how to raise revenue in America. The older priorities of trade and commerce, the balance of economic interests, and the concept of the Empire as an interrelated economic entity gradually gave way to a new emphasis on revenue as a principal end of governmental economic policy and of the colonies' place within the imperial scheme. The colonies would now pay by direct revenues, laws would be enforced, and the subtleties of the balance of mercantile interests for the benefit of all would be of secondary concern in the move toward solvency.

This policy of fiscality was also part of a new overall view of the Empire which had been emerging in the second half of the 18th century, as British expansion had taken place not only in America, with the gaining of French territories, but also in Borneo, China, and India. Explorers had also been sent out, most notably Captain James Cook, to find new continents for exploitation. Cook's voyages had revealed no fabled continent in the South Seas ripe for commercial exploitation, but had included the re-discovery of Australia and New Zealand. If a new, wider empire was envisioned--and it was--then it was necessary to think out the place of the various constituent parts within it. It was in the framework of this futuristic scheme of empire that the concensus emerged in English governing circles that greater direction was going to be necessary to hold the Empire together. One device for assuring cohesion was greater control of the colonial governments from London. This greater control could be effectively assured only by using colonial revenues at the disposal of the Ministry to ensure the appointment and support of officials in the colonies more independent of the colonists and more loyally subservient to the Crown. Consequently, fiscality would assure revenues not only to pay outstanding debts, but also to reorganize the powers of the Crown relative to the existing colonies. The new policy of revenue as a primary goal of policy, then, was not only an economic question, but also a constitutional question, since it involved a change in the established modes of government in the colonies as constituent parts of the Empire, as well as in the rights and privileges of the colonists as understood by them.

This new policy of making revenue the principal purpose of colonial policy, rather than beneficial control, was carried out by George III and a group of loyal supporters made up of officeholders at home and in the colonies. They feared the independent spirit that might grow if political leadership in the colonies, made up of planters and merchants, continued to make gains against royal power in the colonial assemblies. This spirit of colonial independence ran contrary to their idea of a centralized empire directed from London. But in order to carry out this scheme of alteration, the King's party had to have sufficient support in Parliament. Here they found an ally in the largest group in that body, the landed gentry. The landed gentry had endured the burden of taxes in the four wars of the century and were quite willing to see this burden passed off to someone else. Besides, they held it to be just and fair that the American colonists should pay for their own war expenses and for garrisoning their own frontier. The colonies, they argued, were wealthy enough to bear the burden. Thus a coalition was formed between the King's supporters and the landed gentry, which was able to hold together and direct policy from 1764 to 1779, from the beginning of the break with the colonies to the point in time when colonial independence became a distinct reality.

But this policy of fiscality was not without challenge. For a century before 1763, the British merchants had been in major control of governmental policy. This political coalition included not only merchants but also allied manufacturers, bankers, shippers, and insurance interests. This group of influential men favored the Mercantile System as embodied in the Navigation Acts because of the prosperity it brought to the whole realm. They were well aware that the system brought benefits to them as well, and were not inclined to change the system by burdening it with revenue measures. To their minds the status quo was working very satisfactorily and the new imperial scheme might well injure their interests and the economic well-being of the entire nation. But despite their wealth, the merchant party was in the minority and was no match for the King's party-landed gentry coalition, particularly when the coalition could count on support from the higher clergy on the basis of promises made to them of extending the episcopal system to America, with all the new power and influence that that move portended.

In this political situation the merchants gradually lost power in the decades before the Revolution and were only able to modify the various revenue measures somewhat and to swing repeal when it became obvious that one or another measure was not working and was causing more havoc than good. But each time they were able to secure retreat, it took them longer and longer to do so. Consequently, the one group in English government which saw eye-to-eye with the influential American colonists was without effective power to alter the new direction upon which the government embarked in 1763-64.

At the end of the Seven Years' War, then, the fate of England and its colonies rested with a coalition of interest groups, each faction determined to change the status of the colonies within the realm. The stability furnished by William Pitt came to an end in 1763, and leadership fell into the ineffectual hands of George Grenville, First Lord of the Treasury. To Grenville the problem seemed simple. It would take 7,500 troops to garrison North America, and another 2,500 would be needed in the West Indies. The cost would be approximately £200,000 per year. Furthermore, the national debt had climbed from £73 million to £137 million during the course of the recent war. The interest alone on the debt would cost the government £5 million per year on a national budget of only £8 million per annum. Therefore, it appeared clear, the Crown could not pay for the troops out of existing revenues, and ways would have to be devised to raise the money in America instead. New acts calling for new revenues and a vigorous enforcement of the trade regulations would solve the problem. Consequently, the first fateful step was taken that would lead to disagreement, discord, and finally independence. The "cement of empire" as embodied in the Navigation Acts and supported by the British merchant interest group was about to be dissolved.

THE SUGAR ACT. In the spring of 1764, George Grenville introduced into Parliament, and that body soon passed, the Sugar (or Revenue) Act of 1764, a measure that affected the American colonies alone. It contained four basic revenue provisions: (1) rum from foreign colonies could not be imported into America, (2) the duty on foreign raw sugar was retained at five shillings per hundredweight, (3) the duty on foreign refined sugar was raised from five shillings to one pound, seven shillings per hundredweight, and (4) the duty on foreign molasses imported into the colonies was lowered to three pence per gallon, down from the six pence per gallon mandated by the Molasses Act of 1733. The first three provisions caused little stir in the colonies because adequate supplies of rum and sugar could be obtained from the British West Indies, but there was much opposition to the duty of three pence per gallon on foreign molasses. The purpose of the molasses provision was not to cut off the molasses trade with the French West Indies. French molasses was needed by American distillers; and, of equal importance, the American colonies had a lucrative market in the French islands for their exports of provisions, lumber, and livestock. The intent of the act regarding molasses was to set the duty at a reasonable rate and then collect that duty as provided for by the law. Actually the three pence rate represented a rejection by the government of the West Indian planters' desire for a rate of six pence on the product and was a compromise with the American colonial agents' arguments for a two pence rate.

The three pence rate did not do irreparable harm to American trade; the foreign exporters absorbed the additional duty over their duty-free smuggled shipments, but still the act was the object of great controversy. Between 1765 and 1774, the total amount of revenues collected from the Sugar Act was £306,399, or approximately 89 percent of the total of £342,846 collected from all revenue measures during the period. It was £281,760 more than the scant £24,639 collected under the Navigation Acts during the same period. This was obviously a drastic increase in duties for colonies accustomed to paying relatively little. But, of equal importance, more than 70 percent of the tax was collected at only five ports: Boston, Salem, New York, Philadelphia, and Charleston. The remaining percentage was collected at the other thirty-seven ports in the continental colonies. Furthermore, Massachusetts alone paid more than one-fourth of the taxes collected under the Sugar Act; and in New York and Massachusetts the duties from the act equalled or exceeded the collections for all other purposes in time of peace. Thus the burden fell most heavily on the maritime cities and colonies, who, rightly or wrongly, felt aggrieved and took an early lead in opposition to the revenue measure of the Crown. It must be remembered, too, that 1764 saw also the passage of the Currency Act, which seriously reduced the amount of currency available for business purposes, and specified the payment of taxes in specie, always in too short supply in the maritime colonies and their commercial ports. As a result, the business community was hurt in two distinct ways in that fateful year, by the Sugar Act and by the Currency Act.

The Sugar Act was resisted also because of the recognized fact that the duties thus collected would go directly to England. None could be used by the colonies for paying colonial officials. The measure was, then, a general tax on the colonies for the British Treasury over which the colonists had no control, and a device by which their hold over the king's agents in America was seriously weakened. As was recognized at the time, the Sugar Act was a considered attempt to remold both the economy and the political structure of the empire. The act may well have been presented as a means of covering the cost of the armies on the frontier, but it also embodied the principle that the revenue was to be used as the King and Parliament directed for the establishment of a new imperial relationship between the colonies and the Crown. It was more than a case of taxes; it was a modification of the whole system to provide for revenue as a primary goal and for less colonial economic and political independence at the same time.

In addition to being a burden on key maritime colonies and representing a basic change of policy regarding the purpose of the Mercantile System, the Sugar Act also made it much more difficult for those engaged in trade to carry out their ordinary legal functions. While it may be granted that merchants had engaged in smuggling at least to some extent under the system up to that time, particularly during the French and Indian War as they carried out trade with the French West Indies, the enforcement measures outlined in the Sugar Act went far beyond the bounds of the necessary.

More will be said about these regulations and their application by the customs commissioners and Royal Navy through the vice-admiralty courts. But it must be noted that these galling regulations and practices, which forced the honest merchant to undergo great inconvenience and cost in carrying out his legitimate functions, were another important irritant added to the colonial situation in the critical year of 1764. These irksome regulations, combined with the new exactions of the Sugar Act and the unwelcome contraction of the currency under the Currency Act, made protest and opposition inevitable. Indeed, opposition to the foreign molasses provision was sufficient to induce the Crown to reduce the molasses tax from three pence per gallon to one penny per gallon in 1766. This lower rate applied to all molasses imported, including that from the British West Indies, but was low enough not to be a burden, and much of the opposition to the revenue provisions of the Sugar Act passed away. Yet by the Sugar Act the Crown had made clear its change in direction, and the colonies had responded with rumbles of discontent at the new way the Mercantile System was being used.

THE STAMP ACT. When the Stamp Act was passed in 1765, the pattern of fiscality was once again highlighted, and again the colonies reacted strongly against such measures. This time they made Parliamentary taxing power not just a question of revenue-raising, but also a basic question as to whether or not Parliament had a constitutional right to tax. The Stamp Act very clearly caused a fundamental re-examination by the colonies of their place within the British Empire and reinforced the doubts raised by the Sugar Act of 1764.

48

The Stamp Act, imposing duties on such items as newspapers and legal documents, was an "internal" tax, and thus occasioned much opposition throughout the colonies. It was repealed the next year, in large measure because of the non-importation agreement of the Stamp Act Congress. Yet what is frequently not appreciated regarding the background of the act is of equal importance. For example, stamp duties had been used in England for some time, and so Parliament had seen nothing revolutionary about extending them to America. Also, considering the reaction of the colonists to the Sugar Act of the year before, Grenville had delayed the implementation of the Stamp Act so that colonial opinion could be heard on the measure. This way, the government could consider any alternatives the colonists might suggest. But the colonial legislatures would not propose a practical alternative. They chose instead to fight the use of tax revenues for the military, arguing that such taxes, because "internal," were repugnant to their rights. In a word, the colonists spent their time denying the right of Parliament to tax them. These were perhaps valid arguments, but were hardly solutions to the fiscal problems faced by the Crown. The Stamp Act was not sprung on the colonies without warning, or without benefit of consultation. But what is instructive and crucial is that for a second time a fiscal measure was quickly elevated to the higher and more fundamental question of Parliament's right to legislate for the colonies as it saw fit.

Second--and here again the pattern of colonial opposition holds true--despite the fact that the initial opposition to the Stamp Act began with the non-merchant classes (in this case the Virginia planters), the main burden of the act fell on the merchant classes and on the commercial centers. Records show that the strongest opposition came from these men and these areas. It is an often-overlooked fact that the imposition of stamps on legal documents was very hard on the merchant-shippers, because the Sugar Act had mandated the use of so many required documents in both the foreign and domestic trades. Every cocket listing goods shipped, each agreement to pay for transferred goods, and each of the four bonds now required of the shipper required stamps. On the average, total stamps cost £2 sterling per clearance, a very heavy burden, especially on a shipper in the coastal trade. The largest consignment of stamps went to the ocean trade colonies.

In the large coastal cities, the damage was obvious, and customs officials were sometimes persuaded to give notations that "no stamps are available" in order to permit trade to be carried out. But while this device allowed relief in some cases, the general uproar over the duties throughout the colonies was so great that the Crown almost immediately was forced to give second thoughts to the matter. And this time the merchants in most colonial cities went beyond mere remonstrances and with general enthusiasm adopted from the Stamp Act Congress the idea of non-importation. Widespread popular rioting also occurred. The British merchants felt the full effects of the non-importation agreements, and, seeing that trade was going to be seriously damaged, began working closely with the colonies' agents in London for repeal. Under this kind of pressure, the very weak Rockingham ministry was forced to relent, and repeal came in the spring of 1766. The merchants and their non-importation agreements had done their job well. A second revenue measure had been imposed by the Crown, this time "internal," and this time the measure had been repealed through merchant leadership. Thus the merchants, the group hardest hit by the Stamp Act, had shown their strength and had discovered a very effective countermeasure in non-importation agreements.

There is yet a third very important element in the story. The Stamp Act was a revenue measure and thus part of the new policy of the Empire, and the merchant class was thus again forced into a leading role in reacting to this change, yet most argument against the Stamp Act, even by the merchants, was based on the constitutional question as to whether or not Parliament could tax as it wished. As in the case of the colonial legislatures' being asked to suggest substitutes before the Stamp Act was passed, the colonists argued the question only in terms of rights, not in terms of monetary impact. So even though the Stamp Act imposed the greatest burden upon the merchant classes and propelled them into opposition leadership, their reactions, as was the case of most colonists who opposed the measure, reveal that they were thinking in terms not only of profits, but also in terms of time-honored rights. The colonists who objected, whether planter or merchant, whether inland or coastal, or whether gentry or poor, were now arguing in terms of fundamental rights as Englishmen, and asking whether or not these rights were being violated by Parliament's essentially revenue-raising measures. The merchants took the lead in protesting against the Stamp Act, but in doing so were also moving in the mainstream of colonial resistance to policies that would alter the fundamental rights of the American colonists within the Empire. Revenue questions were now clearly becoming constitutional questions; the place and prerogatives of the colonies within the kingdom were being re-examined. The repeal of the Stamp Act in 1766 did not bring this questioning to an end.

THE TOWNSHEND DUTIES. The repeal of the Stamp Act did bring rejoicing in America and relief to both British and colonial merchants, but the basic questions of how the Crown would obtain needed revenues and whether or not it had the right to raise such revenues unilaterally by its power of legislation over the colonies had not been settled. That Parliament would substitute another revenue measure in the form of the Townshend Acts in 1767 was perhaps inevitable, particularly since Charles Townshend, the Chancellor of the Exchequer and the effective head of government as a result of William Pitt's illness, had seen his Parliamentary opposition reduce the taxes on landed estates in Britain and thus leave the government in even tighter straits than before. Accordingly, import taxes were placed on numerous commodities being brought into the colonies, such as fancy wines, textiles, lead, paper, and tea. These new duties represented additional burdens on the shipping and trading population of the colonies, who already felt aggrieved at having been forced to bear the heavy burdens of the Sugar Act. Since the Townshend duties, too, were imposed for raising revenue, rather than for promoting trade within the Empire, the American colonists again fell back on defending the system as they had known it and condemning the new for altering the old mercantilistic purposes. For a third time in less than half a decade, the merchants felt compelled to object to the fundamental changes underway within the Empire.

Since non-importation had worked so effectively against the Stamp

Act, the merchants of the leading commercial cities turned to that device once again. This time there was no great meeting of the colonies to express their united opposition to the new revenue measures, so agreement on non-importation, led by the merchants of Boston, was harder to come by. Philadelphia Quaker merchants in particular were slow in declaring their unwillingness to import English goods, but they finally and effectively joined their peers from Boston and New York in 1769; after that time only three minor ports still allowed the importation or exportation of English goods. Trade again ground to a halt, and again the British merchants helped persuade the government that the duties would have to be abandoned. The Townshend Acts were simply not producing the revenues needed and expected, and they had led to a cessation of almost all trade with the colonies. Non-importation, a legal and effective device, again worked to keep the power of the Crown at bay; the Crown had no choice but to abandon the taxes in 1770, retaining the tax on tea to make clear Parliament's basic constitutional contention that it could levy any kind of tax it desired, the same point made by the Declaratory Act in 1766. The merchants, backed by the popular sentiment they seemed to express--and which at times pushed them beyond where they would comfortably want to go--had for a third time effectively thwarted an attempt to tax the colonies.

But as in the case of resistance to the Stamp Act, the merchants' opposition to the Townshend Acts and their justifications for legal resistance were expressed not in terms of monetary losses, but in terms of constitutional rights. It was not just a case of wrapping a base motive in the trappings of a higher one. When the British merchants made it clear that the opposition of the colonists to the revenue acts would be received more favorably by Parliament if it were couched in terms of inexpediency rather than constitutional rights, the colonial merchants leaders flatly refused to surrender their arguments of principle. Their public utterances and their private correspondence both reveal that to them the revenue question was a constitutional question. By 1770, the change in interpretation of the purpose of the regulations of colonial commerce from that of protection to that of revenue was being met by a constitutional questioning as to whether or not the Crown or Parliament could do just that. Either the government had to acquiesce in the colonists' interpretation of regulation and grant them the sole right to tax themselves, or the colonies had to surrender what they considered to be one of their rights within the British system. If neither side would back down, if no middle ground could be found, a violent clash would be inevitable. William Pitt and Edmund Burke saw this clearly and favored not taxing for revenue in order to avoid the more fundamental question of constitutional rights. Neither George III nor the governments in power during the 1760's and 1770's were willing to avoid the fundamental clash of wills.

THE VICE-ADMIRALTY COURTS. To understand adequately the merchants' opposition to these revenue measures, it is necessary to understand also how, beginning with the Sugar Acts, new regulations were issued to assure that all mandated revenues would be collected; how the vice-admiralty courts were empowered to operate in the colonies; and how abuses within the admiralty court system led to much resentment, not only against the rules and the manner in which they were enforced, but also against the government which would thus burden the merchant-shippers in its American colonies.

During the French and Indian Wars, all colonial trade with the French colonies had naturally been forbidden by the British Crown. A nation does not aid its enemy, and the American continental exports and imports were very important to the economic continuance of the French colonies in the West Indies. However, the customs officials very often did not carry out their duties as specified, sometimes because of their venality, sometimes because of threats to their safety, and sometimes because of the futility of trying to get convictions for violations from local juries not inclined to find their fellows guilty of smuggling. There was apparently widespread collusion among the customs agents, the vice-admiralty courts, and the colonial merchants during the years 1756 to 1763. The local vice-admiralty judges in South Carolina, Pennsylvania, and New York were not inclined to halt illegal trade with the enemy, and in Rhode Island and Massachusetts the merchants and politicians so tied up the judges in legalities and in legal suits against them that the vice-admiralty courts simply could not function effectively. On the basis of the lamentations of the customs officials that they could not enforce the laws of trade, the Crown, at the conclusion of the war, looked to methods of reforming the customs service and the vice-admiralty courts so that the desired revenues would be forthcoming.

During the war, the Crown had empowered officers of the Royal Navy to seize vessels engaged in smuggling. This authority was restated in 1763 when captains and officers of British ships in American waters were granted the right to be sworn in as customs officials with the power to seize and prosecute violators of the acts of trade. A portion of the profits from any legally condemned seizure was distributed to the officers and crews of the naval vessels involved. Soon some fifty-four vessels were stationed off the colonial coast from Newfoundland to the Leeward Islands, their officers now empowered to do the work of the customs service.

The Revenue (Sugar) Act of 1764 contained six sections dealing with revenues, but also some forty provisions dealing with the collection of duties and with the vice-admiralty courts, provisions perhaps more important in their effects than the better-known clauses dealing with revenues. These enforcement sections, like those having to do with revenue, represented fundamental changes in the operation of the Mercantile System and brought forth colonial protests. For example, the law provided for a new admiralty court with jurisdiction over all of the provincial vice-admiralty courts; prosecutions could be heard in any common law court, any provincial vice-admiralty court, or in the new vice-admiralty court with jurisdiction over all areas. This provision allowed the customs officials to have cases heard far from the local juries, which had proved so reluctant to convict their local merchants of smuggling. These procedural advantages granted to the customs service were not peculiar to the colonies or to admiralty law, despite the protests heard against taking cases to the common law courts or out of the provincial admiralty courts. But whatever the merits of the protest against these procedures, the Revenue Act of 1764 also placed the burden of proof of innocence or guilt on the owner or the captain of the vessel, not on his accuser. And if it was revealed that a customs official or naval officer had "probable cause" for making a seizure, the fees for the trial had to be paid by the owner or captain and no legal action was allowable against those involved in bringing the defendant to trial. This rule of law exempted the royal officials from having to pay the costs of prosecution themselves in case of acquittal, and from facing a charge of false arrest in case the captain or owner was found not guilty. But, needless to say, the captain or owner of a seized vessel would hardly look at the matter in that way, since he might be unjustifiably arrested and his ship and cargo seized for a period of time. If he were then found completely innocent, he still might be forced to pay the cost of the trial and would have no recourse against the man or men who had cost him so much anguish and perhaps loss of money.

Furthermore, even if "probable cause" was not declared by the judge, the offending official could still plead "general issue," and the burden of proof would be on the person bringing the charge of false arrest; and triple costs would be paid by the former defendant--now found innocent--if the case was not decided in his favor by the jury or if the case was nonsuited or discontinued. This may have been an effective protection against nuisance suits against royal officials, but it seemed an unfair and discriminatory law to the defendant found innocent of any violation of the trade laws. As an added insult, if the defendant brought his suit at common law against the official and the official was found guilty, the law stated that the maximum damages that could be awarded was a mere two pence. All of these procedures were not unique to British law, but they were unique to the American colonies.

Other provisions of the Sugar Act were equally galling. For example, the law demanded that cockets listing a description of each item of cargo, its contents, who shipped it, and where it was being shipped were required for all ships sailing two leagues or more from shore. Customs officials received fees for the issuance of these cockets. If a ship had no cocket, or if any goods were found on board which were not on the cocket, such goods were subject to confiscation. The two leagues--seven miles--provision brought most coastwise trade under the customs officials because of the difficulty of staying well within the seven-mile limit, considering deep indentations in the coast and the possibility of being forced to sail farther from the coast to avoid navigational hazards, to say nothing of being driven out by winds and currents. The eye of the customs official determined whether or not any vessel was within the seven-mile limit.

In addition to having to obtain a cocket listing all cargo in great detail, a master also had to give bond that no enumerated products would be unloaded anywhere outside the British Empire, and the list of enumerated products was lengthened by the Sugar Act. As almost every cargo would include some enumerated product, the effect of this clause was to force a master to obtain a bond--with a fee attached--as well as a cocket. In addition, a master had to obtain a special bond if he was carrying either iron or lumber, because, while these items were not enumerated, the law required special bonds on iron and lumber to assure that they would not be landed outside the Empire. Since almost all colonial vessels carried either of these two items as part of their cargoes, even in the coastal trade, the practical effect of this law was to force the masters to obtain a special bond or two on every voyage. Furthermore, a master had to give bond that he would not land any non-enumerated product, particularly foreign molasses, in a port outside the Empire, even if he had no intention of doing so or if his ship was not even capable of reaching a foreign port. Thus a master had to have four bonds when sailing: one for enumerated products, one for non-enumerated products, one for iron, and one for lumber. All these, like the cocket, carried a fee.

But even granting the reasonableness of such cockets and bonds for controlling smuggling, the colonial merchants and masters were subject to other regulations under the Revenue Act which made it practically impossible to do business within the law. The law stated that all bonds plus a special permit to load any item of trade had to be obtained before any goods were loaded. This provision covered all vessels, coastwise as well as those engaged in, or even capable of, oceanic trade. Most of the smaller coasting vessels loaded their cargoes bit by bit at various plantations or towns far from the nearest customs house, and at each point made on-the-spot arrangements as to which goods would be carried and in what quantities. These points of loading usually had no warehousing facilities to store the goods until the vessel had obtained the proper bonds and loading certificate, so any cargoes contracted for would be exposed to the elements while proper procedures were followed. Since it might take weeks to secure a normal cargo, this practice would be most ruinous.

Nevertheless, according to the law, a master would literally have to sail to each loading point, determine what cargo he would carry, sail back to a customs house and secure the proper papers and bonds, then sail back to the loading point and load. He could then sail on to the next point and repeat the whole process all over again. And on and on. This was a clearly ludicrous procedure. Indeed, under previous laws requiring loading papers and bonds to be secured, a practice involving no intention to defraud had been worked out between the masters and the customs officials. A master would load at various points, proceed to the nearest customs house, give the necessary bonds and comply with all other regulations, and then continue on his way. But as of 1764 such a sensible solution became a crime punishable by loss of both ship and cargo.

These loading and bonding regulations were another instance of a change of law and custom in 1764. Merchants in the major ports had been used to regulation and had generally complied with it. Loading and bonding regulations were no problem where warehouse facilities and one-stop loading were found. But the laws of 1764, if enforced, would bring the formerly free coastal trade under the law and would do so in a most unreasonable and irksome way. In addition, the careless wording of the law allowed the customs officials to interfere openly with intercolonial trade by arguing that the law specified that no goods could be loaded or shipped in any manner from one colony to another without the same cockets and other legal provisions as were to be applied to water commerce. Customs officials even set themselves on inland freight roads far from the sea and tried to apply the provisions of water transit to freight wagons.

Finally, the Sugar Act provided that in case of conviction for violation of any of these regulations, or any other trade regulations, the ship and cargo would be disposed of according to a given formula: one-third went to the person who informed on the alleged ship or master; one-third went to the governor of the colony where the seizure was made; and one-third went to the British Treasury. Royal Navy officers, now directed to aid in the enforcement of the trade laws, were subject to similar rewards and, as experience soon proved, had virtually no knowledge of the customs rules or of the usual customs practices and carried out their duties with a vengeance.

These matters, which would appear to be strictly trade regulations, were by their nature also important constitutional questions. The law of 1764 placed violations of trade regulations under the jurisdiction of the admiralty courts; and the admiralty courts operated without trial by jury. Only if a defendant brought suit in a court of common law against his unlawful prosecution would a jury be empaneled. It could also be argued--and it was by colonial merchants--that if the Revenue Act of 1764 was a revenue measure and not a matter of trade regulation, it was not properly a matter for the admiralty courts at all. The act was, they argued, a revenue act, and the violation of a revenue law entitled a defendant to trial by jury as was the case in England. Furthermore, they protested that violation of trade laws in England could be heard in the common law Exchequer Court with a jury. This right also was denied them by the Revenue Act of 1764; therefore, the judicial sections of the law were clearly unconstitutional in their eyes. These questions on the constitutionality of Parliamentary law raised the basic question of the rights and privileges of the British government in ruling its colonies on the American seaboard. Questions of application became questions of basic rights; both were being asked after 1764 with the passage of the Sugar Act.

They were asked again in 1765 with the passage of the Stamp Act. Not only did Parliament in this act authorize customs officers to take fees--in addition to their salaries--on clearances, bonds, cockets, entrances, bills of health, etc., to the extent of the table of fees approved by Parliament, but also the act allowed prosecutions under the act to take place under either common law or admiralty law, thus denying colonists the right to trial by jury in the latter instance. Thus the vice-admiralty courts became revenue courts, and though the Crown could argue that this was a logical extension of the revenue acts as some stamps dealt with documents of trade and therefore came under admiralty law, to many colonists the clear fact was that items unconnected with trade could now come under the admiralty courts, where the defendant could be denied trial by jury. This was a valid constitutional question, and objection was made as part of the outcry that greeted the Stamp Act and led to its quick repeal. England's revenue policy was carrying it deeper and deeper into the thicket of constitutionality, and the potential danger of civil war lay in the question of the rights of British citizens in North America.

CUSTOMS RACKETEERING. In 1767, when Parliament passed the Townshend Revenue Act, it was met with the now-familiar protests from leading colonists on the question as to whether or not Parliament had the right to tax, although much of the strength was taken out of the protest by the fact that Parliament had levied an "external" tax and thus avoided the issue of "internal" taxes. But at the same time Parliament provided for a five-man Board of the Commissioners of the Customs for America to oversee the American revenue system, and later in the year provided for four regional vice-admiralty courts in place of the supercustoms court then located in Halifax. This latter act put the judges of the four regional courts of Halifax, Boston, Philadelphia, and Charleston on a salary of £600 sterling to avoid any venality on their part, as might occur under a fee-pay system. Unfortunately for the cause of the radicals who protested that this four-court system would take cases out of local provincial jurisdiction and thus represent a form of tyranny by denial of local jurisdiction, most cases continued to be heard by the local vice-admiralty courts. The regional courts did little business outside their own respective jurisdictions; indeed, only the vice-admiralty judge of Boston collected enough money through condemnations to match his annual salary. The salaries of the other three judges had to be supplemented by taking money from other Crown sources. The new vice-admiralty courts did not in fact present a grave menace to the colonial merchants. Still, the years 1768-70 saw major damage done to relations between England and the colonial merchants, not from the four vice-admiralty courts, as had been forecast, but from the actions of the new customs officials operating in the colonies under the Board of Customs Commissioners. Their actions can only be labeled "customs racketeering"; it served to keep the issues of contention alive.

According to the Revenue Act of 1764 masters of vessels had to give four bonds plus obtain a cocket listing all items; all vessels beyond seven miles had to obtain bonds and clearance papers; customs officials, naval crews, governors, and the Crown shared the proceeds of confiscated goods; and in court the burden of proof was on the accused, who might have to pay all or part of the court costs if the judge declared probable cause. Added to these rules was a provision that the master of a vessel had to report to the customs house and receive a permit to unload before even one item was removed from his vessel. If he "broke bulk" before receiving his permit to unload, his ship was subject to seizure. Within this litany of laws, the new customs officials appointed by the new Board of Customs Commissioners operated for profit during 1768, 1769, and 1770.

During these years, ships' masters were hauled into the admiralty courts for "breaking bulk" by throwing overboard broken or rotten items in their cargoes. When members of the crew, acting according to a time-honored custom of the sea, sold private items carried with them on their ship, the master was charged with breaking bulk. Masters of small, local wood- and lumber-carrying boats were forced to enter into ports and give bonds that they were not carrying their cargoes to non-British ports, when in fact they were engaged only in regional trade and could not have made foreign ports even if they had tried. Intracolonial trade was interfered with even though it was specifically excluded from the Sugar Act, and the customs officials made every coaster pay fees of up to three dollars per clearance, a back-breaking amount for the masters of these small ships bobbing from port to port. The customs officials also brought ships' captains into court for their sailors' practice of selling personal items, not for breaking bulk, but for not having these personal items on the cocket. The customs officials enraged the merchant-traders by using paid informers and by overlooking minor deviations from the trade laws for a period of time and then suddenly arresting them for not giving bonds before placing items on board or for not having items of cargo exactly as listed on the cockets.

When the merchants and vessel owners complained to the Crown, the Attorney-General of England condemned these practices, but the Customs Commissioners deliberately suppressed this opinion and allowed the racketeering to continue. It is interesting to note that in Canada, Governor Guy Carleton flatly forbade such practices. The lower colonies were not as lucky, and the depredations continued, reaching public notice and widespread publicity and comment when the customs officials attempted to ensnare and destroy the influential Henry Laurens in South Carolina and John Hancock in Boston. The attacks on these leading merchants may well have been directed from England for political reasons, but, whatever their purpose, the nefarious practices of the customs officials brought to light by the stout resistance of these two leading merchants went a long way toward bringing discredit on the customs commissioners, who by late 1770 had stirred up so much colonial resistance that they were ordered to call a halt to their attempts to make their fortunes off the system.

But the damage had been done. All up and down the American coast, with the exception of the Virginia, Maryland, and North Carolina areas, where such racketeering was not prominent, the apparatus for raising the new revenues, as well as the revenues themselves, were discredited, and the loyalty of the merchant class to the Crown and its economic system had been severely shaken. Even the repeal of the Townshend duties in 1770 on all items except tea could not repair the damage that had been done. In the last analysis, governments rule by consent and trust; these attitudes on the part of the colonial merchants had been severely strained by the end of 1770 by the customs racketeering.

As the years of decision of the early 1770's approached, then, the bases of contention were clear. The colonists in general and the colonial merchants in particular had had no particular disagreement with the Mercantile System of a century's duration when used for the purpose of protection and growth. But when the System was changed in order to raise revenue and thereby brought to contention the issue of taxation without representation, the situation was fundamentally altered. Furthermore, this new system was now being enforced by customs officials with little understanding or appreciation of the merchant-shippers' customs or sensibilities. The Revolution did not arise from a lack of prosperity and the merchants' reaction to hard times. Indeed, both contemporary reports and trade statistics reveal that the years between the Peace of Paris and the Revolution were times of general prosperity. Fluctuations in prosperity were surely present, but until the outbreak of hostilities times were generally good. The problems were not economic; the problems were Parliamentary taxation to raise revenue, the constitutionality of Parliament's right to exact such taxes, and the gradual breakdown of loyalty to the Crown, particularly within the merchant class.

THE TEA ACT. The pattern of British policy and the colonies' reaction to it as a constitutional objection to revenue measures continued until the outbreak of hostilities in 1774. Despite the fact that there was a goodly amount of smuggling of tea, especially from Holland, to avoid the tax that remained on that commodity after the repeal of all of the other Townshend duties in 1770, it would appear from the evidence available that the colonists' violent reaction to the Tea Act of 1773 was centered on the issue of its being a revenue measure. This attitude is abundantly clear in the case of the strident measures taken against the importation of tea and against the paying of the tax in Boston, New York, and Philadelphia, the leading centers of tea importation for the colonies. The opposition to the monopoly now granted to the East India Company--in itself a violation of the Mercantile System under the Acts of Trade as it had operated since 1663--was clearly based on the issue of revenue, both in the minds of the merchants and among the general public. The Tea Act was seen as a means of forcing recognition of Parliament's right to tax in America; and Boston in particular refused to recognize this right, first by not allowing the tea to be unloaded and the tax paid, and then, when it appeared that the tea would be unloaded anyway, by dumping it into the bay. The record of opposition from New York and Philadelphia reveals that the opposition there was likewise based on paying the tea tax as a revenue measure and on the monopolistic provisions it involved. In all three of these overt cases of opposition to the Tea Act, the merchants were very active. Providence, Rhode Island, too, expressed its opposition to the tea monopoly, and, as in the case of the other port cities, its merchants were dedicated to protesting the act and expressing their support for the actions taken by Boston, New York, and Philadelphia. All cities agreed that the Tea Act and other British measures toward gaining revenues were clearly oppressive and unconstitutional.

POINT OF CONFLICT. By 1774, then, the American colonists stood in opposition as a matter of upholding a principle, namely, that Parliament had no right to enact revenue measures for the colonies without the colonists' consent. What had begun as resistance to single measures embodied in the Revenue Act of 1764 and measures of taxation and enforcement through the Crown's apparatus of the customs service, had been elevated to a basic constitutional question of right. But Britain too was upholding a principle, the principle that it had the power to legislate as it saw fit for the American colonies. From this position it had not budged since 1763. Nor was Britain prepared to waive its rights by recognizing the colonists' claims in 1773-74. So the issue was joined, and Britain, in order to uphold what it considered its rights, accepted the challenge of the colonists in 1773 and determined that they would be brought into subjection, forcefully if necessary, in order that the principle of the authority of the Crown and Parliament be recognized. The colonists could not, in the face of this British attitude, back down; to do so would be to surrender their principle of no taxation without representation. The result was a war that ended by separating the colonies from the mother country. Within a decade of Britain's change of policy of 1763-64, the bonds of loyalty had been stretched and finally broken. Questions of money had become questions of principle. Questions of trade and accepted rights within the imperial system had become questions worth the price of war. Britain's vast commercial empire faced dissolution from a misguided if understandable policy of attempting to convert it from existing for trade protection and encouragement to existing for the purpose of raising revenues for the Crown.

That this was one of the most fundamental issues in separation is revealed in a statement of rights and grievances issued by the Continental Congress in the fall of 1774:

> . . . the several Acts . . . which impose duties for the purpose of raising a revenue in America, extend the powers of the admiralty courts beyond their ancient limits, deprive the American subject of trial by jury, authorize the judges certificate to indemnify the prosecutor from damages, that he might otherwise be liable to, requiring oppressive security from a claimant of ships and goods seized before he shall be allowed to defend his property, and are subversive of American rights.

The outbreak of the Revolutionary War with all of its fateful implications for the peoples involved, and for the history of the world, can thus be traced in large part to a maritime question. America's maritime posture had been a major factor leading it to colonial wealth; now it led to revolution, and finally to independence.

SUGGESTIONS FOR FURTHER READING

Dickerson, Oliver M. The Navigation Acts and the American Revolution. Philadelphia: University of Pennsylvania Press, 1951.

Gipson, Lawrence H. The Coming of the American Revolution, 1763-1775. New York: Harper & Row, 1954.

Harper, Lawrence A. The English Navigation Laws: A Seventeenth-Century Experiment in Social Engineering. New York: Columbia University Press, 1939.

Hutchins, John G.B. The American Maritime Industries and Public Policy, 1789-1914: An Economic History. Harvard Economic Studies, Vol. LXXI. Cambridge: Harvard University Press, 1941.

Jensen, Arthur L. The Maritime Commerce of Colonial Philadelphia. Madison: State Historical Society of Wisconsin, 1963.

Kammen, Michael. Empire and Interest: The American Colonies and the Politics of Mercantilism. Philadelphia, New York, Toronto: J.B. Lippincott Co., 1970.

Labaree, Benjamin W. The Boston Tea Party. New York: Oxford University Press, 1964.

Sosin, Jack M. Agents and Merchants: British Colonial Policy and the Origins of the American Revolution, 1763-1775. Lincoln: University of Nebraska Press, 1965.

Ubbelohde, Carl. The Vice-Admiralty Courts and the American Revolution. Williamsburg: Institute of Early American History and Culture, 1960.

Wahlke, John C., ed. The Causes of the American Revolution. 3rd ed. Problems in American Civilization Series. Lexington, Mass: D.C. Heath and Co., 1973.

60

CHAPTER IV. MARITIME CONFLICT WITH EUROPE: PHASE II--NEUTRALITY AND WAR

The Revolutionary War was not completely ruinous of America's maritime trade, despite the effectiveness of the British fleet in American
waters. The early years of the war witnessed a substantial decline in
domestic commerce because colonial warehouses were short on foreign commercial items when fighting broke out; but by 1778, trade had revived
considerably, including some exchange of goods between Britain and its
rebellious colonies. Even though this commerce was forbidden by both
governments, trade was carried on indirectly by utilizing neutral ports.
Some British goods were obtained also from captured British merchantmen.
After 1778, there was an increase in imports of manufactured goods from
European countries; these products were readily obtainable in most American markets. Likewise, necessary supplies of manufactures were increasingly available from domestic production brought into being in response
to wartime shortages.

The generally healthy economic picture during the closing years of
the war and the continued existence of limited maritime trade with Europe
should not, however, obscure the fact that imports and exports were cut
drastically from their pre-war highs, and that the maritime trades suffered appreciably during the war. The period of conflict cut off the
natural flow of goods and materials between the former colonies and England to a large degree and generally ruined the trading arrangements--
beneficial to both--that had been built up during the 17th and 18th centuries. It is not surprising, then, that with the coming of peace in
1781, followed by the Treaty of Paris two years later, the two former
partners in prosperity would turn to each other once again.

THE POSTWAR MARITIME SITUATION. Despite the claims of some American
colonists in revolution that political independence would bring economic
independence from Britain, with American producers and traders turning to
extensive trade with the whole world without having to rely on the English, the conclusion of the war saw American trade patterns quickly return to those of pre-Revolutionary days. Britain remained both the chief
customer and supplier of the American people. Americans continued to rely
on trade with Britain as the mainstay of their Atlantic commercial system,
partly because British traders knew the American market well and continued
to supply it. Furthermore, British merchants had available the necessary
credit for trade with the capital-starved new republic. Britain was by
far the best market for exported foods from America because of its growing
industrialization and, in turn, the best supplier of manufactures. In addition, Britain was still the entrepôt of Europe for America and therefore
the most convenient and profitable entrée to the markets of the Continent.
The only other important European country that might rival Britain in any
or all of these economic advantages, France, was beset by political troubles that prevented its development along the lines desired by American

traders. Finally, British manufactured goods were not only better, but also cheaper, than those that could be obtained from its Continental rivals. Consequently, American trade fell back into its pre-Revolutionary rhythms after the war and, responding to the pent-up demands occasioned by the trade constrictions brought on by the fighting, experienced an upsurge with the coming of peace.

Much of this increase in commerce came from foreign manufacturers dumping their goods on the starved American market, much to the consternation of, and often to the demise of, local manufacturing built up during the war. But Americans soon found that, although they could renew their trading ties with Britain, the total situation had been changed by their newly-won independent status; and some of their former channels of trade were now closed to them. These two factors--dumping and lost markets--combined with an over-expansion of credit, led to a depression in 1785. But in 1786, with the necessary economic adjustments having been forced by the depression, trade and manufacturing began to revive; and American farmers, businessmen, and shippers looked forward to continuing the prosperity temporarily shattered by the War for Independence. But before that goal was reached twenty-five years later, the maritime trades and the country at large had to undergo periods of economic and political distress. The new United States had to chart its path toward expansion and prosperity amid the pitfalls of conflicting foreign national interests and neutrality, as all of Europe became involved in great wars for survival which encompassed the events of both the French Revolution and the expansionism of Napoleon Bonaparte.

That Great Britain would not continue to grant all the commercial favors to America that the former colonies had enjoyed before the War was to be expected. The commercial policy of a nation, like its foreign policy, must be self-directed, i.e., it must serve the best interests of the country involved. Nevertheless, the commercial status granted to the United States by Britain beginning in 1783 and continuing to 1795 was more favorable than that granted to any other country. This new status was not embodied in a treaty between the two countries, because Britain refused to make a commercial treaty with its former colonies. Rather, the new relationship was spelled out by the Privy Council through Orders in Council beginning in 1783. Basically, these regulations were fourfold: (1) goods entering Britain from the United States had to be in British or American vessels, the same type of nation-and-nation arrangement demanded by Britain of other European countries; (2) certain unmanufactured goods could enter Britain by paying the same duties as those imported from British colonies in America, certain processed goods from the fisheries paid the same duty as when imported from other countries, and all woods with the exception of masts, yards, and bowsprits entered Britain duty free; (3) no "alien duties," i.e., additional duties, were levied on American goods being shipped into Britain on American vessels, whereas other countries' goods had to pay this added tax; and (4) all trade between the United States and the British West Indies had to be carried in British ships alone.

The first three regulations were favorable, rather than restrictive, toward American exports to Britain and thus imposed no particular hardship. The last, however, struck at the very valuable trade between the former colonies and the West Indies and, in effect, destroyed the "sugar triangle" upon which so much of colonial prosperity had been based. The West Indian trade was to be a source of contention between the two countries for years, and American exclusion was not ended until 1830, when non-British shipping was allowed to serve the West Indies. It must be mentioned, however, that this restriction was no departure from British policy; the Crown had reserved shipping to and from its American, Asian, and African colonies to British vessels manned by British seamen ever since the mid-17th century. This provision--now operating against the Americans--had been the basis of their maritime growth during colonial times.

Nevertheless, while some trifling amounts of trade were developed with the Dutch, as with the Danes, the French, and the Spanish possessions in the Caribbean, the fact remained that the rewarding exchange of American fish, lumber, horses, and general foodstuffs for British sugar and molasses had come to an end. The lucrative "long haul" across the Atlantic with surplus products from the Indies being shipped on to Europe was also finished. This loss was hard to replace, and thus British policy toward America, while understandable and even generous in some respects, was deeply resented in the former colonies until adjustments were finally made.

Furthermore, by an act of Parliament in 1788, all importation from the United States into Nova Scotia, New Brunswick, Cape Breton Island, and Newfoundland was prohibited unless in a declared emergency, and no goods were permitted to enter Canada from the United States by sea. This regulation meant that both actual and potential maritime markets to the north were also cut off from the American maritime tradesmen. It was obvious that the British imperial system was still in effect, at least in the Western Hemisphere, and the new United States would have to live economically within the parameters of that policy. These restrictions, plus actions necessitated by the European wartime situation, made the American maritime trades subject to great pressures and restrictions through 1818.

On the other hand, American shippers had some distinct advantages over their European rivals in these critical first years of the republic, advantages which they sought to utilize to their full during Europe's years of conflict. For example, a ship cost from 40 to 60 percent less to build in the United States than in either France or Britain, giving American shippers a decided edge in procuring the vessels of their trade. Also, labor efficiency on American vessels was high, probably enough to offset the comparatively higher wages paid to American sailors. Furthermore, American-built vessels were comparatively durable because of their live oak and white oak construction, and cargo-damage losses were relatively low. The result of all of these advantages was that the American shipper could usually bid for and obtain freights at a lower rate than could his foreign competitors. So while the American merchant marine suffered certain debilities from the country's newly-won independent status, certain factors in its favor could potentially project it to leadership over its rivals in the race for maritime supremacy. Indeed, the very strengths inherent in the American merchant marine were the

reasons for its becoming embroiled in Europe's troubles to such an extent
that eventually the nation itself felt compelled to enter into war to uphold its vital rights upon the seas. Only when the European conflicts
came to an end with the final defeat of Napoleon and, with them, the
reasons for Britain and France's attempts to neutralize this strength or
put it to their own use, would this American maritime potential be able
to assert itself fully.

THE PERILS OF NEUTRALITY. In the summer of 1789 the United States
began its federal life under its new constitution. The country had
learned from sad experience that the weak confederacy formed during the
Revolution by the Articles of Confederation was incapable of performing
many necessary functions expected of it, not the least of which was trying to formulate a concerted foreign trade policy that would have the approval and support of each of the thirteen states. And so, after acri-
monious debate had raged across the land about the merits of the Articles
versus the new Constitution and about what far-reaching changes would be-
fall the country in the event the new document was approved, the requisite nine states approved the new constitution. The new government set
itself to the task of governing the potentially rich and powerful, yet
now-fledgling, republic. That spring, George Washington, the foremost
citizen of the land, took his oath of office as President, and the
houses of Congress organized themselves to chart America's destiny.

Recognizing that America's maritime future was very important to its
economic growth, Congress quickly enacted a tariff law and a navigation
act designed to promote the nation's foreign trade and merchant marine.
In July 1789, it granted a 10 percent discount on tariff duties on all
goods imported in American bottoms and also reduced the duties on Indian
and Chinese tea imported into the country on American ships, the latter
to encourage the developing Far East trade. Later on, in 1804, Congress
also extended the protection given American shipping by levying "light
money" on foreign vessels entering American ports, an additional tonnage
duty of 50¢ per ton being assessed these vessels. The American Congress
was most solicitous of American maritime interests as a valuable key to
America's economic future.

But despite its auspicious beginnings and the hopes the new government engendered for a glorious future, problems were not long in coming.
Within three months of Washington's inauguration, the French nation suffered the beginning of a convulsion destined to involve all of Europe
and much of the world, including the newly-fashioned United States along
the Atlantic shores of North America. The French Revolution was initially a moderate, bourgeois revolution that responded to the frustrations
of a middle class denied power by the existing monarchical system. The
revolutionaries in the first stage of the French Revolution were quite
content to establish a constitutional monarchy under Louis XVI as long as
the power and decision-making processes reflected their needs. Initially the French Revolution evoked a very positive response on the part of
most Americans, for it seemed to embody many if not all of the principles
the Americans had enunciated in their Declaration of Independence. But
many Europeans, and especially European monarchies, looked upon the revolution as a vile contagion to be wiped out before its poison spread.
They thus schemed against it indirectly, prepared militarily because it

threatened to spread to their countries, and impatiently awaited the day when France would return to monarchical sanity. Democracy might well be accepted as a form of government far across the Atlantic in the former British colonies, but to accept it in Europe itself was quite another thing. Europe watched and awaited further developments.

In 1792 the nature of the French Revolution changed radically. In that year and early in 1793, the Parisian mobs arose to overthrow the moderate French government. They declared for a thorough-going egalitarianism and sent both the king and his queen, Marie Antoinette, to the guillotine. Under the leadership of such men as Danton, Robespierre, and Marat, the violent stage of the revolution began, marked in blood by the Reign of Terror. Americans then began to divide on the merits of the revolution, some still seeing in it an extension of American principles, others seeing it as the destruction of law, order, and Western civilization. Of crucial importance, however, was the fact that in February 1793, the revolutionary government, seeking to distract the attention of the French people from their internal convulsions by directing their energies against an outside enemy--and at the same time attacking their enemies before their enemies were in a better position to strike at them--declared war on Great Britain and the members of the Second Coalition of central and eastern European powers. Thus began the twenty-two-year struggle, which ended only in 1815, and only after it had sucked the new American nation into its maw over the issue of neutral maritime rights upon the high seas of the world. President Washington level-headedly issued a Proclamation of Neutrality in April 1793, but it would take more than words to keep the Americans from becoming embroiled in Europe's fights if they insisted on their right to sail the high seas as neutrals to and from the ports of determined belligerents.

Britain was the first to challenge America's rights as a neutral. The French had previously opened their West Indian ports to American vessels to enable foodstuffs to be carried by Yankee shippers from the islands to France. Britain's Order in Council of June 1793 was designed to put an end to this trade by authorizing the seizure and pre-emptive purchase of all foodstuffs on neutral vessels bound for French ports. A second Order in Council, in November 1793, called for the seizure of all ships carrying the produce of, or supplies to, a French colony. The British argued to the legality of these acts on the basis of their Rule of 1756, which stated that commerce illegal in peacetime was illegal also in wartime. The Americans, in turn, argued their Plan of 1776 which stated that "free ships make free goods," a principle advantageous to them as beleaguered belligerents in need of aid in 1776, and now clearly to their advantage as a neutral in 1793. Whatever the merits of these legal arguments, under the Orders in Council the British Navy began seizing American merchant vessels, especially in the Caribbean, and there was nothing the United States could do to protect its vessels, since there was no longer a United States Navy in existence. Such seizures were roundly condemned in the United States.

American anger was both heightened and diffused, however, when the French began to retaliate against Americans allowing their ships to be searched by the British by seizing American vessels themselves. Faced with this situation of both England and France seizing American vessels, Congress passed a thirty-day embargo on all trade with foreign countries and then extended it for a month. But the anger of many Americans, led by the pro-French Jeffersonians, was not sufficient to force Alexander Hamilton, the Secretary of the Treasury, the leading Federalist and the most important influence in the government, into a foolish war against American's best customer, Great Britain. Blocking a Jeffersonian Republican measure in Congress, which would have cut off all trade with Britain, the Federalists instead sent John Jay to England to negotiate a settlement of these maritime differences with Britain. Jay was empowered also to settle the outstanding matters of Britain's refusal to surrender the forts in the Northwest Territory as stipulated in the Treaty of Paris, compensation for the ships seized by Britain, and an opening of the vital West Indian trade once again. If some type of settlement was not reached and the seizures were to continue, the result would very likely be war with Britain. This eventuality would be a great boon to French hopes, but would hardly be in the nation's interests as seen by Hamilton and President Washington.

THE JAY TREATY. John Jay was sent on an impossible mission. The angered American people expected him to make England resist from seizing American ships and thereby recognize American neutral rights. But Britain's agreeing to do that would directly aid its enemy France; and, Britain, having control of the seas, was not about to relinquish its prime advantage against its adversary. At worst, a war with America would be a nuisance, but it was a nuisance England was willing to avoid by making a partial settlement with Jay, despite the inflated hopes of the nation behind him. Besides, the British could not be forced to make any major concessions by John Jay, because the only threat Jay carried with him was America's option to join in a new League of Armed Neutrality with Sweden and Denmark to demand neutral rights under the threat of war. This single point of leverage became useless when Hamilton informed the British that America was not really serious about joining such a league.

Jay came up with the best possible treaty under the circumstances and managed to avoid war despite the personal vilification he had to suffer when the contents of the treaty were leaked to the Republican press while the Senate was debating whether or not to ratify it. Nevertheless, the treaty, toward which President Washington was so lukewarm that he sent it to the Senate without any recommendation, did pass by a vote of 20-10 in June 1795, and the danger of war with Britain passed. In the Jay Treaty the British agreed again to evacuate the forts in the Northwest and to compensate for losses arising from its maritime seizures, the amount to be fixed by a joint arbitration commission, which would deal also with pre-Revolutionary debts to Britons and the Maine boundary line. But Jay had not forced the British to abandon their practice of seizing American ships on the high seas. De facto the treaty recognized their right to do so. The Plan of 1776 was clearly not recognized, and free ships did not make free goods. Thus is explained much of the abuse heaped upon Jay and the treaty he negotiated.

But the British did agree to open their West Indian ports to American commerce to a degree by limiting such trade to vessels of seventy tons or less (a concession angrily rejected by the Senate). Britain also agreed to open its East Indian trade to the United States and to open trade to Americans with the British Isles on a most-favored-nation basis. This arrangement meant that the United States would receive all commercial privileges granted to other nations in their trade with Britain. Thus the treaty was a form of the long-desired commercial treaty with Britain and brought some substantial benefits to American shippers. Most important, whether or not the treaty sufficiently upheld American honor and principle, it did avoid war with Britain, a war that would have been extremely ruinous not only of American maritime commerce, but also of the whole national economy just struggling to maintain itself in the first crucial decades of the nation's existence. The Jay Treaty was obviously better than no treaty at all; it did allow the crisis to pass.

THE QUASI-WAR. For the two years following the Jay Treaty American commerce was basically unmolested by the English and the French, and shipping and shipbuilding showed very strong gains in the United States. The British did not interfere with "broken voyages" between the French West Indies and the French homeland as long as the goods were taken to an American port, unloaded and customs duties paid, and then reloaded for the voyage across the Atlantic. Accordingly, the re-export trade flourished, and by 1798 fully one-third of the customs duties paid at American ports were refunded because of re-exportation. The American merchant marine also flourished in carrying goods between the various ports of the belligerent nations, although Britain continued to stop and search American vessels.

In 1798, however, France decreed that neutral vessels would be "treated exactly as they allowed themselves to be treated by England," that is, as though they were not neutral vessels, and the French Navy began seizing American ships off the American coast. When the American emissaries to France were treated in a very undiplomatic way by Tallyrand, the French Minister of Foreign Affairs, and three unnamed French diplomats, known subsequently only as "Mr. X," "Mr. Y," and "Mr. Z," then approached the American ministers in France, who were trying to work out a solution to the maritime seizures, and informed them that France would be happy to end its seizures if the United States would grant the country a large loan plus a bribe to government officials, the American ministers reacted with an indignation matched only by the indignation of the American people across the sea when they heard about the affairs.

Thus instead of finding itself at war with England over the question of neutral rights, the United States drifted into an undeclared war with France between 1798 and 1800. Between April and July 1798, Congress passed legislation designed to protect American shipping from French depredations. It took the form of letters of marque authorizing American merchantment to carry guns and to capture French privateers or cruisers. Congress also authorized the establishment of a Navy Department, with a force of ships to seize French warships or armed vessels. This legislation specified that the authorization would cease when France agreed to refrain from its lawless acts.

In the ensuing "Quasi-War with France" the Navy brought some thirty-three vessels into service, including the superfrigates Constitution and United States, both of forty-four guns, as well as the smaller Constellation. The Navy, under Benjamin Stoddart, concentrated on protecting the American coast and the Caribbean trade, and did manage to remove the threat of French privateers from these waters. The "Undeclared War" ended with the Convention of 1800, when Napoleon agreed to end his nation's interference with the commerce of the United States. By the time this pact was signed, France had seen one of its frigates captured, one frigate beaten, a hundred and eleven privateers captured and four sunk, and seventy American merchant ships recaptured by the American Navy and some 1,000 armed American merchantmen. France gained nothing by its attempts to force the Americans to work against their own economic good by resisting British inspections. Napoleon's moves had not worked because he lacked the navy to enforce the regulations he tried to impose on neutrals upon the high seas. If the Americans had sacrificed some honor in avoiding war with Britain in the Jay Treaty, the same could not be said regarding their resistance to Napoleon. Thanks to having some sort of a navy created by the situation, the country was now in a better position to insist on its rights as a neutral carrier on the high seas. But its insistence, as fate would have it, next pushed it into conflict not with France or with Britain, but with minor Barbary powers in Africa.

THE BARBARY WARS. During the early years of the republic, American commerce was subject to interference not only by the two great European powers, England and France, but also by the Barbary chieftains of North Africa. For centuries these local rulers had carried out piracy in the Mediterranian and beyond Gibraltar as a favored means of gaining revenues for their kingdoms. Indeed, piracy was the very foundation of their economic and political systems. Various European powers made treaties and gave generous sums of money to the rulers of Algeria, Tunis, Morocco, and Tripoli to protect their nations' commerce in the Mediterranean waters, but the Barbary rulers preferred to have no treaties with some states so that those nations' vessels would be subject to capture. The Barbary rulers were at constant war with one or another European power and received annual presents from those with whom they were nominally at peace. War and piracy brought the rulers confiscated vessels, cargoes, and prisoners for ransom; peace brought annual presents in the form of money, and often military and naval supplies, the price of immunity from future attacks.

Since the total military strength of the Barbary rulers either singly or collectively was no match for the Europeans, who could have driven them from the seas, why did not the European powers launch a concerted drive against them? The answer lay in the fact that the Barbary pirates could be used as handy allies against competitors. For the price of paying an annual ransom and presenting gifts to the potentates as each new consul was presented to the North African courts, peace could be assured and the piratical practices of the Deys, Beys, and Pashas could be loosed on their national rivals.

Within this system the North American colonies prior to independence had built up considerable trade with the countries touched by the Mediterranean. England had usually bought freedom from the pirates, and its American colonies had thus been the recipients of British immunity from attack. As many as 1,200 colonial seamen manning up to 100 ships were engaged in the Mediterranean trade prior to the Revolution. Great quantities of wheat, flour, and fish were exported there, in addition to lesser amounts of rum, rice, and various types of lumber. Large quantities of wines, salt, oils, and leather were brought to American ports in return. The Mediterranean trade was of considerable importance to the Americans both before the Revolution as colonies and afterwards as an independent state.

Faced with the problem of treating with the Barbary piracies as an independent nation during and after the Revolutionary War, the United States first attempted to gain European cooperation in dealing with the depredations. Cooperation was not forthcoming because, although France and the Netherlands favored concerted action, Britain did not. Therefore, the United States began a policy of dealing directly with the Barbary states, and Congress appropriated $80,000 for that purpose. A treaty with Morocco was gained in 1787. But settlements with other Barbary states were not easily obtained. In 1785 the Algerines had captured twenty-one Americans and held them for ransom. But the Dey of Algiers demanded an amount far in excess of the American offer of $200 per man and would not consider a treaty of peace. Negotiations carried on with Tripoli were also aborted by the latter's excessive demands for money. Thomas Jefferson, the American Minister to France, then turned to the Order of the Holy Trinity and Redemption of Captives located at the Church of St. Mathurin in Paris for aid in ransoming the American captives. The Mathurins, a religious order dedicated to raising funds for the redemption of captives, had its agents throughout Barbary and agreed to help, but Jefferson could not obtain funds from Congress to pay the ransom. Nor would the Confederation Congress support Jefferson's plan of forming a league of maritime states to combat piracy--Jefferson already having received favorable assurances from a number of small European states--because it could not guarantee that it could fulfill financial obligations imposed by membership in such a league. Jefferson finally became convinced that power alone was the answer to dealing with the Algerines, but there was little or nothing he or the American nation could do without a navy.

Unable to halt the attacks on American commerce in the Mediterranean by diplomacy, Congress in 1791 finally authorized a naval armament bill. It called for the building of four ships of forty-four guns and two ships of thirty-six guns, but also provided that if a peace with Algiers was concluded the building of the ships would stop. While awaiting the naval force and the power of compulsion it represented, the government continued to negotiate with the Barbary rulers and decided to purchase peace with annual tribute if necessary. When the Dey of Algiers proceeded to capture 100 more Americans, the matter of a treaty took on special urgency, and in 1795 an agreement was reached obliging the United States to pay to the Dey $642,500 in cash and an annual tribute of $21,600 in naval stores. Peace treaties with Tripoli and Tunis followed, and the treaty with Morocco was renewed. Each involved money payments. By 1800 the United States had paid out almost a million dollars in tribute to the Barbary rulers--a strange state of affairs for a nation bragging of "millions for defense, but not one cent for tribute"--but had not gained any concrete assurances of peace and freedom for its Mediterranean trade. The payments seem only to have whetted the appetites of the Barbary pirates for greater riches.

The showdown came in 1801. By then the United States had concluded the Quasi-War with France and had a navy sufficient to enforce its rights if the government so willed. So when the Pasha of Tripoli, disappointed by his share of the tribute, declared war on the United States in May 1801, President Jefferson chose to use force to gain respect for the flag. Jefferson had known of Barbary brutalities for years and as early as 1785 had said to James Monroe in a letter regarding the necessity of fighting them: "The motives pleading for war rather than tribute are numerous and honorable, those opposing them are mean and short sighted." As in 1785, Jefferson now believed that power alone would ensure peace and American rights in the Mediterranean. From 1801 until 1805 American convoys operated in the Mediterranean against Tripoli and the other Barbary states. After two bombardments of Tripoli in 1804, the road to peace opened, and the United States and Tripoli ended hostilities, although America had to pay $60,000 in ransom for American prisoners still held by the Pasha.

From that point on, the war to clear the Mediterranean for American commerce slackened considerably, and the United States was forced to turn to its difficulties with the French and British once again. But with the conclusion of the War of 1812, the United States formally declared war on Algiers, the second greatest Barbary power. Two squadrons of American naval vessels and a blockade of the city of Algiers gradually brought the Dey to the conference table for a peace treaty in 1816. Soon thereafter both Tunis and Tripoli joined Algiers in making recompense for losses to American shipping and the Barbary piracy came to an end. But the Mediterranean had already been effectively cleared for American maritime commerce as early as 1805, and a giant step had been taken in American policy.

Seen as a progression from helplessness, to tribute-paying, to the use of power, the Barbary wars are of great significance. They clearly illustrate that the United States was moving from an essentially passive state of submission to an active state of defending its maritime rights by war if necessary. The same pattern is present in America's being forced to accept Britain's seizures at sea in the Jay Treaty, but actively fighting the French over the same issue in the Quasi-War. America by early in the 19th century had moved to a policy of defending its maritime rights and now had a small navy to enable it to do so. Seen in this light, America's resistance to subsequent British violations of its maritime rights by means of embargo and then by war become more understandable.

ATTEMPTS AT NEUTRALITY. Notwithstanding the losses suffered at the hands of both the British and the French in the course of their great war, and despite the harm incurred during the Quasi-War and the acts of the Barbary pirates, the overwhelming commercial fact was that the American merchant marine was growing at a tremendous rate in the late 18th and early 19th centuries. Thanks was due in no small measure to the reality that American bottoms were needed by both of the major combatants in Europe.

American trade was increasing at the rate of 700,000 tons a year, and in 1801 the imports into the country were four times that of 1792. Exports represented the same percentage of growth. The merchant marine had grown to almost a million tons of ships, and the American trade network had never been stronger. Since the Revolution ended, American sails had surged back to prominence largely as a consequence of the gruesome business of all-out warfare in Europe. When, therefore, Britain and Napoleon signed the Peace of Amiens in 1801--a peace that proved to be only temporary--American business went into serious depression, but it rebounded when war between the powers broke out again in 1803.

With the resumption of warfare, the United States found its position as a seagoing neutral in jeopardy once again, particularly as both powers perceived that commercial warfare upon one another was a weapon they could not now forego in their attempts to dominate one another. France was forced to give up its idea of a direct attack upon England and turned to land campaigns in the East, but it could still direct pressure on its adversary by striking at Britain through neutral trade. England, on the other hand, could not stop Napoleon directly without a land army to aid its continental allies, but could utilize its sea predominance to bring economic stringency to the entire French war effort.

Since Britain had the greater sea power, it is understandable that it was this island power which could and did make the most trouble for the neutral United States and its merchant marine. The British were still relying on their Rule of 1756, which forbade any trade in wartime not allowed in peacetime, to break up the trade between the French West Indies and French home ports. The Americans were still retaliating with their legal argument of the Plan of 1776, which allowed neutral ships to carry any non-contraband to any belligerent port. But the legal arguments were secondary to the argument of power, and the British clearly predominated in this area.

American shippers accordingly adopted the practice of the "broken voyage" between the French West Indies and France by bringing the goods first to an American port, unloading them and paying customs duties, and then reloading them on the same or another ship for carriage to France. The same was also done between the Spanish colonies and Spain. By this device, each leg of the trip was from a neutral port to a belligerent port, or vice versa, and was, it was believed, clearly outside British proscriptions. Britain tolerated this practice until the famous Essex case in 1805. This American ship was taken by the British while on a "broken voyage" and the case of its seizure was taken to the Lords of Appeal in Prize Causes. The British court decided that a legal seizure had been carried out because the ship was in reality on a "continuous voyage" between two enemy ports. In that same year the British imposed a blockade from the Seine to Ostend, a blockade that could be extended if the British so chose. This move further constricted American trade.

Not only was the principle of the "broken voyage" not recognized by the British, but also, since the renewal of the war, the British had resumed the practice of securing seamen for the British navy by "conscripting" British men by force. Considering the low pay, the wretched living conditions on British ships, and the brutal discipline in the Royal Navy, one cannot wonder that such "conscription" was necessary.

71

But with the resumption of the war in 1803, the manning situation became critical, and Royal Navy officers began impressing in earnest. This practice became of major concern to America because the British began taking deserters from British warships off American ships on the high seas. More important, it is estimated that during the long conflict with France the British impressed 8,000 to 10,000 Americans into their navy. This impressment came about because of the carelessness or ill will of the British officers in ascertaining which sailors were American and which were British deserters. Such identification was hazardous at best, and short-handed British officers were none too careful regarding the identity of the men they impressed, especially since it was virtually impossible to tell an American from a Briton in most cases. Furthermore, if a former Briton had in fact become an American citizen and had naturalization papers to prove his new nationality--and, therefore, his right not to be impressed--most British officers refused to accept this evidence. They were aware that enterprising Americans in every port were happy and willing to provide "genuine" naturalization papers for a fee as low as $1 per document. But whatever the circumstances, Americans were impressed into the Royal Navy, and public opinion supported President Jefferson's decision to do something about it.

Jefferson sent to England the Maryland lawyer William Pinckney to aid James Monroe, the Minister to Great Britain, in clearing up these matters of impressment and America's neutral rights. Jefferson insisted that any agreement they made with Britain include a British renunciation of its right to impress from American vessels on the high seas, payment for the Essex seizure, and recognition of the right of broken voyage. The British would grant none of these in the treaty drawn up, nor would they open the West Indian, Canadian, or Nova Scotian trade to Americans as was hoped for. On the issue of impressment, the British promised to avoid molesting genuine American seamen, but would not put the promise into the treaty. On the matter of neutral rights and broken voyages, the best the British would give was to open the broken voyage trade between French and Spanish colonies and their mother countries only if the vessels paid a duty of not less than two percent ad valorem in the American port. This duty would naturally raise the price of the goods thus carried. The Americans were, however, allowed to trade directly with the East Indies.

Despite the fact that this treaty offered nothing of substance and fulfilled none of the conditions demanded by Jefferson, the two emissaries signed it. To make matters worse, when it was revealed at the last minute that Napoleon had issued his Berlin Decree placing the British Isles under blockade, the British informed the delegation that they would not sign the treaty unless the United States refused to recognize the Berlin Decree. Monroe and Pinckney agreed to that, since they wanted a treaty at any price. Jefferson did not; he refused even to forward the treaty to the Senate. Nine months of negotiation as a means of avoiding war had resulted in absolutely nothing, and America was as far from settlement with Britain as ever. Subsequent events drove them further apart.

During 1807 the British committed the degrading act of the attack by the Leopard on the American frigate Chesapeake off the Virginia Capes, an action that infuriated the American nation. And as 1807 drew to a close, the Americans became even more embroiled in the European situation. The

French Foreign Minister announced that, contrary to assurances given
when the Berlin Decree was promulgated a year before, American ships were
now included as vessels forbidden by the French "blockade" of Britain and
subject to seizure. Napoleon hoped to embroil the United States in war
with Britain, for he argued that his move was made necessary by the British Orders in Council. Then in November, Britain issued a new Order in
Council blockading all the ports of France and its allies. The Order
also said that neutral ships trading with those countries were subject to
search and seizure unless the ships stopped in a British port, paid British duties, and obeyed all other British regulations of trade. Britain
was, in effect, demanding regulation of all neutral shipping into and out
of continental Europe.

Napoleon, trying to make his Continental System effective, reacted
by issuing his Milan Decree, which declared that any neutral ship obeying
the latest British Order in Council would be subject to seizure by the
French. He asserted that by obeying such an order the vessel would have
"denationalized" itself and would be then acting as British property.
These orders from the French and British put the American shipmasters in
an apparently impossible situation. If they obeyed the French decrees,
they would be seized by the British; if they obeyed the British decrees,
they would be seized by the French. The increasing vigor with which the
combatants were conducting their war both militarily and diplomatically
forced Jefferson into some kind of response to uphold American neutrali-
ty--if he thought it worthwhile considering the fact that American trade
was prospering despite the noxious regulations and decrees--but war with
both powers was clearly out of the question. Jefferson was thus forced
to use diplomacy and economic coercion as his only available weapons.

THE EMBARGO AND OTHER WEAPONS. Jefferson's first step against the
European powers was an embargo on all foreign trade, announced on December
22, 1807. This act, urged on the Congress by Jefferson, was not one of
desperation or entered into without forethought on his part. As far back
as his resolution of Albemarle County in 1774, and continuing on through
the crises of trade in the 1790's, Jefferson had constantly urged economic
coercion as a viable means of forcing European recognition of American
rights. To Jefferson, embargo would combine impartiality with economy and
would ensure American rights on the high seas and in the ports of belligerents. Britain and France needed American exports; they would capitulate to American rights when denied the services of their valuable neutral
carrier.

But Jefferson's well-intentioned plan did not work. Rather than
softening the attitude of the British, it only hardened it. And the wily
Napoleon turned the Embargo of 1807 to his own advantage by seizing those
American ships that had slipped away before enforcement began by issuing
his Bayonne Decree ordering the seizure of such American ships as "British," since, he argued, they could not be American since American ships
could not be in European waters under the provisions of the embargo and,
therefore, had to be "British ships in disguise." The embargo was also
ineffective because American shippers did everything in their power to
evade being idled. For example, coastal vessels had to give bond that
they would not sail into a foreign port "dangers of the sea excepted."

There thus occurred a virtual epidemic of broken spars and leaky hulls on coastal vessels in 1808, which brought them into foreign ports "for repairs." They were, of course, welcomed by the British. Coastal vessels also made many trips to Passamaquoddy Bay on the Maine boundary and to Amelia Island in Spanish Florida where their goods were transshipped to Europe at sizeable profits. Furthermore, merchants who had ships abroad as of December 1807 kept them there and continued to trade between foreign ports, making very good profits despite British regulations and the Bayonne Decree.

But of critical importance to the failure of the policy was the fact that it caused great economic hardship in the United States. As ships lay idle in the port cities, thousands of sailors were thrown out of work. Many were forced to make their way to British colonies and there enlist in the British navy. By denying the commerce so important to the whole American economic picture, the embargo threw thousands of other workers out of their jobs too and cut the American people off from their valuable imports of sugar, salt, tea, coffee, and rum. Lacking a market, prices for wheat fell from $2 per bushel to 75¢, and the South went into grave economic privation as thousands of hogsheads of tobacco were left to rot on plantation wharves when they could not be shipped to their markets. In the meantime, the price of necessary manufactures climbed higher and higher. New England, the carrier of the nation, naturally suffered greatly, but saved herself somewhat by carrying on illicit trade across the Canadian border, thus reaching foreign markets. More and more vessels ended up in foreign ports for "repairs," and more and more coastal vessels were "blown out to sea" and ended up in foreign ports. When Jefferson then had enacted more stringent restrictions on the coastal trade to prevent such occurrences, he ended up seriously handcuffing the coasters and thereby closed off the valuable and necessary trade in domestics between the North and the South.

As Jefferson's second term of office came to an end, he was able to point to the fact that the embargo had stirred up more local manufacturing, but he had caused great resentments at home. No area of the country really favored his embargo; at the same time, he had not forced either France or Britain to budge one inch. In his last days in office, Jefferson lifted the embargo, in March 1809, and left the problems of American neutral rights in the hands of his fellow Virginian James Madison. Jefferson had put his faith in economic hardship to force the British government in particular to change its policy. But the minor distress in England caused by the embargo in one short year was hardly enough to convince the British people and their government that American neutral rights were of greater importance than their life and death struggle with Napoleon.

If the American people lacked the will to suffer economic privation for principle, the same could not be said for the British. It would finally require five years of economic blockade of the Continent--with all of its attendant suffering for the British people--before the government's policy of weakening Napoleon by maritime strangulation would pay dividends. The British, unlike the Americans, were willing to pay that price. Considering the relative positions of the two countries and what was at stake in each case--national existence vs. neutral rights--it is perhaps no wonder that the British had the will to carry their policy through. But the maintenance of the policy also meant that American neutral rights would continue to be sacrificed to the overall goal of the defeat of Napoleon. The Americans were thus left in their uncomfortable--although still profitable--situation of seeing their maritime rights seriously circumscribed. The question really boiled itself down to whether or not the Americans would suffer the restrictions and indignities in silence until the European situation had normalized itself by peace, with the question of neutral rights then being resolved by default. Such a course of action would demand of the young American nation a great amount of forebearance and a swallowing of much pride. This was a price that the American president and many Americans were not willing to pay.

In place of the ill-fated Embargo Act, Congress substituted the Non-intercourse Act of 1809, which allowed foreign trade to all countries except Britain and France, but with the stipulation that trade would be opened to either (or both) if it withdrew its objectionable measures in force against the United States. Unfortunately for British-American affairs, the British minister in Washington, David Erskine, came to such an agreement with the American government only to see it disavowed by the British government as going too far in giving concessions. This blunder forced President Madison into the very embarrassing position of having to re-close trade with Great Britain after he had announced its reopening. At the same time, Napoleon angrily reacted to nonintercourse by issuing the Rambouillet Decree in 1810, ordering the seizure of scores of American ships in French ports. Nonintercourse was getting the United States nowhere, so the Congress, in May 1810, substituted for it Macon's Bill No. 2. This legislation opened trade with both France and Britain, but included the provision that if either would withdraw its objectionable measures, the United States would cease trading with the other. This device worked no better than nonintercourse. Napoleon cleverly announced through his foreign minister, the Duc de Cadore, that all French decrees hobbling American neutral trade were henceforth repealed and, therefore, the United States would be obliged to cut off all trade with England. Without waiting to see if the French decrees had been in actually repealed, and desiring to make up for his blunder over the Erskine Agreement, Madison announced that nonintercourse with the British would be imposed in three months as provided for in Macon's Bill No. 2. In fact, the French never ceased making seizures. The British therefore concluded that the Americans were playing France's game and became even more embittered at the United States. Naturally, they did not repeal their various Orders in Council. But despite lack of proof of French intentions, and despite the fact that they were severely antagonizing their best customer, the British, the American Congress, in March 1811, officially renewed nonintercourse against Britain.

THE WAR OF 1812. Thus a combination of American diplomacy and French duplicity led the United States by the spring of 1811 into a posture of confrontation with Britain. Perhaps even at this point outright conflict could have been avoided had not three other factors become involved in the tangled situation during the fateful months from March 1811 to June 1812. First, in November 1811, General William Henry Harrison, Governor of the Indiana Territory, an area inflamed with rumors that the British were behind the Indian alliance being formed under the leadership of Tecumseh

and his brother, the Prophet, an alliance that was expected to result
in butchery on the frontier, advanced on the Indians' village at Tippecanoe near the Wabash River. The fight with the Indians that ensued
was hardly decisive, although it was hailed as a great victory by the
Americans. But, of major importance, the troops under Harrison discovered after the battle that the Indians had new British rifles. This
fact was taken as absolute proof--if such was really necessary on a
frontier already convinced that the British were systematically stirring
up the Indians to slaughter the white men--that the conspiracy rumors
were true, and the West became even more inflamed against the British.

Second, the Twelfth Congress, when it convened in the same month as
Tippecanoe, was a very "new" Congress, since almost half of its membership had been turned out in the last elections, many of the losers having been inclined to favor the avoidance of war. Into their places came
many ultranationalists, led by Henry Clay of Kentucky, Felix Grundy of
Tennessee, and John C. Calhoun of South Carolina. These "War Hawks," as
they soon came to be called, were ready to fight for American rights,
particularly against Britain. Smarting from having been denied the
"glory" of warfare their forefathers had experienced, ready to see an
insult to one American as an insult to all, and willing to fight rather
than submit to "national disgrace," the War Hawks were hardly of a tem-
perament to await diplomatic developments to assuage hurt American feel-
ings over being denied their freedom of the seas. The War Hawks were
ready to fight.

Third, ever since 1808 the West and South has been in a marked
economic depression because, as Westerners saw it, their agricultural
goods could not reach their foreign markets. It therefore seemed obvious
to them that the British and their Orders in Council had dammed up American channels of trade and had led to poor economic conditions. They concluded that the best way to open the channels of trade--and at the same
time salvage American honor while removing the Indian menace--was to go
to war with England.

So on June 18, 1812, after weeks of debate, and a marked negative
vote on the part of the representatives from the New England states and
the commercial middle states, the United States declared war on Great
Britain. Diplomacy had failed; embargo and nonintercourse had failed;
America would now assure by the sword an end to impressment and other
British practices that denied it its full neutral rights on the high seas.
The Americans would now "pull John Bull by the nose," and American rights
would be honored. America went to war in 1812 to preserve its rights on
the high seas; common sense took a back seat to national pride. As the
next two years clearly revealed, America was no match militarily for
England.

America might have taken pride in its infrequent victories in the
war, such as those of the Constitution, or of Perry at Put-in-Bay, or of
Macdonough on Lake Champlain, but the overwhelming reality was that the
Americans neither critically hurt the British in their war efforts nor
brought them to a recognition of American rights. Indeed, the burned
capital city of Washington, the illicit trade carried on with the British
along the American coast, and the threat by New Englanders to secede from

the Union because of the damage done them by this imprudent war, bear mute testimony to the futility of this war of national pride. Perhaps the greatest tragedy of this war was that, but for fate, it might have been avoided. American nonintercourse did have some effect in England and pressure had arisen from the manufacturing and commercial communities there to repeal the Orders in Council. But George III had gone completely insane, and months were lost before a regency could be formed and policy dictated. But subsequently Prime Minister Perceval was assassinated by a madman, and more time lost. Suspension of the Orders in Council was not finally announced until June 16, 1812, two days before the United States Senate passed a resolution of war. But there was no way this news could have reached the United States, and thus the country had blindly plunged itself into a war it could not win.

But Britain could not win the war either without a mass invasion of the American continent; so when Napoleon had been defeated in the Battle of the Nations and the great European war was at an end (the Orders in Council having already been suspended), neither Britain nor the United States could see any advantage in continuing the fighting. It was not popular on either side of the Atlantic. On Christmas Eve, 1814, the American and British negotiators meeting in the Belgian city of Ghent agreed to bring the war to an end and restore the situation as it has been before the war. It was not a victor's peace; neither side had emerged victorious. The war had simply been ended. The British consoled themselves with the end of warfare after twenty years; the Americans consoled themselves with Jackson's victory over the British at New Orleans, a battle fought after that peace had been agreed upon. The question of American maritime rights had finally been settled, not by the embargoes, or diplomacy, or war, but by the fact that the European wars, the basic reason for these rights having been denied or at least circumscribed, had come to an end and, with them, the maritime practices that the neutral Americans so resented. With the subsequent signing of the Convention of 1818 between the two countries, an agreement reaffirming American fishing rights on the Newfoundland and Labrador coasts and defining the northern boundary of the Louisiana Purchase territory as the 49th parallel, peace finally came between Great Britain and the United States. Both nations could now look to other matters. Having also finally ended the Barbary piracies, America looked to the continued development of its merchant marine as a key to its prosperity.

SUGGESTIONS FOR FURTHER READING

Albion, Robert G. and Pope, Jennie Barnes. Sea Lanes in Wartime: The American Experience, 1775-1942. New York: W. W. Norton and Co., 1942.

Beirne, Francis F. The War of 1812. New York: E. P. Dutton & Co., Inc., 1949.

Bemis, Samuel F. Jay's Treaty: A Study in Commerce and Diplomacy. New York: Macmillan Co., 1923.

Burt, A. L. The United States, Great Britain, and British North America. New York: Russell & Russell, 1961.

DeConde, Alexander. The Quasi-War: The Politics and Diplomacy of the Undeclared War with France, 1797-1801. New York: Charles Scribner's Sons, 1966.

Horsman, Reginald. The Causes of the War of 1812. Philadelphia: University of Pennsylvania Press, 1962.

Irwin, Ray W. The Diplomatic Relations of the United States with the Barbary Powers, 1776-1816. Chapel Hill: University of North Carolina Press, 1931.

Mahan, Alfred T. Sea Power and its Relation to the War of 1812. Boston: Little, Brown, & Co., 1905.

Mahon, John K. The War of 1812. Gainesville: University Presses of Florida, 1972.

Perkins, Bradford. The First Rapprochement: England and the United States, 1795-1805. Berkeley: University of California Press, 1967.

_____. Prologue to War: England and the United States, 1805-1812. Berkeley: University of California Press, 1961.

Sears, Louis M. Jefferson and the Embargo. Durham, N. C.: Duke Universith Press, 1927.

CHAPTER V.   ON CANALS AND INLAND WATERS

From the beginning of settlement in America, its oceans, bays, sounds, and rivers had been the usual avenues of travel and trade. The ship, the boat, and the canoe carried men and supplies along the coast and into the colonial regions fronting the Atlantic Ocean. The interior lands, or frontier, were penetrated for settlement only where rivers made it possible, because the land mass presented grave difficulties of transit. Few roads were built during the colonial years, and these by and large were but simple "cuts" through the forests, over the hills, or across the grassy plains, often tracing old Indian trails.

The new nation found itself economically anchored to the coastal plain in its first decades of existence. The vast riches of the Northwest Territory and the entire West beyond the Appalachians to the Mississippi gained in the Treaty of Paris in 1783, and to the Rockies after the Louisiana Purchase in 1803, could not be tapped until better means of transportation and communication could be developed. People were gradually settling the West; natural resources were there in abundance. The question was how the people and resources of the area could be tied into the growing and dynamic coastal states, with the Appalachian chain standing as a massive barrier between the East and the West, from New England down to the Georgia plains. It was also recognized that physical and economic separatism could bring in their wake political separatism and chronic regionalism. The Whiskey Rebellion of 1795 and the disquieting propensity of the trans-Appalachian frontiersmen to resist governmental regulation, including the payment of taxes, made it clear that a politically and economically unified nation could not be forged unless the eastern territories could be integrated into the mountain and transmontane regions. Furthermore, waterborne north-south coastal commerce, equally important to the nation, also had many perils. The ocean waters, especially around stormy Cape Hatteras, was far from a perfect link between the emerging manufactures of the Northeast and the agricultural regions of the South. The question was not _if_ the regions--North, South, and West--could be tied together for the betterment of all. The question was _how_ the tie could be accomplished.

Roads could not be the answer. Only three major roads cut the Appalachian highlands, and these were inadequate for expansion and development. There was the Mohawk Valley Road west from Albany across New York; the Forbes Road from Philadelphia to Pittsburgh, which saw trains of packhorses and wagons daily traversing it to and from western Pennsylvania during passable seasons of the year; and the Wilderness Road down the Shenandoah Valley, through the Cumberland Gap, and on to the southern banks of the Ohio. These three inadequate freight arteries imposed an intolerable financial burden upon the Western farmers. They also served as a bottleneck to the cheap transfer of Eastern manufactured goods of all types to markets throughout the young nation. Tench Coxe in 1792 estimated that Western farmers lost from 20 to 50 percent of the value of their crops while transporting them to their seaboard customers. The trade of the great Ohio Valley was inexorably being driven down the Mississippi system by flatboat and then around to the Eastern cities by means of coastal vessels from the Gulf to the Atlantic coast, a long, circuitous, and expensive routing detrimental both to the Western farmers and to their seaboard customers. Roads were expensive and inadequate to the burdens of bulk freight, either in traversing the mountains to reach the West, or in penetrating the mountains to extract their resources, or in transporting the increasing amounts of goods along the Atlantic coast. The nation, then, not surprisingly turned to its heritage of waterways as a solution to its transportation problems. It did so first by improving existing river channels, then by building and improving artificial water roadways called canals, and finally by utilizing fully the natural waterways systems of the Great Lakes and of the Mississippi River and its tributaries.

18TH-CENTURY CANALS. Canals as a solution to transportation problems are as old as the history of man. Both Egypt and Babylon built canals as early as the 16th and 17th centuries B.C. A predecessor to the Suez Canal was built in 1380 B.C. and survived for 1500 years. The Romans built a canal from Rome to the Mediterranean in 102 B.C., and another canal from the Tiber to the sea. They also constructed a channel in Britain from Lincoln to the River Trent; it was later deepened and made navigable by Henry I in 1121. The Moors built canals in the vicinity of Granada after their conquest of Spain. In the East, the Chinese built their Grand Canal of 1,000 miles of canalized rivers and artificial channels in the 13th and 14th centuries. Marco Polo described the locks on the system in his account of his stay in that fabled land. Leonardo de Vinci, the multi-talented Renaissance man, supervised the building of six locks on the canals of Milan in 1487 and also probably built the first canals in France. The Low Countries abounded in canals.

But the 18th- and 19th-century American canal dreamers and builders probably took their inspiration from less distant models. The Languedoc Canal in southern France, completed in 1681 to connect the Bay of Biscay and the Mediterranean (a distance of 148 miles calling for more than 100 locks and fifty aqueducts), was well known on both sides of the Atlantic. England in the late 18th century built a channel between Manchester and the collieries at Worsley and experienced a "canal mania" of building in the 1790's. By 1825, England had more than 2,000 miles of usable canals, the culmination of three decades of well-publicized enthusiam.

America, too, felt the fervor for canals in the 18th century. As early as 1728 the Virginia patriarch William Byrd recommended that a channel be dug from Chesapeake Bay either via the Nansemond or Elizabeth Rivers to Albemarle Sound, a route later to be known as the Dismal Swamp Canal. In 1763 the planter George Washington and five associates bought 40,000 acres of timber land in the Great Dismal Swamp on the Virginia-North Carolina border, and the following year they received a charter from the Virginia Assembly to drain the land and add canals. Within thirty years a grand design for an inland ship canal to enable ships to avoid the hazards of Cape Hatteras had failed, but timber canals, including the "Washington Ditch," had been built, and in the 1790's Virginia and North Carolina began a twenty-mile canal to traverse the area from north to south.

Another obvious project for effecting a shortcut between navigable bodies of water considered during the colonial period was that of cutting a canal between the Chesapeake and Delaware Bays. Such a canal would make it possible to sail from Philadelphia and New Jersey cities to Baltimore and other cities on Chesapeake Bay without making the long trip around the peninsula consisting of Delaware, eastern Maryland, and the Eastern Shore of Virginia. Surveys for the route were made in 1764 and again in 1769. In 1799, the Pennsylvania, Maryland, and Delaware legislatures agreed on a charter for the project, but no aid was forthcoming from the states, and the project languished until the great canal era twenty years later.

The Spanish in the early 1790's completed the Carondelet Canal (or Old Basin Canal) from New Orleans to Lake Pontchartrain, a two-mile shortcut to the Gulf for schooners and batteaux, and in 1794, far to the north in New England, the South Hadley Falls Canal to the Connecticut River was opened. This latter canal included the first inclined-plan canalworks in America. The device was 230 feet long and lifted boats up fifty-three feet by means of a box on three sets of wheels upon which the boat rode. Power was supplied to the lifting device by two sixteen-foot waterwheels. In the meantime, the Santee and Cooper Canal behind Charleston, South Carolina, had been begun two years before in 1792. This artificial route of twenty-two miles between the Cooper and Santee Rivers was designed to enable inland traders to avoid the swamps when bringing their goods from the central parts of the state. The canal was dug by slaves and was finally completed in 1800 at a cost of $750,000.

In 1794 also, the Middlesex Canal in Massachusetts, built to bring New Hampshire timber, granite, and other products to Boston, was started. The Middlesex began on the Merrimac River at Lowell and ran for twenty-seven miles to Boston, thus tying the agricultural and extractive products north of Boston to the city and its harbor facilities. The canal was thirty feet wide and included nineteen locks. It was completed in 1803 at a price of $528,000.

EASTERN CANALS. By the beginning of the 19th century, canal enthusiasts in America had some practical knowledge of how artificial waterways could be created and how natural waterways could be improved upon in order to facilitate the movement of goods and people. An overview of what transportational problems lay before the nation and how they could be solved was well spelled out in Albert Gallatin's Report in 1808, shortly after the National Road was authorized. As Gallatin saw it, both roads and canals should be built at federal expense to "diffuse and increase the national wealth in a very general way." Regarding canals, Gallatin proposed that the nation improve on the configuration of water and land masses by cutting canals in three separate areas. First, the "Four Necks of Land" should be cut through. These were (1) across Cape Cod, (2) across New

81

Jersey to link the New York and Philadelphia areas, (3) across the neck of land between Delaware and Chesapeake Bays, and (4) from Chesapeake Bay across to Albermarle Sound, the latter two projects already having seen preliminary work. Second, said Gallatin, the "Northern Openings" should be cut: (1) from the Hudson River to Lake Champlain, (2) from the Mohawk River in upstate New York to Lake Ontario, and (3) from the Mohawk River to Lake Erie. Third, the "Four Pairs of River" should be joined to penetrate the interior: (1) the Allegheny, Juniata, and Susquehanna across Pennsylvania, (2) the Monongahela and Potomac along the Virginia-Maryland border and into western Pennsylvania, (3) the Kanawha and James to tie Tidewater Virginia to the Ohio Valley, and (4) the Tennessee-Savannah-Santee Rivers configuration to tie the Tidewater South to the Mississippi River Valley.

It is interesting to note that of these "natural" cuts through land masses, three of the four "Necks of Land" were cut through and the "Northern Openings" were completed. The "Four Pairs of Rivers" idea, calling for the greatest distances, time, money, and engineering challenge, never became reality until the coming of the railroads, despite the fact that three of the four junctures were attempted. Gallatin's recommendations were important not because they revealed possible improvements unperceivable by most men (others had envisioned most of these projects), but because they so clearly delineated the existing possibilities for canals and foreshadowed how the canal boom would actually be carried out. Thus the nation, after the dislocations of the Napoleonic War period and the War of 1812, turned to the problem of domestic water-transit and engaged in three great cycles of canal building between 1815 and 1860: the first between 1815 and 1834, the second from 1834 to 1844, and the third from 1844 to 1860.

There were three types of canals constructed for three different purposes. A ship canal was to effect a shortcut for oceangoing vessels; the river canal was to make a river navigable for boat passage; and the barge canal was designed as a slack-water highway for barges pulled by animals walking a towpath. The East in the pre-1815 period had seen ship canals (the Dismal Swamp and the Santee and Cooper), a river canal (the Middlesex), and a river rapids by-pass canal (the South Hadley Falls). In addition, a ship canal from the Delaware to the Chesapeake had been envisioned. In the West, the Corondelet ship canal had been constructed at New Orleans by the Spanish, and a river canal, the Soo Canal, had been constructed by the English in 1797 on the Canadian side of the St. Mary's River between Lake Superior and Lake Huron. It had been built for the Northwest Fur Company with a timbered flume for downward passage and a lock with a nine-foot lift for the passage upstream. The Soo Canal had been blown up by American troops in 1814 during the war.

The East during the Canal Era concentrated both on ship canals to make possible easier transit up and down the coast between the major trading cities, and on barge canals to expedite the gathering of the riches of the Appalachian range. By 1812, the Dismal Swamp Canal project, designed to avoid Cape Hatteras and carried out by Virginia and North Carolina, had been improved with a feeder ditch from Lake Drummond in the heart of the Great Dismal Swamp. With this improvement and its locks, it

was functional as a ship canal built on five different levels. Although
the canal promoters were to meet failure in their expansion of it by a
spur canal to Currituck Sound between 1828 and 1831 (the spur was constantly closed by shifting sands), still the main canal was gradually improved over the years with the addition of stone locks. Its final length
of twenty-nine navigable miles carried barges, steamboats, and schooners
on their commercial routings.

The success of the Dismal Swamp Canal, however, engendered imitation,
and between 1855 and 1859 the rival Albemarle and Chesapeake Canal was
built to the east of it. The Albemarle and Chesapeake Canal took greater
advantage of natural bodies of water as it moved to the southeast from
Norfolk by the Elizabeth and North Landing Rivers to Currituck Sound and
then by the North River to Albemarle Sound. Consequently, it had fewer
maintenance problems and lower costs. But both canals were successful
for years.

It was also during the Canal Era that the Chesapeake and Delaware
Canal between those imposing bodies of sheltered waters came to fruition.
The idea for this canal, abandoned, as we have seen, in 1799 after the
Pennsylvania, Delaware, and Maryland legislatures had granted a joint
charter, was revived during the canal mania of the 1820's and, with
generous amounts of money subscribed by the federal government and by
private investors, opened in 1829. Over thirteen miles long, it had
three locks and cost a total of $2,250,000. It was a sound investment
for the public and private investors because it bore heavy traffic not
only during the Canal Era, but also until 1880, when it became too narrow
for ship traffic. It was, however, expensive to operate since the summit
level could only be maintained by pumping water up into it. The federal
government purchased the canal in 1919 and eventually converted it into a
sea-level canal of great importance to moderate-sized vessels traversing
the Atlantic coast.

The Delaware and Raritan Canal was a barge canal between New Brunswick, New Jersey, and Bordentown, New Jersey, on the Delaware River forty-
two miles away. It also included a twenty-two-mile feeder ditch. In effect, this eight-foot-wide canal, with thirteen locks, connected the major
urban areas of New York City and Philadelphia with the interior. Its
construction was authorized in 1830, and it opened to traffic four years
later. It enjoyed almost instant success by carrying the large amounts of
coal that reached the Delaware River from the canals of eastern Pennsylvania on their way to the major cities of the East. The Delaware and
Raritan was enlarged in 1846 and reached its peak of activity in 1859,
when it carried more than 1.7 million tons of freight, including 1.3 million tons of anthracite coal. In that year it handled 1,400 coal boats
on its waters, most of 180-ton capacity. The canal was effectively
strangled in 1871, when the Pennsylvania Railroad bought it and denied
it its coal traffic. It languished until 1933.

The remaining major Eastern canal was the Morris Canal, running from
the mouth of the Lehigh River for 102 miles across New Jersey to New York
harbor. Unlike the Delaware and Raritan, the Morris did not enjoy great
success, partly because its penetration into the foothills of the Alle-
ghenies demanded that it climb 914 feet to its summit from the east and

then drop 760 feet to the west. A cumbersome system of twenty-three inclined planes and twenty-three locks was required. More important, the Morris Canal and Banking Company was almost constantly engaged in shady financial speculation. As a result, it went into bankruptcy in 1841, only ten years after the canal was completed. After 1844, when the company was reorganized and engaged in a rebuilding program, the Morris Canal belatedly began to play a significant part in the anthracite coal trade and reached some moderate financial success. Like the Delaware and Raritan, the Morris lost out to rail competition in the post-Civil War period. Other Eastern canals were the Cumberland and Oxford in Maine; the Blackstone from Providence, Rhode Island, to Worcester, Massachusetts; the New Haven and Northampton from the Connecticut port city to Northampton, Massachusetts; the Delaware and Hudson from Honesdale, Pennsylvania, to Kingston, New York, half way up the Hudson from New York City; and the Delaware Division from Easton, Pennsylvania, to Bristol, New Jersey. All enjoyed moderate success during the Canal Era.

CANALS TO CUT THE MOUNTAINS. The Eastern canals played a large part in expediting trade up and down the coast and in transporting the natural resources of the Appalachians, especially coal, to the seaboard cities. But the canals that captured the imagination of a generation of expansive Americans and led to untold interregional economic growth were those cutting through the forbidding mountains to link the East with the West. Justifiably, the most famous of these, and the one that set off a reaction of frenzied imitation in a "race" to reach the West, was the Erie Canal from Albany to Buffalo, completed in 1825.

Even before the beginning of the 19th century, an imperfect link between the grand economic pathway of the Hudson River and the interior fronting Lake Ontario had been accomplished by the Western Inland Lock Navigation Company. This company carried a series of river improvements and short canals between the Mohawk River and the streams running into Lake Ontario. The partially-developed system was far from satisfactory, however, because of its very limited capacity, and the company soon ran out of funds. Although Gallatin had recommended both a riverway to Lake Ontario, such as the one already attempted, and another to Lake Erie, the latter seemed too formidable; and the New York legislature in 1808 refused even to authorize a survey of a "grand canal" to Lake Erie. Apparently many observers agreed with President Jefferson that the projection of a three-hundred-fifty-mile canal through the wilderness was a century ahead of its time. The project was shelved and forgotten.

In 1815, however, DeWitt Clinton, seeking a means of recouping his political fortunes after the Tammany organization in the Democratic party had ruined his career by having him removed as Mayor of New York, seized on the issue in his race for governor as one that would bring him support from all factions and parties in the state. Using the canal issue to best advantage at mass meetings, Clinton won the governorship, and the canal was assured. When the federal government refused to aid the state in the project, New York began it alone, and in April 1817, the state legislature authorized the construction of the middle portion of the "grand canal" from the Mohawk to the Seneca Rivers via Canastota, and another from the Hudson to Lake Champlain, two of Gallatin's "Northern Openings" at one time.

Appropriately, work was begun on July 4, 1817. Working with enthusiasm and dispatch, by October 1825 the workmen had completed the canal across the state. It was 363 miles long and forty feet wide and had eighty-three locks and eighteen aqueducts. It cost $11 million. To symbolize the importance of the feat of building the great canal from just north of Buffalo in the West (to avoid the Niagara escarpment) across the state to the Hudson, the natural water highway emptying into the greatest harbor in the Western Hemisphere at New York City, Governor Clinton and his party left Buffalo on October 26 with two kegs of Lake Erie water on the Seneca Chief to traverse the canal and the Hudson. On November 4, 1825, he poured the water from the kegs into the New York harbor waters. The East and the West had been joined.

Even before the project was completed, it was obvious that it would be a tremendous success. Local traffic immediately began to use the finished portions of the canal, and the toll receipts began to mount up. But more startling and hopeful to New York and to the nation was the fact that freight rates and passenger rates immediately dropped to reflect this new, cheaper mode of travel and transit. Freight costs plummeted from $120 per ton from Buffalo to New York to $4 per ton, and passengers found that they could get comfortable accommodations, including bed and board, across the state at the rate of only 4¢ per mile. Soon some 20,000 boats of up to thirty tons capacity were being towed along the canal, carrying goods and people on this new vital artery of East-West commerce.

As the years went by, the Erie was widened and deepened so that it could accommodate canal boats of up to 240 tons capacity. Because the Erie was such a resounding success, other parts of the state demanded their share of the blessings that only canals could bring. Spurs were authorized to the north. These were the Black River Canal and the spur to Oswego on Lake Ontario. To the south were the Chenango Extension and the Chemung Canal, the Cayuga and Seneca Canal in the Finger Lakes region, and the Genesee Valley Canal to Olean near the Pennsylvania border. Although these secondary canals never paid for themselves and drew off much of the excess revenues from the profitable main canal, still the Erie made a profit. It served to accelerate the rise of New York City as the major port in the East and to open the entire upstate New York area to both people and development. It also occasioned a rash of imitators, the most rash being the effort of neighboring Pennsylvania.

As New York labored to complete the Erie Canal, Pennsylvania was already moving to tap the riches of the Appalachian interior through two canals. Between 1816 and 1825, the Schuylkill Canal from Philadelphia westward to Reading, then northward to Mount Carbon above Pottsville, was completed. It included fifty miles of slack-water pools and almost fifty-eight miles of canal. This combination required thirty-eight dams, thirty-two short canals, one tunnel, and 116 locks to make possible a 588-foot drop in elevation from the western end of the canal to Philadelphia. Despite its engineering complications, the canal was successful, first with freight consisting of timber and agricultural products, and later with anthracite coal. Likewise, the Union Canal, which tied into it at Reading and ran seventy-seven miles to Middletown to the west, was also a grand engineering feat. The Union included ninety-one locks, numerous reservoirs and pumps, a long aqueduct, and even a 729-foot tunnel. It was begun in 1821 and completed in 1827.

But the canal that fired the imaginations of the Keystone citizens, and upon which they pegged their hopes for prosperity by tapping the riches of the Western trade, was the Main Line Canal across the state. As projected at its inception in 1826, the Main Line began at the western end of the Union Canal near Middletown and ran across the entire state to Pittsburgh, a total distance of 359 miles from Philadelphia to the western terminal point. Water traffic could then follow the Ohio River, formed by the juncture of the Monongahela and Allegheny Rivers at Pittsburgh, to the rich markets of the West. The eastern end of the line consisted of the Schuylkill and Union Canal systems bringing the goods to and from Philadelphia. In building the Main Line, spurred on by the Erie Canal to the north and the building of the Baltimore and Ohio Railroad and two other canals to the south, Pennsylvania took on a prodigious feat because it required breasting the Appalachian chain at its highest and widest points. Moving through central Pennsylvania was only moderately difficult, the canal running parallel to the Juniata and Conemaugh Rivers, but the rest of the way was very hard, and at the crest of the mountains it was necessary to construct a railroad to carry the canal boats over the mountains' summit. The Allegheny Portage Railroad began at Hollidaysburg to the east of the crest and ran 10.1 miles up the side of the mountain by a system of five inclines and five levels to the 1,398-foot peak. From there down to Johnstown to the west the drop of 1,171 feet necessitated 26.5 miles of track, again with five levels and five inclines.

The state also found it necessary to turn to railroads to supplement the system in the east because the Union Canal was found to be too narrow for the Main Line boats. An eighty-one-mile railroad had to be built from Columbia to Philadelphia between 1828 and 1834. Consequently, freight and passengers beginning in Philadelphia started their journey by rail, had to be transferred to canal boats at Columbia, moved by canal 172 miles to Hollidaysburg, were there lifted by the Portage Railroad thirty-six miles across the crest to Johnstown, and were then towed another 105 miles through the canal again to Pittsburgh. Eastbound freight had to follow the reverse process. As an interesting development of this procedure, a short-lived but unique mode of passenger transportation, advertised in Philadelphia as being able to carry passengers all the way to Pittsburgh by boat, was inaugurated. This all-boat transit was accomplished by loading the passengers into half-boats in Philadelphia and carrying the half-boats to Columbia by rail; there the boats were locked together to make the water trip to Hollidaysburg, where they were halved again for the Portage Railroad segment of the journey; they were then locked together again for the canal tow to Pittsburgh. Enterprising as this procedure might be, it could hardly compete with the comparative ease of the Erie Canal route; and, indeed, it illustrates the fundamental problem associated with the Main Line Canal. It was too cumbersome and inefficient, and with branches added to the north along the northern and western branches of the Susquehanna, and another branch attempted from the Ohio River beyond Pittsburgh north to Erie, the financial burden was too much for the freight and passenger revenues. The Main Line alone cost $12 million, but the other 314 miles of additional canals cost the state another $6.5 million.

To try to increase the traffic on the Main Line, Pennsylvania in 1836 began the Susquehanna and Tidewater Canal from Columbia to Havre de Grace on upper Chesapeake Bay. This short forty-five-mile section was opened in 1839, flooded out, and had to be partially rebuilt. When it reopened in 1840, it picked up considerable traffic because of its larger lock dimensions, and by 1843 it carried more than half of the Main Line freight from Pittsburgh. But this canal, of course, carried the freight away from Philadelphia toward Baltimore and the Chesapeake Bay cities, so it was decided to enlarge the Union Canal. The enlargement cost another $6 million. By 1857 the whole system was in serious trouble because of its inability to compete with the Erie Canal and the expanding railroads. In that year, the Main Line was abandoned and sold to the Pennsylvania Railroad. It had by then cost $16.5 million; it had lost $6.7 million. The western portion of the canal was operated only until 1864, and the other canals that made up the eastern sections of the system rapidly declined to nothingness in the 1860's. Pennsylvania's grand attempt to compete for the Western trade by canals had failed miserably, although its antracite-carrying canals in the eastern part of the state continued to carry freight and show profits for many more years.

Pennsylvania built its trans-Appalachian canal and failed. Virginia and Maryland's attempts to do the same to the south were never even completed, and were soon superseded by the railroads. The idea for what eventually became the Chesapeake and Ohio Canal dates from 1749-50, when it was first planned that a road be built along the Potomac and then down the Monongahela to the Ohio valley. In 1774 the idea was changed to one of improving the Potomac River for 150 miles above tidewater; but this plan was abandoned when the Revolution intervened. After the war, in 1785, the Potomac Company was incorporated to improve that river, particularly around the Great Falls above the nation's capital. The resulting canal on the Virginia side of the river was begun at Washington's insistence and was hailed as one of the greatest engineering achievements of the time. It opened in 1802 and was gradually improved so that by 1808 there were five short canals along the river bypassing the rapids between Washington and Harpers Ferry. The extension of the canalized river system began on July 4, 1828, when the Chesapeake and Ohio Company took up the project with money provided by the federal government, the State of Maryland, and the cities of Washington, Georgetown, and Alexandria. President John Quincy Adams turned the first spade; but, it has been ominously noted, on that same day the Baltimore and Ohio Railroad began its construction to the West, a railroad that eventually doomed the trans-mountain canal idea. Nevertheless, by 1850 the Chesapeake and Ohio Canal had been completed to Cumberland, Maryland, at the cost of over $11 million and was capable of carrying canal boats of 100 tons. The canal reached its peak in traffic only in 1872, but then declined. It was finally abandoned in 1924, never having traversed the mountains, but having proved extremely valuable for local traffic in the Potomac Valley.

A similar fate awaited the more southerly James River and Kanawha

Canal. The idea of canalizing the Virginia rivers to reach the Ohio would seem to have originated with George Washington in the 1750's; but not until 1784 was Washington able to advance his scheme after making a 650-mile tour of the area. He returned with great enthusiasm for the project, and in 1785 the James River Company was incorporated. The very busy Washington would accept only the title of Honorary President of the company, and, as a result, Edmund Randolph was named to fill the active presidency. By 1789 the company had built a seven-mile canal around the rapids of the James from Richmond to Westhampton, and between 1796 and 1801, the canal was advanced to Crow's Ferry, 220 miles above Richmond. From this point on, the canal project fell on hard times. The State of Virginia took over the floundering project between 1823 and 1826, but then abandoned it, deciding to build a turnpike instead across the Allegheny crest. By 1832 the canal was back in private hands in the form of the James River and Kanawha Company, but with three-fifths of its capital belonging to the state. By 1851 the canal had been extended to Buchanan, the farthest it was ever built, and the branch canal to Clifton Forge had been almost completed to Eagle Rock when work stopped in 1856. The canal with its various branches carried heavy local traffic and was a valuable economic aid to those areas touched by it. During the last year of the Civil War, General Phil Sheridan's forces cut the banks of the canal and destroyed some of its locks; the canal never recovered from this destruction. In 1880, what was left of the canal was sold to the Richmond and Allegheny Railroad, soon to become the Chesapeake and Ohio Railway, and tracks were laid along its grade. Like its northern counterpart, the Chesapeake and Ohio Canal, the James River and Kanawha Canal never cut the mountains and never tapped the riches of the Middle West.

MIDDLE WEST CANALS. The Midwestern canals built during the Canal Era were designed mainly to bring the agricultural products of the interior up to Lake Erie, there to be transshipped via the Erie Canal to the East, or down to the Ohio River, to the cities on that waterway or on down to New Orleans. The most important of these canals was the Ohio and Erie Canal in Ohio. Authorized for construction in 1825, the barge canal went from Lake Erie at Cleveland down the Cuyahoga, the Muskingum, and the Scioto Rivers, to intersect with the Ohio at Portsmouth. The federal government contributed $1.2 million for the Ohio canals, and this amount was supplemented by considerable state and private funds. The Ohio and Erie was completed in 1832 at the height of the canal craze in America. It was 308 miles in length with over 1,200 feet of lockage to attain its two summit levels. Its cost was estimated to be almost $8 million. While it never carried much traffic between its terminal points on Lake Erie and the Ohio River, it proved to be especially valuable for local business.

The Miami Canal from Cincinnati to the north also was authorized in 1825, and by 1829 the Miami River had been canalized as far as Dayton. In 1831, authorization was given to extend the canal to Lake Erie, and by 1843 the canal had been completed all the way to Toledo. Like the Ohio and Erie, the Miami Canal was very valuable for local traffic. The State of Ohio authorized six more canals during the late 1830's and the 1840's. These were the Hocking Valley Canal; the Whitewater Canal from Cincinnati into east-central Indiana; the Ohio and Pennsylvania Canal from Akron to New Castle, Pennsylvania; the Sandy and Beaver Canal from Boliver on the Ohio and Erie Canal to Beaver, Pennsylvania, on the Ohio River; the Wabash and Erie Extension to tie in that Indiana canal to the Miami Canal along the Maumee River; and the Muskingum Canal from Zanesville to Marietta on the Ohio. None of these secondary canals was particularly successful; and like the two main Ohio waterways, the Ohio and Erie Canal, and the Miami Canal, they fell victim to railroad competition in the 1850's.

Ohio's enthusiasm and eventual lack of success were matched and even exceeded by Indiana. Indiana first authorized the building of the Wabash and Erie Canal in 1832, to tie the heart of the rich agricultural state into the Lake Erie commercial network. However, enthralled by the early signs of success of canals throughout the United States, Indiana in 1836 passed a $13 million internal-improvements bill that included two canals and two railroads, plus either a railroad or a canal between Ft. Wayne and Lake Michigan. The $13 million pledged to these projects represented about one-sixth of the entire wealth of the state. The next year the Panic of 1837 hit. The state struggled back from this paralyzing depression and gradually completed the Wabash and Erie, the canal finally making a juncture with the Ohio River at Evansville only in 1853. In the meantime the Whitewater Canal into Cincinnati had been completed with private funds in 1846, only to be partially destroyed by floods in 1847 and again in 1848. The Whitewater struggled on until 1865 when it was paralleled by a rail line. In 1860 the lower half of the Wabash and Erie was closed. By the 1870's the entire system had been abandoned. Indiana had mortgaged its future on its canals and had lost. The railroads would treat the state more kindly.

Illinois' only attempt to enrich itself by canals came in the form of the Illinois and Michigan Canal from Chicago to LaSalle and juncture with the Illinois River. The project was authorized in the enthusiastic year of 1835, only to be abandoned with the coming of the Panic two years later. The Illinois and Michigan Canal then proved to be very prosperous for a number of years. In 1871 it began to act also as a sewage canal for the city of Chicago, but it carried its peak of freight as late as 1882. In 1892, the Chicago Drainage Canal was begun and with its completion in 1900, the sturdy Illinois and Michigan Canal was filled in and forgotten.

Michigan's sole canal project was the canalization of the St. Mary's River at Sault Ste. Marie between Lake Superior and Lake Huron. This extremely important project was carried out by the state in 1855 and proved to be a wise investment in money, not only for the state but also for the entire Great Lakes area shipping complex coming to fruition during those years.

IMPACT OF THE CANALS. Between 1815 and 1860, virtually every state from Virginia north to New England participated in one way or another in building canals to improve its commerce. During the first cycle of 1815 to 1834, 2,188 miles of canals were built with $58.6 million invested. The second cycle, 1834-44, saw 1,172 miles completed, for an investment

of $72.2 million. The third cycle, 1844-60, accounted for only 894 miles
completed but saw investments of $57.4 million. All totaled, the 4,254
miles of American canals cost $188.2 million. During these years the
various states, local governments, and the federal government contributed
approximately $432 million to internal improvements; 43.5 percent of
these monies went into canals. In addition, part of the states' proceeds
from the sale of public lands within their borders went into canal projects; many states also applied the federal government's distributed
surplus revenues to the canals; and the federal government also gave
direct gifts of land to be used on various internal improvements, including canals. During the decade 1850-60, these land grants amounted to
22.5 million acres. How much these lands sold for, and how much of the
proceeds of the sale of public lands and the distribution of surplus
revenues were applied to canals cannot be calculated. Whatever the
figure, it is clear that many, many millions of dollars went into the
building of canals. The question, then, must be confronted: what did
the nation gain by the construction of these canals too soon to be superseded by the more technically efficient and dependable railroads?

The answer cannot be given in dollars and cents. It is clear, however, that the canals were instruments of tremendous benefit both economically and politically. First of all, the canals led to sharp declines
in transportation costs. Not all reductions were as dramatic as those
following the opening of the Erie Canal, and the extent of the declines
varied according to the time and place. Nevertheless, transportation
costs on the East-West lines and from the interior to the Atlantic coast
were lowered significantly because of the canal routes.

Second, the canals allowed the West to dispose of its surplus in the
higher-priced markets of the East and in foreign countries. For example,
in 1835 only 268,000 barrels of flour moved from the Western states to
New York City. By 1840, the figure stood at more than one million barrels; by 1850, more than three million barrels were shipped; and by 1860,
more than 4.3 million barrels moved along the canals. And this increase
represents only one product. At the same time, the ready availability of
the Eastern markets to the West allowed the West to shift from subsis-
tance agriculture to commercial agriculture, a change that in turn enrich-
ed not only the Western farmer, who produced more goods at lower cost for
greater profit, but also allowed the food-consuming public--East, West,
and South--to eat better for less and thus apply a greater money surplus
to hard or soft consumer goods. Industry, in turn, was spurred to greater
growth.

Third, the Eastern market for manufactures was widened by the lower
transportation costs and by the higher level of income in the agricultural
West. There naturally followed a higher level of investment in the East
and a greater demand for Western products in the non-food-producing areas
of the country.

Fourth, lower transportation costs, especially via the Erie Canal,
led to more Western settlement. With more people living in the West,
there was a growing demand for both Western foodstuffs and Eastern manufactures. In 1820, only 8 percent of the population of the nation lived

in Ohio, Indiana, Illinois, and Michigan; by 1850, the figure had climbed to 18.1 percent. More people meant more production and more consumption at lower cost throughout the nation. How can the economic benefits of these developments be measured accurately? Overall, how does one accurately measure the effects of commercial agriculture in the West made possible by access to Eastern markets, or how does one measure the impact of industrial growth aided by the widening of the market for manufactures made possible by the canals? The effects of the economic stimulus of the canals, then, while not measurable in dollars, were tremendous and are still with us today in the form of our highly-developed national industrial economy.

Would the nation have advanced economically without the canals? Surely it would have, but at what rate? Would not the railroads have had the same effects when they came into being? Surely they would have, but how does one calculate how much would have been lost economically by the time-lag of a decade, since the railroads were incapable of broad expansion in the 1820's and 1830's? The canals may have been superseded by the railroads at almost the very moment of their greatest extension, but one cannot then conclude that the canals made no lasting contributions. The canals laid the economic groundwork upon which the railroads built in the decades after the 1840's. The canals were in a real sense the transportational pioneers on the American landscape. They led the way economically; therein lay their contribution.

Finally, the bonds of economic unity and interdependence forged between the states of the East and the West by the narrow ribbons of water called canals played a large part in destroying forever the political regionalism and separatism so prevalent at the beginning of the 19th century. By the 1840's an economic marriage of mutual convenience had been forged between the East and West, a marriage that continued to grow into one of the strongest pillars of economic and political well-being. The pioneer canals, fated by their technological limitations to be abandoned within decades of their birth in favor of better means of travel and transit, nevertheless played a premier and glorious role in forging this unity. They helped the nation to become one economically, politically, and socially.

THE GREAT LAKES. The tremendous economic and political advances induced by the building of the canals were complemented by equal developments both on the Great Lakes and on the Mississippi River water systems. In the same way that economic unity and interdependence through the interior and along the Atlantic coast were advanced by the canal systems, so too economic unity and interdependence were fostered by equally revolutionary advances on the great natural waterways of the emerging West.

The Great Lakes are collectively the largest body of fresh water in the entire world. Encompassing a total of 96,000 square miles of water, over half of all the fresh water territory on the globe, their drain basin covers an area of more than 291,000 square miles of the interior of the United States and Canada. It is 1,157 miles from Duluth at the farthest point west on Lake Superior to the eastern end of Lake Ontario, and 2,342 miles from Duluth to the Atlantic Ocean via the St. Lawrence

River. The Great Lakes, then, as had been discovered in the 17th
century, range far into the interior of the American land mass and represent one of the largest navigable water bodies in the world. Their
shoreline totals 8,300 miles. The water-blessed Great Lakes states constituted the heart of the Old Northwest and drew thousands of people to
make their homes there in the first decades of America's national existence.

Settlement on the Lakes really began when General Moses Cleaveland
[sic] established a town at the mouth of the Cuyahoga River on the
southern shore of Lake Erie in 1796. Soon other towns began to be
formed: Detroit, on the river-lake chain of water between Lakes Huron
and Erie; the villages of Buffalo, Ogdensburg, and Oswego in New York
on Lakes Erie and Ontario; and, slightly inland from Lake Ontario, the
village established by Col. Nathaniel Rochester and his Maryland friends
at the falls of the Genesee River. The Western Reserve of Connecticut
on the southeastern shore of Lake Erie saw towns being built early in
the 19th century. All were on rivers or lakes, and all looked to bright
futures because of their advantageous locations on navigable waters.

Some of the earliest vessels on the Lakes were powered not by sail
but by steam. The Canadians launched the first steam vessel on the Lakes
in 1816, the 700-ton Frontenac, and the Americans in 1817 at Sackets
Harbor west of Watertown, New York, launched the 200-ton Ontario. But
the vessel that gripped the imagination of the Lakes sailors was the
Walk-in-the-Water launched at Black Rock near Buffalo the next year.
This 135-foot sail-with-auxiliary-steam vessel was the first steam craft
on Lake Erie and won instant acclaim for its efficiency until unfortunately breaking up in a storm in 1821. Yet the workhouse vessels of early
Lakes development were not the fragile steamers, but the stout sailors.
The topsail schooner was the most popular vessel on the Lakes, but three-
masted barks and barkentines and square-rigged brigs and brigantines also saw service, carrying stores and provisions for the towns and military
posts scattered around the edges of the broad Lakes system.

With the opening of the Erie Canal and the steady migration of people into the Lakes region on the heels of that momentous event in 1825,
the region bloomed. Pioneering families both old and new turned to commercial agriculture as their livelihood. Thousands of acres of lush
woodland were cut so that the land could be turned to the plow. The
Midwest soon became the center of cereal production in America. In 1840,
more than one million barrels of flour reached New York City from the
West. This amount exceeded that reaching the city from western New York
lands. As we have seen, by 1850 the amount of flour shipped from the
West had almost tripled to more than three million barrels and topped
four million barrels by 1860.

Economic expansion began first in Ohio and along the southern shore
of Lake Erie and then moved into northeast Indiana via Toledo. Then
southern Michigan and the Illinois and Wisconsin shores of Lake Michigan
felt the surge of economic activity and population growth. By 1842 the
$4 million worth of food products moving through Cleveland was quite as
large as that of New Orleans, and the repeal of the British Corn Laws in

1846 stimulated grain production and shipment even more. Buffalo, the leading receiving point for the Lakes grain and flour moving to it by hundreds of vessels large and small, received 1.2 million bushels of grain and flour in 1836, but by 1851 the figure had climbed to 17.7 million bushels, a figure easily eclipsed throughout the remaining years of the decade; and by 1860 the total stood at more than 37 million bushels of flour and grain. This quantity was in addition to great amounts of pork, bacon, and other provisions being shipped from the Lakes region to Eastern cities.

But the Great Lakes states in the decades prior to the Civil War exported more than food stuffs. Millions of feet of Midwest lumber were used to build the expanding towns and cities of that area, but by 1860 one hundred million feet of lumber and 23 million barrel staves also moved through Buffalo on the way to Eastern markets. Copper was first shipped from the Lake Superior region in 1845, and by 1860 8,000-plus tons of the precious metal were being carried on the Lakes. Iron began to be transported from the same region in 1855, and only five years later at least 100,000 tons of ore and 5,000 tons of pig were crossing the waters of the Lakes annually. In addition to this essentially east-bound traffic from the Lakes region, westbound traffic on the Erie Canal to the emerging West climbed from $9.7 million in value in 1836 to $94.2 million in 1853. The upper Midwest was coming alive economically in these decades and tying itself to the South as well as to the East. The ties were made possible by transportation, and transportation in these years beyond Buffalo meant water transportation on the Lakes or by the Lakes-canal combinations.

The growth of lakeside cities in the upper Midwest reflected the importance of their water functions. Buffalo, the entrepôt of goods moving on the Erie Canal and on Lake Erie, had a population of 80,000 by 1860, and as early as 1845 handled more grain, flour, and livestock than any other city in the United States. Cleveland managed the farm products from the agrarian states of Ohio and Kentucky, as well as manufactures from Cincinnati and Pittsburgh. Toledo, at the western end of Lake Erie and the transit point for goods moving up the Wabash and Erie Canal and the Miami Canal, shipped more grain than any other city on the Lakes with the exception of Chicago. Detroit was the grain, livestock, wool, and lumber port for the State of Michigan. On the western side of Lake Michigan, the activities of Milwaukee were topped only by those of Chicago. Chicago in 1860 had a population of 100,000 persons--the city was not even mentioned in the census of 1830--and shipped out some 20 million bushels of grain and flour. Chicago also received more than 300 million board feet of lumber per year from the Lakes area for use in the cities of the Illinois and Wisconsin interior.

All of this trade in the middle decades of the 19th century was made possible by the vessels of various types which traversed the Lakes in the business of commerce. There were heavy, sturdy, and flat-bottomed "canallers," found especially in Lake Ontario and Lake Erie. There were a few square-riggers and 100- to 500-ton brigs. Most prominent of the sailers were the clipper-type schooners of the 1850's, known simply as "lakers." These vessels were of distinctive design, having a retractable centerboard in the keel. Most were two-masted, although three masters also evolved. In addition to the sailers, there were steam vessels, most notably the <u>Vandalia,</u> a 138-ton sloop launched at Oswego in 1841; this was the first commercial ship to use John Ericsson's propeller. By 1856 there were no fewer than 118 propeller-driven ships and 120 conventional paddlewheel steamers, in addition to more than 1,100 sailing vessels, on the Lakes. Great Lakes vessels, which totaled only 4,000 tons in 1830, had reached the figure of 393,220 tons by the time of the Civil War. The Lakes had clearly been conquered by sail and steam, and Western commerce had taken on a new and vital dimension by the effective use of these waterways.

By contrast with the saga of the canals, however, the coming of the railroads did not adversely affect the Great Lakes maritime network. The railroads actually stimulated water trade by their rapid and inexpensive transporting of the flood of immigrants into the area, who proceeded to develop it with great rapidity. Furthermore, the various railroad lines, instead of ruining the Lakes lines to take away their trade, actually went into the passenger-steamship business themselves in order to complete their lines and make better connections between various points in the Lakes region. For example, a traveler could journey from Buffalo to Detroit on one of their water routes and complete the remainder of his journey to Chicago by rail. Until the rail lines paralleled the Lakes shores and advanced to the point where they could offer clear economic advantages over the water routes, the Great Lakes vessels continued to dominate the long-distance transit of the entire area.

Ancillary to the Great Lakes maritime developments were various improvements made upon the St. Lawrence River, the great channel through which flow the waters gathered by the Lakes system. To tame the various rapids of the river and to by-pass somehow the 325-foot escarpment of Niagara to permit water travel, not only locally but along the entire river and into the Great Lakes, had been a dream of enterprising men for centuries. A one-mile canal around the Lachine Rapids above Montreal was attempted as early as 1700, and the British built four short canals between Lakes St. Louis and St. Francis near Montreal during the Revolutionary War. However, the undeveloped state of both the American and Canadian West had precluded any further work on the potentially valuable waterway.

After the War of 1812, William Hamilton Merritt, a St. Catherines, Ontario, merchant, chagrined at how the Niagara Portage Road had fallen so easily and frequently into American hands during the war, decided that a water by-pass a safe distance inland would have to be built. After many difficulties, Merritt organized the Welland Canal Company, and between 1824 and 1829 construction of the first canal by-pass of Niagara Falls was completed. Beginning at Port Dalhousie on Lake Ontario, and using natural creeks and rivers where possible, the Welland Canal emerged into the Niagara River upstream from the fall. Its forty wooden locks, each 110 feet in length, effected a 258-foot lift. The value of Merritt's canal soon became obvious, and various improvements were made. In 1833 the route of the canal was changed to bring about a fairly straight north-south cut from Port Dalhousie to Port Colborne on Lake Erie 27 1/2 miles away, thus by-passing not only the falls but the sometimes-perilous Niagara River too. A second and larger canal was built between 1841 and 1845, this time with locks of larger dimensions. The end of the 19th and the beginning of the 20th century saw a third, and then a fourth, Welland Canal built along approximately the same route.

In addition to accomplishing this conquest of the most difficult of all barriers to water commerce on the Great Lakes-St. Lawrence system in the early years of the 19th century, the Canadian government also built the Cornwall Canal around the Long Sault Rapids in 1842-43. The Beauhornois Canal and the Lachine Canal around other navigational obstructions were both built in the 1840's. By 1848 a navigable channel with a nine-foot depth existed all the way from the Atlantic to Lake Erie. These improvements were never enough to compete seriously with or deflect trade away from the Erie Canal and the railroads further south, but important steps had been taken in canalizing the mighty St. Lawrence. In addition, the Reciprocity Treaty of 1854, whereby the two neighboring countries agreed to mutual navigation of the St. Lawrence, set a pattern of cooperation that bore fruit a century later in the building of the St. Lawrence Seaway.

THE MISSISSIPPI RIVER SYSTEM. The basin drained by the Mississippi River and its tributaries includes all or parts of thirty-one states from western New York to Idaho and from Louisiana to the Canadian border. It includes almost 15,000 miles of navigable waterways. The distance from the Gulf up the Mississippi and the Missouri, which is its longest tributary (believed by many geographers to be the true upper channel of the river), is 4,190 miles, longer than either the Amazon or the Nile. It is truly a wondrous natural navigational system into the heart of America and a natural resource equal to any with which the United States has been blessed.

Early river traffic on the Mississippi and in its wide basin was very limited. During the pre-Revolutionary period, an unsuccessful attempt was made in 1766 by a Philadelphia firm to set up a trading station at Kaskaskia in the Illinois Country. In that same decade the merchants of Natchez, then in British West Florida, carried on sales to the Spanish Creoles along the river's banks in "floating stores," but little commercial traffic other than the occasional travels of Western fur traders was seen. But with the end of the Revolutionary War and the Americans gaining clear title to the lands between the Appalachians and the Mississippi, people rapidly began to fill in the land mass and the need for commercial intercourse followed in their wake. In 1790 only a little over 109,000 people lived in the West. Two decades later, in 1810, the number had topped one million. In the meantime, the Louisiana Purchase had been negotiated by President Jefferson in 1803, with the result that the new nation now held undisputed control of the entire Mississippi basin. Growth of the river trade and internal commerce was now assured.

Free navigation of the Mississippi River and its tributaries to all the people of the country without state interference was first assured in the Ordinance of 1787. The Ordinance included provisions that the navigable waters leading into the Mississippi were to be common highways and that no taxes or duties could be levied on those who used them. When the new federal Congress adopted the Ordinance in August 1789, the legal foundation for free waterways was assured within the new national structure; and because the Southwest Territory and all acts of admission of new states included these provisions, the Mississippi and its tributaries were assured to be free highways of commerce for all who would use them.

At the same time, Congress in the early 19th century, moved by a desire for internal improvements and anxious to please the Western voters, declared its right to appropriate money for water courses, as well as for roads. It inaugurated its river-improvement legislation in 1820 when a survey of the Mississippi and Ohio Rivers was authorized. Early improvements of the natural inland waterways consisted primarily of the removal of snags, logs, boulders, and sunken vessels from the rivers, in addition to clearing the channels by the dredging of sand, gravel, and rock from the river bed. Between 1824 and 1844, the federal government spent $2.5 million, primarily on the Ohio and Mississippi Rivers, although the stolid resistance of the dominant Democratic party and the events leading to the Civil War prevented any improvements from 1846 to 1866.

But with or without federal aid, transit on the system in the interest of commerce grew by leaps and bounds. Predominant of all craft that navigated the Mississippi and the Ohio were flatboats. By the 1780's, these great, clumsy boxes, knocked together out of rough lumber, sometimes reaching lengths of 100 feet and widths of twenty feet and averaging between forty and fifty tons, were floated downstream guided by oars, or sweeps, or were steered by a long oar pivoted at the stern on a forked stick. They came down the rivers by the thousands, especially in the fall and spring with the higher waters, with goods and often immigrants from Wheeling, Pittsburgh, Olean, and other points on the upper rivers. In 1813 it was recorded that 1,306 flatboats reached New Orleans; this figure may have been but half of the true count to reach the Crescent City. By 1846-47 the number was up to 2,792. Although the flatboat declined as a river bulk-vessel thereafter, it continued in use until the outbreak of the Civil War. As freight carriers that could be broken up upon reaching their destinations, the flatboats could hardly be topped, and by them untold tons of coal, lumber, staves, pig iron, salt, stone, brick, and varied agricultural products reached the many river towns all the way to New Orleans during the expansive decades of the early 19th century.

Also of importance in carrying both freight and people were the keelboats, long, narrow vessels of light draft especially valuable for the shallow waters of the rivers. Unlike the boxy flatboats, the keelboats were built on keels, had ribs, and were covered with planking. They reached up to eighty feet in length and were sharp on both ends. They drew only two feet of water even when fully loaded with as much as fifty tons of freight. But, unlike the flatboats, the keelboats were designed to move both down and up the rivers. Accordingly, they included cleated footways around the gunwales for the crew to walk on as the men poled the boat upstream. Upstream passage was sometimes accomplished by warping, that is, pulling the keelboat from the shoreline by means of long ropes. A keelboat could make the journey downstream from Pittsburgh to New Orleans in four to six weeks, but it took four months or longer to make the return journey. Larger keelboats were known as barges. These often carried a mast or two for square sails and a crew of up to fifty men. Some of the later barges were up to fifty tons in weight, carried 170 tons burden, and even had swivel guns for use against the Indians if attacked.

A third type of nonpowered river vessel was the raft. These giant, flat, timbered configurations moved in season out of the Allegheny, the Kanawha, and the Big Sandy Rivers onto the Ohio. They came out of the St. Croix onto the Wisconsin and out of the Black onto the Mississippi, bringing valuable timber to market and sometimes even cut lumber. Some were broken up at intermediate points, but others went all the way downriver to St. Louis or to New Orleans. It was estimated that in 1857 some 660 million feet of lumber were floated down the Allegheny River to Pittsburgh alone by this means.

With the utilization of the flatboats, keelboats, and barges and rafts, the economy of the Mississippi and Ohio Valleys began to spurt. The more advantageous steamboats did not begin to replace the nonpowered vessels until the mid-1820's. By that time Cincinnati had already become a city of 10,000 persons, largely on the basis of trade, and soon moved to play a major part in the building of steamboats and steam engines. Louisville was the center of the tobacco trade, and St. Louis, with 5,000 people, was already the commercial center of the trans-Mississippi West. Farther to the East, Pittsburgh had a population of 7,000 persons and was fast becoming an iron-producing center, in addition to serving as a center for coal, lumber, and various manufactures. At the same time, cotton production was booming in the river valleys of Alabama, Louisiana, Mississippi, and Tennessee; and the Southern river-craft carried the valuable crops to ocean ports. River-craft also brought to the cotton areas vast amounts of grain, pork, flour, and manufactures from the Ohio Valley. These were items that the South was coming to depend upon as it turned more and more to its dominant and dominating crop. Horses, mules, and hay in great quantities were also carried to the South from the Midwest.

Despite these gains, the real key to major interior development lay in the adaptation of steam power to river transportation. Steam turned the rivers into the principal means of internal transportation because it overcame the great problem of human strength being the only propellant upstream. Steam-powered vessels could carry great amounts of goods and people both downstream and upstream with greater dispatch and in relative safety. Although steam-powered vessels were first used on the Eastern rivers in the early years of the 19th century, in particular on the Hudson by Robert Fulton and Robert Livingston, and on the Delaware by John Stevens, it was in the West with its winding rivers, which made sailing impractical, that the steamboat came to its most important domestic use.

Steamboat service on the Western waters was first planned by Fulton

and his associates for use between Pittsburgh and New Orleans. To that
end, they ordered a survey of the rivers and the building of a suitable
steamboat. In October 1811, the New Orleans of 371 tons began its journey from Pittsburgh to the Gulf of Mexico to inaugurate the service.
Other steamboats followed in rapid succession; and by 1817 fourteen
steamers were working between Louisville and New Orleans. By 1819,
thirty-one steamboats were operating on the Western rivers. The man
generally acknowledged as the foremost leader in Mississippi steamboat
development was an early pioneer, Henry Miller Shreve, who in 1816 built
the Washington, into which was incorporated some very important design
innovations. Shreve's vessel was an overgrown keelboat of 403 tons with
a flat, shallow hull. He placed the boilers and engines on top of the
planked-over deck rather than in the hull and strengthened the hull with
a trusslike arrangement of heavy timbers at angles fore and aft some
eight feet above the deck for two-thirds of the 148-foot length of the
vessel to control its flex. This arrangement came to be known as a "hog
frame." With the addition of a double deck and two stacks with ornamen-
tal crowns, Shreve had created such a functional vessel that it became
the basic design for the American steamboat which revolutionized travel
on the Western rivers. By 1834 there were 230 steamboats on the Mississippi and Ohio Rivers, and their total tonnage was 50 percent greater
than the steam tonnage in the entire British Empire. In the early 1830's,
at least 1,000 steamboats arrived at New Orleans annually, bringing
valuable goods from upriver and returning upstream with Southern products
and with imports. By 1860 the number of arrivals at New Orleans had escalated to 3,245 per year, or an average of about nine per day. The
shallow-draft steamboats had conquered the Western rivers.

Before this conquest was possible, however, it was necessary to make
one major improvement in the Ohio River, the principal tributary to the
Mississippi. The goal was to remove the rapids at Louisville, known as
the Falls of the Ohio, a drop of twenty-two feet in a two-mile stretch of
water over a series of rock ledges. It was possible for vessels to shoot
the rapids at high water, but at low water that could not be done safely;
and it was practically impossible for the steamers to make their way up
the river over the rock ledges. This barrier to navigation was a great
benefit to Louisville; it made the city the head of practical navigation
on the lower Mississippi system and the stopping point for upper-system
steamboats. The city thus became the locale of transshipment, storage,
and forwarding businesses by the score. But the rapids still stood as
the major obstacle to commerce between the upper and lower stretches of
the system. Despite the backing of the citizens of Cincinnati, the major
city on the Ohio, the attempt made between 1816 and 1819 to construct a
canal around the Falls on the Indiana side of the waterway did not succeed.
A second attempt by the Louisville and Portland Canal Company, with the
financial support of both Congress and local citizens, proved to be successful. Begun in 1825, the Louisville and Portland Canal opened in 1830
along the Kentucky shoreline for a total cost of $750,000; it consisted
of a short canal and three locks to carry vessels around the rapids. It
proved to be successful navigationally, and also showed enormous profits
from tolls. It was enlarged in the 1850's and again improved in the
1860's, before being taken over by the federal government in 1872.

With the completion of the Louisville and Portland Canal in 1830, steamboats moved up and down the Mississippi and Ohio waters. They also steamed up the other tributaries of the Mississippi, such as the Arkansas, the Missouri, and the Wisconsin, in addition to the dozens of smaller rivers making up vital parts of the inland system. A measure of their success is the fact that between 1820 and 1860, almost 6,000 steam vessels were built on the Mississippi-Ohio system, particularly in the cities of Pittsburgh, Cincinnati, and Louisville. These cities alone built 75 percent of the steamboats by number and 81 percent by tonnage between 1820 and 1880, and steamboat manufacturing became leading industries in these emerging urban economic centers of the Midwest.

The steamboats on the Western waters, engaged in essentially non-romantic economic functions, with an incontestable air of romance nevertheless, were either of the side-wheeler or the stern-wheeler type. The side-wheelers were the favorite of the traveling public and became the Western river steamboats par excellence. By 1830 they had pushed the stern-wheelers from the rivers largely because of their superior steering and handling qualities. It was possible to vary the speeds of each of the giant, side-mounted wheels--which were sometimes up to thirty feet in diameter and twelve feet in width--for a sharper turn, or even to run the wheels in opposite directions. With greater turning leverage from their position on the sides of the vessels and the ability to vary the speed or even reverse the direction of the paddles, the side-wheelers caught the fancy of the captains, the owners, and the general public riding them. But the stern-wheelers had the advantage of greater protection of the fragile paddles from driftwood and logs by their position at the rear of the vessels. They also allowed a wider beam, and therefore a shallower draft, to vessels equipped with them. This was a very important consideration not only on the major rivers during slack water, but also on the secondary waters of the system. It meant more cargo space and a longer season; so the stern-wheelers never died out. In fact, the stern-wheelers staged a revival after 1840, especially in the 1850's, when two paddle-wheels were placed in the stern side by side, each being independently operated to give almost the same maneuverability as could be found on the side-wheelers.

But whatever their placement of paddles relative to their hulls, the great, shallow-draft steam vessels, with their tall superstructures decorated with fashionable "gingerbread" and bright paint enclosing the functional low-pressure (and then high-pressure) steam engines, became longer and wider with less draft and more power as the decades wore on and as steamboats responded to the demands for more profitable transportation on their native waters. By 1860 the average smaller steamboat of 100-125 tons was 132 feet in length with a breadth of more than twenty-four feet. Its average draft had decreased from 6.3 feet to 3.7 feet. The 400-500 ton behemoths of the Mississippi-Ohio waters averaged 216 feet and were more than thirty-five feet wide, but drew no more than six feet of water.

Despite the steamers' popularity and their contributions to commerce and American folklore, even during the "Golden Age of Steamboating" in the 1850's, the signs were present that an age was passing. More and more passengers and freight traffic were diverted to the railroads, which could move faster in all weather with greater flexibility of routing. The resulting fervid competition between steamboats and railroads happened to occur during a decade when the rivers were plagued with a number of "low-water depressions" and when towboats and barges first began to demonstrate their economic superiority to the steamboats for bulk freight. As the railroads made rapid connections possible between Pittsburgh and Cincinnati, between Cincinnati and Louisville, and between St. Louis and the East, almost all the passenger and fine freight business abandoned the great steamboats. The steamboat operators were still able to keep much of the heavy freight and to extend their services by plying up the secondary rivers to the frontiers. They rendered valuable aid to those developing areas, but never again would the steamboats serve as kings of Mississippi commerce.

The riverboats, like the canals and the Great Lakes sailers, were fated to be replaced by improved means of both water and land transportation. They all faded into near oblivion in the post-Civil War years. But all had played vital parts in transforming the economic, social, and political life of the American heartland, and had consequently helped to form a base for greater progress in the years following the fratricidal bloodletting that engulfed the nation in the 1860's. All had assisted, in particular, in forming the vital and interlocking system of commerce between the East and the West and between those areas and the Cotton South. The canals and inland waters had helped to create a new America; and with the increasingly valuable oceangoing maritime network carrying American men and goods to the farthest reaches of the globe, they had played a part in making a new world.

Albion, Robert G. The Rise of the New York Port, 1815-1860. New York: Charles Scribner's Sons, 1939.

Andrews, Israel D. Report . . . on the Trade and Commerce of the British North American Colonies and upon the Trade of the Great Lakes and Rivers. U.S. Congress, 32-1, Sen. Exec. Doc. 112. Washington: Robert Armstrong, Printer, 1853.

Baldwin, Leland D. The Keelboat Age on Western Waters. Pittsburgh: University of Pittsburgh Press, 1941.

Beasley, Norman. Freighters of Fortune: The Story of the Great Lakes. New York: Harper & Bros., 1930.

Brown, Alexander C. The Dismal Swamp Canal. Chesapeake, Va.: [Norfolk] Historical Society, 1971.

Couper, William. Claudius Crozet, Soldier-Scholar-Educator-Engineer (1789-1864). Southern Sketches, No. 8, First Series. Charlottesville, Va.: Historical Publishing Co., Inc., 1936.

Drago, Harry Sinclair. The Steamboaters: From the Early Side-Wheelers to the Big Packets. New York: Dodd, Mead & Co., 1967.

Goodrich, Carter. Government Promotion of American Canals and Railroads, 1800-1890. New York: Columbia University Press, 1960.

_____; Rubin, Julius; Cranmer, H. Jerome; and Segal, Harvey H. [Carter Goodrich, ed.] Canals and American Economic Development. New York: Columbia University Press, 1961.

Gray, Ralph D. The National Waterway: A History of the Chesapeake and Delaware Canal, 1769-1965. Urbana: University of Illinois Press, 1967.

Hahn, Thomas F. George Washington's Canal at Great Falls, Virginia. Sheperdstown, W. Va.: American Canal and Transportation Center, 1976.

Haites, Erik; Mak, James; and Walton, Gary. Western River Transportation: The Era of Early Internal Development. The Johns Hopkins University Studies in Historical and Political Science, 93rd Series. Baltimore and London: The Johns Hopkins University Press, 1975.

Harlow, Alvin F. Old Towpaths: The Story of the American Canal Era. New York: D. Appleton & Co., 1926.

Hatcher, Harlan. The Great Lakes. New York: Oxford University Press, 1944.

Hunter, Louis C. Steamboats on the Western Rivers: An Economic and
    Technological History. Cambridge: Harvard University Press, 1949;
    reprint ed., New York: Octagon Books, 1969.

Hutchins, John G.B. The American Maritime Industries and Public Policy,
    1789-1914: An Economic History. Harvard Economic Studies, Vol.
    LXXI. Cambridge: Harvard University Press, 1941.

Johnson, Emory R. et al. History of Domestic and Foreign Commerce of
    the United States. Vol's I & II in one volume. Washington, D.C.:
    Carnegie Institution, 1915.

Kirkwood, James J. Waterway to the West. [n.p.]: Eastern National
    Park & Monument Assoc., 1963.

Merdinger, C.J. "Canals through the Ages," The Military Engineer,
    Parts I-III, 49, 330-32 (July-Dec., 1957), 77-89.

Shaw, Ronald E. Erie Water West: A History of the Erie Canal, 1792-
    1854. Lexington: University of Kentucky Press, 1966.

CHAPTER VI: THE SLAVE TRADE AND THE COTTON TRADE

The practice of holding other human beings as chattel, i.e., as property, is as old as civilization. Human bondage has been found in the Western world from at least the time of the ancient Egyptians, Greeks, and Romans. Slaves gained by warfare or purchase performed a myriad variety of tasks, both menial and consequential, for their owners in the ancient world, from the back-breaking rigors of the building of the pyramids to the privileged conducting of academies of learning in Rome. But with the passing of the Roman Empire and the advent of Christianity as the dominant influence in Western Europe, the practice of holding bondsmen fell into decline, although the idea of a stratified society with the lowly serving the mighty remained an integral part of the Christian world that emerged in the period we call the Middle Ages.

With the coming of modern times, slavery as such had almost disappeared from the European world, now tenuously expanding itself by exploring the Atlantic reaches with hearty adventurers sent out by the various European nations. But the discoveries of the New World, combined with the demands for labor created by the new industrial and commercial economic world emerging in the 16th century, fashioned a set of conditions that brought slavery back into prominence in the European colonies being created on the western shores of the Atlantic Ocean. Economic necessity and human greed produced a revival of slavery, and slavery took its place--for good or for ill--in the economic, political, and social systems of the nations of the Western Hemisphere. The United States, both in its colonial stage and in the first six decades of its existence, shared in this re-emergent slavery and was the recipient of its economic benefits, as well as its tragic consequences.

SLAVERY AND THE ATLANTIC SLAVE TRADE IN COLONIAL TIMES. Although it was the British who eventually earned the greatest "credit" for developing and perfecting the maritime industry known as the slave trade, the Portuguese under Prince Henry the Navigator first re-introduced slavery into Europe in the mid-15th century. Some fifty years before Columbus made his voyage of discovery, the leaders of a Portuguese expedition cruising the northern Guinea Coast shipped back to their Prince ten Africans as examples of African life they had discovered there. By 1444, some 250 more African men, women, and children had been landed in the port city of Lagos. They had been distributed among the nobility under the watchful eye of the Regent. These early African captives were well treated by the Portuguese; they were baptized and educated. They might well have been slaves in the ordinary sense of the term, but the Portuguese interest in them seems initially to have been in bringing them to Christianity. But the early motive of Christian charity was soon overcome by the base motive of greed, and by early in the 16th

103

century, it was clearly recognized throughout Western Europe that profit could be made by enslaving and selling the African natives.

The slave trade received its start in the New World in 1517 when a Dominican priest, Bartolome de Las Casas, moved by compassion at the mistreatment of the native Indians in the lands claimed by Spain in the New World, and hoping to save them from being exterminated, sent a request to King Charles V of Spain. Las Casas' petition, which he later greatly regretted, was for twelve Africans to be sent to the New World for each Spanish colonist there. Charles V accordingly granted the Asiento, the privilege of carrying 4,000 Negroes per year to the Spanish colonies, to one of his courtiers, who subsequently sold it to a syndicate of Genoese merchants. Thus began a veritable flood of slaves being shipped to the New World. With Spain and Portugal in the lead, although with some challenge from the French, English, Dutch, Swedes, and others, the slave trade quickly developed, and by 1540 some 10,000 Africans per year were being transported to the West Indies and Latin America. By the end of the 16th century, some 900,000 Blacks had been shipped into the West Indies, into Mexico, and into the other Latin American colonies. These natives of the western coast of Africa, from Senegal to Angola, mostly of Negroid type, were forced to work the mines and fields that brought the Spanish and Portuguese the riches of the Americas. The pattern was clear. Spanish and Portuguese development of their New World colonies required a sizeable supply of tractable labor which could be provided by slaves brought from Africa.

Thus at the very birth of Western civilization in the New World, slavery and the slave trade were indispensable parts of the process of growth. Wherever the Spanish explorers went, slaves went with them. They were with Balboa in the discovery of the Pacific, with Cortez in Mexico, and with Pizarro in Peru. Apparently the first slaves in what became the United States were those one hundred with Lucas Vasquez de Ayllon in 1562, when he attempted to found a settlement on a site probably located in what is now South Carolina. Negro slaves were in St. Augustine in Spanish Florida after 1565.

The first African slaves to be conveyed to the English colonies were twenty nameless persons brought by a Dutch man-of-war to the fledgling colony at Jamestown in Virginia in 1619. Some eleven years later, in 1630, the captain of an English ship, the Fortune, exchanged the bondsmen he had captured from a slaver out of Angola to the Virginians for a quantity of tobacco. The Dutch settlers in New Amsterdam also entered into the slaving business as early as 1625, following the monopoly grant to the Dutch West India Company in 1621 of the slave trade to the New World. It is recorded also that the English colonists likewise engaged in the slave trade; in 1638, the Desire out of Salem carried a cargo to the West Indies including seventeen Pequot Indians for sale and returned with various items of produce "and negroes."

But in these early years of the 17th century, the number of slaves imported into the northern continental colonies was very small. Apparently no regular slavers sailed with exclusively black cargoes. As late as 1650, there were only 300 slaves in Virginia and very few in New England and the Middle Colonies. When the British Crown chartered the

Royal African Company in 1672, the government encouraged the colonies
to buy the human cargo of this lucrative royal monopoly; the slave trade
into the English colonies then began in earnest. By 1700, about 1,000
slaves per year were being imported. Since the northern colonies were
not adaptable to the plantation system of agriculture, and since northern agriculture was supplemented with commerce and home industry in
which slaves would have no real economic advantage, those few slaves
bought and held in the northern colonies were primarily as household
servants of the wealthy few. But the requirements of working the expanding fields of rice and tobacco in the south created heavy demands
for slave labor there; and this, combined with the almost insatiable
demand for slave field-hands on the sugar plantations of the West Indies,
resulted in so great an urgency for slaves that the Crown in 1698 threw
open the door to all who desired to deal in the African commodity, not
just the Royal African Company. Clearly, by the end of the 17th century,
slavery had established itself in both the West Indian and continental
English colonies; the demand for labor had been met by transporting
unwilling Africans into bondage across the waters of the Atlantic.
Slavery and the slave trade were as much a part of the English colonial
economic system as they were of the Spanish and Portuguese systems.
Christian solicitude for baptism and salvation for the African natives
had been complemented by economic necessity in the expanding and self-
confident colonies being created in the New World by rulers, merchants,
planters, and shippers on both sides of the Atlantic.

Who were these black victims of European avarice transported
across the ocean to bondage in the Western Hemisphere? Were they being
forced into a life completely unknown and foreign to them? The answers
are varied. Slavery itself was surely widespread in Africa long before
the European slavers touched the shores of that continent to deal in
human cargo. Most of the slaves shipped to the New World were probably
prisoners of native wars. Many were criminals sold by their own chiefs
as punishment, and not a few were individuals sold by themselves or by
their families in times of famine. Some were definitely persons kidnapped by the European slavers or, more often, kidnapped by native
gangs to be sold at the seaports in exchange for Europeans goods or rum.
Even though slavery had long been known throughout Africa, including a
thriving slave trade on the eastern coast with the Arabs, never before
had the victims of the system been transported far across the unknown
seas, with no chance at all of returning to their lands and tribes.
The Europeans had added an element of perpetuity to a system already
inhumane in its consequences.

On the other hand, the question must be asked as to the status of
these Blacks in the New World, and more specifically their status in
the English colonies on the American continent. Were they to be essentially servants for life, unlike the indentured servants who were coming
to the English colonies from the Old World, but who would serve for only
a time in exchange for their passage, usually four years? Was it ever
possible for a Negro slave to become a free man in the English colonies?
Did baptism confer freedom on a black slave? In the early decades of
the 17th century these questions were pondered by the leadership of the
colonies, and only gradually did responses emerge. The responses favor-

ed the white majority and cast the African Black into perennial bondage. Virginia in 1661 declared all Negro slaves to be perpetual servants, and two years later neighboring Maryland declared all Negroes to be regarded as slaves. Maryland also forbade all racial intermarriages and decreed that if a free-born English woman married a slave, she too would become a slave. Later in the 17th century, the various colonies affirmed that baptism did not confer freedom on the Blacks. Thus race and color were firmly tied to enslavement in the evolving colonial world of the 17th century. That Blacks could be free of enslavement was possible, but not probable, other than through manumission. For the vast majority of these bound laborers imported into the colonies directly from Africa, or from the West Indies after "seasoning," their color and their legal status had been indissolubly bound together. They were to be slaves; they were to be chattel; they were to be property.

This decision against the freedom of the slaves was arrived at not only out of a feeling of racial superiority, but also because of certain economic realities operative in the colonies. The economy in the southern agricultural colonies was rapidly expanding, based on the staple crops of tobacco, rice, and indigo. Land was cheap; capital was available; what was needed was labor to round out the process of agricultural production. The type of labor needed was that which would be suitable for large-scale production. The work was routine and did not require a high degree of training or skill. Very important, too, the labor supply had to be constant and, hopefully, cheap. On all of these scores, slavery was preferred. White servants were in too short supply, always chafed under harsh duties and punishment, and were lost to the planter after their terms of indenture. Furthermore, the planters, always fearful of losing their dominance in society, were well aware of the fact that white indentured servants became free citizens upon completion of their contracts and had a tendency to move into the small-property or property-less lower classes in the colonies, there perhaps to incite resistance to the control practiced by the planter aristocracy. A few generations of temporary white servitude would lead necessarily to political, economic, and social challenge thrown up by the nonplanter population. Thus slavery represented a solution to one of the English colonies' most pressing problems, an adequate and submissive supply of labor, and also helped guarantee the social and political order.

Because slavery seemed the best answer, it was adopted during the colonial period with the cooperation of the mother country, which cared little enough for the moral implications of bondage as long as slave labor met the needs of the emerging Empire. Given the wealth and power flowing to England from its colonial expansionism, particularly in the Caribbean sugar colonies, it is hardly a wonder that it would have few second thoughts about the implications of slavery in the American southern colonies. And so the number of slaves imported into the colonies increased, and the planters flourished. In Virginia, where one-twentieth of the population consisted of Negro slaves in 1670, the numbers grew so rapidly that by 1730 the proportion was one-fourth. Maryland, the Carolinas, and Georgia were not far behind. The low price of slave labor had won out over all other considerations, and slavery was clearly established in the colonies by the end of the 17th century. The 18th century saw an acceleration of slavery and the slave trade.

But the use of slaves in the Sugar Colonies and on the tobacco, rice, and indigo farms of the American colonies, important in itself, was important also to the English and colonial domestic economies. The English slave trade was centered first in London and Bristol, but gradually shifted to Liverpool. Liverpool gained a near monopoly of the trade, which usually followed a triangular pattern. Manufactured goods from English mills, such as linens, iron, copper, gunpowder, and muskets, were loaded in British vessels and sent to the African coast to be exchanged for slaves. The slaves, in turn, were sent to the West Indies, and occasionally directly to American, to be sold. The receipts from these sales were used to buy sugar, cocoa, coffee, indigo, and ginger. These goods were transported home to be sold for further profits in the domestic markets. In this fashion the African slave trade represented an outlet for British manufactured goods, as well as a source of profit on products for which there was a strong demand at home. These facts help to explain both the enthusiasm of the government for the trade and its reluctance to repress it in any way.

At the same time, the American colonies, chiefly those of New England, also enthusiastically joined in the slave trade for the benefit of their domestic industries, particularly rum. Yankee vessels often left their home ports for Africa with a cargo chiefly or entirely made up of rum. Sailing to Africa, they exchanged the rum for as many slaves as could be purchased from the local chiefs or from European traders at the coastal barracoons--the going rate often being 200 gallons per slave--and then sailed to the West Indies with their black cargo. Part of the proceeds of their sale of the slaves in the Indies was used to buy molasses, either from the British or, more often, from the traders in the French or Spanish islands. The molasses was brought back to New England, there to be sold and converted into rum. Thence the whole lucrative rum-slave-molasses triangle would begin again.

By 1750, Massachusetts alone had sixty-three distilleries converting 15,000 hogsheads of molasses into rum, and Rhode Island had thirty more distilleries. By 1763, Rhode Island was sending eighteen vessels a year to Africa, representing an exportation of about 1,800 hogsheads of rum per annum. These New England vessels, in addition to carrying slaves to the Indies in the rum triangle, sometimes carried slaves from Africa or from the West Indies to the colonies for sale. In the second half of the 18th century, Boston and Salem, Massachusetts; Portsmouth, New Hampshire; New London, Connecticut; and Newport, Providence, and Bristol, Rhode Island, were the principal New England slave entrepôts for the colonies.

Other variations on the Africa-West Indies-New England slave triangle could be found. For example, slaves were sometimes carried to South Carolina in exchange for naval stores used in the shipbuilding industry. Other times, New England ships carried local goods to the West Indies in return for the valuable molasses. But whatever the variation, the sale of slaves was part of the entire trade and manufacturing complex of New England and was dearly appreciated as such. The slave trade provided much of the capital for the industrial revolution carried out in New England. Rhode Island became the largest and most active slave-trading center in America, and the colony's leading citizens and shipowners prospered as never before. Such prominent men as Esek Hopkins, Aaron Lopez, and the four Brown brothers of Providence--"John and Josey, Nick and Mosey"--built their fortunes partially on the rum and slave trade.

With slaves furnishing the laboring power for southern plantations, as well as for the sugar islands in the Caribbean, while also constituting a most valuable and necessary item of trade in both British and American colonial trade patterns, it is no wonder that the slave trade flourished as never before in the 18th century. After the Treaty of Utrecht in 1713, at the end of the War of the Spanish Succession, the British gained effective control of the West African coast from Gambia to the Congo and could freely carry its enslaved inhabitants throughout the world. The treaty also granted to the British the Asiento, the legal right to supply 4,800 slaves a year to the Spanish possessions in the New World. The British slave merchants (which included the King's subjects in America) thus had a clear field in the slave trade and made the most of it. From that year until the end of the century, an average of 70,000 Blacks were transported from Africa to the New World each year except during times of war. While most of these slaves were carried to the Caribbean, especially to Jamaica, rather than to the continental colonies, the American colonies' slave population, both by importation and by natural increase, underwent a dramatic increase. In 1714 there were only 59,000 slaves in continental British North America; by 1754 the figure stood at 298,000, an increase of more than 500 percent; and by 1790 the total number of slaves stood above 697,000, a further increase of at least 100 percent and an increase of almost 1,200 percent over the figure at the end of Queen Anne's War in 1713. In 1790, slaves represented 17 percent of the American nation's population.

While complete figures are lacking on importations during the 18th century, it is known that Virginia between 1710 and 1769 imported 52,504 slaves and that South Carolina from 1733 to 1785 imported 67,769, not including an untold number brought into the colony via the overland slave routes from St. Augustine. These were used primarily in the rice colonies of the Carolinas. The numbers brought into Georgia are not obtainable, but contemporary descriptions of Savannah picture it as a smaller version of bustling, slave-trading Charleston and an important slave center for the planters of rice, indigo, and sea-island cotton. There is simply no question that the slave trade formed a valuable item of trade in the foreign commerce of the North American colonies, in addition to furnishing the necessary labor for the expanding staple-plantation agricultural system of the colonial south. Nor is there any question that the Black population, especially in the southern colonies, grew very rapidly in these decades. Probably most of this increase came from natural fecundity and the demographic fact of more births than deaths among the slave population; yet the slave trade not only set up this laboring system in the first place, it also kept an adequate supply of black laborers available for the colonial plantation economy throughout the period.

THE MOVEMENT TO ABOLISH THE SLAVE TRADE. Of the perhaps ten million or more Blacks who were taken from Africa to the Western Hemisphere from the 16th through the 19th century, the great majority were transported to the Caribbean and to South America. Most of these ten million persons were of Negroid origin. Few Bushmanoid, Pygmoid, Mongoloid, and Caucasoid (or "Hamatic") Africans were sent to the New World during the days of the slave trade. The predominance of Negroid Africans is explained by the fact that they were native to western African lands from Senegal south to lower Angola, the favorite haunt of the European and American slave ships. Of the Negroid peoples forcibly removed, most were of the "true Negroid" sub-group, as opposed to the Banti sub-group found further to the south and east. But whatever their sub-group or exact place of origin on the western coast of Africa, the slaves torn from their homelands were forced to undergo the horrors of the "Middle Passage" from Africa to the western lands.

Captured slaves in Africa were marched to a coastal slave station perhaps a hundred miles or more from home. At the stations they were herded into pens with other unfortunates to be kept until a slave ship arrived and a bargain was struck between the master and the local chieftain or slave trader. Some of the slaves had never seen the ocean or a ship and believed that their capture had been carried out so that they would serve as food for the strange-looking men on board the vessels. Many were so frightened at being carried away across the ocean in a ship that they dropped into shark-infested waters to avoid meeting the horrifying fate they believed awaited them on board the ship or across the seas. Slave traders found that the slaves often had to be bound hand and foot while being transported to the ship and until they were safely stowed away and held by chains, or many would surely kill themselves trying to escape.

The hold of a typical slaving vessel was approximately five to six feet in height. Since this distance meant a waste of valuable cargo space, a shelf about six feet in width was built from the sides of the ship. This shelf allowed another row of slaves to be stacked into the hold on the shelf. It is estimated that on a typical slave ship each man was allowed a space six feet long, sixteen inches wide, and about thirty inches high; women received a space five feet-ten inches by sixteen inches; boys and girls received correspondingly less. It was in accommodations of these dimensions that the slaves might have to endure a week or a month until the vessel was completely loaded at the various slave stations, and then another month to six weeks or more in transit until the western shore of the Atlantic had been reached.

The business nature of the whole process can be illustrated by the existence of two rather distinct schools of thought regarding stowing of the slaves for the Middle Passage. Some Guinea captains were called "loose packers." They gave more room to the slaves on the voyage, and perhaps better food, arguing that this practice reduced mortality and brought a better price per slave in the West Indies. Other Guinea captains were "tight packers," that is, they allowed less room per slave, but reasoned that even with higher mortality rates they would still complete the journey with more live slaves and thus make more money from each trip. The tight packers seem to have come to dominate the trade as time went on. Given such conditions, it is no wonder that the

Middle Passage has been characterized by one author as a "crossroads and market-place of diseases." Smallpox, measles, "bloody flux," hookworm, yaws, and elephantiasis and other forms of leprosy were in some degree present on every trip across the Atlantic. Add to these hazards the poor food, the melancholy, the almost non-existent sanitary facilities, and the personal abuse suffered by the slaves at the hands of the crews (themselves the most wrethed and inept types of sailors available), and one begins to appreciate why volumes of personal reminiscenses stall at finding words adequate to describe the horrors of the Middle Passage.

In 1789, a Privy Council estimate held that about 12.5 percent of the slaves died on the Middle Passage, another 4.5 percent died in the harbors before being sold, and an additional 33 percent died during the Caribbean "seasoning" process. If this estimate is correct, 50 percent of the Africans never lived through the processes of the slave trade, although some modern authors place the mortality rate slightly lower.

The figures for the white crews of the slaving vessels show that between 1784 and 1790, a full 21.5 percent of all slaving seamen from Liverpool and Bristol died on the voyages, undoubtedly because they were on the unhealthy ships for the whole journey, rather than just on the middle leg across the Atlantic; thus they were more exposed to scurvy, a deficiency disease caused by their course and monotonous rations. But in addition to those who died of disease, there were those sailors who were discharged before completing the voyage (so the captain would not have to pay them), who simply deserted in some port, or who were intentionally or unintentionally left behind. These brought the total crew loss on a typical voyage to about 40 percent, much higher than in any other branch of the merchant marine, or even in the notorious Royal Navy, whose seamen were hardly better than slaves. That the Middle Passage was a perilous time for both cargo and crew is perhaps best illustrated by the common warnings to mariners to sail at least five miles downwind of a slaver to avoid the stench. The horrors of slaving are revealed also in the practice of some masters to not reveal to their crews that they were to sail to Africa for slaves until after the men had signed on and were well out to sea.

If a slave was fortunate enough to survive the Middle Passage, or if he was lucky enough to be carried on one of the rare ships in which the captain really cared for his cargo, he still had to undergo sale at some South American, West Indian, or American port. Sometimes the entire cargo was consigned to a single planter or group of planters. More commonly, sale was carried out by a "factor," who received a commission on his sales. Sometimes the captain was forced to carry out the sale himself in the town square. But the most common method of sale was at public auction "by inch of candle" or by "scramble." Usually the less healthy slaves were sold by the former method. They were marched to some public place, and bids were received on them until an inch of candle had burned; then the bidding was stopped. Those unhealthy slaves who were not sold by the time the candle had burned down were sometimes left to die on the wharves without food and water. The healthy slaves were often sold by "scramble." By this method, a fixed price for each man, woman, girl, and boy would be set, and the purchasers, at the sound

of a gun, would scramble onto the ship to claim the hardiest looking of
the lot up to the number they had bought. After sale by any of these
means, the purchased Blacks would be led away by their new owners, leaving behind family, friends, often their very identities, and even the
dismal security of the slaving vessels. Slaves were obviously items of
commerce; understanding this is the key to understanding the Atlantic
slave trade.

But despite the fact that the slave trade could be looked upon as
only a dealing in commodities, there were those in the American colonies
who could not view it in that way. From the very beginning there were
those who felt repugnance at both slavery and the slave trade. Massachusetts abolished slavery in the colony in 1641; and Rhode Island did
away with slavery for life in 1652, decreeing that every slave in the
colony would be free after ten years or at age twenty-four. Early in
the 18th century, the Quakers in Pennsylvania protested against both
slavery and the slave trade, only to see their steps to prevent importation of slaves into the colony vetoed by the Privy Council. But the
Quakers persisted, and in 1761 a duty of £10 per slave imported into
Pennsylvania was imposed, effectively ending the slave trade there.
There was opposition to the trade even in the southern colonies, which
depended upon slaves as a labor supply. Although Georgia apparently had
no qualms of conscience over the trade, there was some opposition in the
Carolinas and Virginia out of fear of an insurrection with the growing
number of slaves in the colonies, as well as from some moral repugnance.
The Virgina House of Burgesses tried again and again to restrict the
slave trade during the 18th century, not only because the colonists
feared slave revolts, but also because of an anxiety over an oversupply
of slaves in the colonies, which would lower the value of the existing
bondsmen.

The colonies had to be firmly instructed in 1770 by King George III
that they could not prohibit importation of slaves, but they were clearly restive under both the political and economic burden of an increasing
number of slaves and the moral implications of the existence of the institution within their colonies. Henry Laurens of South Carolina had
engaged in the slave trade, but gave it up as evil. The Virginia
planter and political leader George Washington had doubts over the institution of slavery and provided for emancipation of his slaves at his
death. And Thomas Jefferson regretted the presence of the institution
within the colonies and included in the first draft of the Declaration
of Independence a condemnation of the trade in slaves being carried on
by England as a "cruel war against human nature itself," although the
clause had to be omitted from the final draft because of the opposition
of South Carolina and Georgia delegates and of northern slave traders.

But with political independence from Great Britain, a growing sensi-
tivity to the horrors of the trade, and a continuing awareness of the
oversupply of slaves, various states moved to prohibit or restrict slavery and the slave trade within their boundaries. In 1778, Virginia
forbade the importation of slaves for sale; Maryland did the same in
1783. In 1780, Pennsylvania legislated the gradual abolition of slavery;
and Massachusetts forbade slavery in its new constitution. New Jersey
prohibited the importation of slaves, and North Carolina placed a prohi-

bitive duty on slaves imported, both in 1786. Even South Carolina joined in restriction the next year when it forbade any importation for a
five-year period. With all of these states legislating to restrict or
forbid slavery and the slave trade within their borders, it was obvious
that the trade was going to be severely curtailed if not eventually ended before too long. The reasons may have been economic and pragmatic,
as well as humanitarian, but the effect would be the same.

But, in the meantime, despite this negative sentiment against the
trade, it still flourished where there was adequate reason for it to do
so. It was still legal in Georgia; it flourished also in North Carolina
despite the high duty imposed, and South Carolina re-opened the trade in
1803. Furthermore, the slave trade still thrived in New England. Rhode
Island, Massachusetts, and Connecticut may have forbidden slavery within
their states, but they had not forbidden the slave trade; and the commerce in human beings was still carried on in Salem, Providence, Newport,
and New London. As a matter of fact, importations of slaves into the
United States rose steadily after the formation of the government in
1789 under the new Constitution, which forbade the curtailment of the
slave trade through 1807. President Jefferson signed the bill abolishing the slave trade in March 1807, the prohibition to become effective
on January 1, 1808; but it is instructive to note that in 1807, the last
year of the trade, no fewer than 15,676 slaves were imported into the
country. Nevertheless, the wishes of the majority of the country had
been heeded, and the slave trade legally came to an end within a decade
of the passage of the new Constitution.

Slavery was still in existence and flourishing, but the slave trade
had fallen victim to its own inhumanities, to economic necessity, and to
the fear of insurrection. Many Americans surveying the scene looked forward in confidence to the day when slavery, too, would be a thing of the
past. Perhaps with the further increase in the white farming population
and a decrease in the importance of plantation agriculture in indigo,
tobacco, and rice, slavery too would fall victim to economic imperatives
and die away. Such was the hope; such was not to be the reality.

THE IMPACT OF COTTON. Prior to the 1780's, small amounts of cotton
had been grown in the South, but all had been used for domestic purposes
and none had been exported. It was of the "short-staple" or "upland"
variety, of limited use because of the difficulty of separating the fibre from the seens. Even a skillful person could not prepare more than
a bale (about 225 pounds) per year for the factory, and this tedious and
time-consuming process made the resulting cotton fabrics too expensive
for common use. By 1790 "long-staple" or "sea island" cotton also had
come into cultivation in the South Carolina and Georgia coastlands.
This type of cotton produced a considerable demand for fabrics made
from it, but the tiresome process of removing the seed still existed as
an obstacle to widespread production despite the favorable market. In
addition, it could be produced only in a very limited region. Southern
agricultural leaders were well aware of these problems and began a
search for some method of cheaply and efficiently extracting the seed
from the fibre to break the technological bottleneck to profitable cotton production.

As is known by every schoolchild, Eli Whitney, a Connecticut school-teacher on his way to a position in South Carolina, was apprised of the problem while in Georgia and turned his considerable inventive talents to it. The result was his invention, patented in 1793, the "saw gin," a revolving cylinder with saw-teeth that drew the cotton through a fine screen and thus removed the seeds. Even a hand-powered gin could process fifty times more cotton in a day than could a person separating the seed from the lint by hand, and a machine run by horsepower could process from 300 to 1,000 pounds a day. By Whitney's invention the bottleneck was broken, and cotton growing responded to the market imperatives in existence at the time.

The combination of the discovery of a rapid and inexpensive method of ginning the cotton, the growth of textile technology, which allowed the making of the fabric in large quantities at relatively low cost, and the popularity of the cotton cloth throughout the Western world resulted in the greatest expansion of the textile industry in the history of the world. As an integral part of this rapidly-expanding industry, the South rapidly turned to cotton as its major export to the markets of the northern United States and to Europe, especially Britain. Since upland cotton could be grown in many areas throughout the South, multi-crop farming tended to be rapidly displaced as planters and investors turned more and more to the growing of the valuable vegetable fibre. Vast areas of the South that had formerly been marked by small, subsistence farming were converted to cotton farms in response to the market. Tobacco, rice, and the still-profitable crops of sugar (especially in the Mississippi delta region) were not abandoned, but simply gave way as the leading staples of the South. With the rising prices and profitability of cotton, the South came to rely on cotton as the very backbone of its economy and was soon dominated by it.

Cotton prices began to rise in the late 1790's and the early 1800's, because the increasing demand for cotton in the textile areas could not be matched by an adequate supply; and even though cotton prices fell as the 19th century progressed, as the supply came closer to meeting the demand, cotton growing remained a very profitable enterprise. Briefly stated, cotton growing expanded rapidly, but not as rapidly as worldwide demand, resulting in a generally favorable price for raw cotton despite some seasonal variations. The increasing size of the cotton crop in the South after 1790 makes this picture clear. In 1791, only 2 million pounds of cotton were grown in the United States. One decade later, the total had grown to 40 million pounds; and by 1811, this had doubled to 80 million pounds. By 1821 the total crop stood at 177 million pounds, and then almost doubled again in five years to 330.5 million pounds. By 1834 it stood at 457.5 million pounds. All of the Southern states shared in the new enthusiasm for cotton, although South Carolina and Georgia made the most spectacular gains as they rapidly abandoned diversified farming. South Carolina, for example, went from 1.5 million pounds grown in 1791 to 65.5 million pounds in 1834. In the same years, Georgia went from 500,000 pounds to 75 million pounds. The older planter states of Virginia and North Carolina increased their crops only about 100 percent from 1801 to 1834.

Equally important to the growth of the cotton economy in the South during these decades was the expansion of cotton growing into frontier areas. By 1834 the new states of Tennessee, Louisiana, Mississippi, Alabama, Florida, and Arkansas were far out-producing the older cotton states. For example, Mississippi, which had grown no cotton as late as 1811, by 1834 was producing 85 million pounds per year. Alabama in 1834 showed the same total, coming from only 20 million pounds just thirteen years before. Both of these new states were out-producing South Carolina and Georgia, next in line in total production. In fifth place was Louisiana, which had gone from 2 million pounds produced in 1811 to 62 million pounds in 1834. Farther down the list were Florida and Arkansas, but the total amount of cotton produced in the South had risen from 2 million pounds to 1791 to 457.5 million pounds in 1834, as we have seen. Most of this increase came in the new cotton lands of the Southwest. The newer Southern states in 1834 were producing 297.5 million pounds, compared to the older Southern states' 160 million pounds. By 1860, the total amount of cotton produced in the United States was in excess of 2.24 billion pounds.

Looked at another way (although with some inaccuracy because the typical bale of cotton increased in weight from 225 pounds per bale in 1791 to 461 pounds per bale in 1860), total bales produced in 1790-91 were 8,889; by 1859-60 the total was 4,861,292 bales. Total bales increased from 2,333,718 in 1849-50 to 4,861,292 ten years later on the eve of the Civil War, an increase of 108 percent in one decade. Obviously cotton production was rapidly increasing right up to the time of the Civil War, despite the fact that by 1860 domestic prices had dropped to about one-half their levels from the period of rapid expansion of 1803 to 1807, and to about one-half to one-third their foreign levels at the same earlier date.

The first prerequisite to large-scale production of cotton, demand, was obviously present as indicated by the expansion of cotton production and the maintenance of a price level adequate to assure profit and expansion. The second factor, large areas of land available for expansion to meet demand, was also clearly available, as is indicated by the spread of cotton production into the Deep South and into the Southwest. The third factor, labor, was supplied primarily by slaves. Slave labor was ideal for the production of cotton--as well as the other Southern staples of tobacco, rice, and sugar--not only because of the lower cost of slave labor as opposed to indentured labor, but also because these staple crops could be most efficiently produced on plantations. Rice and sugar in particular required large capitalization, and cotton and tobacco were best produced by slaves more adaptable to routine plantation work than to the varied tasks of general farming supplemented by household manufacture. Furthermore, the planters seem to have been more interested in commercial farming on a large scale and could more easily obtain the credit and land necessary for this type of agriculture. In addition, a small farmer could increase his productivity and profits by opting for the specialization in commercial staples, and thus become a planter too. But this shift could only be done successfully by the acquisition of considerable slave labor, since free white labor was in short supply and always more expensive, to say nothing of being less tractable than bonded slaves.

114

Slave labor gave the added advantage of making available the efforts of the entire slave family at one task or another. The father, the mother, and even the children could be utilized in cotton, rice, tobacco, or sugar production. This practice was not possible under the free labor system without added expense. Free labor came to be rapidly displaced by slave labor in much of the economy of the South in the first half of the 19th century. The great bulk of the staple crops of the region came to be produced on plantations using slave labor. All of the sugar and rice, most of the tobacco, and more than three-fourths of the cotton came from the plantation-slavery system.

Thus the slave system grew with the cotton-and-other-staple plantation system dominating the South. By 1860, Alabama had 453,000 slaves (45 percent of its population) and Arkansas had 111,115 slaves (more than 25 percent of its population); Florida had only 61,745 slaves (almost 45 percent of its population), but neighboring Georgia had 462,198 (about 44 percent of its people). Kentucky had 225,483 slaves (19.5 percent of its population) and Louisiana had 331,726 (over 46 percent). Maryland had 87,189 slaves (12.6 percent of its population) and Mississippi had 436,631 (55 percent). Missouri in 1860 had 114,931 slaves (9.7 percent of its population), and North Carolina had 331,059 (about 33 percent). South Carolina had 402,406 slaves (the highest proportion of all with 57 percent of its population being slave), and Tennessee had 275,719 (24.8 percent). Texas, admitted to the Union only a decade before, had 182,566 slaves (30 percent of its population), and Virginia led the South and the nation in numbers with a total of 490,865 slaves (more than 40 percent of its population). In the South as a whole, slaves constituted 33.6 percent of the population.

THE SLAVE TRADE CONTINUES. In abolishing the slave trade in 1807, the United States was not alone in the Western world. Denmark had already done so in 1802, and Britain, after years of agitation against the trade led by Thomas Clarkson, William Wilberforce, and the Society for the Abolition of the Slave Trade, finally outlawed the trade in 1807. Sweden followed suit in 1813, followed by the Netherlands in 1814, Spain and Portugal for areas north of the equator between 1815 and 1818, and finally France in 1818. But despite the legal prohibitions against the trade, it continued to exist in response to a continuing market for the contraband, though it was greatly diminished in volume from the levels of the late 18th century.

Some American slavers continued in the trade despite a series of American restricting laws dating back to 1794. To outfit for the trade, to build a ship for the trade, to be a member of the crew of a ship in the trade, as well as to be caught with slaves in possession, were all illegal and punishable by fines and imprisonment. Finally, in 1820, an act was passed declaring that anyone engaged in the trade would be liable to the penalty of death. And yet the trade continued. Until 1818, Florida served as the base of operations, and a slave ferry ran regularly between Havana and Pensacola. From there the slaves were taken up the Escambia Riber into Georgia for sale and dispersal. Governor David B. Mitchell of Georgia estimated in 1817 that 20,000 Blacks were being smuggled into Georgia each year by this and other routes. The purchase of Florida in 1819 and its occupation in 1821 put an end to this trade.

Before the trade was effectively ended, the pirate and slave dealer Jean Lafitte operated out of Barataria Bay south of New Orleans, and later Galveston served as an emporium for slaves until the local slave fleet was captured by an American warship in 1821. During the 1830's, some northern ports, such as New York, Baltimore, Boston, and Portland, Maine, served as bases for ships engaged in the slave trade, and Texas served as a channel of the trade after gaining its independence in 1836.

Part of the reason the slave trade persisted was that, while attempts were made to break up the trade on the coast of the United States, very little was done to suppress it on the African coast. Four United States warships were sent to the West African coast in 1820; there they found heavy American slave trading going on, but the squadron's effectiveness was severely hampered by the fact that it could search and take into custody only American slavers; and all American vessels equipped themselves with flags and papers of various nationalities and denied American jurisdiction over them. Of course, British slavers claimed American registry when convenient, too, in order to escape search by British warships and subsequent punishment. It seemed obvious that only American and British cooperation on the African station could bring the slave traffic to an end, and yet here is where the gravest difficulties lay.

Americans, still smarting under the violations of American neutrality and sovereignty from the years of the embargoes through the War of 1812, were in no mood to allow the British one inch of latitude on search and seizure on the high seas. Secretary of State John Quincy Adams mounted a vigorous protest when British naval commanders in 1818 boarded a slaver under the American flag and took her into Sierra Leone for trial. The 1820 agreement between the two nations for cooperation in the African Squadron had completely broken down by 1823. The following year a treaty with Great Britain was drawn up allowing for cooperation through mutual right of seizure and subsequent trial by the nation of the owner of the vessel, but the Senate added so many amendments to protect American sovereignty that the British would not accept it. When Britain finally agreed to sign in 1831, the American Secretary of State refused to do so.

As a result of this refusal to cooperate with the British and the inefficiency of the American African Squadron, assigned both to break up the slave trade and to keep British cruisers away from American merchantment (but based on Porto Praia in the Cape Verde Islands far away from its patrol area and often able to put only one vessel in service), the slave trade continued. It has been estimated that in 1839 as many as 150,000 slaves were still crossing the Atlantic--as compared to an average of 100,000 per year when the trade was legal! Of course, few of this aggregate were coming to American shores, but American efforts at ending the slave trade either alone or in cooperation with other nations were meager at best. The original appropriation for the anti-slave patrols had been passed in 1820 in the amount of $100,000. In 1823, it was reduced to only $50,000, and from that point on the appropriations dribbled off to virtually nothing, reaching a mere $5,000 in 1834. From that year until 1842, no monies were appropriated. Sensitive to any violation of the American flag, and unwilling to take effective action against the illegal traders, the American government was condoning by its inaction the efforts of honest ment to suppress the inhuman--and clearly illegal--traffic in persons. Even when two slavers flying the American flag were stopped by the British in 1839, and it was clearly proved that the ships were Spanish and flying the American flag only to escape punishment, the United States government still protested that the British could not have known for sure that the ships were not American until after they had boarded them and, therefore, that the British action was illegal.

Because the conflicts between the patrolling British cruisers and the heavily-armed slavers began taking on all the aspects of a naval war, the Americans and the British finally agreed formally on "joint suppression" by "joint cruising" off the African coast, in the Webster-Ashburton Treaty of 1842. But from this date until 1857, there were on average only five American ships assigned to the patrol (the British maintained four to five times that number) and, stationed in the Cape Verde Islands a thousand miles away and stopping and searching a vessel only if it flew the American flag and only if slaves were actually on board, the patrol was of negligible value. By 1857, the joint suppression and the joint cruising clearly constituted a farce. The British were aided by a law of 1839, which allowed their squadrons to condemn a vessel for slave trading if the officers found a slave deck, shackles, grated hatch openings, an excess supply of water casks, or slaving trade goods; but the hard-pressed and miniscule American squadron did not have even this reasonable "equipment clause" in its favor.

It has sometimes been charged that the reason this illegal slave trade was not suppressed was Southern opposition, which found voice in the actions of the federal government. While this contention may contain some truth, it would appear that equally important was the fact that there was no national imperative to enforce the laws. The number of slaves coming into the United States was relatively small, the cost of real enforcement would be high, and enforcement could hardly find a place among the various reform movements sweeping the country during these years--such as temperance, abolition, and public education--to say nothing of the conflicts over the spread of slavery and the possibility of secession. But even without effective American help, the British persisted; and by 1850 they had closed down about half of the West African coastline. The number of slaves illegally exported was down to about 37,000 per year, with the British squadron having captured about 700 slaving vessels in a decade.

The 1850's saw the heyday of American participation in the illegal slave trade. Many factors were working in the traders' favor. The demand for slaves was increasing not only in the United States, but also in Cuba, Brazil, and much of South America. Furthermore, the African market was still open, with the English factors having been replaced by French, Spanish, and Portuguese merchants plus native mulattoes. And profits were great. While the cost of slaves in the over-supplied African market dropped to as low as $10 per man, the price in the high-demand market in Cuba could be as high as $625 per man, with the usual selling price ten times the cost. In addition, improvements in maritime technology in the form of "clippers" out of Baltimore and New England shipyards meant that a modern slaver with a fair breeze could even out-run the new steam frigates sent in pursuit of him. These factors, com-bined with American testiness over the searching of a vessel under the American flag or under American registry (even if the captain made an on-the-spot "sale" of the vessel to an American crewman for $1), helped assure a lucrative continuance of the trade. Despite the pleas to the humanitarian instincts of the American people by Commander Andrew F. Foote, USN, who had been assigned to the African Squadron and who wrote a moving book about the slave trade entitled Africa and the American Flag, the trade into Latin America and the United States continued in the 1850's.

New York City was one of the largest centers of operation, with the "Spanish Company," the "Portuguese Company," and later the "American Company," owned and operated by American businessmen, continuing their operations. American vessels alone probably accounted for about 11,000 slaves a year being brought into the Western Hemisphere in the years immediately preceding the Civil War. The total importation of slaves by vessels of all nations during the 1850's is variously estimated at between 30,000 and 40,000 per year. How many of these slaves were im-ported into the United States during the 1850's is impossible to deter-mine. It was not until 1861 and the outbreak of the Civil War that the United States finally made a determined effort to stop the slave trade. With little opposition in Congress, the Southern states having seceded, $1.8 million was appropriated for the purpose, and the following year the United States and Great Britain signed a treaty allowing full rights of mutual search and seizure (including the recognition of the "equip-ment clause"), with courts representing both nations for trial of slave-runners. The combination of the war and vigorous enforcement meant the virtual end of the slave trade in the Western Hemisphere.

During the colonial period, approximately 275,000 slaves had been brought into the American colonies; between 1791 and 1808, another 70,000 were imported; from 1808 to 1861, probably another 54,000 were brought in. Thus from its opening to its demise, the slave trade brought approximately 399,000 Blacks into the country. This amount of importa-tion, coupled with a high rate of natural increase (the only available figures show the white increase rate at an average of 26.7 percent per decade from 1830 to 1860 and the Negro rate at 22.1 percent for the same period--not a great difference) accounts for the figure of at least 3.9 million slaves in the United States in 1860.

What the effects were of the exportation of at least 10 million of the healthiest, youngest, and ablest Africans from their homelands can only be guessed. The social, economic, and political consequences of the removal of the flower of African manhood in these centuries cannot be imagined. The impact of the importation of almost 400,000 of these people into the colonies and the United States has already been discuss-ed. Without these slaves and their progeny, the entire socio-economic Southern plantation system could not have come into being, based as it was on the growing commercial staples, especially cotton. The rise in cotton produced from 2 million pounds in 1791 to 2.4 billion pounds in 1860 led, in turn, to the creation of the cotton trade with the North and with Europe. This new branch of domestic and foreign commerce had effects upon the South and upon the nation which helped transform both into economic giants by the middle of the 19th century.

THE COTTON TRADE. The dimensions of the cotton trade and its impact on the national and international economic scene are astounding. In the decade of the 1790's, the average cotton crop per year was only 52,000 bales. Of this, 37.7 percent was usually exported outside the United States. During the first decade of the 19th century, the cotton crop was almost 284,000 bales per year, and 57.2 percent on an average was exported. This 57.2 percent represented an average value of $8.7 million per year and constituted about 23 percent of the value of total exports from the country. Between 1811 and 1820, the crop had grown to an average of 409,600 bales, of which 58.2 percent, worth $15.7 million, was exported. This constituted an average of 31.7 percent of total national exports by value.

In the 1820's, the average figures were 831,000 bales, 76.5 percent exported, worth $25.6 million per year, and 47.6 percent of the value of national exports. In the 1830's, the crop averaged 1,368,000 bales, 82.5 percent exported, valued at $52.8 million, and 58.5 percent by value of total exports. During the 1840's, the average figures were 2,164,000 bales, 78.7 percent exported, $55.3 million in value, and 50.2 percent of exports by value. In the final decade before the Civil War, the averages climbed to 3,394,100 bales, 76.6 percent exported, worth $123.2 million, and 53.3 percent of the value of American exports. Cotton thus came to dominate the export trade as tobacco, rice, and lumber products declined; manufactures also showed a substantial gain but could never challenge cotton in volume or in value in either domestic or foreign trade.

As the cotton trade developed, it called forth a vast increase in the merchant marine to carry the cargo. While the exact amount of tonnage cannot be precisely determined, it was estimated in 1852 that the foreign trade in cotton alone engaged some 800,000 tons in American shipping and provided employment for at least 40,000 men. In addition, the domestic coastwise shipping of cotton called forth another 1.1 million tons of shipping and 55,000 men. In all, probably 47 percent of the registered American foreign fleet and 55 percent of the coastal fleet were engaged in the cotton trade. The size of the fleet and the construction of larger ships of greater length with broad bottoms to navigate the shallow water of the Mississippi River to New Orleans, gave the American freighters a distinct advantage. As a result, 75 percent to 80 percent of American cotton sent to foreign ports was shipped in American vessels.

Most of the cotton exported was shipped to Great Britain, which was in the process of building a giant textile industry on the basis of a series of textile machinery inventions. Britain consistently consumed at least one-half of the world's cotton, raising its American imports from one million bales in 1839-40 to 2.3 million bales twenty years later, an increase of 130 percent. But continental Europe, too, was an expanding market for American cotton. During the same two decades, con-

119

tinental imports of cotton rose 136 percent as the demand for cotton increased in Prussia, Austria, Russia, Switzerland, Belgium, Holland, Spain, and the Italian states. Yet the most rapidly expanding market for the South's cotton was Northern textile mills. The mills' consumption of bales increased from 336,000 bales in 1839 to 953,000 bales on the eve of the Civil War, an increase of 184 percent. It was the combination of the expanding cotton crops being carried to the expanding textile industries in Europe and in the northern United States that created the "cotton merchant marine."

Probably a majority of the cotton vessels in the trade followed a triangular route, sailing first from New York or New England some 700 or 800 miles down the coast to Charleston or Savannah with manufactured goods or foodstuffs to the staple-rich but manufacturing-poor South (or sometimes going a full 1,700 miles to the Gulf ports of Mobile or New Orleans instead). From one of these Southern ports, the ships sailed with the cotton cargoes to Liverpool or Havre. There they would load with European manufactures needed in the United States (or very often with immigrants), and return to their original ports in the North to begin the process once again.

Yet a considerable amount of the cotton was brought coastwise to New York and then transshipped to Europe. The return cargoes of European goods would also be routed through New York and carried to the South by coastal vessels. The reason for this distortion from a direct trade to and from Europe lay in the emergence of enterprising and dynamic New York shippers who established regular packet service not only up and down the eastern coast of the United States, but also across the Atlantic. New York-based packets gathered tobacco from the Chesapeake, rice from Louisiana, naval stores from the Carolinas, and especially cotton from Charleston, Savannah, Mobile, and New Orleans and then brought then to New York. From there the products were distributed in the Northeast or sent by packets or tramp freighters to Europe. The roundabout procedure was reversed for shipping from Europe and for Northeastern manufactures being sent into the South.

Whether the cotton was exported as part of the "cotton triangle" of Northern ports-Southern ports-European ports, or whether Southern cotton and European manufactures reached their final destinations via a 200-mile detour into New York, the New Yorkers built their emerging trade network on Southern cotton and its transport, which was tremendously profitable for New York, then emerging as the premier American port. It also meant that the Northern metropolis enjoyed a remarkable command over Southern commerce, with its interests and agents and credit facilities lubricating the whole cotton trade and, incidentally, drawing off much of the potential Southern profits into Northern pockets. In addition to losing freight revenues to Northern shippers, the South found itself dependent on the North for domestic manufactures, such as coarse textiles, ready-made clothing, saddlery, furniture, and even locomotives--to say nothing of large quanitites of foodstuffs. Thus while the South provided a majority of the foreign shipping via cotton and helped create the rapidly-expanding merchant marine, it also grew more and more dependent upon the North because of its agricultural specialization in staples, particularly cotton.

<u>THE IMPACT OF THE SLAVERY AND COTTON TRADES</u>. The impact of slavery
and the cotton trade on the South was quite different from their impact
on the rest of the nation. As the South shifted from diversified farming into cotton, it wedded itself to the plantation-slavery system.
Most planters of necessity invested very heavily in slaves, thus converting their circulating capital into fixed capital. In turn, the
Southerner typically had to rely on the capital of local merchants for
food, implements, and even luxuries; the merchants in turn were dependent upon Northern industrial and food-producing states. Liquid capital not sent into the North was very often sent to the Border States
for additional slaves in response to the unceasing demand for labor in
the Deep South. This situation was created when the upper tier of
Southern states, finding themselves with agricultural resources of lessening value, turned to some grain production as a substitute, but also
to the sale of slaves to the growing cotton regions of the Deep South
and the Southwest. But the Border States, in turn, were still dependent
upon the North for manufactures and some foodstuffs, to say nothing of
transportation services; so the liquid capital thus gained by the upper
tier of Southern states also tended to flow northward.

Another loss to the South resulted from its cotton trade. If an
export of any kind requires substantial investment in transportation,
warehousing, port facilities, etc., it necessarily creates complementary
and subsidiary industries which in turn create more capital investment,
more specialization, and more urbanization in and around the ports and
areas of export. Yet the cotton trade required only a few centers for
collection and exportation and therefore did not encourage the development of subsidiary industries, markets, and urbanization. Furthermore,
any specialization and investment in transportation needed by the South
to export cotton rested firmly in the hands of Northern businessmen and
shippers, so even this potential economic gain was lost.

On the other hand, the South's loss in opting for staple agriculture, especially cotton, as the basis of its economy was the Northeast's
gain. Not only did the Northeast dominate the cotton and staple export
trade through its ships, merchants, banking, and insurance, but it also
used the South's cotton to convert itself into a major textile-produc-
ing area. From the successful textile operations begun by Samuel Slater
in Pawtucket, Rhode Island, in 1790, Northeastern textile manufacturing
blossomed into a major industry. As it did so, it used more and more of
the South's cotton. In the decade of the 1830's, the average yearly consumption of cotton for domestic use was 223,100 bales. During the 1840's
the average had almost doubled to 434,800 bales a year, and during the
1850's the average had reached an astounding 752,100 bales a year in domestic consumption. While the gains from the growing of the raw cotton
accrued to the Southern planters (minus their losses in goods and
services to the North on whom they were so dependent), the gains from
the conversion of the raw cotton into a finished or semi-finished state
went almost entirely to the Northeast. The Northeast, then, became not
only a greater maritime area thanks to cotton and the cotton trade, but
also a greater manufacturing, banking, and merchandising area because
of the South's great staple.

121

The developing West also was able to make tremendous economic gains because of cotton and the South's agricultural system. As the South moved from subsistence farming into staple farming, it made no move to develop commercial agriculture to any great extent. With the Northeast turning to manufacturing and to small-crop specialization, the expanding West found great wealth and a solid economic base by turning to large-scale commercial farming to provide the grains, meats, fruits, and dairy products demanded by both the Northeast and the South. The West as a food-exporting region sent food to the Northeast in exchange for manufactured goods. It also sent food to the South, receiving in exchange primarily bank drafts drawn on the North, which were used to buy more manufactures in the East and within its own boundaries and thereby created a larger urban market in the East and at home for its foodstuffs.

Thus the slavery-plantation-cotton system of the South played a major part in creating a national trade network, as well as an international trade network, in the six decades between independence and the Civil War. The South with its staple agricultural system but without local shipping and manufacturing services, the Northeast as the leading force in manufacturing, merchandising, banking, and shipping services, and the West as the evolving commercial food-producing area serving both the South and the East, together produced a regional interdependence and thereby an economic organization that rapidly propelled it to world leadership in agriculture, manufacturing, and maritime shipping. Cotton and the cotton trade, built on the slave trade and slavery, was one of the most important elements, if not the most important element, in the process of dynamic economic evolution experienced by the United States in the first half of the 19th century.

SUGGESTIONS FOR FURTHER READING

Albion, Robert G. Square-Riggers on Schedule: The New York Sailing
    Packets to England, France, and the Cotton Ports. Princeton:
    Princeton University Press, 1938.

Curtin, Philip D. The Atlantic Slave Trade: A Census. Madison: Uni-
    versity of Wisconsin Press, 1969.

Davis, David B. The Problem of Slavery in Western Culture: Ithaca:
    Cornell University Press, 1966.

DuBois, W. E. B. The Suppression of the African Slave-trade to the
    United States of America, 1638-1870. New York: Longmans, Green,
    and Co., 1896.

Gray, Lewis C. History of Agriculture in the Southern United States to
    1860. 2 vols. Washington, D.C.: Carnegie Institution, 1933.

Howard, Warren S. American Slavers and the Federal Law, 1837-1862.
    Berkeley and Los Angeles: University of California Press, 1963.

Hutchins, John G. B. The American Maritime Industries and Public Policy,
    1789-1914. Harvard Economic Series, Vol. LXXI. Cambridge: Harvard
    University Press, 1941.

Mannix, Daniel P. and Cowley, Malcolm. Black Cargoes: A History of the
    Atlantic Slave Trade, 1518-1865. New York: Viking Press, 1962.

North, Douglas C. The Economic Growth of the United States, 1790-1860.
    New York: W. W. Norton and Co., Inc., 1966.

Pope-Hennessy, James. Sins of the Fathers: A Study in the Atlantic
    Slave Traders, 1441-1807. New York: Alfred A. Knopf, 1968.

Scherer, James A. B. Cotton as a World Power: A Study in the Economic
    Interpretation of History. New York: Frederick A. Stokes Co.,
    1966.

Taylor, George Rogers. The Transportation Revolution, 1815-1860. The
    Economic History of the United States, Vol. IV. New York: Holt,
    Rinehart and Winston, 1951.

Wells, Tom Henderson. The Slave Ship Wanderer. Athens: University of
    Georgia Press, 1967.

Williams, Eric. Capitalism and Slavery. Chapel Hill: University of
    North Carolina Press, 1944; reprint ed., New York: Capricorn Books,
    1966.

Woodman, Harold D., ed. Slavery and the Southern Economy: Sources and

Readings. Forces in American Economic Growth Series. New York: Harcourt, Brace and World, Inc., 1966.

CHAPTER VII. DECADES OF MARITIME GREATNESS: THE PACIFIC

During its colonial years America depended upon the seas for its existence and progress. The Atlantic Ocean sustained its people through fishing, shipbuilding, and commerce. Without access to and opportunities for growth upon the oceans, the American colonists would have been unable to effect the high level of economic maturity they attained through their efforts and the mercantile rules of Britain. Indeed, this dependence on the sea and the changing of the mercantile rules proved to be pivotal factors in leading the American colonists to resistance to their mother country, and subsequently to independence.

But independence in the political realm did not guarantee independence in the economic and maritime realms, and the new nation soon found that the European powers showed little regard for American neutral rights during their momentous struggles for national existence between 1792 and 1814. The attitudes of smaller and weaker powers, too, such as the Barbary rulers, illustrated the truism that national rights are honored only when a nation can and will enforce those rights. Thus the United States was forced through the travail of the embargoes, the Barbary Wars, and the War of 1812 to defend its rights upon the seas. But if the nation did not wholly enforce respect by dint of diplomacy and armed might in all of these cases, still it did not suffer economic and political ruin and proved it was a power to be reckoned with, at least in the Western Hemisphere. It was during these same years of international crisis for the new nation and in the first six decades of the 19th century that American maritime prowess not only continued to grow in the Atlantic regions, but also spread itself across the blue waters of the Pacific. This Pacific expansion brought in its wake wealth, crises with other nations on the western shores of North America, and a deep interest in affairs halfway around the world in the lands of the fabled East. As a result, America, a second-rate Atlantic power in 1781, became a first-rate Atlantic and Pacific power by 1860.

SEALS AND SEA OTTERS. In the years after independence, leading shipowners and merchants of the port cities of Boston, New York, Philadelphia, and other major shipping areas endeavored to reestablish their Atlantic commercial network, severely damaged by the Revolution and by that loss of British trading privileges which victory had brought. In a similar move to rebuild, many lesser merchants in these and in minor ports from New England to Long Island Sound decided to attempt to make their fortunes in the seal trade, first in South Atlantic and then in Pacific waters. Gleaning from the recently-published journals of the great English explorer Captain James Cook and other European explorers the great demand in the Orient for the warm hides of the seal, as well as information as to where these animals could be found in abundance, these merchants sent their captains to search for the mammals in the southern waters off the Western Hemisphere, from Patagonia on the Atlantic on around to the Pacific islands.

In the South Atlantic, the sealing vessels sought their prey in the Falklands, on Staten Island, and on South Georgia, taking as many as fifty thousand skins on a single trip. By 1797 the hunt for seals had moved to Pacific waters, and the islands of Juan Fernandez, 500 miles off the coast of Chile, became the favored haunt of the seal hunters. Here, as on the barren shores of the South Atlantic islands or on the isolated coasts of Patagonia, thousands of helpless seals were clubbed to death and stripped of their skins, the valuable pelts being shipped by the hundreds of thousands to the markets of Canton. After 1798 the center of the sealing industry was a small island, only seven miles long and four miles wide in the Juan Fernandez group, known as Mas Afuera ("more to sea"). Along the rocky coasts of this and other islands in the group, dozens of Yankee vessels anchored while their crews carried out their slaughter of the seals in three great waves, in 1798, in 1800, and in 1803.

Often leaving part of their crews on the islands to hunt the seals while they sailed on to Canton--the crews being more than willing to burn parts of the islands to drive the seals within reach of their clubs if necessary--the sealing expeditions decimated the seal population within a matter of a few short years. When in 1805 the Spanish destroyed the Yankee settlements on Mas Afuera and later turned the island into a penal colony, the seals had already been largely wiped out. It has been estimated that between 1793 and 1807, more than 3.5 million pelts were taken from Mas Afuera alone. The total number of pelts taken from the islands of the South Atlantic and South Pacific is impossible to determine, but the numbers of seals slaughtered must have been astronomical. The seal trade with China as thus developed from these areas, and the other sealing voyages of the time that carried crews as far into the Pacific as Easter and Pitcairn Islands (where they discovered the widows and children of the mutineers of the Bounty), illustrate the scope and dynamism of American merchant-mariners as they breasted the South Atlantic and Pacific waters early in the 19th century in their thrust for markets and wealth; and, by doing so, they helped open the gates of the Orient to American trade.

While the seal harvest was in full swing in southern waters between 1792 and the first decade of the new country, a similar enterprise was also being carried out far to the north. Captain Cook's reports not only had talked of southern seals and the China market, but also had highlighted the fact that pelts could be obtained from the Indians on the northwest coast of America. But the real enthusiasm for the Northwest Coast was initially sparked by a deserter from the Cook expedition, one John Ledyard of Groton, Connecticut, who jumped ship at Long Island and gave a fascinated world an eye-witness account of the great explorer's death in Hawaii in 1779. He related also how ragged furs obtained for a few trifles on the Northwest Coast had been sold for a hundred dollars each in Canton and how Cook almost had a mutiny on his hands at one point as his crews wanted to return to the coast for more pelts. When Cook's journals were published and it was found they confirmed Ledyard's story, the race for the sea-otter pelts of the Northwest was on, with Ledyard leading the enthusiasm. He asked only that he be

126

dropped off on the coast of Oregon, there to make his way across the continent to prove that a land route to the wealth of the Northwest Coast was possible. Although Ledyard never made his journey, his projections of the wealth to be gained by the sale of Northwest furs at Canton--now verified by Cook's journals--were enthusiastically explored by others.

The Americans entered the Northwest Coast-Canton fur trade in 1787 when two small trading vessels from Boston, the Columbia and the Lady Washington, their crews armed with sea letters from the United States government and passports from Massachusetts, made their way around Cape Horn and arrived at Nootka Sound south of the Straits of Fuca the next year, to subsequently discover the Columbia River. After spending eleven months trading with the Indians for sea-otter pelts, the Columbia under Captain Robert Gray made its way to Canton in 1789, where her crew exchanged the sea-otter furs for teas and then completed a circumnavigation of the earth by returning to Boston in August 1790. Captain Gray and the crew of the Columbia created a sensation not only by their trading exploits, but also by carrying back with them a native of the Sandwich Islands (Hawaii), who brought bedazzlement by his shining raiment to the comparatively dreary streets of Boston. More important in the long run, by her voyage of almost 42,000 miles, the Columbia began the Northwest fur trade which the Americans soon came to dominate.

Armed with copper, cloth, clothes, shoes, nails, chisels, blankets, and firearms to trade to the sometimes-dangerous Indians in exchange for sea-otter pelts, the small sixty-five-to-ninety-foot vessels generally left the New England coast in the summer and arrived on the Northwest Coast the next spring. After bartering for months with the Indians until their holds were filled with the precious pelts, the Yankee vessels sailed for Canton by way of the Sandwich Islands--valuable for both relaxation and sandalwood. After trading the pelts for teas in Canton, the vessels returned to Boston with typical profits of $200,000 for a single voyage. Hundreds of vessels sought out the Northwest Coast for sea-otter pelts for the markets of Canton, and many Boston fortunes were made as a result of this triangular trade early in the 19th century.

Although Spanish, English, French, Russian, and Portuguese fur traders also were active along the Northwest Coast, the Americans easily prevailed over their competitors from 1790 to 1815. Dominance was easy because the European nations were involved in almost constant warfare during these years, and the British fur traders, potentially the strongest rivals to the Americans, could not legally trade with China because of the monopoly on the Chinese markets enjoyed by the East India Company, a monopoly held until 1834. The Russians, another rival in the Northwest, were not allowed by the Chinese government to enter any Chinese port, so had to ship their furs back to Siberia and then overland into China, or else send them to Canton on American ships, an option they usually chose.

Even though the British were usually an unimportant factor in the trade, at times they could be quite troublesome. Such was particularly true in the case of John Jacob Astor's settlement at Astoria, established in 1811 with the encouragement of Thomas Jefferson at the mouth of the

Columbia River. Astor's Pacific Fur Company sent two groups of men to establish the fur-trading post, one by way of Cape Horn in the Tonquin and one overland. The settlement was reinforced by more men in 1812. But the outbreak of the War of 1812 brought news that a Canadian vessel, the Racoon of twenty guns, was being fitted out in London to take Astoria, so the Canadian managers of Astor's outpost sold the post and its stock of furs to Britain's Northwest Company in 1814 for $58,000 rather than lose it all by conquest. As a result, the American flag was hauled down as the Racoon arrived, and Astoria became Fort George.

But the fall of Astoria did not end American dominance in the Northwest because firm commercial connections had been established in the region. The Russian-American Company was forced to rely on the American sailors and merchants for necessary supplies--by an agreement of 1812--and for shipment of their furs to Canton. Furthermore, Britain's Northwest Company was involved in constant feuding with the Hudson's Bay Company, was not interested in supplying the Russians, and was not allowed to supply furs to the China market anyway. Thus American interests were safe, although the sea-otter trade declined after the war because of the scarcity and high prices of pelts caused by the overkill of the animals by American, British, Russian, and other nationals in the Pacific Northwest.

Even if the sea-otter trade declined early in the 19th century after forming a vital link between the United States and the Canton market, its years of fruition had formed a second vital link between American interests on the Atlantic coast and the American economic potential on the Northwest Coast, an interest the American government was not willing to lose to anyone. Thus when the time came in 1818 to settle with Britain the question of the ownership of the Oregon Territory, the United States would not grant British preeminence. It only agreed that the area north of 42° parallel from the "Stony Mountains" to the Pacific would be equally and freely accessible for ten years to the vessels and the citizens of both Britain and the United States. The subsequent negotiations of 1826-27 continued this principle of joint occupancy indefinitely, and through the 1830's and into the 1840's the United States maintained an avid interest in and a right to use this Oregon Territory, whose natural riches and whose function as the way station to China had been revealed by the fur traders of forty years before.

PACIFIC WHALING. Having fully developed their industry during the colonial period in Atlantic waters, and having moved into the South Atlantic on the eve of the Revolutionary War--only to see their livelihood ruined by that conflict--New England whalers again took up their hazardous trade in the 1780's and 1790's. But in the second great period of whaling, begun after the Revolutionary War, the primary hunting grounds for the giant mammals were not in the Atlantic Ocean but on the far reaches of the Pacific.

The first whaler from an American port to round Cape Horn was the Beaver from Nantucket in 1792, long after Atlantic whaling was well established. But so abundant were whales in the Pacific that by the first

128

decades of the 19th century the American whalers had largely abandoned the Atlantic waters--leaving only the little "plum-pud'ners" of Rhode Island in pursuit of whales off Greenland--and in larger and more efficient ships were engaged in voyages extending as long as two to three years. They swarmed into the Pacific buoyed up by confidence in the rising price of sperm oil and the high demand for spermaceti for candles. In 1819, American whaling vessels landed in Hawaii, and in that same year they sought their valuable prey off the coast of Japan. By 1821 some thirty vessels were working off the Japanese coast. In the 1830's, Americans opened the whaling grounds off the Northwest Coast (filling the economic gap left by the gradual decline in the fur trade in that region) and off the Kamchatka coast. In 1848, an American whaling vessel penetrated the Bering Straits to hunt the bowhead whale in Arctic waters. During these same decades American whalers touched New Zealand, Tasmania, Java, the Solomons, Guam, the Philippines, the Fijis, and the Galapagos Islands. The Hawaiian Islands were the center of their far-flung Pacific whaling grounds.

One primary target for the whalers was the right whale, the "right whale" to catch because of the baleen lining of its mouth, which gave whalebone of great commercial importance, and because it produced a great quantity of oil. Another prime target was the sperm whale, with its valuable long head, the upper part a rich reservoir of oil, the lower part packed with spermaceti. The whalers also sought the humpback, the finback, the sulphur bottom, the bowhead, and the smaller killer whales. But whatever specie they killed to be cut apart at boatside-- its precious sperm oil to be ladled out, its blubber to be boiled down on the deck of the ship for oil to be stored in barrels below decks, its whalebone to be preserved to bring high prices on the commercial market-- the result was a period of unrivaled expansion beginning in 1815 and extending into the 1850's.

Whereas in 1815 there were 1,230 tons of whaling vessels afloat from American harbors, by 1820 some 36,445 tons were listed; and from 1830 to 1860, the average aggregate tonnage utilized per year was 190,500. During these last three decades, from 1830 to 1860, when whaling was at its zenith, the whaling fleet averaged 600 vessels, and annual imports averaged 117,950 barrels of sperm oil, 25,193 barrels of whale oil, and more than 2.3 million pounds of bone for a total value of more than $8 million a year. The high point for number of total vessels used was 1846, when the fleet consisted of 736 vessels worth something in excess of $21 million. They furnished employment in the industry for 70,000 persons. The total value of the industry that year was estimated as being over $70 million.

The spin-off effects of whaling on the American economy were considerable. Whaling voyages accounted for a consumption of 500,000 barrels of flour a year, and a like amount of pork and beef, plus millions of staves and millions of tons of cordage, thus benefitting the American farmer and merchant too. The industry contributed also to the cotton and woolen industries, with one-third to one-fourth of all the spermaceti oil from whaling being used in the production of these textiles. The export of whale oil and bone constituted 3.6 percent of all American merchandise exported in 1845, a figure typical of these years.

While hunting more and more in waters off the Northwest Coast and in Alaskan-Russian waters, America's 763 whalers constituted almost 82 percent of the total of 900 whaling vessels operating throughout the world in 1846. In peak years, 10,000-plus whales were taken by the ships of the American whaling fleet. They operated primarily out of New Bedford, Nantucket, Sag Harbor, and New London and Fairhaven, Connecticut. These five harbors furnished more than 83 percent of the total ships in the American whaling fleet. These same boom years of the 1840's saw Nantucket, the colonial whaling leader, reach its peak and then give way to New Bedford as the premier American whaling port. Nantucket was a victim of choosing to stay longer with the vanishing sperm whale, as opposed to other species, and of having a forbidding sand bar at the mouth of the harbor, necessitating the use of ingenious "camels" between 1842 and 1849 to lift heavily-laden vessels over the bar and tow them into port. New Bedford rushed to leadership with some 20,000 persons in the industry in 1850, including 10,000 seamen on 320 vessels.

Even when the whaling boom began its decline in the 1850's, the Northwest Coast whaling grounds continued to be profitable, being based on the hunting of the bowhead whales in the Okhotsk Sea, along the Kamchatka coast, and in the Bering Strait. This North Pacific whalery continuing to grow in the 1850's as other areas declined was largely responsible for an increase in the value of whale products from $18.7 million to a total of $89.3 million in this decade alone.

Whaling went into precipitous decline in the 1860's, a victim of the petroleum industry and of the Civil War, during which the whaling fleet dropped 50 percent in number of vessels and 60 percent in tonnage. Many ships were captured by the Confederate cruisers or were simply taken out of service. In addition, other industries became more attractive to New England capital because whaling voyages were becoming longer and longer, were costing more and more for fitting out and provisioning, and were less likely to turn a handsome profit. The number of sailing whalers declined steadily until by 1906 only forty-two were left in the trade, but in their heyday the Pacific whalers played a major part in America's Pacific destiny. Whaling continued to focus the nation's attention on the Pacific coast and its importance to the country as the fur trade declined. And the protection of the whaling industry was brought up again and again in Congress in the debates over the Oregon question, where it was pointed out that America's destiny was tied to the Pacific and the Far East. Whaling may, indeed, have been a minor industry in the total American picture even in its zenith years of the 1840's and 1850's, but its high visibility, its obvious vulnerability, and its political impact eminating from New England congressmen made it a major factor in America's interest both in the acquisition of the Oregon Territory and in the advancement of American influence in the Far East.

AMERICAN INTERESTS IN HAWAII. In their carrying of goods to and
from the markets of Canton, in their search for pelts held to be of such
great value in the Orient, and in their hunt for whales, American ships
sailed throughout the reaches of the far Pacific. The natives of the
Marquesas Islands, the Fijis, the Admiralties, the Carolines, and the
Philippines, as well as those of New Guinea, Wake, Guam, Tahiti, and
Samoa, all saw American vessels visit their shores for trade goods such
as tortoise-shell and mother of pearl, for sandalwood, sharks' fins,
and bêche de mer (a slimy sea-slug highly prized by the Chinese for use
in soups), and for provisions for their crews. American vessels of all
types were as at home in the Pacific of the 19th century as they had
been in the Atlantic in the 17th and 18th centuries. The center of this
Pacific commerce was the Sandwich Islands, which developed into a focal
point of American interest in an increasingly-Americanized ocean. Vessels from the United States bound for Manila or Canton, vessels from
the Northwest Coast on their way to or from China or American eastern
ports, vessels leaving unsold goods for later sale or transshipment elsewhere, vessels owned by Americans trading throughout the Pacific, whalers
going to or from their hunting grounds in the northern or southern seas
or off the coast of Japan, all made Hawaii the foremost seaport and
entrepôt of the Pacific.

American vessels had been calling in Hawaiian waters from the
earliest days of the Republic on their voyages to and from the Orient,
but Americans were not the only nationals who recognized the economic
and strategic importance of the islands. In 1794, Captain George Vancouver, following up on the work of Captain Cook, and having made two
previous visits to Hawaii since 1790, talked of encouraging the British
government to settle some West Indian planters in the islands to culti-
vate sugar there without recourse to slavery. Vancouver made a treaty
with King Kamehameha at Hilo that year, which the officer regarded as a
formal cession of the islands to Great Britain, although it is probable
that the King only believed he was putting the islands under British
protection. Whatever the case, the serious illness of George III, the
occupation of Parliament with other matters, and Vancouver's early death
ended any further assertion of British sovereignty over the islands at a
time when such a claim could probably have been upheld against any other
challenger.

Russia also made a claim to Hawaii some time later when, in 1815,
Georg Anton Scheffer, a German physician working for the Russian-American
Company, was ordered by its chief agent, Alexander Baranov, to obtain
land and construct a fort at Honolulu. Ordered out by King Kamehameha,
Scheffer went to Kauai and obtained permission from the local chief to
build two blockhouses there. He was also granted a monopoly of the
sandalwood trade. But the Russian government disavowed his actions in
1816. Both Scheffer and the Russian-American Company later tried to
convince Czar Alexander I to add the Sandwich Islands to the Russian
Empire, but they failed in their efforts, and Russian claims to the islands were never seriously resurrected.

But as in the case of the Northwest Coast, where the primacy of one
of the outside powers would be determined not by diplomacy but by econo-

mic penetration, in Hawaii the Americans took the lead. Because the islands lay across their Pacific trade and whaling routes, American interests soon came to dominate there, aided, strangely enough, by Protestant missionaries whose goals were antagonistic to those of the traders, whalemen, and merchants becoming increasingly prominent in the islands.

On April 4, 1820, the ship Thaddeus tied up at Kailua, having on board a small band of New England missionaries sent out by the American Board of Commissioners for Foreign Missions of the Congregational Church to establish a Christian civilization in the Sandwich Islands. By 1840 six more companies of missionaries were active, and 20,000 Hawaiians had become converted to Protestantism. Two years later, nineteen mission stations were in operation in the islands, employing sixty-nine workers, many of them staffing six Christian schools in the islands, which had already educated at least 15,000 Hawaiians of all ages. As these missionary enterprises grew, the church workers, not from intention and design but from example and education, tinged the native Hawaiian civilization with American mores and values. The early missionaries had great influence over the native chieftains in a direct way, and as the years progressed many of the missionary workers were prevailed upon to leave the missions and enter directly into governmental service in order to aid the kings in the increasingly complex governmental affairs of the kingdom. Thus by the 1840's, American influence had become dominant in directing the Hawaiian government. Furthermore, many members of the missionary bands left their Christian work to enter directly into landholding and other economic affairs. The sons of missionaries emerged as leading planters and merchants in Hawaii as the century progressed. Through such developments, hardly intended by the early Calvinist enthusiasts who came only to spread God's word, American values and American influence increased in the island kingdom--to work hand in hand with increasing American economic interests.

The first great item of trade that brought the Hawaiian Islands into the American commercial orbit was sandalwood. This particular wood, which harbors at its heart an oil valued as an ingredient for exquisite perfume, was discovered to be valued highly in the Canton market in the late 18th century. This discovery was very important because the Western powers lacked items of exchange for the Chinese teas, for which there seemed to be an insatiable demand as the Atlantic world went through a "tea revolution." With the discovery of sandalwood from the Marquesas to New Zealand and Australia in the south and to Hawaii in the north, the commercial exploitation of the tree--possible only by digging the trunk completely out of the ground to get at the greater quantity of oil at the base--began in earnest. By 1804-05 some 900 piculs (a Chinese measure of weight equalling 133 1/3 pounds) were being imported into Canton annually, and between 1810 and 1818, with an abundant supply in the Pacific islands and a high demand in Canton, the sandalwood trade boomed. American ships seeking sandalwood arrived in Hawaii at the rate of four a month, and Kamehameha, having a monopoly on the trade, ordered his people into the forests to collect the precious wood, allowing his chiefs to keep about 4/10th by weight for themselves.

The American sandalwood traders brought out to the islands British printed cottons, broadcloths, and hardware, which they sold to the natives at high prices. They then invested their gains in sandalwood for the Canton trade. Other American ships sailing from the Northwest Coast loaded with furs stopped off at Hawaii to top off their cargoes with sandalwood collected for them by agents they had left in the islands on their way to the Northwest. But since by 1816 the greater part of the wood sold in China by American traders was from Hawaii, the statistics of this trade clearly reveal the transitory nature of this item of commerce. In 1817-18, nearly 16,000 piculs of sandalwood were marketed at Canton by American merchants; by 1820-21, only 6,000 piculs were sold. The sandalwood trade was on the decline, but not before the American merchants had received about $400,000 for the wood in the Canton market. The sandalwood trade, then, was both wasteful and transitory and, all in all, had little direct long-range effect on the Hawaiian economy.

Yet the sandalwood era was still a very important episode in Hawaiian history. Above all, it had a disastrous effect on the Hawaiians, because this item of trade first brought the foreigner to the islands in great numbers. This influx resulted in a shattering of native health from venereal disease, measles, influenza, cholera, mumps, and other afflictions. It has been estimated that almost one-half of the native population of 300,000 was wiped out by either a cholera or a bubonic plague epidemic in 1804. Also, the social effects on native mores, with the revolution in values introduced by the shift from a subsistence economy to a commercial economy, were reported to be devastating and resulted in alcoholism, deep-seated pessimism, and a destruction of native codes of conduct. Economic gain and a cheap ostentation with cloths, tobacco, alcohol, money, and guns and ammunition became the marks of the native chiefs, who drove their people deeper and deeper into the forests in search of the sandalwood. But also of tremendous importance to Hawaiian and American history, the sandalwood trade marked the beginning of intensified American interest in the archipelago. With the buildup of the sandalwood trade, influential Americans began to recognize for the first time the immense commercial advantages of the islands. This interest, reinforced by the missionaries' efforts, continued to grow because of Hawaii's importance to the expanding Pacific whaling industry, which rose to prominence as the sandalwood trade was declining in the 1820's.

Located in the middle of what became the three principal whaling areas of the Pacific--the area off the coast of Japan, the area south of Hawaii along the equator, and the area off the coasts of Alaska and Kamchatka--Hawaii was bound to grow with the whaling industry. It was estimated that in the 1820's almost 200 whaling ships were calling in the islands annually; by the mid-1830's, this number had doubled; in the boom year of 1846, 700 or more whalers visited Hawaiian ports, especially Honolulu. Since each of these whaling vessels spent from $800 to $1,500 per visit for provisions, equipment, and repairs, the economic effects of whaling on Hawaii were tremendous. By the 1840's, this business represented between $3 and $4 million invested in the islands. With the creation of merchant houses to provision the whalers, as well as to expedite the trade between the United States and various parts of the Pacific world carried on by merchant vessels, Hawaiian commercialism and Hawaiian capitalism were born.

The semi-annual visits of the whalers, combined with Hawaii's position as the entrepôt for Chinese, Northwest Coast, American, Mexican, Manilan, and English trades in many items, had transformed the Hawaiian economy and culture completely by the fourth decade of the country. The simple exchange of provisions, hides, and sandalwood in the early days of Hawaiian trade gave way to warehouses containing hardware, bread, flour, shoes, books, furniture, California hides, nankeens, tea, silks, rice, cigars, rope, coffee, lumber, spars, and salmon. The exchange of specie and bullion took place when suitable items of trade were not available. An instructive measure of the effects of trade on Hawaii can be found in the fact that by 1840, Honolulu had twenty-four merchandising houses, two hotels, two taverns, twelve boarding houses, two billiard rooms, and seven bowling alleys. By the next year there were reported to be fifteen wholesale and thirty-two retail houses, and suitable lots for building were selling at $8,000 each. By 1850 the number of retail firms in Honolulu had risen to seventy-five.

With all of this commercial interest manifested in Hawaii, it was natural that diplomatic interest would follow. In 1826, Captain Thomas ap Catesby Jones of the U.S.S. Peacock was ordered to Hawaii to protect commerce there and to relieve the islands of American deserters from whaling vessels. He proceeded to negotiate a treaty with the regents of the eleven-year-old king, obliging the Hawaiians to permit trade, to aid the crews of wrecked vessels, to suppress desertion, and to protect the rights of American citizens. Unfortunately, the treaty was not even submitted to the Senate because it would have implied recognition of Hawaiian independence, but Americans in the islands regarded it as valid anyway and the Hawaiian rulers seem to have followed its provisions.

Whatever the status of the "treaty" of 1826, President John Tyler, in a message to the House of Representatives on December 31, 1842, enunciated the policy of his administration toward the islands. The President stated that American interests in Hawaii were dominant over that of any other power and pledged to uphold the security and independence of Hawaii. It was in fact an extension of the fundamental principles of the Monroe Doctrine into the Pacific and a direct application of them to Hawaii, creating there in fact in American sphere of influence. The "Tyler Doctrine" of 1842 was well received in the United States, for it fit in well with growing interests in the Oregon Territory and in the widening China market. A combination of missionary efforts, economic penetration, and fears of British and French interests in the islands had moved the United States toward a rather bold assertion of its rights in the Pacific.

Whether or not the doctrine would be honored by foreign competitors was answered the next year when Lord Paulet, in command of a British warship, took over control of Hawaii in order to protect the rights of all foreigners and to prevent seizure of the islands by the French

Pacific Fleet sent to safeguard the rights of Catholics there. The action was met by an outcry by the American public and a protest from the government. Whether the tumultuous reaction of the Americans was the true reason for his actions or not, Lord Aberdeen, the British Foreign Secretary, assured the government that the seizure was unauthorized and disavowed any knowledge of it. Within months the Hawaiian government was restored, and the British later followed this action by an agreement made with the French that neither would take possession of the archipelago. Whether intended or not, the French-British declaration reinforced the unilateral Tyler Doctrine, and American primacy in the islands was never seriously questioned thereafter by the European powers.

A formal treaty for "reciprocal liberty of commerce and navigation" between Hawaii and the United States was signed in 1849; it included de facto recognition by the United States of the government of Hawaii, although it did not guarantee Hawaiian independence. All in all, it placed the relations between the two countries on a more satisfactory basis and was maintained for the next fifty years until annexation. It must be added, though, that the Tyler Doctrine of 1842 remained in force throughout the period, being specifically reaffirmed by President Zachary Taylor in 1849 and by President Millard Fillmore in 1851.

Hawaii was definitely within the American sphere of influence from 1842 on, even though the missionary and planter interests failed in their plot to have the islands annexed to the United States in 1854, and the sugar interests on the islands were stifled by Louisiana sugar interests and Congress in their attempts to obtain a reciprocity treaty in 1857. As in the case of the Oregon Territory, economic interests were paramount by the 1840's, and American interests continued to grow in the entrepôt of the Pacific, especially with the boom in trade of foodstuffs to California in 1850 as the Hawaiian merchants shipped great amounts of sugar, beans, onions, potatoes, etc. to the unprepared bonanza state of California, long on gold and short on food. Although whaling gradually declined in the 1850's, Hawaii continued to thrive on its fast-growing agricultural exports, especially sugar. As whaling had taken the place of sandalwood, now sugar took the place of whaling in the 1850's, and Hawaii was again on the high road to prosperity--and walking down that road hand in hand with American interests. Hawaii had become an American entrepôt and an American outpost in the Pacific. Time would make it a possession.

AN OPENING IN CHINA. As American interests sought economic recovery by the pelt trade in the South Atlantic, the South Pacific, and the Northwest Coast in the decades after the American Revolution, and as whaling vessels moved to take advantage of the rich harvests to be found in Pacific waters in the same years and created Hawaii as a vital supply station in their work, so too did they find that one of the chief sources of recovery lay in the China trade. Indeed, it can be argued that the China trade was the very key to Pacific greatness during these years because the trade with Canton made the search for furs possible and, with whaling, made Hawaii the trading center of the Pacific. China was, in the last analysis, the market for the furs, the sandalwood, and the products

of American enterprise and, in return, the source of the fabulous tea
trade, which helped lift American maritime commerce to world leadership
in the 19th century. The China trade fired the imagination of the American people to create a great empire in the Pacific.

Aware that they were unnecessarily dependent upon London for their
goods from China and India, some American merchants decided at the end
of the Revolution to begin direct trade with the East without relying
on the East India Company and the British trading network. Accordingly,
with the backing of Robert Morris, the New York financier of the Revolution, a 360-ton privateer now renamed the Empress of China was sent to
Canton for tea in 1784 in exchange for ginseng (a medicinal root) from
the forests of America. Sailing by way of the Cape of Good Hope, Captain John Green made the passage to the Orient and returned in May 1785,
with a cargo not only of tea but also of nankeens, chinaware, silk and
the herb cassia. Although the profits of 25 percent realized on this
voyage were not considered great, the voyage of the Empress of China
awakened a great interest in Oriental trade and proved that the East
India Company's monopoly could be broken. Within one year no fewer than
five ships had made their way to the Far East, and the pattern of trade
was set. The cottons, silks, and teas of India; the teas, silks, and
chinaware of China; and the spices of the East Indies began to flow into
American ports, each item kindling more interest in the trade with the
fabled Orient.

Within a few years, ships from New York, Philadelphia, Boston, and
Providence were regularly making their way to the anchorages of Whampoa
below Canton. But Salem merchants, led by the house of Elias Hasket
Derby, usually left the Northwest fur trade and the Pacific waters to
Boston and the other cities and struck out across the South Atlantic and
around the Cape of Good Hope to seek their fortunes in the East Indies.
Gathering a cargo of goods from American, European, and West Indian ports,
the Salem ship captains made their way around Africa and across the Indian Ocean to Mauritius, Calcutta, the Dutch East Indies, and Manila,
trading as they went and sometimes touching Canton too. While Salem was
in the lead in the East India trade, Boston dominated the Northwest Coast
fur trade and the China trade. Boston prospered mightily, protected by
the much lower tariff rates and port dues on American vessels than on
foreign vessels arriving from China, which had been built into the tariff
legislation of 1789.

By 1790, the Far Eastern trade accounted for approximately one-
seventh of the nation's imports. Here there was no British competition,
demand for Oriental goods was high, and fortunes could be made. In exchange for furs, ginseng, cotton goods, flour, whale oil, candles, lumber,
tobacco, and specie from America, imports from the British East Indies
grew from $742,500 in 1795 to $3.4 million in 1800, from the Dutch East
Indies from $26,700 in 1795 to $4.4 million in 1801, and from China from
$1 million in 1795 to $4.6 million in 1800. By 1810, the American traders
were averaging more than ten voyages a year to Canton and were challeng-
ing the trade advantages held by the East India Company.

The War of 1812 disrupted this lucrative trade as American shipping at Whampoa came to a halt. The British were able to drive American vessels off the Northwest Coast and away from Hawaiian waters because the American government had no navy to protect national maritime interests. Indeed, the American government had a hard time not being completely defeated by the British in this needless war for American maritime rights. Nevertheless, when the war came to an end, American trade with the East quickly revived, and within five years of the Treaty of Ghent, forty-seven American vessels were to be found in the Canton market, more than ever before.

From 1815 until 1841, the second period of the old China trade, total imports to and exports from China remained almost static, averaging about $10 million per year from 1821 to 1841. But although the China trade did not appreciably increase while total American foreign commerce multiplied itself six times over, during this period American competition in the Orient was sufficient to compel the British to cancel the East India Company's monopoly in 1834 in order to allow Englishmen to compete on equal terms with their American rivals. The American China merchants were clearly a power in Canton by the 1830's and thus were able to take advantage of the events of the Opium War, and the treaties that proceeded from it, to further their interests.

To understand the opening of China to the West, in which the United States played a minor role, it is necessary to examine China's history. The Chinese reacted to Western intrusions into their country within the context of their own attitudes and institutions. As the various Western powers, led by the British, sought to gain entry into China for trading purposes in the latter 18th and early 19th centuries, the Chinese treated the Western powers as though they were not the West but a continuation of the Inner Asian barbarians from whom the Chinese had received tribute for a thousand years. The Westerners were to approach the Chinese emperor as barbarians bringing tribute and, as such, were expected to perform the kowtow, the ceremonial knocking of the head upon the ground as an act of surrender in three separate prostrations, part of the Confucian ceremony of subordination, which symbolized all relationships of life. But, more important, this bringing of tribute had served as a cloak for trade by the barbarians entering China over the years. Trade was seen as distinctly subordinate to tribute and allowed only as a boon granted to the barbarian, by which he could share in the bounty of China. As such, trade was beneath the dignity of the official duties and policies of the emperor.

But trade with the West continued to grow and thus found itself within the confining traditions of a tribute system in which the barbarians were allowed to trade only with the sufferance of the emperor who was more interested in the moral value of tribute than the material value of trade. The Chinese attitude of superiority toward the barbarian, built up through centuries of contact with the barbarians of Inner Asia and the tribute system as an extension of it, represented a time-honored attitude by which the Chinese faced all outsiders. Of equal importance, lacking a more realistic response based on power confrontation with equal or superior force, it also constituted the only defense that the Confucian monarch held out against the inroads of the West. When this system of subordination of all outsiders as barbarians and of imperial disdain for trade, was cracked and finally broken in the mid-19th century by the Western nations, China lay helpless before those powers who took advantage of its economic potential for their own ends.

Since trade was beneath the dignity and attention of the Chinese emperors, and since they perforce had to control the troublesome and undesirable commerce somehow, they devised a system whereby monopolies on foreign trade were sold to Chinese merchants called "cohong" or "hong" merchants. Never more than thirteen in number from their foundation in 1721 until the system ended in 1840, the cohong merchants were mutually liable for one another and were given complete control of all foreigners, their property, and their trade. The cohong were responsible for the enforcement of all trade regulations, too. Foreigners were forced to live outside the walls of Canton in "factories" and had to deal through "Compradors" for all supplies both on shore and for their vessels, while officials known as "linguists"--who knew no foreign language at all!--were in charge of securing the sampans to load and unload the ships. Over these lesser officials were the cohongs, who served the needs of foreign trade while answerable to their emperor.

All in all, the system worked well during its century of existence, and American traders held the cohongs--especially the famous Houqua--in high esteem, despite petty annoyances caused by the greed and corruption of the Chinese officials. And so the American China traders made their way to the Chinese coasts, ran a gauntlet of piratical junks, sailed past the old Portuguese factory at Macao, moved beyond the Bogue Forts with their immovable guns firmly anchored in stone sockets designed to "protect" Canton, and then sailed up the Pearl River to the foreign anchorage at Whampoa, twelve miles below Canton itself, there to deal with the cohong and to purchase teas, silks, nankeens, and chinaware in exchange for their Western merchandise of sandalwood, furs, and specie.

Despite the fact that American merchants cooperated well with the Chinese system, and with the hong merchants who represented the emperor to the Western traders, the system was doomed to extinction by British pressure and military force. Because the East India Company, with its monopoly over Far Eastern trade, worked to the disadvantage of others competing with "John Company," those merchants in the "country trade" between India and China raised so much opposition to the monopoly, aided by British manufacturers who thought that golden opportunities awaited them with the abolition of the Company's monopoly, that Parliament destroyed it in 1834. But when the expected golden opportunities did not arise, criticism turned instead to Chinese trading arrangements, and in particular to the cohong system, as the source of difficulties. When, therefore, the Chinese emperor subsequently chose to stamp out the opium imports from India and other regions (a source of great profits for British merchants and for a few American merchants, such as Perkins & Company and Russell & Company out of Boston), he inadvertently gave the British a perfect opportunity to war upon China and to break its closed trading system.

Thus there occurred the first Anglo-Chinese War, better known as the Opium War, which began in 1839 and ended with the Treaty of Nanking of 1842. By this treaty the British were given the rich prize of Hong Kong; the four ports of Shanghai, Amoy, Ningpo, and Foochow were opened in addition to Canton; British consuls were established in the Chinese ports to oversee British trading rights; the Chinese paid in an indemnity of $21 million; and the monopoly of the cohong over foreign trade was ended. Nothing was said about the trade in opium, which continued as before, much to the physical and mental detriment of the Chinese citizenry.

Apprised of the Anglo-Chinese situation by the visit of Commodore Lawrence Kearney, who arrived on the Chinese coast in 1842, and unaware that the Chinese government issued a proclamation three months after Kearney's departure for home granting the same commercial privileges granted to Britain in the Treaty of Nanking to all other nations, President John Tyler, with the approval of Congress, sent Caleb Cushing as Commissioner to China in 1843 to secure a like treaty for the United States. Cushing, a Newburyport, Massachusetts, lawyer and politician long experienced in the China trade, embarked for China with four warships carrying gifts for the emperor such as a pair of six-shooters, a model of a war steamer, and the Encyclopaedia Americana. Cushing managed to negotiate a favorable treaty with China in 1844, not because of these rather condescending gifts or the patronizing letter from President Tyler accompanying them, nor from Cushing's threatening to go directly to Peking rather than deal with the emperor's emissaries--as is often asserted--but from the simple fact that the Chinese saw that they could not resist and preferred to grant trading rights directly to foreign countries and thus win their gratitude rather than allow Britain to claim the credit.

In July 1844, the Treaty of Wanghia was signed in the little village of that name outside Macao. By the terms of the treaty, all privileges granted to the British two years before were also given to American nationals. The treaties differed in that the Americans asked for no cession of territory (as the British had gained at Hong Kong); there was no indemnity asked or given; and the opium trade by Americans was definitely proscribed (American citizens engaged in it or in other contraband trade were allowed to be dealt with by the Chinese government without any protection from the United States). Furthermore, customs collections were left in the hands of the Chinese government, rather than in the hands of foreign nationals, and the principle of extraterritoriality (providing that Americans would be tried by Americans for crimes, and Chinese by the Chinese) was included. Extraterritoriality was thought by the Chinese to be only a temporary expedient, but it was not so identified in the treaty, and the issue became a source of friction and hostility as the century progressed. Likewise, the Treaty of Wanghia, and the treaties subsequently negotiated with other nations, also included most-favored-nation clauses. This principle, which had worked very favorably and with no harm to China when dealing with the barbarians of Inner Asia, became a one-way street when dealing with the superior Western powers. The ratchet effect of this provision, whereby every trading privilege given to one treaty nation was automatically granted to every other treaty nation, soon bound China into a series of legal trade concessions from which it could not escape.

The immediate effects of the Treaty of Wanghia on American commerce with China were very positive. American trading vessels in Canton averaged about sixty annually, an increasing number of vessels visited Shanghi and the other treaty ports, and American consulates were established in most of the port cities. Spurred on by this opening of lucrative markets, Americans were soon utilizing the famed China Clippers, which would load the precious teas in their holds and then begin their races to London against one another and against British vessels. So superior were these clippers that they almost monopolized the tea trade between China and Europe in a short time.

Despite American superiority via the clippers, British trade with China was always larger than American trade. This fact helps explain the continued British interference in Chinese internal affairs, such as the Taiping Rebellion from 1850 to 1864 and the second Anglo-Chinese War from 1856 to 1860. Still, American trade with China grew to its highest point in the 1850's and was sufficient to call for a re-guaranteeing of American commercial rights, and even extending them somewhat, in a second treaty signed in 1858, known as the Tientsin Treaty. The American China trade, then, while distinctly minor in scope to that of the various European powers in the 18th and 19th centuries, especially to that of Great Britain, led the United States to permanent and important commercial interests in that country. These interests, beginning in 1790 and gradually expanding until 1860, were, in turn, well understood by the American nation. In conjunction with American whaling and trading rights in other Pacific areas, the China trade was a prime determinant in America's acquisition of the Oregon and California coasts as stepping-stones to wealth and power in the Pacific.

ACQUISITION OF THE WESTERN COASTS. With the growing American commercial interests in the Far East, reinforced by several editions of the Narratives of Charles Wilkes of the Wilkes Expedition of 1838-42 which told in great detail not only of Antarctic and Pacific lands, but also of the Oregon Territory, the Columbia River, the Cascade Range, the California coast, and San Francisco, America fixed its eyes resolutely on the Pacific coast. Leadership in this interest came from Atlantic coast merchants and whalemen who saw the Pacific coast and its ports as absolutely necessary for continued American expansion in the Pacific. But this maritime vision of Manifest Destiny was also enthusiastically shared by expansionists from the Mississippi Valley and the Old Northwest, who looked to Oregon and the Strait of Fuca as a link between the Mississippi Valley, with its surplus grains, and the teeming millions of the Orient. Oregon could be a new entrepôt for the exportation of American surpluses in return for the teas, spices, and other goods of the Orient. Possession of the Oregon Territory, preferably all the way to 54°40' north latitude, would mean a greater hold on the Pacific.

The "Oregon fever" set off by the migration of a thousand settlers each year in both 1843 and 1844 to the Willamette Valley overland by the Oregon Trail, as picked up and expanded by the commercial interests of the Northeast and Middle West, escalated into a national epidemic. That Britain also had a claim to the area was hardly a deterrent, but rather an incentive to prevent the territory from falling into alien hands. The "Oregon convention" held in Cincinnati in 1843 rejected all proposals for a settlement with England and demanded, rather, that the United States take the whole western coast. President James K. Polk, swept into office on a wave of enthusiasm directed toward putting both Texas and all of the Oregon Territory under the American flag, told England in no uncertain terms that "our title to the country of Oregon is clear and unquestionable."

Yet for all the campaign talk of "Fifty-Four Forty or Fight," Polk was a realist. He let it be known in British diplomatic circles that he would settle at 49°, a continuation of the northern limit of Louisiana agreed upon in 1818, rather than insisting on the whole of Oregon. When Lord Aberdeen, the Foreign Secretary, had been given sufficient time to convince the British public that British interests would be well taken care of by not pushing their claims to lands south of 49° as long as Vancouver Island and passage on the Columbia were assured, an Anglo-American treaty was drawn up in 1846, and the United States had its clear title to lands on the Pacific coast south of 49°. American commercial interests and skillful diplomacy had gained for America in the Oregon Treaty lands that Britain could not have gained other than by force anyway and, therefore, never tried very hard to keep.

The acquisition of California was even easier and came as a consequence of the Mexican War. The great harbors of San Francisco and San Diego had been known by Americans since the early days of the hide trade, early in the century. The commentary of Wilkes' Narratives had merely reinforced what American Pacific whalemen and traders had long known, that San Francisco in particular would be a key to the fulfillment of American hopes for commercial dominance in the Pacific. Located on or near the major crossroads of the Pacific, the bay appeared to be potentially another great center of trade between the Pacific coast and the riches of the East. Therefore, when (with the connivance of John Charles Frémont) an independent California was declared by the American residents there in the "Bear Flag Revolt" at Sonora in 1846, the American governmental leaders were more than willing to recognize the republic and then formally acquire the territory in the Treaty of Guadalupe-Hidalgo with Mexico in 1848. American Pacific interests, combined with adroit diplomacy for Oregon and grand opportunism in California, gave America its continental frontier on the Pacific.

America's commercial hold on California was reinforced with the discovery of gold in the Sacramento River Valley in 1848. The California gold rush quickly brought thousands of gold enthusiasts to San Francisco, in addition to the much smarter merchants who really "struck it rich" not by mining for gold but by selling food and supplies to the needy miners, who usually saw their fervid efforts result in nothing. In 1849 alone, more than 90,000 persons from all walks of life disembarked at San Francisco. While countless others traveled overland, these California enthusiasts sailed by ship to Panama, trekked across the isthmus to Pacific waters, then boarded ship again for San Francisco; sometimes they sailed directly to the California coast by way of Cape Horn. In 1849 and 1850, some 760 ships of all types rounded the Horn from Atlantic ports heading for California. So great was the migration by sea and overland by any conveyance possible that, by 1849,

141

California had surpassed the requisite number of 60,000 inhabitants for statehood. Upon making application for this new status, the new citizens of California not only thereby illustrated America's lock on her newly-acquired Pacific coast, but also set off a ten-year struggle over the question of slavery, which was temporarily shelved by the Compromise of 1850 but finally ended only with the outbreak of the Civil War.

The California gold rush resulted also in the golden days of the "clipper ship era." With a premium being placed on speed, the long, clean, sharp-built clippers, with their high masts and massive spars supporting hundreds of yards of white billowing canvas sails, were the immediate and obvious answer to the fevered haste to reach the California coast with men and supplies.

These clippers, the evolutionary result of adaptation from the earlier Baltimore clippers, had long been in use in the China trade, where they had proved their worth by carrying their precious cargoes of tea from the Orient around the Cape of Good Hope to American ports, often in less than one hundred days. Such famed clippers as the Ann McKim had played a large part in increasing the importation of tea from 6.6 million pounds in 1822 to 19.3 million pounds in 1840. The tea trade, which represented only 36 percent of the total imports from China in 1822, had climbed to a dominating 81 percent of imports from China by 1840. American ships took their precious cargoes not only to America, but also to Russia, Brazil, Holland, various German ports, and, after the repeal of the British Navigation Acts in 1849, to the major tea port of London.

The rush to California thus spurred an already-blossoming clipper trade into a short-lived but extremely lucrative alternative of sending the swift clippers around Cape Horn to California. Extra earnings could be made by carrying persons and provisions at very high rates to San Francisco in exchange for specie, which would be carried to China to be used to purchase tea. The clippers then returned home to their Atlantic ports, usually New York, in most cases by way of the Cape of Good Hope and across the Atlantic, to begin the profitable circuit over again. The clipper era reached a high point in 1853, when 145 clippers sailed from eastern ports to San Francisco, with twenty-five of them reaching the city in 110 days or less, but the record of only 89 days had been established by the famous Flying Cloud two years before. Fifty-one clippers were built in 1853 alone.

From this point on, with speed being less important, with greater cargo space returning greater revenues to owners, and with steam-powered ships as major competitors in key trading areas, the clipper ships' days of prominence in both building and use gradually faded. With the Panic of 1857, the clipper ship era came to a virtual end. Many of the fine, stately vessels served out their usefulness as guano carriers from Callao or Chinchas, off the South American coast, to various world ports. But in their brief days of glory, the clippers were major factors in the China trade and in the rapid growth of the California coast. They also represented, perhaps, the most romantic and picturesque days of sail and the high point of American dominance of the seas.

142

A third competitor to the United States along the Northwest Coast and Alaska since early fur-trading days was Russia. Fearful of American designs on the area, Czar Alexander I closed the entire area claimed by Russia by imperial ukase in 1821, but found even at that early date that American commercial interests were too great to be excluded. Instead of having the effect of bringing prosperity to the government-sponsored Russian-American Company as intended, the Russians found that their colony still depended heavily on American ships for food and supplies. As a result of this dependence, Russia signed a treaty with the United States in 1824, allowing Americans to fish and trade in the area for a ten-year period. The treaty, a complete victory for Secretary of State John Quincy Adams, called for the withdrawal of the exclusionary ukase and a dropping of Russian claims to the American coast south of 54°40'. It was a clear sign that American commercial interests were becoming dominant in the Northwest area. The American acquisition of Oregon and California two decades later clearly solidified this position.

By 1852, Bostonians had major interests in the trade and fishing on the Alaskan coast, and merchants from San Francisco and the Puget Sound area had stepped into the vacated shoes of the Hudson's Bay Company, which had given up its claims to Alaska. By that time lucrative commercial contracts had been signed for ice to be shipped from Sitka; and during the Crimean War it was the San Francisco-based American-Russian Commercial Company which supplied the Russian-American Company with general supplies and allowed the Russian colonists to survive. The American company obtained a twenty-year contract in 1854 to buy ice, coal, and fish from the Russian colony. With all of this commercial activity being carried on, American advocates of the purchase of Alaska pointed out its value to the fishing and whaling trades, as well as its use as a natural bridge to the commerce of the Pacific and Asia.

It was, then relatively easy after the Civil War for the expansionist William Seward, with the support of the influential Charles Sumner of maritime Massachusetts, to convince the Senate to approve a treaty of annexation and the House of Representatives to approve the $7.2 million purchase price without considerable difficulty in 1867. Only those who knew nothing of maritime and commercial matters saw Seward's purchase as "folly." From the Russian point of view, persistent expansion of American commercial rights in the North Pacific and the United States government's support of these rights had finally convinced the Russian government that it could either sell Alaska to the Americans or see it taken by them anyway. Eighty years of American pressure finally persuaded the Russians that they had over-extended themselves in North America. It had been a contest of unequals, and America by 1868 had added another Pacific possession to its expanding domain.

By the 1850's, then, Hawaii was clearly in the American commercial orbit; China had been opened to American trade; California and Oregon had become American territories; and Alaska was under American commercial dominance. The Pacific trade network was approaching its zenith.

THE OPENING OF JAPAN. Japan had been known to the West since the

16th century. By the close of that century, the Portuguese had developed a considerable commerce with the islands, and many Japanese had been
converted to Christianity. Early in the 17th century, the Dutch began
to trade in the islands, and the English in 1613 set up a factory at
Hirado. However, fearful of Western encroachments and the influence of
Christianity, the Japanese rulers in 1638 closed the country to foreigners, banished all aliens there, proscribed Christianity, and forbade
their subjects to travel overseas. Only a very limited trade with the
West was allowed by granting a small trading post to the Dutch on the
island of Deshima in the Bay of Nagasaki, to which two ships per year
could be sent. For two centuries the Japanese nation thus lived in
self-imposed confinement, until it was penetrated by the Americans in
the 19th century.

Over the years since 1791, when Captain John Kendrick (who three
years earlier had opened the Northwest fur trade with Canton) first
tried to gain admission to Japan and was firmly rebuffed, few direct
contacts were made between the American people and the Japanese. But
as early as 1819, American whalers pursuing their quarry had discovered
the whaling grounds east of Japan. Attracted by excellent hunting in
the area, scores of whaling vessels were soon frequenting these waters.
Although whaling afforded little direct contact with the kingdom, occasional shipwrecks cast the crews upon Japanese shores, where they were
promptly arrested and transported in close confinement to Nagasaki,
there to be turned over to the Dutch at Deshima for deportation. Sto-
ries of American hardships at the hands of the Japanese filtered back to
the United States, undoubtedly in rather exaggerated form, and caused
much protest and popular indignation. In whaling and commercial circles,
there were demands that the government take steps to force the Japanese
to treat such victims of shipwreck with consideration. What added
particular stridency to the demands were reports that the sailors had
been forced to step on tablets bearing a likeness of the Cross or of the
Virgin and Christ Child. This practice, known as fumi-ye, was an assertion of Japan's continuing fear of Christian influence and caused
even more consternation than the Chinese kowtow.

Despite protests to the American government, the urgings of missionary groups who saw in Japan a field of great potential for their prose-
lytizing, and occasional unfruitful plans to send representatives to
Japan, the nation remained closed to Americans. The attempt by Commodore James Biddle in 1846 to negotiate an opening of Japan was met with
a blunt refusal by the Japanese authorities. Under orders not to excite
any hostile feeling toward the United States, Biddle sailed away and
Japan maintained its isolation.

This was the situation until Commodore Matthew Perry was sent to
Japan in 1853 to gain guarantees of Japanese protection of American seamen and the opening of one or more Japanese ports for trade and use as
coal depots. Perry needed no urging to make contacts with the Japanese,
and thus freeze out British commercial ambitions, or to open the islands
to commerce. His belief in a benevolent American imperialism clearly
included Japan, and few American attitudes were different from his. The
Japanese government and advisors were adamantly opposed to opening their

144

islands to outsiders, but the presence of Perry and four American vessels, including two steamers which awed the Japanese, made it obvious to them that some arrangement had to be made with the foreigners. Negotiations over the meeting place deadlocked, and Perry sailed his vessels within sight of the capital at Yedo to show his determination to force the issue of Japanese relations with the United States. When Perry in subsequent negotiations gave clear indications that he would use force if necessary to get a treaty, the Japanese had no choice but to capitulate, and the Treaty of Kanagawa, of March 1854, was agreed upon. According to the articles of the treaty, crews of shipwrecked vessels would no longer be imprisoned, and two consular ports (Shimoda and Hakodate) were opened to American ships for supplies. This was not a commercial treaty, as it contained no specific provisions for further trade. It did not include extraterritoriality, but it did include a most-favored-nation clause. The Treaty of Kanagawa was important only as a first step, but it did crack open the Imperial Kingdom to the West.

Four years later, a second treaty was negotiated by Townsend Harris, the American Consul General to Japan. This treaty of 1858 opened Japan to American trade and added two more ports to those designated earlier. Furthermore, it set a schedule of tariff rates and included an article of extraterritorial rights for Americans. This second treaty was a genuine commercial treaty between the two countries. It also included a provision that the President of the United States would act as friendly mediator if the Japanese became involved in a dispute with any European power. Japan was at last clearly open to American trade. England, France, Russia, and Holland quickly followed suit with similar treaties. However, Japan was not seen by the United States and by these other nations at that time as an area of great commercial opportunity, as in the case of China, but more as a convenient port of call lying across the sailing routes of the Pacific. But even without developing into a great center of American trade in the immediate aftermath of the treaties, Japan's opening represented to the United States a completion of its Pacific interests.

American vessels now sailed by wind and steam from one end of the great ocean to another in their business of whaling and commerce. Around the ocean's shores in a great arc stretching from southern California, up the coast to Alaska, across the Bering Sea to Japan, and down to China, American interests reached their Pacific zenith in the 1850's. This great arc of influence, anchored on the premier ports of San Francisco and Honolulu and closely tied to the pulsating maritime activity in the Atlantic, represented America's seafaring activity in all its strength.

SUGGESTIONS FOR FURTHER READING

Bradley, Harold W. The American Frontier in Hawaii: The Pioneers, 1789-1843. Stanford: Stanford University Press, 1942.

Caruthers, J. Wade. "The Seaborne Frontier to California, 1796-1850," The American Neptune, XXIX, 2 (April 1969, 81-101.

Clark, Arthur H. The Clipper Ship Era. New York: G. P. Putnam's Sons, 1910.

Dulles, Foster Rhea. America in the Pacific: A Century of Expansion. 2nd ed. Boston & New York: Houghton Mifflin Co., 1938.

_____. Lowered Boats: A Chronicle of American Whaling. New York: Harcourt, Brace and Co., 1933.

_____. The Old China Trade. Boston & New York: Houghton Mifflin Co., 1930.

_____. Yankees and Samurai: America's Role in the Emergence of Modern Japan, 1791-1900. New York: Harper & Row, 1965.

Fairbank, John K. Trade and Diplomacy on the China Coast: The Opening of the Treaty Ports, 1842-1854. 2 vols. Harvard Historical Studies, Vol. LXII. Cambridge: Harvard University Press, 1953.

Graebner, Norman A. Empire on the Pacific: A Study in American Continental Expansion. New York: Ronald Press Co., 1955.

Kirker, James. Adventures to China: Americans in the Southern Oceans, 1792-1812. New York: Oxford University Press, 1970.

Kushner, Howard I. Conflict on the Northwest Coast: American-Russian Rivalry in the Pacific Northwest, 1790-1867. Westport, Conn.: Greenwood Press, 1975.

Latourette, Kenneth S. The History of Early Relations between the United States and China, 1784-1844. Transactions of the Connecticut Academy of Arts and Sciences. New Haven: Yale University Press, 1917.

Morgan, Theodore. Hawaii: A Century of Economic Change, 1778-1876. Harvard Economic Studies, Vol. LXXXIII. Cambridge: Harvard University Press, 1948.

Morison, Samuel Eliot. "Old Bruin," Commodore Matthew C. Perry, 1794-1858. Boston & Toronto: Little, Brown and Co., 1967.

_____. The Maritime History of Massachusetts, 1783-1860. Boston: Houghton Mifflin Co., 1921.

Paullin, Charles O. American Voyages to the Orient, 1690-1865; An
    Account of Merchant and Naval Activities in China, Japan, and the
    Various Pacific Islands. Annapolis, Md.: United States Naval In-
    stitute, 1971.

Stackpole, Edouard A. The Sea-Hunters: The New England Whalemen during
    Two Centuries, 1635-1835. Philadelphia & New York: J. B. Lippin-
    cott Co., 1953.

Stevens, Sylvester K. American Expansion in Hawaii, 1842-1898. Harris-
    burg, Pa.: Archives Publishing Co. of Pennsylvania, Inc., 1945.

Tyler, David B. The Wilkes Expedition: The First United States Explor-
    ing Expedition (1838-1842). Philadelphia: American Philosophical
    Society, 1968.

CHAPTER VIII. DECADES OF MARITIME GREATNESS: THE ATLANTIC

The six decades of the early 19th century witnessed the American maritime empire expanding into areas of the far Pacific virtually unknown to Americans during colonial times. The western and northwestern coasts of the continent, the Hawaiian Islands, and Chinese ports all saw American vessels in profusion, vessels carrying with them, in their search for whales, or commerce, or glory, the seeds of American influence into areas destined to be entwined with American interests and policies from that time forward. Yet it was not on these Pacific waters, but on the more familiar Atlantic, that American greatness most dramatically manifested itself as the young nation struggled to economic maturity.

OPENING FREE TRADE THROUGH RECIPROCITY. Aware of its strong position in world trade made clear by its role as the world's leading neutral trader during the wars that ravaged Europe from 1793 to 1815--a leadership that led the nation to war first with France and then with England during those years--and of the American merchant marine's ability to more than compete with other maritime powers because of its advantages of lower shipbuilding and manning costs, the United States in the decades after 1815 moved to assure itself of a more prominent place in the Atlantic and world trade networks. It could help accomplish this by taking the lead in breaking down the restrictive barriers to free competitive transit erected by self-seeking and self-protective national trade policies. The United States could now compete--indeed, would be forced to compete now that it was excluded from many of the benefits of the closed British trading system--and the first consequence was that it would have to break down the existing obstacles to the free transit of goods with Britain and its colonies.

Accordingly, the Navigation Act of 1815, often called the "Reciprocity Act," was passed. It provided that ships of any nation carrying the goods of that nation would be allowed into American ports on the same terms as American ships would be allowed into its national ports. This move quickly led to a reciprocity treaty with Britain that same year. By the terms of the treaty, each nation's vessels were granted free entry into the ports of the other. In effect, it established a free highway between United States and British ports, with fair and open competition between vessels. However, the treaty did not provide for American entry into the British West Indies, leaving the Americans still burdened with the narrow restriction to vessels of seventy tons or less as provided for in the Jay Treaty of 1795.

This disadvantage was keenly felt by American farmers, fishermen, and exporters, not only because it limited their markets in this rich area, but also because it established for the British a very profitable

triangular trade route with Britain, the United States, and the British
West Indies as its vertices. Heavy bulk goods were brought into the
United States in British vessels; these vessels would be loaded with
provisions, lumber, and stock and then sail to the West Indies; finally,
the ships would load with sugar and molasses for Britain, thus completing the triangle. A variation was to leave the West Indies for New
Orleans, there to load with cotton and tobacco for importation into
Britain. Given the existing British trade provisions which excluded
Americans from the Indies trade, American vessels could not compete in
the triangle and were forced to sit by helplessly while British vessels
carried the valuable cargoes. To make matters worse, British vessels
on the first leg of the triangle across the Atlantic could compete with
American vessels at ruinous rates, because any revenues lost on this
part of the journey could be made up on the other two, where there was
no competition. Many American vessels were returning from Britain under
ballast while British vessels carried the trade items that might otherwise have been theirs.

But if British vessels were forced to trade directly with the British West Indies without touching American shores they would have few
items for shipment on the outbound leg of the journey and would lose
their advantage. Furthermore, the Indies depended upon the United
States for much of their provisions and would suffer greatly if trade
with the Americans was curtailed. Thus the British ostensibly seemed to
have all the advantages under the existing situation, and the Americans
seemed to have few; but the Americans had leverage in the form of cutting
off the British West Indies from American sources of supply. The Americans used this leverage to force an opening of the West Indian trade in
the years between 1817 and 1830.

After forbidding any imports into the United States from the Indies
except in American or British West Indian vessels in the Navigation Act of
1817, and then declaring American ports closed to British vessels from any
colony closed to American vessels in the Non-Intercourse Act of 1818--both
of which measures failed to have the desired effect--Congress in the Non-
Intercourse Act of 1820 closed American ports to all British vessels from
all British colonies in America (not just from the West Indies) unless the
items of trade were totally colonial in origin and imported directly into
the United States. This, in effect, forbade shipment of West Indian goods
indirectly to America via Britain and was detrimental to British shipping,
since West Indian products could not be carried in British ships to America either directly or indirectly. It was a deliberate attack on the
British colonial system in order to force the Crown to grant reciprocity
regarding the West Indian trade. Unlike the early attempts to pressure
the British into a change of policy, the Act of 1820 began to have positive
effects. It injured the British West Indian planters, who soon protested
vigorously in London against the British navigation system, which was too
restrictive for them under these conditions.

In the ten years that followed, both the United States and Britain
engaged in a number of moves and countermoves, with proposals and
counterproposals in trying to resolve the problem. By 1824 the British
were willing to give in on most items of dispute, but they refused to

allow identical terms for American vessels as for British vessels sailing into the West Indies, i.e., full reciprocity. Diplomatic negotiations finally reached a complete impasse when President John Quincy
Adams issued a proclamation in 1827 interdicting all trade in British
vessels from all British colonies in the Western Hemisphere in retaliation for an Order in Council of the year before, which forbade all
trade in American vessels with all British colonies. It was a complete
standoff, with all British colonial ports closed to all American vessels, and all American ports closed to all British vessels from the
colonies.

The diplomatic and maritime logjam was finally broken in the "Reciprocity Treaty of 1830," in which President Andrew Jackson, responding
to the pressure against the closing of the West Indian trade and carrying out his campaign promise to do something about it, was willing to
accept a compromise. By the agreement, British West Indian commerce was
completely opened to both American and British vessels, and virtually
all American produce and manufactures were allowed into the islands.
Similarly, all West Indian exports were allowed into the United States.
American vessels could now carry unlimited American goods to the West
Indies, and carry West Indian cargoes to any foreign country, not just
to American ports. Thus the treaty involved substantial gains for the
United States, although the British insisted on higher duties on American vessels entering the West Indies--as they had insisted all along--
and the treaty also allowed British shippers to re-establish the old
triangle of Britain-United States-British West Indies, which worked to
their maritime advantage. But this advantage flowed from geography and
from the British national right to impose discriminatory duties if they
so chose, and there was no way the Americans could have forced the British to give up their advantage except by nonintercourse, which would
probably have been more detrimental to the United States than to Britain.

Nevertheless, by this agreement and by others concluded with other
countries in the meantime, American vessels by 1831 could sail with substantial freedom and assurance of fair competition to Britain and its
possessions in the Far East, and to France, Norway, Sweden, Holland,
Prussia, Hamburg, Bremen, Lubeck, Russia, Austria, Denmark, and Brazil,
reciprocity treaties having been made with these countries. The United
States had not been able to break the British colonial system regarding
the lucrative West Indies, but it had met with overwhelming success
elsewhere and had become the world leader in the development of a free
navigation policy upon the oceans. This lead it never relinquished, although the United States, like other countries with an adequate merchant
marine, still reserved its coastal trade to ships of its own flag.

CARIBBEAN AND LATIN AMERICAN TRADE. American trade with Latin
America began during the British-French wars at the end of the 18th century, when Spain, on one side or the other throughout the wars, opened
its colonial ports to foreign vessels out of sheer necessity. Between
1795 and 1799, exports from the United States to the area climbed from
$1.3 million to $9 million. The level of imports stood even higher.
Britain at times seized American vessels in the trade, but it still remained profitable. In 1808 Brazil opened its ports, and Americans made

151

further gains between 1810 and 1825 as Spain's Latin American colonies successfully declared their independence. Even during the wars of independence, American trade with the ports of Mexico, Columbia, Chile, and Peru was carried out, and at the conclusion of the fighting the United States was in an excellent position to take on much of the foreign commerce of the newly-independent republics.

Between 1825 and 1860, approximately 20 percent of all exports from the United States went to Latin America, in addition to the exports to Cuba and Puerto Rico. This commerce was made up of medicines, furniture, foodstuffs, boots and shoes, iron, carriages, machinery, horses and mules, and India shawls and China silks exported directly or indirectly to the southern nations. In return, about 20 percent of American imports came from Latin America. Imports were dominated by sugar, coffee, and hides for the Northeastern boot and shoe industry.

But the three Latin American territories most important to American trade were those still under foreign rule: Cuba, Puerto Rico, and Brazil. Early in the 19th century Cuban trade with the United States consisted of both sugar and coffee, but gradually sugar came to dominate the trade. This shift was finally accomplished when a hurricane hit the island in 1844 and uprooted virtually all the coffee trees. The Cuban landowners never returned to the growing of the coffee bean in any appreciable amount and turned to sugar as their major export crop. Sugar became Cuba's major item of trade, along with tobacco and cigars, and brought the island into ever closer ties to the United States. With Cuba becoming the foremost sugar producer in the world, and the United States as its chief customer, the island fell into economic dependency on the United States and existed in a relationship to it much like the dependency of the Southern cotton growers upon New York and the North for their shipping and credit. Spain's other Caribbean possession, Puerto Rico, was almost identical to Cuba in its economy and in its dependence on the United States.

Brazil, upon gaining its independence in 1822, became the world's leading coffee producer by taking advantage of a combination of liberal trade policies, favorable soil and climatic conditions, and the continued importation of slaves. Rio de Janero became the center of the coffee trade, and New York and New Orleans owed a sizeable amount of their importing fortunes to the Brazilian coffee growers, as did Baltimore, Philadelphia, and Boston.

The importance of Caribbean and Latin American colonies and nations to the United States by the late 1850's can be illustrated by the fact that during the period 1856 to 1860, some 30 percent of all imports into the United States by value and 18 percent of all exports from the United States by value were with Caribbean and Latin American colonies and countries, including the British West Indies. The Atlantic trading world had added a whole new region to its domain in the first half of the 19th century and had established itself in an enviable position in the Latin American economic world.

THE COASTAL TRADE AND THE FISHERIES. Protected first by discrimina-

tory port dues and then, after 1817, by a federal statute that forbade
the carrying of goods between domestic ports by foreign vessels--the
cabotage laws--America's coastal merchant marine continued to grow as a
major means of domestic commerce during these same years. The coasters
carried lumber, coal, domestic and foreign manufactures, and general
merchandise up and down the Atlantic and Gulf coasts between the seaboard cities and towns. After 1820 there was consistently more tonnage
engaged in coastwise trade than in foreign trade, although after 1840
the tonnages employed in the two branches were approximately equal.
Much of the valuable coastal trade, as we have seen, was made up of the
shipment of cotton which was centered in New York by the exertions of
that city's merchants and shippers, who carried Northern and foreign
manufactures down the coasts to the major Southern cities and brought
back cotton either for Northern textile mills or for foreign export.
But, in addition to this forced detour in the cotton trade, the coastal
trade also saw heavy trade between New England and the mid-Atlantic
states by moving foodstuffs, lumber, stone, coal, firewood, textiles,
and shoes to ports where coastal and interior demands had created markets
for these valued items of commerce.

By the late 1830's, more than a million tons of shipping was engaged in the coastal trade. By the late 1850's, the total had climbed to
well over two million tons. The coastal trade, while hardly as romantic
as journeying to far-off Canton or Hawaii, or to the exotic ports of the
Mediterranean, nevertheless continued to serve, as it had since early
colonial days, as one of the major bases of the expanding commerce and
wealth of the nation.

As the coastal trade emerged from the colonial period to continue
its position of strength, so too did the fishing industry. Like the
coastal trade, the fishing industry, centered in New England, saw a much
increased prosperity and expansion in the period 1789 to 1860, especially
after 1815. The cause was largely the increased demand for fish arising
from the rapid growth in population that the nation experienced in those
years. The processes of industrial and commercial growth along the Atlantic seaboard and in the interior accounted for the increase in population in these areas, and natural fecundity aided by wholesale immigration
from Europe helped produce a larger food-consuming public.

Cod was still the most important product of the industry. The annual tonnage employed in the cod fisheries increased from 60,000 tons in
1820 to 136,000 tons in 1860. Massachusetts continued to lead the industry until the 1850's, when Maine assumed that position. Massachusetts
was in the process of gradually turning from the fishing trades to industry as its major concern during the pre-Civil War decades. That was
particularly the case in Boston, which abandoned the fishing industry almost completely between 1835 and 1855, and in the South Shore and Merrimac
regions, which also saw notable declines in their cod industries during
these years. But Gloucester and Cape Ann continued to be active in the
industry and emerged as the premier fishing areas by the end of the period.
In 1859 Gloucester sent out 301 schooners to harvest the cod; the fleet
employed about 3,500 men and boys.

It was also in this period that the New England fishermen altered
the usual location of their activities. By the 1830's they had begun
to abandon the Newfoundland Banks in favor of Georges Bank farther
south, a hundred miles east of Cape Cod. By fishing waters closer to
home, the fishermen were able to keep their catch alive in salt-water
wells in the boats until they reached port. There the fish were iced
and sent inland by rail to the major cities of the nation. By making
these changes, the industry was able to make gains in distribution impossible in earlier times and to increase its market thereby.

Mackerel fishing between 1820 and 1860 underwent an expansion that
brought it equal in importance to cod in the New England fishing economy. By 1851 there were more than 350 sail engaged in the mackerel
fisheries, though there were large fluctuations in the catch because
the quantities and locations of the great schools of mackerel varied
considerably from year to year. The fluctuation in tonnage in the
mackerel fisheries matched the elusive habits of the fish. The tonnage
varied from a low of only 28,000 tons in 1840 to a high of almost 74,000
tons in 1849. Still the catch per year averaged about 200,000 barrels,
and mackerel continued to be a major commercial fish. With growth in
the herring, halibut, menhaden, oyster, and lobster fisheries to match
the growth of cod and mackerel, the New England fisheries enjoyed prosperity throughout the period. Continued population growth, transportational improvements, and better means of preserving the fish resulted
in the New England fishing industry's continuing to show substantial
growth in the last half of the 19th century.

Although of lesser extent in tonnage employed and in total harvest,
the fisheries of the mid-Atlantic and Gulf areas also grew in both
halves of the century. By the 1840's, fishing was an industry of some
importance in Maryland, Delaware, Virginia, and North Carolina, and the
harvesting of oysters had become very important to the fishermen of New
Jersey, New York, and the Chesapeake. These tendencies continued in the
post-Civil War decades, so that by 1908 the New England, Atlantic, and
Gulf fishing industries represented a capital investment of $29 million
with an annual catch worth $40 million or more. The fisheries employed
109,000-plus persons at that time.

The fisheries in the 19th century grew absolutely, but not relatively. While they still represented rather substantial local industries along the Atlantic and Gulf seaboards, by early in the 20th century, fish represented only .5 percent of value of exports, and the
whale, cod, and mackerel fisheries utilized less than 2 percent of the
total American vessel tonnage in the maritime fleet.

SAILING PACKETS. During the colonial period and into the 19th
century, there were two basic types of sailers on the Atlantic trading
routes. Transient, or tramp, vessels were the more common type. They
sailed on no fixed routes or schedules, usually under a merchant-
captain or supercargo, either carrying his own goods or operating as a
common carrier. These tramps might voyage for two or three years
wherever the fortunes of profitable trade might take them and touch a
dozen ports before returning to their points of origin. Regular traders,

on the other hand, operated between fixed ports and were usually owned by merchants transporting their own goods. Sometimes, like the tramps, they also acted as common carriers. These vessels, typically of 300 to 400 tons, were especially prevalent between New York and Liverpool, London, or Le Havre. Regular traders were preferred for passengers and mails because of their regularity in routing.

In the second decade of the 19th century, however, a new type of trans-Atlantic service was introduced, the packet service. Packets (the name "packet" referred to the mail packets or pouches they carried on set schedules) were like regular traders operating from set ports, except for the important fact that they left their assigned harbors at stated, regular dates "full or not full." Their greater regularity of transit avoided the sometimes lengthy delays caused by difficulties in attaining or loading cargoes for the journey. Because of this crucial feature, the packets came to play an ever-increasing part in Atlantic trade in the next three decades prior to the Civil War.

The precedents for packet sailings could be found in the British mail packets, or "coffin brigs," which had been moving across the Atlantic carrying government dispatches and mail on regular schedules since 1755, and also in the popularity of the regular river and bay steamers, which began service after 1807 on the Hudson River between Albany and New York and on other bodies of water on the Eastern seaboard thereafter. Their regularity stimulated passenger and freight traffic and illustrated that such service might well prove to be profitable on the ocean trades too.

The first experiment with trans-Atlantic packet service came in 1818 with the establishment of the Black Ball Line, to run between New York and Liverpool. Black Ball began its service with four well-built little ships of about 500 tons, the Amity, the Courier, the Pacific, and the James Monroe. Flush-decked, full-rigged, and painted black, one ship would leave from each of the two ports on either side of the Atlantic on a scheduled day each month. They sailed "full or not full" in order to attract the "fine freight" from Liverpool to New York, especially woolen and cotton cloth, at $10 per ton; to attract the cabin passenger trade at a forty guinea rate (approximately $186); and to capture the profitable mail and specie traffic. If the captains could not gain enough of this premium trade, they filled their holds with steerage passengers and heavy freight.

This sailing schedule of once per month from each port necessitated making one winter trip each year despite the storms and westerlies that would be encountered--regular traders usually tied up during this stormy part of the year--but the experiment was successful, and in March 1822, the Black Ball Line doubled its fleet to eight ships and its sailings to two per month from Liverpool and from New York. With this move, the Black Ball Line became known as the "Third Line," though it was also frequently referred to as the "Old Line."

The success of the Black Ball Line brought forth a number of imitators. In January 1822, the "Second Line," or "Red Star Line," began

service between New York and Liverpool, followed in September by the
Blue Swallowtail Line on the same route. In 1822 and 1823, two lines
were also established to run between New York and Le Havre, these known
simply as the "First Havre Line" and the "Second Havre Line." The year
1822 also saw the inauguration of service to London with the establishment of the "Black X Line," and a second New York-London service began
in 1824, known as the "Red Swallowtail Line,"

The years from 1818 to 1838 were the heyday of the sailing packets.
They carried most of the fine freight, cabin passengers, specie, mail,
and news back and forth across the North Atlantic between Europe and its
burgeoning former colony in North America. Late in this period of popularity, another line was added between New York and Liverpool, the
"Dramatic Line," established by Edward K. Collins. It drew its name
from Collins' practice of naming his ships after famous figures of the
stage: the Shakespeare, the Garrick, the Sheridan, the Siddons, and the
Roscius. Then in 1843, a fifth line was added to Liverpool, the "New
Line," fated to be absorbed by the senior Blue Swallowtail Line only six
years later.

The popularity of the packets on the three major trans-Atlantic
runs to Liverpool, to London, and to Le Havre was reflected in their
numbers. In 1818 only four ships were running on a packet schedule; by
1825 the figure stood at twenty-eight, by 1830 at thirty-six, by 1840 at
forty-eight, and by 1845 at fifty-two. By this last year, the packets
averaged three sailings from and three sailings to New York each week.
New York was the American focal point of the Atlantic packets. Philadelphia, Boston, Baltimore, and Charleston tried to establish lines to
rival the New York packets during the period, but met with little success.

Sailing from America to Europe, the packets were "going downhill all
the way" because of the favorable prevailing winds and currents. Whatever their European destination, the packets all followed basically the
same route along the North American coast past Newfoundland and across
the North Atlantic until they were off the British Isles. There the
packets bound for Liverpool might take the southern route past Fastnet
Rock on the southwest coast of Ireland and move into St. George's (or
the South) Channel. From there they would clear Holyhead and the jutting
peninsula of Wales and move into the Irish Sea, thence into the Mersey
River and the huge stone docks of Liverpool at high tide, there to be
safely harbored twenty feet above the low-tide sea with the sea gates
shut behind them until their departure at high tide. The northern route
to Liverpool would take the packets around the northern coast of Ireland
and down through St. Patrick's (or the North) Channel, on past the Isle
of Man into the Irish Sea and into the Mersey and Liverpool.

Those packets bound for London would cut past the Scilly Islands
off the Cornish peninsula at Land's End, along the southern coast of
England and thence on up through the Straits of Dover to the Thames and
London. Packets bound for Le Havre would scoot past the Scilly Islands
and then go straight across the English Channel and around the Cher-
bourg peninsula to the great port of Le Havre, located at the mouth of
the Seine, the waterway to Paris. The speed and convenience of the east-

bound passage to Liverpool, London, or Le Havre was matched by the lack of speed and the inconvenience of the westbound passage. Going west was known as "going uphill all the way" because of sailing into the westerlies, a navigational fact of life that made it necessary to tack most of the way. As a result, it was usually about 500 miles longer going from Europe to America than going the other way.

Yet even in the face of winter sailing and the necessity of sailing into the prevailing westerlies, "going uphill," the packets maintained their appointed schedules through the years. Much of the credit was given to the crews and captains of these rugged sailing vessels. The crews were necessarily tough, because the packets' schedules demanded speed and all sail possible was crowded on despite any inclemencies of weather. Most of the sailors were reported to be under thirty years of age and as hailing from New York and New England. They did their duties well, but it was noted that there was a progressive deterioration in the quality of the crews, especially in the 1840's and 1850's, as steam competition drove the packet companies harder and harder to maintain their runs, and better berths could be gained by the competent sailors on the steam vessels.

Being an officer on a packet was the peak of ambition for any sailing man in the 1820's and 1830's, and all knew of the normal progression from packet mate to master. The few dozen packet captaincies were the most desirable commands on the seas until the advent of the clipper ships and steam vessels in the 1840's and 1850's. Command of a packet brought both honor and wealth, and some of the very best men in the profession made noteworthy careers in this manner.

A major reason for the profitability of a captaincy on a packet was the mail service function carried out by the vessels. After their inauguration in 1818, the packets soon carried most of the mail across the Atlantic because of their speed and regularity. Indeed, the British mail brigs between New York and Falmouth were withdrawn in 1828 because of packet competition. On the packets the mail revenue, or "letter money," was the prerogative of the captain and was a lucrative source of income. It was estimated in 1818 that "letter money" brought each master an average income of $180 per year over and above his contracted wage, but by 1822 the amount had risen to $360 per year. By 1833 it had almost tripled to about $900 per year, and at the height of the packets' popularity it brought in $1,500 per year to each commander. This was a small fortune for the times and explains the fabled wealth of the packet captains, although the coming of faster steam vessels in the 1840's brought an end to this bonanza for the men commanding the sailing packets.

But the owners of the packets enjoyed large profits too. In the mid-1830's, it was estimated that for three trips per vessel per year, each vessel would earn about $20,000 annually in freight earnings. Passenger and specie revenues would bring in another $30,000 for a gross income of $50,000. Subtracting between $10,000 and $20,000 for wages, insurance, food, etc., for the three voyages, each vessel would still earn as much as $30,000 a year. Considering that a typical packet cost

157

$40,000 to $50,000 to build and would be in service for eight to ten years (thus making between twenty-four and thirty voyages in its life-span), and that each year the vessel would make between $25,000 and $30,000, the net earnings on a vessel over its lifetime would approximate $200,000 to $300,000. Furthermore, despite being driven hard, there were relatively few losses of ships through shipwrecks, which would have considerably cut into a line's profitability. For example, New York-based packets suffered only twenty-two losses in more than 6,000 Atlantic crossings. The remarkable fact emerged that the sailing packets had fewer shipwrecks than ordinary traders despite their regular winter crossings--undoubtedly a tribute to the skill of their captains and crews.

In addition to carrying out the very important functions of transporting freight and mails with speed and regularity, the packets also made a contribution in carrying passengers across the Atlantic waters. In 1820, only 10,311 passengers debarking in America had chosen the packets; but by 1840 the figure was over 90,000 per year. This number was easily eclipsed in the years that followed, and by 1850 at least 300,000 passengers from Europe were choosing to travel by packet. The peak year was 1854, when 460,474 disembarked in America from packet vessels. Many, if not most, of these passengers in the early years were cabin passengers able to pay the premium rates for the speed and convenience of the regular packets; but as the years progressed, more and more packets carried more and more poor immigrants to America--especially in the 1840's, when competition with steam dropped the cabin rates down to $75 for the westward passage, and steerage rates for the immigrants dropped accordingly. It was the packet vessels and the regular cotton traders which expedited the great mass migration out of Northwest Europe to America in the decades prior to the Civil War.

Although steam packets in the late 1840's and 1850's presented a serious challenge to the sailing packets, the increase in traffic across the Atlantic both eastbound and westbound more than supported both. Packets still sailed with regularity and dependability and could demand higher freight rates than the irregularly sailing vessels, still had able commanders able to effect fast passages in their ships (now of up to 1,500 tons register), could still obtain their vessels at lower prices than could their British competitors, and still carried the great bulk of passenger traffic both ways across the ocean. Yet after 1857, the sailing packets went into decline, and they finally went out of existence in the 1870's. One reason for their demise was the development of low-priced, iron-hulled British immigrant steamships operating on the Atlantic sea lanes; they denied the packets important revenues and drove them to a marginal position. As early as 1862, only 62 percent of the passengers arriving in New York came by sail. This was a decline from 96 percent as late as 1856. Eastbound passengers, too, began to turn to the more efficient and commodious steam vessels. Fine freight was gradually shifted to the steam vessels, and the packets were forced to carry the lower-revenue bulk items such as iron, coal, and other heavy freights. After 1855, only five ships were built for the established packet lines. By the 1870's the remaining packet lines were that in name only, as they had given up sailing "full or not full" in order to get what cargoes and passengers they could in their declining days.

Yet the sailing packets in their decades of service had rendered valuable aid to the nation's growth, and the fact of their demise in no way diminishes their stellar service to America's commerce and development. The sailing packets captured the revenues of fine freight across the Atlantic; they instituted fast and dependable mail service between the Old World and the New; they carried hundreds of thousands of passengers, both cabin and immigrant, to their businesses or new lives in America; and they illustrated the possibility and advantages of fast, regular, and dependable service across the North Atlantic. It was on the basis of the packets' pioneer service that the steam vessels of the age began their meteoric rise to commercial importance, eventually revolutionizing ocean transportation in the decades after 1860.

STEAM AND IRON ON OCEAN WATERS. Steam power, the propellent of the maritime vessels that came to dominate the oceans, lakes, and rivers of the world during the late 19th century, had its beginnings almost a century before. The man who first attempted to apply James Watt's steam engine to water transportation was James Rumsey, an innkeeper at Bath, Virginia (now Berkeley Springs, West Virginia). After failing in his attempts to apply steam to paddlewheels and to a device on a boat that featured poles to be pushed into the river bottom and thus propel the boat against the current, Rumsey in 1784 developed a steam engine to push water from a jet in the rear of a boat and thus propel the vessel through the water at a speed of four knots. Working with the backing of such notables as George Washington, Benjamin Franklin, and Dr. Benjamin Rush, Rumsey also invented the water-tube boiler. Rumsey died in London while addressing the Society of Mechanical Arts on his ideas, but left a lasting legacy with his water-tube boiler and feathered paddlewheels.

Another early pioneer in steam navigation was John Fitch of Pennsylvania, who developed a paddlewheel steamboat in 1790. With the paddlewheel in the stern of his little vessel, Fitch was able to make eight miles per hour in still water, and his boat made thirty trips as a packet, actually carrying paying passengers between Philadelphia and Trenton, but the venture paid no dividends, and Fitch drifted into insolvency. He journeyed to Ohio to try again, but there he met with no success and finally committed suicide.

In this decade of the 1790's, however, success was finally achieved when an American artist and draftsman, Robert Fulton, fascinated by the steam inventions he studied in England, gave up his other work and devoted himself to the mastery of the principles of steam. For a time he labored on the idea of a submarine and tried to get the backing of Napoleon for the project, but the French ruler was not interested. Happily, however, Fulton did receive the support of the American minister in Paris, Robert Livingston. In 1803, Fulton tried out his first steamboat on the Seine, but it sank because the engine was too heavy for the hull. A second boat with a heavier hull was successful, and Fulton's principle had been proved. In the meantime, Livingston had gained a twenty-year monopoly on steam navigation within New York; and, with his backing, Fulton soon had a vessel ready for its maiden voyage. This was the North River Steamboat of Clermont, popularly called the Clermont, named after

Livingston's home on the Hudson. It was 130 feet in length and was equipped with two fourteen-foot side paddlewheels. It was powered by an engine with twenty-four-inch cylinders and a four-foot stroke, built for Fulton and Livingston by Boulton and Watt of Soho, the foremost steam-engine builders in England. On August 17, 1807, the Clermont, to the delight of the curious crowd of onlookers, belching sparks and smoke as it went, moved up the Hudson against the current. Within twenty-four hours the boat had moved 110 miles up the river to Clermont, and the following day it steamed on to Albany at the speed of five miles per hour.

Fulton's success with the Clermont, which subsequently went into operation as a regular New York-to-Albany packet, led to the building of three other steamboats for the Hudson River service before the War of 1812 intervened. Fulton and his backers, as we have seen, also took steps to place steamboats in service on the Mississippi-Ohio system. Fulton died in 1815, and Livingston's monopoly on steam navigation in New York was broken by competition with the steamers of the enterprising Cornelius Vanderbilt and the decision of the Supreme Court in Gibbons v. Ogden in 1824. Yet so successful were the early experiments in steamboating that by 1819 there were at least 100 steamers in operation in the Hudson and the Delaware on the Eastern seaboard and on the Great Lakes and the Mississippi systems in the interior. During the 1820's, the steamboat came to hold a prominent and permanent place on the waterways of the West and on the rivers, bays, and sounds of the East. Protected from foreign competition by the cabotage laws, regular steamers ran from New York to New Haven and from New York to Providence, as well as between the major cities of the seaboard East.

But if steam could carry a boat across bays and sounds and up rivers, why could it not also carry men and freight across the ocean? With this question in mind, Captain Moses Rogers of New York, the leading steam mariner in the country, began his enthusiastic campaign for trans-Atlantic steam travel. Rogers had commanded Fulton's Clermont on its maiden voyage up the Hudson and had operated John Stevens' paddlewheeler, the Phoenix, on its maiden voyage from New York to Delaware Bay, the first ocean-going trip by a steam vessel. In 1818 he obtained the backing of two Savannah, Georgia, merchants and began the Savannah Steam Ship Company with a capital of $50,000. He bought a typical 319-ton square-stern sailing vessel of 100 feet in length in New York and added collapsible paddlewheels and a seventy-two-horsepower steam engine. The vessel, christened Savannah, was full-rigged in addition to having its steam apparatus.

After sailing the vessel down to Savannah, and there taking President James Monroe on an excursion to Tybee Lighthouse and back, the Savannah left for Liverpool on May 24, 1819. It arrived in Liverpool on June 20, having made the first trans-Atlantic crossing partially under steam power in twenty-nine days. During this time Rogers used steam power for eighty to ninety hours on parts of eighteen days and caused somewhat of a local sensation when the Cape Clear, Ireland, semaphore station sent out a cutter to aid the Savannah on the mistaken belief that she was on fire. But after futile attempts to sell the vessel to the King of Sweden and to

Czar Alexander I of Russia, Rogers sailed the little vessel home, his dream of trans-Atlantic steam travel from Savannah to Liverpool shattered. The Savannah subsequently had her engines removed, and she was converted into a coastal sailer to live out her days of usefulness.

Rogers' failure was largely a matter of technology. It was recognized that the large supply of coal and cordwood necessary to power the steam engine on the Savannah left little room for paying freight. But this was but one of the technological problems that had to be solved before steam crossings of the oceans would become practical. The early steam engines were crude and heavy, and their great weight demanded extra-strong hulls in the wooden vessels into which they were place. A high-standing walking-beam apparatus with a shaft on one end attached to the engine's cylinder and a shaft on the other end attached to the paddlewheel, while practical for the Mississippi shallow-draft riverboat, was impractical for oceangoing vessels because it required an opening in the deck, which would allow water into the hold and would interfere with the proper placing of the necessary auxiliary sails and masts. The walking beam would also make the center of gravity too high and would leave the engines exposed to the weather.

Steam engines also required a supply of fresh water to be converted into the precious steam. If salt water was used out of necessity, it then became mandatory to blow the boilers frequently to remove the brine, a procedure that required a complete stopping of the engines, allowing them to cool, and then a refilling with cold water before getting up steam again. It was also discovered that the side paddlewheels were often inefficient on the high seas because of the problem of maintaining them at the proper depth when the ship was rolling. In addition, if the steam engine used coal, there was less room for cargo; if it used wood, they would also lose cargo space and would have to stay relatively near bases of supply. Added to these problems was the fact that American marine engineering was at a very low state of development at this time, with few skilled machinists and poor equipment. The cost of buying European engines instead was virtually prohibitive because of shipping charges and because the tariff on iron manufactures was very high, running between 23.5 and 30 percent in the years 1833 to 1857.

If American marine steam enthusiasts were laboring under rather severe handicaps during the 1820's, 1830's, and 1840's, the same cannot be said of the British. They rushed into the lead in these decades and left American maritime development in steam far behind, as this new power source came to conquer the Atlantic. As early as the 1780's, steam vessels were pioneering in Britain, and in the 1790's several small steam vessels were operating regularly in Scotland. In 1801 the little stern-wheel tug, the Charlotte Dundas, began operating on the Forth and Clyde Canal. After 1812 the British moved into a clear technological lead over their American counterparts with more efficient engines and propelling mechanisms. By 1820 there were thirty-four steam vessels operating in Britain; by 1830 the figure had reached 298 steamboats, and by 1835 had jumped to 503 vessels. The figure would reach more than 2,000 vessels in domestic and foreign service in 1855.

A Canadian vessel, the Royal William, in 1833 made what was probably the first passage of the Atlantic solely under steam power, completing the trip from Pictou to Gravesend in twenty-five days; but it was not until 1835 that the British really began to exert themselves to adapt their successful steam experience on the home waters to the broad expanses of the oceans. In that year, the British and American Steam Navigation Company was founded with a capital of £500,000 by Junius Smith, an American living in England. His plan was to build two British and two American steamships to sail the Atlantic on a bi-monthly schedule. Accordingly, contracts were awarded for the building of the Royal Victoria, but the project was constantly plagued with delays, and the builder of the engine, the most critical component of the vessel, went bankrupt when only two-thirds done. In the meantime, the Great Western Railway Company obtained a charter from Parliament to build a railroad from London to Bristol; but at the suggestion of a young engineer in its employ, Isambard Kingdom Brunel, the company decided to supplement it with a steamboat service to New York. With this development, the race to see who would first steam the Atlantic was on, although the distinguished Rev. Dionysius Lardner of the British Association for the Advancement of Science, editor of an encyclopedia and author of a book on steam engines then in its fifth edition, solemnly warned those planning steam service from Liverpool to New York that they "might as well talk of going from Liverpool to the moon."

By 1838 Smith's British and American Steam Navigation Company, still determined to be the first across the water under steam, chartered from a company running vessels from Cork to London the tiny, 703-ton Sirius of 320 horsepower to sail under its sponsorship for New York on March 28. Its competitor, the Great Western Railway Company, had already launched its Great Western of 1,320 tons, also to be the first, and announced it would sail on March 31. But the elegant Great Western was delayed by a fire on board at Gravesend and finally began its successful Atlantic crossing only on April 8 from Bristol. The Sirius was the first to arrive in New York on April 23, but only twelve hours ahead of the Great Western. The Sirius had made the passage in eighteen days from Cork; the Great Western had made it in fifteen days from Bristol. In a real sense, both had won the race, but, of greater importance, they had proved beyond a doubt the practicability of trans-Atlantic steam travel. By the end of that year alone, there had been eleven steam vessel sailings from New York, five by the Great Western and six by four other British vessels. The Sirius made but one more trans-Atlantic crossing before being sold to a line to run to St. Petersburg.

Steam made its first clear conquests of the Atlantic, and average passage times by 1839 cast an ominous shadow over sailing vessels on the northern routes. In that year the average time for sailing vessels on the westward passage was no less than thirty-four days; the average passage time for steam vessels was only seventeen days. On the eastward passage sailing vessels took 22.1 days as compared to 15.4 days for steam. While the long-range effects of this technological revolution might be obscured by the persistence of sailing vessels for another three decades because of the abundance of trade, the final outcome was foreshadowed in these figures. More immediately, the presence of steam vessels on the North Atlantic sea lanes forced the sailing packets to reduce their passenger fares drastically to compete with the faster steamers; and even then the sailing packets were almost completely deserted by cabin passengers on the longer westbound runs within a short period of time.

The British conquest of the Atlantic by steam with the Sirius and the Great Western was, however, but the first step toward steam dominance of the trade on that ocean. The British government after 1836 moved to aid the steamship industry through contractual operating subsidies because of a desire to aid economic infants to build to economies of scale; to gain nationally, economically, politically, and militarily from improved communications; and to aid national defense by having superior ships convertible for wartime use. A combination of private industry plus government subsidy, the government believed, would lead to greater efficiency at lower cost. That the policy paid rich dividends became evident in the 1840's and 1850's, as British steam lines moved to dominate the North Atlantic sea lanes.

In 1840 the British granted a mail subsidy to the Cunard Lines, the company founded by Samuel Cunard, the Nova Scotian native who had learned the shipping trade while working in Boston. The seven-year subsidizing contract called for bi-monthly service between Liverpool, Halifax, and Boston. Cunard's paddlewheelers with side-lever engines were able to make a steady 8 1/2 knots and soon moved to preeminence on the Atlantic. The United States did not even respond to the Cunard challenge (or to the challenge posed by the Hamburg-American Line begun in 1847 by Herr August Bolten to run between Hamburg and New York) until 1848. In that year it granted a subsidy to the Ocean Steam Navigation Company to operate two large steamers to Bremen via Southampton or to Havre, but this company languished in the early 1850's. In 1849 the government granted a subsidy to the New York and Havre Steam Navigation Company to run from New York to Cowes and Havre.

Only in 1850, with the establishment of the New York and Liverpool Mail Steamship Company by the former sailing packet entrepreneur Edward K. Collins, did the United States directly try to capture the lucrative steam trade between the United States and England. But the "Collins Line," which began its service with a rich subsidy and four new wooden-hulled, richly-appointed paddlewheel steamers, fell on hard times despite increases in its subsidies; and, with the loss of its Arctic in a collision in 1854 and the disappearance of its Pacific in 1856, the experiment was ended with the cancellation of all mail subsidies in 1858. The Collins Line could not survive despite its minimum passenger and freight rates and despite a brand new "superliner," the Adriatic, and the pooling agreement it had with Cunard between 1850 and 1855.

The British in 1850 increased their hold on the trans-Atlantic steam traffic by chartering the Liverpool, New York and Philadelphia Steamship Company, generally known as the "Inman Line" (after its founder, William Inman of Leister). Inman specifically designed his ships to accommodate immigrant passengers, as well as cabin passengers, and made an important technological advance by building his fleet on the use of iron vessels using the screw propeller. Although he began by using Philadelphia as his American terminus, Inman switched to New York in 1857 and increased his flourishing business even further.

By the time of the Civil War, the British had clearly stolen the march on the Americans in the steam merchant marine, not only by their careful use of subsidies, but also by their better steam engines; their movement to iron hulls, which could better accommodate machinery, and, with greater buoyancy, gave a larger internal capacity; and by their adoption of the screw propeller which was more economical of coal and caused no drag as paddlewheels did. Britain had conquered technologically and economically on the high seas. Time would expand its advantage over the Americans.

SHIPBUILDING. The Americans had excelled in shipbuilding during colonial days. The advantages of location, timber supplies, skilled workmanship, and high demand had been theirs. They had capitalized on it to create a major industry on their shores. These advantages continued to serve them well into the early decades of the 19th century, indeed, as long as wooden ships and wooden shipbuilding dominated the ocean trades.

From the early 19th century to 1830, the demand for sailing ships was strong. The inherent economies in the American merchant marine operations led to the shipowners' ability to carry more goods at a lower price. This advantage led to higher yields on their investments and thence to increased ship demands. At the same time, the tremendous increases in foreign and domestic trade and in fishing also led to a strong demand for the output of the shipyards. American shipbuilders had to pay higher wages than their European counterparts, but the plentiful supplies of oak timbering, oak and hard-pine planking, and pine for masts was enough to overcome the higher wage costs. Even the British regulations between 1786 and 1849, which closed the right of British citizens to buy American-made ships, and the French regulation of the same type enacted in 1793, did not hurt the shipbuilding industry. These regulations, by compelling American shipbuilders to sell in a closed market, forced the prices of ships down, leading to more shipping and a greater long-run demand for ships. During these first three decades of the 19th century, shipbuilding was scattered all along the Atlantic coastline, though New England was still in the lead, with Maine the most prominent state in shipbuilding, followed by Massachusetts. The Hudson River Valley and the Chesapeake Bay regions also saw much ship construction. American shipbuilding was still highly decentralized and was carried out on a very small scale. This de-centralization and smallness of scale, however, did not mean any loss of efficiency in the American yards; and with adequate timber supplies and a reputation for building ships of superior durability, American-built merchant ships cost 40 to 60 percent less than similar vessels in England or France.

The next thirty years until the Civil War saw an increase in demand with some peaks and troughs; 1847-57 was the peak period of wooden-ship construction. Overall business conditions were good; the Irish famine led to greater demand for immigrant accommodations; the British repealed their Corn Laws in 1846, and North American grain was rushed to fill their demand for foodstuffs; and the cotton trade was greater than ever before. In addition, 1849 saw the rush to California and the advent of the China clippers. In 1854, Lloyd's registration rules were changed, with the result that British shipowners could now buy American vessels without penalty. The next year saw the peak tonnage built, with 583,000 gross tons coming off the shipways of America. Between 1847 and 1857, at least four million gross tons of shipping were built, about 50 percent of all tonnage built between 1815 and 1860.

Despite all of these positive signs, however, there were indications of serious trouble in the wooden shipbuilding industry, at which the Americans excelled. Deterioration may have been held off for a time by superiority of design and by the price differential, but there were clear indications that the industry would find itself in serious trouble in the decades ahead. By late in the period, there was a serious shortage of timber on the Atlantic coastline; and shipbuilders were importing it from the Great Lakes area, the interior coastal regions, and the South, but all at higher prices than they had ever paid before. The cost of labor was rising, too, with a shortage of skilled shipbuilders caused by the high labor demands and high wages of the growing manufacturing cities and the continued westward migration of much of the populace. For example, ship carpenters in city yards in the mid-1840's averaged $1.75 to $2.00 per day; by the mid-1850's, they were averaging $2.00 to $4.00 per day. As a result of these increasing costs of supplies and labor, the price of American-built vessels rose sharply, while the cost of European-built vessels rose only slightly. By 1860 a British-built, first-rate wooden ship cost between $83 and $105 per ton, while an American-built clipper cost somewhat more than $70 per ton. The price differential was still in America's favor, but the gap was closing rapidly. This factor, combined with America's economic and technological lag in the building of steam and iron vessels, foreshadowed the hard times into which the American shipbuilding industry would fall in the second half of the 19th century.

FOREIGN TRADE OVERVIEW. In 1815, at the end of the European wars, American foreign trade consisted of $52.4 million in exports and $113 million in imports, for a total of $165.5 million. The amount of trade increased steadily through the years, especially in the prosperous 1850's, so that by 1860, exports totaled $333.6 million and imports totaled $353.6 million, for an overall foreign-trade value of $687.2 million (an increase of 415 percent in the forty-five years between 1815 and 1860).

To carry this increasing trade, the American oceangoing merchant marine enlarged from 824,295 registered tons engaged in foreign trade in 1815 to 2,379,396 registered tons in 1860, an increase of 288 percent. Because the total amount of trade was growing faster than the tonnage of American ships carrying that trade, the percentage of American imports and exports carried in American bottoms declined by value from 92.3 percent in 1825 to 66.5 percent in 1860--still a significant amount, but also a telling decline, which portented trouble ahead for the foreign-trade merchant marine.

Imports into the United States showed a steady reliance on European countries. The amounts of trade grew significantly, but the percentage imported from various countries stayed approximately the same except for a notable drop of imports from the West Indies. America in the period 1821-25 imported $118.3 million worth of goods from the United Kingdom for 46 percent of its imports, from France $33.7 million for 9 percent, from Russia and Germany 3 percent each, from Cuba 9 percent, and from the West Indies $69.9 million for 19 percent. In the period 1856 to 1860, imports from the United Kingdom were $601.6 million for 37 percent, from France $212.5 million for 13 percent, from Russia .4 percent, from Germany 5 percent, from Cuba 10 percent, and from the West Indies $205.9 million for 13 percent. Imports by continents in the period were also rather constant, in 1860 showing 19.2 percent by value imported from North America, 9.9 percent from South America, 61.3 percent from Europe, 8.3 percent from Asia, 3 percent from Oceania, and 1 percent from Africa. Leading items imported that year were cotton manufactures, 9 percent; woolen manufactures, 11 percent; silk manufacture, 10 percent; flax manufactures, 3 percent; iron and steel products, 6 percent; tea and coffee, 8 percent; sugar, 9 percent; hides and skins, 3 percent; and alcoholic beverages, 3 percent. America's imports, then, growing from $113 million in 1815 to $353.6 million, or 313 percent, in 1860 were primarily manufactures and foodstuffs and were mainly from Europe and from the Caribbean and South American areas .

Exports, too, showed relatively little change in the countries to which they went. Typical are the percentages for the period 1856 to 1860, which showed 49 percent of exports by value going to the United Kingdom, 12 percent to France, 7 percent to the non-British West Indies, 7 percent to British North America, 5 percent to South America, 4 percent to Cuba, 4 percent to Germany, 2 percent to the British West Indies, and 1 percent to the Netherlands. By continent, 74.8 percent went to Europe in 1860, 15.7 percent to North America, 4.7 percent to South America, 2.4 percent to Asia, 1.5 percent to Oceania, and 1 percent to Africa. The commodities exported during the 1856-60 period by value consisted of raw cotton, 54 percent; domestic manufactures, 12 percent; wheat and flour, 11 percent; raw tobacco, 6 percent; pork and pork products, 4 percent; corn and corn meal, 2 percent; beef, tallow, and hides, 2 percent; timber products, 2 percent; rice, 1 percent; and fish, 3 percent. The percentages by value remained almost the same throughout the period while total value in dollars climbed from $52.5 million to $333.6 million, an increase of 635 percent. Cotton and European consumers clearly dominated the expanding American export market.

The American merchant marine was primarily employed on Atlantic waters, but boasted strong Pacific, coastal, and inland components. In 1860 the total tonnage of the American maritime interests in all employments totaled 5.3 million tons, almost equal to the total tonnage of the entire British Empire of 5.7 million tons. American waterborne commerce had played a major part in bringing the nation to both unity and economic strength at home and in making it a major influence in the far-flung areas of the world, from European port cities and capitals half way around the world to the distant reaches of the Far East. America's maritime strength, especially on the ocean waters, was at its zenith.

SUGGESTIONS FOR FURTHER READING

Benns, Frank L. The American Struggle for the British West Indian
Carrying Trade, 1815-1830. Indiana University Studies, Vol. 9,
Study No. 56. Bloomington: Indiana University Press, 1923; re-
print ed., Clifton, N.J.: Augustus M. Kelley, 1972.

Bowen, Frank. A Century of Atlantic Travel, 1830-1930. Boston: Little,
Brown, and Co., 1930.

Buck, Norman S. The Development of the Organization of Anglo-American
Trade, 1800-1850. New Haven: Yale University Press, 1925.

Flexner, James T. Steamboats Come True: American Inventors in Action.
New York: The Viking Press, 1944.

Hidy, Ralph W. The House of Baring in American Trade and Finance: English Merchant Bankers at Work, 1763-1861. Harvard Studies in Business History, Vol. XIV. Cambridge: Harvard University Press, 1949.

Hutchins, John G.B. The American Maritime Industries and Public Policy,
1789-1914: An Economic History. Harvard Economic Studies, Vol.
LXXI. Cambridge: Harvard University Press, 1941.

Innis, Harold A. The Cod Fisheries: The History of an International
Economy. New Haven: Yale University Press, 1940.

Johnson, Emory R. et al. History of Domestic and Foreign Commerce of
the United States. Vol's I & II in one volume. Washington, D.C.:
Carnegie Institution, 1915.

Lane, Wheaton J. Commodore Vanderbilt, An Epic of the Steam Age. New
York: Alfred A. Knopf, 1942.

Morison, Samuel Eliot. The Maritime History of Massachusetts, 1783-
1860. Boston: Houghton Mifflin Co., 1921.

Sloan, Edward W., III. "The Machine at Sea: Early Transatlantic Steam
Travel," in Benjamin W. Labaree, ed., The Atlantic World of Robert
G. Albion. Middletown, Conn.: Wesleyan University Press, 1975.

Taylor, George R. The Transportation Revolution, 1815-1860. The Economic History of the United States, Vol. IV. New York & Toronto:
Rinehart & Company, Inc., 1951.

Tyler, David B. Steam Conquers the Atlantic. New York: D. Appleton-
Century Co., 1939.

CHAPTER IX. IMMIGRATION: THE OCEANS AS A CONDUIT OF PEOPLE

During the century from 1815 to 1914 there occurred one of the greatest mass migrations in the history of the world. Impelled by declining economic conditions caused by the agricultural revolution, the industrial revolution, political revolutions, and the basic desire to assure a better future elsewhere for themselves and their progeny, fifty million Europeans left their homelands to begin again in another country. Of these fifty million people with their fifty million hopes and dreams, approximately thirty million sought a new life in the United States, while the remaining twenty million emigrated to Canada, South Africa, Australia, New Zealand, and South America. Without ocean transport this mass migration could not have occurred, and without the existence of a commercial network across the Atlantic this oceanic transfer of peoples would never have attained the flood stage it did in the latter half of the 19th century and the first decade of the 20th century. In some measure America became a social, economic, political, and religious heterogeneous melting pot because of the international character of the merchant marine which conducted this traffic in migrants across the seas from their European homelands.

IMMIGRATION BEFORE 1860. The American colonies saw the coming of newcomers to their shores from the first immigrants in 1607 until the Revolution. This phenomenon was part of their daily existence, for conditions in Europe in the 17th and 18th centuries brought a constant flow of both English and non-English immigrants to the colonies. Their reception in the New World was one of welcome tinged with misgivings over social dislocations that might be caused by their presence. But the ambivalence of the colonial leaders was matched by their knowledge of the importance of the newcomers to the developing colonies, so the process continued as a solution to the shortage of skilled labor and to the need to promote land settlement thereby to develop the colonies. Immigrants were sometimes urged or allowed to settle the frontier areas to act as a barrier against the Indians, the French, or the Spanish.

But in the years 1775 to 1815, the flow of people slowed to a trickle. The years of the Revolution were followed by a decade of uncertainty and then by almost two decades of insecurity and warfare in Europe. Only about 250,000 immigrants came to America between the end of the war and 1815. The number averaged about 6,000 per year from 1783 to 1793, then about 10,000 per year until the last years of the century, only to fall to 3,000 annually during the Napoleonic wars, and then stop entirely during the War of 1812.

From 1815 and the end of the War of 1812 to the opening of World War I in 1914 a century later, however, the United States became the destination of a massive migration of peoples to its shores. The immigrant tide came in three waves, each larger than before. From the 1830's to 1860, the first wave was predominantly Irishmen, Scots, Englishmen, Welsh, and Germans from the Upper Rhine Valley, who sought American shores, reaching a peak in the years 1847-54. The second great wave came in the three decades between 1860 and 1890, reaching its greatest surge in the last ten years of the period. This second period saw a majority of English, Scottish, and Irish agricultural workers among the newcomers, but also great numbers of Scandinavians, Prussians and Saxons from Germany, and Bohemians from Austria. The third period, from 1890 to 1914, saw not only a continued flow of peoples from northwest Europe, but also a predominance of southern and eastern Europeans from Russia, Italy, Greece, and the Baltic areas. It peaked in the last five years before World War I. These three waves brought thirty million foreigners to American shores and changed the nation profoundly during its century of greatest growth and development.

The first great exodus from Europe began after the Napoleonic wars as the European economy went into depression with the ending of the conflict. Manufacturing contracts were ended, wages became depressed, and unemployment emerged as a serious problem. The weight of the accumulated war debts fell on the small farmers and also on the large landowners, who passed on the burden to their tenants in the form of higher rents. At the same time, the enclosure movement continued to claim waste and common land and remove it from public use, much to the disadvantage of small-scale farmers. In the cities, both the established urban classes and the displaced farmers looking for alternate employment as they fled from the land were confronted with a rapid transition to machinery, which in some industries displaced as many as five-sixths of the work force. And so machinery was smashed and factories were burned in isolated incidents in the cities, to match the smashing of threshing machines and burning of barns in the countryside, as the lower classes struggled against economic forces they could neither understand nor control. Many finally came to the decision that emigration to another country was the only choice for themselves and for their families.

In these same early years of the 19th century, the governments of the various European countries began to remove restrictions on the emigration of their people. In 1825 the British repealed their regulations forbidding artisans to emigrate, and two years later all restrictions on emigration were removed, mainly because of the increasing volume of struggling Irish peasants who were not allowed to leave the Kingdom and were threatening to "deluge Great Britain" by their very numbers. From 1820 to 1848, the various governments in the Germanies allowed emigration, but actively discouraged it. With the revolutions of 1848, however, they opened the gates of their countries as a safety-valve against further agitation within their kingdoms. Sweden repealed its restrictions in 1840 out of fear of pauperism. And so it went as the first surge of emigration began to be felt in Europe and the first large numbers of displaced Europeans sought American shores.

If conditions in Europe induced many of its people to leave, conditions in America induced many of them to come. As the upturn in the number of emigrants began in the late 1820's, the United States was experiencing a severe labor shortage, especially for the unskilled. Canals were being built, factories were desperate for hands, construction expansion demanded thousands of willing backs, and the great acreages of the West were now open for development and transit thanks to the Erie Canal and to the Lakes and river systems. To those willing to work and sacrifice, America meant economic opportunity and a chance to escape to freedom from restrictive laws, customs, and guilds. These factors, combined with severe winters in 1825, 1826, and again in 1829, plus the dislocations and uncertainties caused by the revolutions in the Germanies, Belgium, and Poland, forced many people out and set off the first of the three tidal waves of Europeans to America.

German emigration to the United States began in earnest in the 1830's and reached a peak between 1846 and 1855. The majority of the German emigrants were from the southwestern provinces of Württemberg, Baden, and Bavaria. Those who joined the "Auswanderer Movement" were primarily victims of heavy taxes and crop failures. Most were small farmers caught in the burden of debt, although many wealthy farmers joined in the flight. Population was on the rise, and fear of unemployment crept through the ranks of the populace as it seemed the burden of public taxes would continue to increase. Perhaps the greatest fear of the eventual "Auswanderers" was that of losing their precious land and being forced to join the wage-labor class, the proletariat, in the cities. From various sources of information, primarily from Germans who had already emigrated to America, they found that labor was scarce in that developing country across the Atlantic and that they could be free artisans or perhaps own their own land in America. So they went, leaving behind them the insecurity of the Old World for the security of the New.

Sizeable British emigration began after 1815 and continued heavy through the years until 1860. In those forty-five years, approximately 750,000 Britons, almost one-sixth of all arrivals in America, abandoned their native land. The majority were farmers and landless agricultural workers who found themselves underbid by the desperate Irish immigrants fleeing across the Irish Sea to find work at any price. The majority of the British farmers were small landholders and, like their German counterparts, felt crushed by the burden of taxes. Perhaps the greatest force impelling them to leave Britain, however, came in the 1840's when the repeal of the Corn Laws in 1846 convinced thousands of small farmers that the inevitable effect of the repeal would be the flooding of their grain market by Continental and North American wheat and other grains. That flooding did not take place until the 1870's, but still the fear of this dislocation was enough to force many to take passage to America, where no such development could occur. The forces of the industrial Revolution and the factory system also drove out a significant proportion of skilled workers in the 1820's. British woolen operatives; carpenters; coal, lead, and copper miners; and potters joined thousands of iron puddlers in the exodus to America, where their skills and energies would bring them livable returns on their labors in an economy often desperate for their particular job talents.

Ireland was a land of poverty in the early 19th century. Its six million peasants were impoverished year after year owing to a mixture of government mismanagement, a dependence on the potato as the mainstay of the Irish diet, a continued subdivision of the scarce lands until the plots could not sustain their peasant owners, and the high population-growth rate. Famine and disease stalked the land every five or six years as the potato crop fell short of demands for human consumption. Yet the Irish stubbornly clung to their little plots of ground until 1845, when the blight ruined the potato crop, and 1846, when it failed completely. It is estimated that in one year alone almost a half million Irish died of famine and pestilence in the wake of this agricultural disaster. But the potato famine also forced thousands upon thousands of Irish to break loose their bonds with the soil and their native land at last.

Between 1846 and 1854, approximately one million desperately poor Irish peasants left for America, in addition to the untold thousands who emigrated to Britain, there to worsen the position of the already burdened English farmer and farm laborers. Much of the emigration was directly impelled by the Irish landlords who between 1849 and 1856 alone evicted 50,000 families from their homes and forced them to leave the country. The landlords were pushed to this action because in 1847, as a measure of relief, the Poor Law was applied to Ireland. It obligated the landlords to pay taxes to the parishes for poor relief. When the landlords attempted to raise the money for taxes by increased rents and found that the peasants could not pay them--most could not even afford to eat--the landlords simply drove them off their lands by the power of the law and had their poor cabins "tumbled" to prevent the peasants from returning to their homes. The landlords called it "shovelling out." The population of Ireland in 1841 was 8.2 million; by 1851 it stood at only 6.5 million. Considering the birth rates at the time, which would normally have pushed the population to over 9 million persons during the decade, the total loss to Ireland was about two-and-a-half million persons during the ten-year period, and 822,000 more emigrated in the years 1851-54.

There was also some migration to the United States during these decades from North America. Between 1815 and 1860 approximately 250,000 Canadians moved to the United States. The movement from Canada began after 1837. Some were political refugees from the abortive Canadian rebellions of the 1830's. Other Canadian emigrants came from the Maritime Provinces, where the free trade measures of the British government in the 1840's led to depression in the timber, shipbuilding, and provisioning industries. The largest number of Canadian emigrants came from Quebec where the growing French-Canadian population experienced difficulty in obtaining lands from engrossing speculators and began a movement into the upper Midwest and into New York and New England.

American immigration figures of the pre-Civil War decades clearly reveal the increasing popularity of emigration as a solution to the economic problems faced by European peoples and the popularity of the United States as a refuge from their problems. In the 1820's, only about 151,000 entered the country. By the 1830's the number had almost quadrupled to 599,000 for the decade. The 1840's saw almost a tripling of that figure up to 1,713,000, and the high point for the pre-Civil War years came in the 1850's, when 2,314,000 emigrants entered the United States from foreign countries. The five million people who entered the country from abroad between 1815 and 1860 were greater in number than the entire population of the country in 1790. America was the recipient of most of Europe's fleeing millions.

Yet important as the causes of this great migration might be, the Atlantic commercial system was the basis of the whole transfer system. Atlantic commerce, building to new heights during these decades, provided an inexpensive and fairly reliable means of transportation for virtually all of the five million people who left their homelands for America. By the 1820's, there were over a thousand vessels carrying timber between Canada and the Maritimes to Britain, and the next decade saw more than a thousand vessels also carrying cotton to Liverpool. As these and other commercial vessels completed their eastbound voyages, they found that for the westward leg of the journey they had space available because of the lesser bulk of the manufactured and processed goods coming to America. Rather than returning in partial ballast, enterprising captains discovered that immigrants made good cargo. They sought this cargo openly, and the immigrant trade was soon an organized and lucrative part of the Atlantic commercial network.

Even in the early years, passenger brokers appeared, and emigrants sailed from virtually all ports in northwestern Europe as cargo to America. But with better commercial connections developing with the use of rails and coastal steamers, emigration soon came to be concentrated at larger ports such as Liverpool, Le Havre, Bremen, and Hamburg. Competition between the traders sent fares plummeting, and by 1830 they often stood at one-fourth to one-tenth their levels of fifteen years before. Immigrants as essentially self-loading, self-caring, and self-unloading freight were items not overlooked in Atlantic trade.

PASSAGE BY SAIL. By the beginning of the first surge of immigrants in 1830, the Atlantic maritime base had been firmly established, and the European refugees had become a critical part of that commercial network. By that time, the packets were sailing in greater numbers and were more than willing to carry the emigrant passengers to America. Furthermore, the competition from packets for fine freight forced the regular traders also to enter the immigrant-transit business in order to fill their holds. During the 1830's the number of passengers carried by American vessels increased fivefold as the captains of vessels found thousands of the willing emigrants waiting for passage at ports both in the British Isles and on the Continent. American sailing companies moved to capture the traffic by setting definite routes and sailings to accommodate them. Rates for passage also saw reductions because the tobacco, cotton, and grains making up the eastbound freight earned such good revenues that it was possible to transport the emigrants on the return westbound voyages at substantially lower rates. In the 1840's, too, with more cabin passengers moving to steam vessels because of the much faster time going "uphill" to America on these ships, the sailing packets carried even more "steerage" emigrants in the bottoms of their vessels on their return voyages from Europe. By the late 1840's, American vessels were carrying more than twice as many emigrants to North America than were the British and Irish vessels in the Atlantic trade network. This American dominance of the immigrant trade continued into the 1850's, when 360 of the 405 vessels in the North Atlantic trade bore the American flag.

With the immigrant trade being superimposed on the existing and expanding Atlantic maritime network, the immigrants were often forced to follow the paths of commerce. For example, the great number of poor Irish found in New England in the pre-Civil War period can be explained by the fact that most of them came to North America on vessels in the lumber trade between New Brunswick and Britain. The Irish would book steerage passage on the lumber vessels returning to St. John or St. Andrew's. From there they would travel on the coastal sailers carrying plaster of Paris, or gypsum, from the Maritimes down to Boston, Providence, New London, or some other New England Port. The gypsum-carrying sailers ran regularly down the coast because the mineral was an important fertilizer of high demand in the northeastern United States. Again, a large number of German immigrants disembarked at New Orleans because of that port's commercial connections with Le Havre in the important cotton trade. From New Orleans, the immigrants could make their way in safety, at a comparatively low cost, up the Mississippi to the Midwest on the steamboats plying the river. From this source, cities such as St. Louis and Cincinnati developed their large concentrations of German-speaking immigrants in the decades of the early 19th century.

New York, of course, continued to be the primary point of entry for most European immigrants because of its extensive trading connections with all major ports in Britain and on the Continent. Philadelphia, Boston, Baltimore, and other Atlantic seaboard cities saw considerably fewer immigrants because of their lesser roles in the trans-Atlantic trade network. New York in 1855 received about 70 percent of the immigrants; New Orleans was next with 8.6 percent, followed by Boston with 7.4 percent, Philadelphia with 3 percent, and Baltimore with 2.6 percent. Thus almost 92 percent of the immigrants arrived at five American ports, New York claiming the lion's share.

On the European end of the conduit, Liverpool, as the center of the packet trade for the British Isles, became the primary embarkation point from the Isles and from Scandinavia. The city had grown with the slave trade in the 18th century, then continued into the cotton trade and the packet trade, to emerge as an immigrant point too, seeing about two-thirds of the emigrants from northwest Europe depart from its docks in the 1850's. The city retained its lead in the emigrant trade throughout the century. On the Continent, Le Havre, with its extensive contacts with New Orleans through the cotton trade and with the interior of Europe, handled a sizeable number of emigrants, especially Germans, although Bremen began its rise in the emigrant trade with the successful conclusion of its reciprocity treaty with the United States in 1827.

The passage of the emigrants to America in steerage, particularly in the earlier decades of the 19th century, nearly defies description. Many emigrants had spent almost their entire funds just getting to a seaport. They waited for days or weeks for a ship to leave, often living in unsanitary and even dangerous hostels surrounding the dock areas of the cities. Sometimes they bought tickets for themselves and their families for passage, only to find that the tickets were fraudulent. Sometimes the meager food supplies hoarded by the emigrants for their three weeks' journey by sea were exhausted even before taking ship, and they were at the mercy of the ship's captain and the prices he would charge for enough food to sustain life until America was reached.

On board, after frequently being overcrowded into the holds with rough-built lumber shelving serving as bunks, sometimes two or three tiers high, the emigrants found themselves with even worse problems during their time at sea, when they were entirely under the control of the captain. The food provided was often rotten and entirely inadequate, the water casks were often so foul that vinegar would have to be added to the water to make it drinkable; toilet facilities were almost nonexistent; rats abounded; and cooking had to be done on small stoves, if allowed at all.

When storms were encountered, the terrified immigrants often found themselves confined in the holds without any ventilation for days and even weeks on end. Disease and mortality were only too frequent companions of the emigrants on the sailing vessels, although the speed of the packets and the competition for the emigrants between the various companies mitigated the deplorable conditions somewhat. Still, fire and shipwreck in North Atlantic waters sometimes occurred, to haunt the minds of those who would follow across the waters.

Conditions upon arrival in America--or in Canada for those vessels traveling to that British possession--were hardly better, with neither country making adequate provision for the reception of the unfortunate victims of European economic and political change. Most immigrants, unless they were met on the docks by friends or relatives who had preceded them, and who knew from bitter experience the helplessness of the immigrants as they disembarked in the new country, found themselves accosted by "runners" from hostelries determined to take every last pence or mark from their unsuspecting "guests," either legally or illegally. If this type of fleecing by the crimps was avoided, there was still the problem of acquiring proper tickets for the journey to their eventual destination, again with the constant danger of being sold bogus tickets to nowhere. All in all, the journey by sail from European countryside or squalid city across the Atlantic Ocean to a new start in America was marked by suffering, fatigue, hunger, sickness, dishonesty, and sometimes even death for the immigrant.

It was for this reason that first the British and then the Americans moved to impose regulations upon the immigrant trade. The first British measure, the Passenger Vessel Act of 1803, mandated that one passenger could be carried for each ton of ship's register, a surgeon had to be on board, and adequate food provisions had to be carried. But the law was easily evaded, and the allowable practice of figuring children under fourteen years as only part of the adult allocation led to continued overcrowding. The Act of 1817 tried to grant greater space by making the formula one passenger per 1 1/2 tons, but the practice of adding passengers after embarkation and dumping them before disembarkation rendered the law completely ineffective. The Act of 1823 lowered the allowable passengers to a one-person-per-five-ton ratio, but it too was generally evaded; the Act was amended in 1826 to exempt the Irish from its provisions. Faced with an increasing need to rid the Islands of surplus population, yet with some compassion on the emigrants on the nation's ships, subsequent British laws were passed in 1828, 1835-36, 1842, and 1847, but were poorly enforced, even though many provisions for adequate space, better food and water, sanitation standards, and lifeboats were included. It was not governmental regulations, but the passing of the sailing ships in favor of the steamers, which finally improved conditions on the journey. Competition for passengers and the size of the larger steam companies, which squeezed most of the unscrupulous operators out of the trade, were much more effective than well-intentioned but easily evaded and inadequately enforced laws.

American control acts, on the other hand, while fewer in number, would appear to have been more rigidly enforced. Beginning with the Immigration Act of 1819, the basis for federal supervision in the field and the beginning of official immigration statistics as mandated by the law, and continuing through the Act of 1855 (which repealed the three earlier acts of 1819, 1847, and 1848), American law held to the lower formula of two passengers per registered ton until a flat fourteen-square-feet-per-passenger formula was finally adopted. The later laws also controlled all ships bringing immigrants to America by specifying such matters as the number of tiers of bunks allowed, adequate ventilation, minimum food and water, ranges for cooking, and sufficient privies. The Act of 1855 extended these same regulations to steamships. Laws passed by the seaboard states beginning in the 1820's levying head charges on shipmasters according to the number of passengers brought in, the money to be used for the immigrants' care if they became indigent, were also enforced. Because they were enforced, the American laws had some effect, although not as much as the twin forces of competition and the steamship.

One of the more effective benefits ever given to the immigrant horde came when New York City in 1855 opened Castle Garden near the Battery for the protected reception of the immigrants. Its thirteen-foot walls kept out the crimps from the boarding houses as well as the perveyors of counterfeit tickets. The runners, hotel owners, and crooked brokers tried in every way possible to work their way into the refuge. Their efforts were uniformly in vain, and the immigrants were at last presented with decent treatment and genuine help in getting started in America.

THE LATE 19TH-CENTURY SURGE. During the years 1860 to 1915, the United States received approximately 25 million migrants, most of them from Europe. This tide of humanity helped to swell the nation's population from 31.4 million at the beginning of the Civil War to almost 92 million on the eve of World War I. These years not only marked the period when the pre-war number of immigrants quadrupled to bring the immigrant tide to its fullest swell, but also saw a distinct shift in the areas in Europe from which the immigrants came. As northwestern and central European immigration steadied and even lessened in some

176

cases, the numbers arriving from southern and eastern Europe rose tremendously. This shift came in the 1880's and 1890's, when fewer Irish, English, Scandinavian, Swiss, and German citizens came to America, and more and more Russian, Italian, Austro-Hungarian, and Balkan peoples sought American shores. This mis-named "new immigration," the term cannoting a less cultured, less skilled, and less permanent group of people than those who came earlier--judgments which have been proved to be very questionable validity--reached flood proportions in the decade 1900-10, when 70 percent or more of all immigrants came from these southern and eastern European regions to take their places in the factories, mines, and cities of the expanding American industrial scene.

Much of the impetus for this surge of twenty-five million people out of their homelands came from the tremendous rise in population taking place in the Western world as a result of better nutrition and health care brought about by both the Industrial and Agricultural Revolutions. Italy, for example, experienced a natural population increase in the early 19th century of approximatly three persons per thousand population. Yet in the 1870's, the figure had jumped to six persons born per thousand population; and by the 1880's it had almost doubled to eleven births per thousand persons. At the same time, the death rate was dropping. Italy in the forty years from 1875 to 1915 saw the death rate decline from thirty persons per thousand to less than twenty per thousand. This combination of an increase in the birth rate and a decrease in the death rate resulted in a population expansion that severely strained the peninsula's ability to maintain itself on its limited natural resources.

Poland went through a similar birth-rate increase and death-rate decline during the same period with similar results. Between 1850 and 1870, the population of Poland rose by one million persons. But in the next two decades between 1870 and 1890, it rose by two million-plus; and between 1890 and 1910, it rose another three-and-a-half million. With some variations in detail, the same was happening all over Europe, and this, combined with other factors, was a major reason for the great exodus from the Continent.

The agrarian and economic revolutions, bringing with them the collapse of the old agrarian order and the rise of factories clustered in cities, had been the distinctive features of northern and western European life in the earlier decades of the 19th century; the same dual revolution now began to work its way into southern and eastern Europe. Peasants found themselves being driven inexorably toward the status of propertyless day-laborers as their peasant agricultural ties with sufficient and beneficent land-holdings became tenuous. The peasants of Austria-Hungary found themselves subdividing their meager land holdings among an increasing number of families until they approached the point of not being able to sustain adequately the persons and families working them and dependent on them for food. At the same time, these peasants were faced with rising protective tariffs on agricultural goods, which cut them off from their former markets. Not because they understood these economic forces encroaching upon them, but because they sensed that their future could not be improved on land-holdings dimin-

ishing in size and bringing forth crops of less value, the Czechs, Bohemians, Poles, Galicians, Slovaks, Magyars, Croats, Serbs, and Slovenes
of the troubled Empire began to look outside their beloved valleys for
a future promising some security.

Italy also saw excessive subdividion of the land in the face of
population growth, but the Italians' problem was compounded by a continuance of their unscientific farming methods, which brought forth no
higher yields for their efforts. The fate of the Italian peasant was
further directly endangered because of a loss in the export market for
citrus fruits because Florida and California were developing these
crops and thus lessening America's dependence on foreign imports. Italy
also saw France raise its tariffs on wine to protect the French wine
industry and thus decrease the market for the Italian variety. In
Greece, the French protective tariff imposed on currants collapsed the
industry there and led many Greek farmers to look elsewhere as their
economy went into decline.

On the fringes of the great Russian Empire, political policy played a major role in expelling the non-Russian peoples from their homelands. After the assassination of Czar Alexander II in 1881, the
Russian state moved to a determined offensive against subversion by
forcing all peoples within the polyglot empire into the Russian mold.
This became a strident campaign for "Russification." Among the first
to feel discrimination were the Russo-German Mennonites from the Volga
River and Black Sea areas, invited into Russia during the reign of
Catherine the Great a century before, who now found themselves under
severe restrictions.

More gruesome was the campaign carried out in the Empire against
the Jews, who were not only denied free participation in the state, but
also were refused access to education, the professions, and land ownership, and were forced to live within struct geographic limitations
known as the Pales of Settlement. This tactic gave way to terror campaigns against them called pogroms. Under this pressure, thousands of
Jews left their native land for political and religious freedom in the
West, particularly in the United States. Other various Russian peoples
on the Russian borderlands, while never suffering such persecution as
experienced by the Jews, moved out under the campaign of Russification,
many eventually to settle in America.

Turkish oppression of the Slavic Christians in European Turkey west
of the Straits for political and economic reasons also led to mass migrations of these people, already bowed low by poverty, in the late 19th
and the early 20th century. This exodus from the Balkans was aided by
the defeat of Turkey in the Russo-Turkish War of 1877, which led to a
breakdown in the severely restrictive legislation imposed by the Porte,
because many areas of the Balkans achieved political independence in
the Treaty of San Stefano and at the Congress of Berlin that followed.
A clear breakdown in prohibitory regulations was a factor in other
southern and eastern migratory movements. Regulations against emigration in the Italian states became a thing of the past with the attain-
ment of Italian unification in 1867. The 1867 political settlement in

Austria-Hungary known as the Ausgleich led to the same freedom to emigrate, as well as to greater Slavic dissatisfaction with their status within the Empire, as the German-speaking Austrians were given dominance in Austria and the Magyars, or Hungarians, came to rule as master people in the Hungarian section of the Dual Monarchy.

With the added factor of the popularity of liberal free trade ideas permeating governmental policies (albeit protected by tariffs where necessary for national interests), governmental regulations of emigration were first modified, then gradually repealed or ignored. "Free trade in labor" became as accepted a doctrine as free trade in goods, because it allowed a shift in manpower to areas where resources had to be developed; and emigration out and immigration in were understood and even encouraged until the 20th century, when national ambitions for greatness saw these liberal ideas curbed in favor of more restrictive policies.

Added to agricultural distress and to this change in attitude on the part of the European governments was continued industrial distress in northern and western Europe. Germany in the early 1880's fell into depression, and coal miners, iron and steel workers, and textile workers sought a way out of their economic helplessness. The same was true in Britain as textile and woolen workers, as well as coal miners and iron puddlers, abandoned their industrial disabilities and set out for the New World as others had done before them. Workers from other northwestern European countries did the same; they were joined by thousands of agricultural workers as distress in the farming segment of the economy persisted, as it had in the earlier decades of the 19th century.

Thus in the brief period 1901 to 1910, more than 8.1 million emigrants came to America from Europe, the largest influx in the whole immigration history of the United States. They included 2.1 million Austro-Hungarians, 2 million Italians, 1.6 million Russians, 388,000 Englishmen, 341,000 Germans, 339,000 Irishmen, 249,000 Swedes, 190,000 Norwegians, 167,000 Greeks, 120,000 Scots, 80,000 persons from European Turkey, and 53,000 Rumanians. By 1915 more than thirty million immigrants had entered the country in only one century. In the later years, steam passage of the Atlantic made it all possible.

PASSAGE BY STEAM. A major factor in the surge of twenty-five million people across the North Atlantic in the fifty-five year period after 1860 came from the improvements in transportation, for it was in these decades that steam conquered the Atlantic. To the immigrants, the result was that the crossing presented almost no serious hazards, despite the fact that during the period 1840-90 some 120 steamers were lost on the Atlantic. The mortality figure dropped to almost nothing as hundreds of ships criss-crossed the ocean on thousands of voyages. The new steamship lines, too, by altering their routes and further catering to the passenger trade for the first time, made it possible for most Europeans to sail from their homelands directly to America. Steamships also made seasonal migration possible, since faster and safer passages at low cost removed the ocean as a major impediment to job mobility. Above all, steam travel made the journey speedier and

179

more commodious, and by these factors alone removed the greatest hardships formerly associated with the Atlantic voyage.

As the steam passenger vessels gradually replaced the sailors in the years 1850 to 1870, the ships became larger and more comfortable. Although first- and second-class passengers received the best of service and comforts on the journeys, immigrants were no longer a sideline in any sense of the word, and the passenger lines competed for their favor. At the same time, the control of passenger traffic and of the immigrant trade passed to larger lines better able to handle the hordes of immigrants. Such famous European steamship lines as Cunard, Hamburg-American, North German, Holland-American, Red Star, Compagnie Générale Transatlantique (C.G.T., or the "French Line"), White Star, and Inman came to dominate the lucrative trade.

These companies not only avidly competed with one another through local agents scattered throughout Europe for the convenience of the department citizens, and throughout America to expedite the sale of pre-paid tickets and the transfer of funds for relatives and friends about to make the journey, but also took pains to give aid and direction to the immigrants during their voyage from their old lands to their new. The British lines, for example, organized the North Sea crossings from Scandinavia to the point of having company personnel meet the emigrants and arrange their passage to Liverpool, there to begin their trip across the Atlantic. Similarly, the Hamburg-American Line met Scandinavian passengers at Lubeck in order to aid them in meeting their trans-Atlantic connections. The Compagnie Générale Transatlantique arranged special trains from the Italian border to Le Havre for the emigrants from that country. Some of the lines also obtained control of lodging houses for the emigrants' convenience and organized their transportation through every step of the journey. Cunard Lines acquired a size-able complex of houses in Liverpool, which could accommodate 2,000 persons at a time, and hired foreign-speaking staffs in order to aid their customers. Hamburg-American early in the 20th century went even further by organizing a large village as an immigrant waystation complete with every facility the travelers would need, including a church.

It was also important for the southern and eastern European emigrants late in the 19th and early in the 20th century, that both the British and German lines organized regular routes from various Mediterranean ports to America. These allowed emigrant travelers to make their journeys without the necessity of a detour to a northwestern European port. Obviously, immigration had come a long way since its days as a cheap-freight alternative to regular commercial cargo; it had become an important item of commerce in itself, and the European transportation lines were responding to its demands.

Although much was written early in the 20th century--when resistence to the "new immigration" was at its height--about the machinations of the steamship lines in advertising throughout Europe to induce an "unnatural" migration of peoples to America, it is clear that such reports hold little truth. In fact, almost all of the steamship advertising consisted of mere newspaper announcements detailing times and locations of sailings. Charges of lurid advertising would appear to be the result of xenophobic fears rather than careful analysis. The advertising used by the lines was primarily informational, not promotional.

It was also charged that the steamship lines, along with American railroad companies, scattered thousands of agents throughout the European continent in order to ensnare the real or potential emigrant into the agencies' hands. It is true that the various lines had agents throughout Europe. In 1890, for example, the five British lines had more than 3,600 agents in the British Isles, and C.G.T. was reported to have had some 11,000 agents in France and Switzerland. It was also charged that 4,000 various agents were active in the southern provinces of Italy at that time. These figures are probably accurate. However, apparently the great bulk of these agents were merely storekeepers selling tickets to emigrants and working on a commission basis. They were clearly not full-time agents scouring the countryside for customers. Furthermore, they could hardly have openly encouraged emigration, since such fostering of emigration was forbidden by almost every European government. They need hardly have done so anyway, because the evidence would indicate that the emigrants offered themselves to the agents without any prompting. Selling passage to America by pressure tactics was not necessary in view of the economic and political conditions of the time.

It is also true that by the 1890's virtually every town in America had an agent for at least one of the steamship lines to expedite the arrival of relatives and friends of the immigrants already in the country. For example, Hamburg-America had approximately 3,200 agents in America, and Red Star had 1,800. These agents were particularly important to the immigrant trade because, to a great extent, they sold pre-paid tickets, the dominant mode of transfer in the last years of the great migration. It might be noted, too, that rail agents on both sides of the Atlantic offered reduced steamship tickets too, a clear case in point of the railroads' cooperation with and final dependence on the steamships as the vital link in the lucrative immigrant network during the years of the heaviest flow of human cargo across the wide ocean.

As the lines moved to capitalize on the immigrant flow and to aid the European migrants on their journey both in Europe and in America, they also made the journey across the Atlantic more pleasant by introducing larger ships. Technology and commerce combined to the benefit of even the lowest class of Atlantic passenger. In the 1860's and 1870's, ships had grown from early steam tonnages of 2,500 registered tons to ships of double that size. The 5,000-ton giants could carry 150 to 300 first-class passengers and from 1,000 to 1,500 passengers in steerage. The days of the inhumanly cramped steerage voyage in unventilated holds without adequate food and water, to say nothing of sanitary facilities, were over. The new steerage passengers, while hardly traveling in luxury, were at least safe and comfortable during their two-week voyage to New York or to one of the other American ports. A Congressional investigation of the immigrant trade in the 1870's found no serious abuses. Iron hulls instead of wood, and screw propellers instead of the old sidepaddles, worked basic changes in the Atlantic trades; and even the lowest-class passengers benefitted from the changes.

By the 1880's the average speeds for passenger vessels on the westward voyage--going "uphill all the way" having lost its meaning with
the death of sail--were averaging fifteen knots; and with twin screws,
two-deck superstructures, and 12,000 to 15,000 registered ton vessels
being introduced in the 1890's, the Atlantic lost its terror as technology bested its mass, currents, and winds. But even these advances
soon appeared to be elementary because the early part of the 20th
century saw ships of up to 30,000 or 40,000 tons introduced on the
Atlantic trading routes. These giant vessels, sometimes 800 feet or
more in length, could cruise at up to twenty-five knots, had three or
four screw propellers, and could carry up to 3,000 passengers in steerage.

Maritime architecture was reaching larger sizes and improved safety standards such as were never dreamed of scant decades before, and
was dwarfing the efforts of the steam pioneers of the 1820's and 1830's;
such vessels as the pioneer Great Western became pleasant if not forgotten memories of the infantile stage of the Atlantic passage by steam.
The giant passenger vessels exceeding 30,000 tons, with their smaller
companions in the 10,000-to-20,000-ton range, now crossed the waters
from northwest Europe to America in ten days, and from the Adriatic to
America in only twenty-one days. The crossings by sail in danger and
squalor, lasting anywhere from one to three months, were gone; and the
mortality rate on the North Atlantic run had dropped to an infinitesi-
mal .05 percent. The Atlantic passenger trade, now the mainstay of the
revenues of the European-owned North Atlantic lines, determined the
routing of the vessels and, at the same time, made it possible for the
late 19th and early 20th centuries to move back across the waters to
Europe, too, in response to economic demands or to the longings of the
heart for the Old Country. Still, the great majority of the immigrants
went to America and stayed, there to build their lives anew in more
economic, political, and social freedom than could be found in the
homes of their childhood. As they did, they helped transform America
during its century of growth and change.

IMPACT ON AMERICAN DEVELOPMENT. The inflow of these thirty million
immigrants into the United States in the century after 1815 brought
forth distinct blemishes on the history of the American people, blemishes caused for the most part not by the immigrants but by the reactions of those already in America--many of them former immigrants or
children of immigrants themselves--to those newcomers seeking its
shores. In the pre-Civil War era, America experienced two waves of
nativist hostility to the foreigners in the land.

In the 1830's an anti-foreign enmity swept the land, directly in
particular at the growth of Roman Catholicism in the predominantly
Protestant land. The large multitude of immigrants from Ireland had
clung tenaciously to their faith in the New World, and their numbers,
augmented by a considerable number of Catholic immigrants from Germany,
quite naturally led to the growth of more dioceses and clergy in the

United States. The growing presence of the "foreign" religion in the land seemed a threat to American institutions, and the nation witnessed and thrilled to the cries of Rev. Lyman Beecher in his A Plan for the West (1835) that the Pope and the Holy Alliance were engaged in a diabolical plot to send Catholic immigrants to America, and particularly to the Mississippi Valley, to capture that rich territory for Catholicism and to set up a separate Catholic kingdom in America's midst.

The Rev. Mr. Beecher's warnings, however, were no match in titillation and sensation to Maria Monk's Awful Disclosures of the Hôtel Dieu Nunnery of Montreal (1836), in which the "escaped nun" revealed the sensational sexual practices to be found within that nunnery and, by inference, behind the closed doors and high walls of the rectories and convents of Catholicisms's celibate religious leaders. The fact that it was rather early and easily proved that Maria Monk was demented, and that the disclosures were the product of the mind of a Catholic-hating supporter of the woman, did little to dampen the ardor with which the anti-Catholic natives clung to their belief in her story.

The 1850's saw the spread of the Know-Nothing party in America. This super-patriotic society reached its peak in 1855 with the slogan "America for the Americans." It included in its platform the barring of pauper and criminal immigrants, extending the residency requirements for aliens before being granted citizenship to twenty-one years, and restricting the privilege of officeholding in the United States to native-born citizens alone. Yet it would appear that the Know-Nothing movement was less an attack on immigrants as such than an attempt to reaffirm American institutions and act as a political refuge and core of national unity in the tumultuous times amidst the tremendous dislocations set off by the passage of the Kansas-Nebraska Act a year earlier. Whatever the reasons, the immigrants of the 1850's were made to bear the brunt of the nativists' attacks until unity was reaffirmed by the Civil War and the "foreigners" proved their loyalty by fighting for the Union cause.

Early post-Civil War nativism was directly mainly at Chinese immigrants, brought into the country to work on the trans-continental railroads. This anti-Chinese agitation finally resulted in outright exclusion in 1882, after the 300,000 Oriental immigrants to the West Coast served as the target of violent outbreaks against them led by Denis Kearney, an Irish-born agitator, in the San Francisco Sandlot Riots of July 1877. Yet the bulk of the nativist sentiment in the late 19th century was directed against the swelling tide of European immigrants, especially against the newer immigrants from southern and eastern Europe, who seemed more "foreign" and "unable to assimilate."

Nativism became particularly strong in the aftermath of the Haymarket Riot in Chicago in 1886. Haymarket, mistakenly seen as the work of foreign anarchists, was followed by a national wave of hysteria against foreign agitators. It was during the 1880's that Americans first began to regard immigration not as a means of national success, but perhaps as a national problem. Although this may be seen as a sign of the immigrants' success and numbers in one sense, the anti-immigrant sentiment of those decades would appear to be more an indication of industrial strife and economic depression combined with a desire for social reform. These forces made Americans aware of the class cleavages that did in fact exist among them and propelled them away from their earlier, perhaps naive, view of the rapidity and ease of assimilation. Put another way, the American dream of an all-enfolding unity and success began to be re-examined for its validity, and apparent trouble spots were identified for correction. America for the first time discovered "lumps in the melting pot."

Whatever the reasons for the anti-immigrant sentiments that came out of the 19th century, whether the causes were to be found in social dislocation, a challenge to Protestant domination, the closing of the frontier, or industrial violence, during the post-World War I era America finally closed its doors to the mass of Europeans seeking entrance. The Quota Law of 1921, which was intended to curb further incursions of southern and eastern Europeans in particular, was followed by the Quota Law of 1924, which discriminated against them even further by allowing only 165,000 immigrants to come to America each year. After four decades of gradually-building agitation against the continued flow of aliens into the country, the United States for all practical purposes ended its "open door policy" toward immigrants in 1924. An era had ended. Emma Lazarus' stirring words engraved on the pedestal of the Statue of Liberty, "Give me your tired, your poor, your huddled masses yearning to breathe free . . ." became a proud boast and an enshrined memory without much substance to 20th-century America.

Difficult as it may be to argue statistically or with great precision because of the paucity of data available, and because immigrants, like most Americans, never recorded their successes and failures for posterity to examine in great detail, there is no question that the thirty million immigrants, the largest percentage of them crossing the Atlantic from Europe, made tremendous contributions to the building of America in its most productive century. They helped transform it from an agricultural frontier, a neophyte in the affairs of nations, into the richest agricultural-industrial country in the world. The immigrants provided much of the labor for the construction of the transportation networks of canals and railroads, which transformed the country and led to accelerated economic growth. The immigrants in increasing numbers manned the factories and worked the mines of America. Throughout the century, more than half of the immigrants who entered the United States reported they had "no occupation," and by far the greatest number were between the ages of sixteen and forty-four, their years of greatest productivity. This largely unskilled yet productive base, combined with capital available from domestic and foreign sources, provided the bone and sinew of the emerging industrial works throughout the northeastern sections of the country.

At the same time, the thirty million immigrants and their offspring were not only producers but also consumers. Immigrants and the children of immigrants bought goods and services, as did their native counterparts, and thus helped produce an even larger demand for foods, manufactured items, transportation and educational facilities, and other services. This, in turn, provided even more dynamism to an economy based as much on population growth as on the exploitation of natural resources and on the increase in world markets.

While most of the immigrants remained in the cities of the East because of the demands there for low-paid, unskilled factory labor, large numbers moved into the interior to develop the inland heartland. In the pre-Civil War era, they journeyed to Ohio and to the Great Lakes region by means of the Hudson River and the Erie Canal, by the Pennsylvania Main Line Canal, up the Mississippi River from New Orleans by steamboat, and in the 1850's by rail too. In the post-Civil War decades, they went almost exclusively by railroad, sometimes by special cheap cars provided for them by the railroads, and even by whole train-loads if demand required. They went in response to the railroads' advertising, and also because of the encouragement and help given them by the Western states' immigration bureaus, set up to encourage their settlement. The states, too, had advertising, pamphlets, and special agents, and, working hand-in-glove with the land-grant railroads in the 1870's and 1880's in their campaigns to sell their granted land for cash and customer development, created compact, homogeneous settlements of immigrants of like nationality throughout the Midwest and on the western plains.

Those immigrants who did not enter the American agricultural scene by direct means and by direct inducement, entered nevertheless in less spectacular ways. Often families came one by one across the ocean, and then frequently moved piecemeal into agriculture, with a factory or min-ing job serving only as a temporary way station on the journey to a farm. Members of a family stayed behind in industry to earn more money, as first one and then another member settled on the land, usually dis-placing a native pioneer farmer moving on to untapped land resources farther west. In the 1820's and 1830's, the immigrant farmers moved into New York, Pennsylvania, and Ohio. In the 1840's, they followed the departing pioneer into Missouri, Illinois, and Wisconsin. The 1850's and 1860's saw them take up the land being abandoned in eastern Iowa and Minnesota, and the decade of the 1870's felt their presence on the far prairies. But whether the immigrant farmers came by wagon, canal boat, or rail, and whether they came as part of an organized ef-fort or as enterprising individuals seeking something better for them-selves and their families, they became part of an agricultural system so expansive that it could form the economic base for the industriali-zation of the nation and still have enough excess products to make the United States one of the more important grain- and food-exporting nations of the world.

In industry, in agriculture, in construction, and later on in the professions and the arts, the immigrants and their sons and daughters make their mark. Between 1820 and 1950, 39.3 million immigrants enter-ed the United States. More than 33.2 million of them came from Europe, with only 3.1 million emigrating from Canada and the British North American colonies. Only a trifling few came from Mexico. Almost none came by air until after World War II. Thus the overwhelming majority of immigrants to America reached their new land from the European continent by water. The Atlantic transportational network, first responding to the immigrant tide as a supplement to its commercial trade and then beginning to specialize in that trade, made it possible for these millions of people to make their way to a new life. The convenient bridging of the Atlantic by ships of greater size and efficiency made the process of immigration possible. European economic, political, and social conditions may have provided the impetus to these thirty million people to leave, and the American industrial, agricultural, and transportational systems may have provided the final means of distribution and achievement once they arrived, but the Atlantic maritime system, increasingly dominated by European vessels, provided the crucial and indispensable transportational link between the aspirations and dreams of the Old World and the accomplishments of the New.

SUGGESTIONS FOR FURTHER READING

Bowen, Frank C. A Century of Atlantic Travel, 1830-1930. Boston: Little, Brown, and Company, 1930.

Coleman, Terry. Passage to America: A History of Emigrants from Great Britain and Ireland to America in the Mid-Nineteenth Century. London: Hutchinson & Co., 1972.

Guillet, Edwin C. The Great Migration: The Atlantic Crossing by Sailing Ship since 1770. 2nd ed. Toronto: University of Toronto Press, 1963.

Handlin, Oscar, ed. Immigration as a Factor in American History. Englewood Cliffs, N.J.: Prentice-Hall, Inc., 1959.

Hansen, Marcus Lee. The Immigrant in American History. Edited by Arthur M. Schlesinger. Cambridge: Harvard University Press, 1942.

_____. The Atlantic Migration, 1607-1860: A History of the Continuing Settlement of the United States. Edited by Arthur M. Schlesinger. Cambridge: Harvard University Press, 1940.

Jones, Maldwyn A. American Immigration. Chicago History of American Civilization Series. Chicago: University of Chicago Press, 1960.

Tylor, Philip. The Distant Magnet: European Emigration to the U.S.A. New York: Harper & Row, Publishers, 1972.

Tute, Warren. Atlantic Conquest: The Ships and the Men of the North Atlantic Passenger Services, 1816-1961. London: Cassell & Co., Ltd., 1962.

Walker, Mack. Germany and the Emigration, 1816-1885. Harvard Historical Monographs, Vol. LVI. Cambridge: Harvard University Press, 1964.

Ward, David. Cities and Immigrants: A Geography of Change in Nineteenth-Century America. New York: Oxford University Press, 1971.

CHAPTER X. MARITIME DECLINE IN THE LATE NINETEENTH CENTURY

During the first half of the 19th century, the American merchant
marine had grown so substantially that by the 1850's it has become a
major asset and symbol of pride for the young nation. American ships
dominated the country's import and export trade. They challenged Britain for the maritime crown of the world. Wherever ships sailed the
seas, there was the American flag and the American challenge. The soaring masts and billowing canvas of the swift clipper ships had become
particular symbols of American determination, craftsmanship, and genius
in the eyes of its people.

Even though few Americans probably knew--or were interested in--
such statistics as were available in government reports, most were aware
of the obvious: America was becoming the new Queen of the Seas. That
Great Britain and the other major maritime nations had a major competitor was clear. Such instinctive knowledge had a solid basis in fact.
In 1855 approximately two-thirds of all the net tonnage entering and
leaving the country's ports was carried in American bottoms, leaving
foreign shippers only one-third. If measured by the value of foreign
commerce rather than by the tonnage capacity of the vessels, the figures were even higher--more than 75 percent.

The irrefutable testimony of the cold statistics reinforced the
more colorful evidence of forests of tall masts in every seaport, large
and small, along the American coasts, tangible signs of American maritime greatness. American foreign trade was strong and vigorous; its
coastal trade, closed by law to foreigners since the earliest days of
the Republic, was even stronger. Statistics of the coastal trade showed 2.5 million tons of shipping vessels registered, slightly more than
that found in foreign commerce. These coasters moved the freight of
the nation up and down the Atlantic coast with its dozens of major harbors and uncounted hundreds of minor ones, around the Florida peninsula
to and from the Gulf ports, around Cape Horn into Pacific waters, and
up and down the Western shores. America had every right to be proud
and confident when it came to both its foreign and coastal merchant
marine in the 1850's.

EVIDENCE OF WEAKNESS. Yet perceptive observers could not have
failed to notice clear signs of trouble on the horizon, signs of maritime decline in the foreign maritime trade, which increasingly showed
that American maritime prominence was perhaps illusory and that degen-
eration might in fact be setting in. Within two generations the American foreign merchant marine slipped to second-rate status, and the
nation found itself early in the 20th century at the mercy of foreign
shippers and unable to care for its own needs.

189

An astute observer would have noted in 1855 that the United States had slipped 5 percent in net foreign tonnage entered in American vessels and 4 percent in tonnage cleared since 1845, and that both of these figures actually represented a brief resurgence from a general decline that had set in during the early years of the decade. He would have perceived that the 75 percent of commerce carried by value was actually down about 6 percent from a decade before. If he had compared the number, tonnage, and types of ships built by foreign countries from 1845 to 1855, especially by Great Britain, he would have noted not only that foreign merchant powers were building more vessels, but also that they were steadily switching over to iron and steam. The American foreign merchant fleet was growing absolutely, but was it growing relatively? The clear answer was "no." These and many other indicators would have told him that the American oceangoing merchant fleet was possibly in trouble. Future events would show that what he suspected and feared would become reality.

By 1914 the United States had only about half the number of ships engaged in foreign trade as it had had in 1855. But more important, since the mere number of ships does not reflect their possibly larger size and increased tonnage, it must be added that by 1914, American gross tonnage had declined from almost 6 million tons to only a little more than 3 million tons. Furthermore, by 1914 American merchant vessels carried only 26 percent of total tonnage entering and 26 percent of total tonnage clearing the nation's ports. Foreign vessels had captured almost 75 percent of the tonnage capacity in and out of the country.

But was an overall decline in foreign commerce the reason for the decline in the merchant marine? Most assuredly not. The total value in dollars of foreign commerce in 1855 was almost $477 million, up from almost $220 million only ten years before. By 1914 the figure stood at $3.75 billion, an increase of 794 percent. American high seas merchant tonnage had been halved while its foreign trade had multiplied eight times over in a fifty-year period. The additional startling fact that only 9.7 percent of all foreign trade by value being carried in American vessels on the eve of World War I stood as undeniable testimony that the nation had abandoned the sea lanes of the world.

All economic indicators show that the United States in the fifty years after the Civil War went through tremendous expansion in almost all areas of its economic life. The statistics of productivity, personal and corporate income, capital investment, industrial and transportation expansion, and domestic and foreign commerce--indeed, virtually all measurements of wealth and expansion--showed strong upward tendencies. America went from being a predominantly agricultural nation to being one of the leading industrial nations of the world in the five decades after the Civil War. But its oceangoing merchant marine went into precipitous decline. Why did it happen? Who, or what, was to blame? The answers to these questions, vital to national security and economic growth, as well as to those directly involved in the sea trades, are difficult to trace and often more difficult to prove conclusively. Yet reasons must be sought if we are to understand not only the maritime weakness of the nation on the eve of World War I--and since--but also because they might well reveal answers to the perennial questioning as to why and how nations fall into economic and political vulnerability.

BRITISH ADVANTAGES IN THE PRE-CIVIL WAR ERA. As long as wooden sailing vessels were predominant on the trade routes of the world, the United States had a distinct advantage. One sees this in its preeminence in the English shipbuilding industry during colonial days and, after independence, in its rapid rise to prominence on the ocean highways in its challenge to Britain's merchant marine. But when advancements in technology pointed to the building of iron hulls and using steam for propulsion, the United States lost the upper hand. In the building of such ships in the two decades prior to the Civil War, Britain had many clear advantages and capitalized on them. As far as ocean-going vessels were concerned, Britain was more advanced in iron engineering and in the application of steam as a propellent, having been building effective steamers since the early decades of the century. Furthermore, Britain could supply its shipbuilders with iron more cheaply than could American suppliers because of the nearness of its mines and mills to its shipways. This factor, coupled with advanced steam engineering, meant that Britain could build metal steam vessels more cheaply than could Americans. American shipowners, governed by the law of 1789, could not buy ships from foreign countries and, therefore, lost the ability to purchase British technology in the form of more advanced vessels to thus make up for local deficiencies.

Great Britain, beginning an era of industrial dominance after the Napoleonic wars which extended throughout the 19th century, was gradually moving away from a protectionist-mercantilist economic policy to a free trade policy whereby it would use its domestic capital and labor primarily for manufactures and rely on other countries for foodstuffs and for markets for its manufactured goods. This policy, which eventually emerged victorious with the repeal of the Corn Laws in 1846, necessitated giving aid to its merchant marine to facilitate the importation and exportation of goods to and from the island kingdom.

Therefore, in the 1830's the British government made the crucial decision that it was in the national interest to subsidize British steamship lines from the public treasury, where such help was needed both to aid the shipbuilding industry and the nation at large and to ensure rapid and dependable communication with all areas of the Empire. It was England's belief that the maritime industry needed developmental aid on those shipping lanes where British commercial and military interests benefitted. Thus a contract ocean-communications system under the direction of the government was created, and aid was given where it was deemed necessary. The aid policy was designed not to rival other nations as a matter of national prestige, but to give substantial benefits to the national economy and to the merchant marine on a pragmatic basis.

The British government began its policy of granting subsidies through mail contracts with its agreement with the Peninsula and Oriental Steam Navigation Company in 1837. For an annual subsidy of $144,000, the company was to give weekly mail service to the Iberian Peninsula as far down as Gibraltar. Three years later the company was authorized to extend its service to Alexandria for $184,000, and in 1842 it began a line between Suez, Ceylon, Madras, and Calcutta. This line was later extended to Singapore and Hong Kong. Early in the 1850's, the company added services from Suez to Bombay and then to Australia. The Peninsular and Oriental Company, operating with adequate subsidies over routes where there was little competition and where service could not be profitably extended for passenger and freight revenues only, proved that good results could be obtained and that such a line could be run economically.

The British subsidized also the Royal Mail Steam Packet Company beginning in 1840 in the amount of $1,168,000 a year for mail service to the West Indies. In 1852 the line was extended to Brazil, and the subsidy was raised to $1,314,000 per year. The British subsidized also the Pacific Steam Navigation Company beginning in 1840 to serve the west coast of South America from Panama to Valparaiso, Chile. These packet lines, like the Peninsular and Oriental Company service, gained for the country better speed and transit of the mails, improved communication within the Empire, and steamship operations in areas where steamship lines could not have arisen without aid. Furthermore, they did not adversely affect established shipping in the areas they served. British steamship and mail subsidy aid to these three lines was well thought out and effective.

The same could be said for British maritime subsidies across the North Atlantic. After early and unsatisfactory experiments with the Great Western Railway Company, the British and American Steam Navigation Company, and the Transatlantic Steamship Company, ventures that held no great hope of long-range success, the government signed a contract with Samuel Cunard of Halifax for bi-monthly service to Halifax and Boston for a sum of $292,000 a year. The contract was to run for seven years. The Cunard Line furnished four large paddlewheel steamships and began its service in 1840. The line was very successful, and to encourage it further the government raised the subsidy in 1848 to $705,600 a year. Thus the number of voyages was raised to meet freight and passenger demands. By 1489-50, the British government was subsidizing the four steamship companies on their respective world routes in the amount of $3,696,905 and was enjoying improved communication, distinct trade advantages, and military aid from use of the steamships in wartime--as would prove to be the case during the Crimean War.

PRE-WAR SUBSIDY FAILURES. Faced with British steamship competition, particularly in the North Atlantic, the United States government was forced to react to the challenge. Essentially it could have responded in one of four ways. It could simply have adopted a hands-off policy and allowed the British their dominance, thereby reaping the benefits of faster and more regular service for American passengers, mail, and freight (whatever the effects might have been on American shipping over the North Atlantic). Or it could have discriminated against the British steamers by imposing higher duties upon them (a move that would have denied the country the benefits of better service and wrecked existing reciprocity agreements). As a third possibility, it could have supple-

mented the established British steamship routes by complementing them
with routes not yet established but still important to its own economic
well-being (a plan that would not have been too expensive and would
have enabled the United States to extend its services over areas that
would have been profitable without competing with British services unnecessarily). Finally, it could have attempted to rival the British
subsidies with countervailing subsidies of its own (a tactic that would
attempt to build American lines and check British advances).

Unfortunately, the government chose the last course of action in
most cases and thus incurred large expense and small success in trying
to establish American lines of oceangoing steamships in the very teeth
of well-established British competition. In adopting this policy, the
United States government also overlooked the fundamental economic fact
that competition in steamships across the North Atlantic would force
freight and passenger rates down by the law of supply and demand, and
thus either additional subsidies or economic losses would be inevitable.
American failure in the subsidy race with Great Britain was not long in
coming.

In 1846 Congress accepted a contract with the Ocean Steam Navigation Company to send four steamers semimonthly from New York, alternate-
ly to Bremen in Germany and Le Havre in France, for a subsidy of
$450,000 per year. The voyages began in 1848, and the contract was re-
newed in 1852. But with American ships costing more to build and
operate, and with these American ships being too slow to compete with
the vessels of other countries for the European mail business, Ocean
Steam Navigation never attained a competitive position and soon languished.

A second, bolder attempt to compete on the North Atlantic came
about in 1847, when the New York and Liverpool Mail Steamship Company
was granted an annual subsidy of $385,000 for ten years to carry the
mail from New York to Liverpool on a schedule of twenty round trips a
year. This run was in obvious direct competition with the Cunard Line.
The founder of the line, Edward K. Collins, had extensive experience in
trans-Atlantic shipping as the founder of the Dramatic Line of sailing
packets and was sure his "Collins Line," as it came to be called, would
suceed. However, Collins underestimated the cost of construction and
needed a $385,000 loan from Congress to get his initial vessels in
operation. The first four vessels, all of over 3,000 gross tons, wooden-
hulled, and very heavy and extravagant, were probably uneconomical by
any standard. They also went beyond the demands of the contracts and
were far more expensive than British-built vessels. Each cost about
$735,000 instead of the estimated $400,000.

When Collins' vessels began the trans-Atlantic service in 1850 in
direct competition with the Cunarders, the first result was that passenger and freight rates dropped to one-half their previous levels, thus
depriving Collins (and Cunard) of valuable revenues. Collins' first
forty-one voyages lost an average of $16,929 per voyage despite the sub-
sidy of $19,250 for each trip. Faced with this desperate situation,
Congress raised the Collins subsidy to $858,000 a year, and the British

pushed up the Cunard subsidy to $843,600 a year. Still the advantage was undoubtedly with the smaller and more economical Cunard steamships.

Then in 1854 the uncompartmented wooden Collins side-wheeler Arctic collided with the small French iron steamer Vesta, equipped with watertight bulkheads, off the coast of Newfoundland and foundered, taking with it to its watery grave more than 300 persons. It was the worst ocean tragedy in the Western world until the loss of the Titanic in 1912 and, unfortunately, was marked by cowardice and panic on the part of the crew of the Arctic. In 1856, Collins' Pacific simply disappeared in the North Atlantic while steaming from Liverpool to New York. These tragedies occurred just as Congress was having second thoughts about competition with the Cunarders through the Collins Line. In 1855 Congress had already dropped the Collins subsidy back to its original figure, and in 1858, deep in the Panic of 1857 and representing a nation being torn apart by the all-consuming crises of slavery and possible civil war, Congress cancelled all mail subsidies.

The failure of the Ocean Steam Navigation Company and the Collins Line, however, did not mean that all subsidized American lines, or even the principle of subsidization, was necessarily a failure, although Congress may have interpreted it that way. In 1847 the United States Mail Steamship Company was organized to carry the mails from New York via Southern ports and Havana to Panama for a subsidy of $290,000 a year. Although there were numerous problems with the company because of its not providing the ships and services as stipulated in its contract with the government, United States Mail was moderately successful until its demise in 1859. Its success, of course, was aided by the fact that the California gold rush placed heavy demands on it and provided paying customers and freight at a critical time in its history. It was aided, too, by the fact that it was not trying to compete directly with an existing subsidized company.

The most successful American subsidized line was the Pacific Mail Steamship Company, or "Aspinwall Line," named for its principal founder, William H. Aspinwall of New York. Its contract for $199,000 per year called for it to maintain service from Panama up the western coast of the United States to Astoria in Oregon. The company was very successful in supplying the western end of the gold-rush traffic with rapid and dependable transportation. It increased its service in 1851, armed with the higher subsidy of $348,250 a year. The line operated profitably and with regularity.

By these two subsidies, the United States gained regular high-speed service for mail, passengers, and freight to its new areas on the Pacific. Passengers deserted the proud clipper ships with their 100-to-150-day trips around the Cape for the 21-to-30-day service via Panama furnished by the United States Mail and Pacific Mail companies. The companies also enjoyed success because they were not in competition with subsidized foreign steamers and enjoyed practically a monopoly position along their routes, the exact conditions that made the British companies so successful. The cancelling of the mail subsidies in 1859 did not end the Pacific Mail Line; it steamed successfully into the later decades

of the 19th century on its own. The United States Mail Line fell to
domestic competition engendered by its earlier success.

Yet despite the success of the Pacific-bound lines, subsidies were
abandoned by Congress in the late 1850's. Congress may have been chiefly at fault for not having a long-range view of what it was trying to
accomplish and where and how it should be done. It was surely negli-
gent in not demanding economy and service as planned. Congress may also have been short-sighted by demanding that all mail steamers be convertible to warships of similar class. This requirement increased the
cost of construction and cut down on passenger and freight space. Congress may have been unwise in allowing subsidies to vessels operating
on sea lanes where they could not possibly have competed. It may also
have been overly influenced by the failure of the Collins Line. But
wherever the fault lay, in Congressional confusion, in Collins' extra-
vagance, or in the attempt to compete where competition was ruinous,
the overriding reality was that, by 1859, the total outlay of tax
monies to the subsidized routes had amounted to $14 million and revenues
had repaid only about 50 percent of this cost. Congress and the general
public were ready and willing to write off the whole experiment as a
bad mistake.

Consequently, at the most critical time of its development, ocean
steamship service--the obvious future course of the ocean merchant
marine--was denied the help it needed. In addition, the mail subsidy
experience of the 1840's and 1850's cast a long shadow over other attempts to aid the merchant marine in the decades to come. Much argument
would have to be marshalled before the United States would again decide
that ocean navigation companies, like the railroads, were more than
simply ordinary economic enterprises and would need sustained government
aid to build, service, and provide their essential functions for the
good of the country as a whole. Even in the second period of subventions,
1864-77, and, four decades later, after 1891, Congressional aid was still
parsimonious and half-hearted, and the ocean merchant marine languished
until the crisis of World War I.

EFFECTS OF THE CIVIL WAR. The Civil War between 1861 and 1865,
coming on the heels of the debacle of ship subsidies, brought disastrous
results to the ocean carrying trade of the United States. In 1860 American vessels still represented more than 70 percent of tonnage capacity
of vessels entering and clearing from American ports, leaving foreign
flags about 30 percent. But by 1865, American vessel capacity entering
had declined to only 47 percent, and vessels clearing to only 45 percent.
Furthermore, by value of foreign trade in dollars, the American percentage of imports and exports fell from 66.5 percent to 27.7 percent in
the same five-year period. This constituted the greatest single freight
decline in American maritime history, a decline arrested only briefly
before resuming its downward slide to less than 10 percent by the end of
the century.

The Confederacy had virtually no navy in 1861 and was well aware of
its weakness. The Union had most of the nation's merchant ships in its
possession, which could continue to carry cargo or could be converted

into gunboats and other naval auxiliaries, as well as the capacity to
build a considerable naval force which the South could never match.
Given the North's predominance in these fields, the war on and for the
seas would be very important to the South. The Confederate leaders
recognized that the Union could continue to ship its goods to European
customers and would eventually extend a blockade around the entire
South. It therefore followed that if the Confederacy could not outbuild the Union in merchant and naval vessels, it could surely raise
the price of Union victory by destroying as much of the Northern merchant fleet as possible on the high seas. In the broadest perspective,
the South could hope to win the war only if it made the price of victory
too high for the Union. To turn, then, to the time-honored practice of
commerce raiding would, on the one hand, curb or seriously curtail the
Northern maritime advantage and, on the other hand, would not cost the
South much in the limited amounts of money or manpower that it had
available.

In this endeavor, the Confederacy was very successful, seizing and
destroying Northern merchant vessels on the sea lanes of the world. As
a result, 110,000-plus tons of Northern merchant vessels were captured
or destroyed during the course of the war by Confederate raiders. But
this Southern strategy had effects beyond the capture and destruction
of valuable tonnage. In the first place, it drove insurance rates on
American vessels to unheard-of heights. This effect, coupled with
lower freight rates on foreign vessels to begin with, meant that by the
second half of the war it cost as much as 25 percent more to ship on
American vessels than a foreign ships. Yet captured or destroyed vessels and higher costs were only part of the problem raised by the Confederate raiders.

One obvious method for American shipowners to prevent capture and
destruction or confiscation of their vessels and cargoes was to give up
flying the American flag. According to recognized international law,
a ship of one belligerent (in this case the Union or the Confederacy)
was liable to capture and destruction by the forces of the other. But
a ship flying a neutral flag had free access to the ports of either
belligerent or anywhere else. It followed, therefore, that if a Union
shipowner changed the registry of his ship from American to that of any
other country, he could ship unhindered wherever he might, safe from
confiscation or destruction by either the North or the South.

It is not surprising, then, that during the course of the war some
800,000 tons of American merchant vessels--more than 1,000 ships--were
either sold to foreigners or otherwise legally passed into foreign registry and sailed on under a foreign flag, usually British. This shift,
combined with the 110,000 tons lost to Southern raiders (one ship, the
C.S.S. Shenandoah, virtually decimated the Pacific whaling fleet), represented at least 34 percent of all American tonnage engaged in foreign
trade prior to the war, an appalling loss at a critical time. The economic benefits of one-third of the American foreign fleet thus passed
into foreign hands. These valuable ships were never to return because
of the law of 1797, which stated that if an American vessel was sold to
a foreign national or obtained a license under a foreign flag it then

could not be repatriated. The law remained in effect during the war,
and after Appomattox the victorious American Congress was in no mood
to forgive those American shipowners whose "disloyalty" to the Union
cause had been so obvious. Thus one-third of the pre-war American tonnage left American registry and was forced to remain under foreign
flags. However understandable the Congressional attitude in the immediate aftermath of the fratricidal contest might be, the result was devastating for the American merchant marine.

The Civil War also had adverse effects on the cotton trade, one of
the most important branches of American foreign commerce and one in
which it had clear and profitable dominance. On the eve of the war,
American vessels clearing New Orleans with cotton outnumbered foreign
vessels by about four to one. But the Union fleet's blockade of this
valuable Southern port reduced cotton exports from 3.5 million bales in
1859 to only 10,000 bales two years later. Thereafter, even less cotton
was shipped. The death of the cotton trade meant the abandonment or
sale of virtually the entire cotton fleet. Cotton exports did not regain their pre-war levels until 1879; when they did, there was no cotton
fleet to carry the bales. British iron screw cargo ships now dominated
the trade, aided by Canadian vessels and by American-built vessels sold
to Britain. American shippers never regained more than one-third of
this valuable segment of American foreign trade.

When these factors are considered, then, it becomes obvious that
the Civil War was the second great blow to the American oceangoing merchant marine. The Mississippi steamboat network also was decimated during the conflict. The Civil War may have resulted in the end of slavery,
the victory of centralism over states' rights, the final moment of glory
for the Old South, the triumph of Northern capitalism, and many other
events of major importance in American history. It was also a second
giant step in the decline of the oceangoing maritime fortunes of the
United States during these crucial decades.

FOREIGN ADVANTAGES AND AMERICAN DISADVANTAGES. When mail subsidies
were abandoned by Congress in 1858, the United States was left with only
seven steamers in its foreign trade, compared with 120 steamers under
British registry. England continued this lead for many reasons. One of
these was the fact that Britain had developed iron and steam technology
long before the Civil War and continued to maintain that lead in the
years thereafter. Iron vessels had first been built on a regular basis
in England in the 1830's, and the government, recognizing the advantages
of this type of vessel, had adopted a policy of indirect help. It did
so by ordering iron ships for the Royal Navy, thus giving its private
yards practical experience in the construction or iron ships, which
proved to be invaluable as time went on. Tools, machinary, and various
skills for building iron ships were necessarily acquired by British
shipbuilders. Thanks to French and Dutch inability to follow suit and
America's unwillingness to do so, British shipyards enjoyed a practical
monopoly in the building of iron steamships.

Iron ships had many advantages. For example, according to ship
disaster records they had only one-seventy the risk of sinking as did

wooden vessels because of their stronger construction. Furthermore, because of technological improvements as the decades progressed, the amount of space necessary in a vessel for machinery and coal gradually declined. The net result of more voyages by safer iron-steam vessels with more usable cargo space was that the amount of tonnage carried per seaman (or the seaman efficiency ratio) continued to climb, meaning greater profits per man-hour employed than on wooden vessels. Stated succinctly, iron ships employing ever-improving steam engines as driving power were, for good economic reasons, in the process of dominating the ocean carrying trades. British interests in particular, because of advanced technology fostered by government aid, could outbuild American shipyards and outsail American wooden vessels with comparative ease throughout the 1860's and 1870's.

But this was only part of the British advantage. One might surmise that with the increase in size and technological expertise experienced by American industries in the later decades of the 19th century, these foreign advantages in shipbuilding and ship operation might be overcome. In point of fact, they could not because of many factors that militated against attaining a competitive position in the oceangoing merchant marine, as opposed to the always-protected and reasonably secure coastal trade.

One of these factors was the continuing higher cost of building ships in American as opposed to British yards. This differential has been carefully estimated as running as high as 25 to 30 percent more for American-built ships than for British-built ships throughout the 19th century. While it is true that the number of American yards decreased significantly during the 1860's and 1870's, and thus the size and facilities of the remaining few increased to attain some economics of scale, the gains by consolidation were never sufficient to overcome the relatively high wages that prevailed in American shipyards. For example, in the early 1880's, the average skilled worker in an American yard received a wage of about $14 per week, which was necessarily comparable to the wages then prevailing in the iron, iron fabrication, and engineering industries from which most skilled shipbuilders were drawn. This wage could hardly have been lower, given the labor market. Yet $14 a week was about 44 percent higher than the rate prevailing in Scottish shipyards. Since labor costs represented between 40 and 50 percent of the total cost of a ship, it is obvious that foreign shipbuilders could maintain a substantial advantage, even though American shipbuilders tried to cut wage differentials by various labor-saving devices. But no devices of technology or of full plant utilization could overcome these wage differences.

Perhaps sufficient economies of scale could have been attained by the government intervening to organize the entire industry on a large enough scale, and by a complete rationalizing of facilities to prevent wasteful duplication of efforts between yards and, more important, duplication of the very costly equipment necessary in metal and steam shipbuilding. Only full utilization of facilities and of expensive equipment (perhaps by directed specialization of building of ship types in the various yards) could have put the United States in a competitive position. But such streamlining by state control over costs, prices, plant utilization, products, and profits was clearly unthinkable, given the free-enterprise outlook of the industry, the government, and the nation during the late 19th century. Even had such steps been taken, it is doubtful that it could have overcome such a huge price differential as 25 to 35 percent per ship.

Furthermore, even if American ships could have been built competitively, the costs of operation would still have been greater. American wages were higher, and food and crew facilities in American vessels were better and more expensive. Exact figures on the cost difference between American and British ships are impossible to obtain (one authority estimates the figure to be between 25 and 50 percent), but one shipowner calculated late in the century that it typically cost about $1,000 more per voyage to pay American wages to a crew. This amount was in addition to paying higher repair and supply bills in American ports, which amounted to about $8,000 per vessel each year.

Hearings of a Congressional committee in 1870 included testimony that the approximate cost of manning and supplying an American ship of 1,000 gross tons was between $1,100 and $1,250 a month; an English ship, between $650 and $800 a month; and a German ship, between $600 and $750 a month. In 1881, British freighters had a manning scale of one man per 51 gross tons; the American manning scale was one man per 40.25 gross tons. In 1901, wage expenditures on three comparable express trans-Atlantic steamers (one American, one British, and one German) stood at averages of $29.49 per man each month on the American vessel, $23.16 per man each month on the British vessel, and $15.43 per man each month on the German vessel. There was simply no way an American shipowner could compete with foreign operators when American shipbuilding costs were 25 to 35 percent higher and running costs of vessels stood at 25 to 50 percent higher.

Given this situation, it is no wonder that profits in foreign trade declined approximately 75 percent in the last quarter of the century. Gross capital formation in the nation rose $84 billion between 1869 and 1901, but American capital was not attracted to such a risky venture as American shipbuilding or foreign commerce. Taxes on capital goods (such as ships and shipbuilding materials) remained high, the cost of iron ships was prohibitive, running costs were high, and the government refused to give subsidies to make up the differences in the building and operation of vessels. When earnings by interest on bonds and by dividends on stock were typically running from 5 to 10 percent in rails, metals, metal fabrication, mining, clothing and textiles, and dozens of other industrial areas--to say nothing of the capital gains realized through increased value of stock in these enterprises--it is no wonder that capital was hardly attracted to such uncertain enterprises as shipbuilding and foreign commerce. Nor would it be until investors large or small could be assured somehow of a fair return on the capital.

The result of all of these cost factors was clear. Shipbuilding went into serious depression, particularly after 1878. Those Americans still engaged in foreign commerce continued to rely on the relatively cheap but very inefficient wooden square-riggers and schooners. Building of metal sailing vessels, as with steam vessels, was also more expensive in the United States than in Britain, and Britain dominated this type of shipbuilding too. Few American ships sailed the routes where steamships predominated by their greater efficiency.

The considerable amount of American capital invested in shipbuilding and foreign commerce was employed chiefly in financing and managing ships under foreign flags where reasonable profits could be expected. By 1901, small shipowners seeking lower-priced ships, large shipowners seeking to retain their business, capitalists desiring to employ their capital funds profitably, and American railroads seeking to extend their influence in foreign trade in the only way possible, had pioneered the use of "flags of convenience" through long-term charters and the establishment of foreign subsidiaries to gain ownership of 136 ships totaling 672,000 gross tons of foreign-flag shipping, an amount almost equal to the 880,000 gross tons of the American merchant marine remaining in foreign commerce.

FUTILE ATTEMPTS TO AID THE FLEET. As the total oceangoing maritime industry (with the singular exception of the coastwise trade) fell into the doldrums, those chiefly concerned began to raise their voices to protest the deteriorating situation. Shipowners, shipbuilders, manufacturers for the shipbuilding industry, exporters, and, later, naval personnel and the seamen's union began to argue before the general public and before Congress that the decline had to be reversed. They pointed to the merchant marine's importance to national defense and to the fact that increased merchant marine strength could extend foreign trade. They warned against the nation's being caught without shipping facilities in the event of a European war and the subsequent withdrawal of foreign-owned ships from the American carrying trade. They also bemoaned the loss of employment by American citizens in the shipbuilding and maritime industries. Yet while all interested parties could agree that something had to be done, they could not agree on the best course of action. Nor could the Congress and the Presidents come up with an acceptable solution, because the whole issue became caught up in the tariff question, and therefore in partisan politics.

Basically the shipowners in the post-Civil War era were originally in favor of "free ships"; that is, they desired that Americans should be able to buy their ships anywhere in the world, rather than being confined to domestic shipyards as had been mandated under the navigation law passed in 1789. They argued that subsidies either to themselves or to the shipbuilders would only result in higher costs of shipping; and since higher costs would make the nation less able to compete with foreign shipping, fewer goods would be shipped in American bottoms and the decline in merchant shipping would continue. In the main, the Democratic party, with its major sources of support in the agrarian South and West, which cared little about who carried the mails or freight, was inclined to favor the "free ships" policy--adopted by Britain in 1849--although Democrats in shipbuilding districts were an exception. To the Democrats, free ships and a repeal of the restraining navigation laws fit in nicely with their party's basic opposition to the high tariffs then in force. They were thus in the comfortable position of opposing subsidies and bounties, both favored solutions of the Republicans.

The Republicans, firmly committed to the principle of high protective tariffs since the Morrill Tariff of 1864, held to a maintenance of the navigation laws to protect the shipbuilders. If tariffs would have to be maintained--as they would be, of course, by the Republicans--and help was needed by the shipowners and shipbuilders, then bounties should be given to the builders, to the owners, or to both. This tactic would bring the party the favor of both the shipbuilders and the iron interests, so important in its inner councils. Yet the Republican party recognized that, with the public opposing favoritism to big business in any blatant manner, direct payment would be politically unpopular and that it would be ballot-box suicide to vote for such direct subsidies. The party was stymied in its search for some means of giving aid.

Thus from the Civil War until the late 1880's, with the tariff question constantly confusing the issue and the two major parties basically at odds over the question of how to aid the merchant marine--to say nothing of the parties' also being caught up in Reconstruction, political corruption, the growth of trusts, third-party sentiment, farmer agitation, and many other major issues of contention--neither party could do anything to halt the decline of the merchant marine. No positive policy could win sufficient support in the Congress or in the White House. All possible solutions perished in hopeless partisan wrangling and endless debate. In the meantime, deprived of any meaningful help, either of free ships and free trade or of subsidies, the merchant marine continued to slip toward insignificance.

Finally, after 1885, the few owners left in American trade, aware that they could not win with words and that even with cheaper foreign-built ships they could not overcome the second problem of higher running costs from wages, supplies, etc., decided to join with the shipbuilders and demand subsidies as a solution. The coastal shippers, too, seeing that repeal of the navigation laws would likely mean competition up and down the coasts from new companies equipped with foreign-built ships if such ships were admitted to the oceangoing trade (the one would be the opening wedge for the other, they feared), also decided to join the shipbuilders in a demand for subsidies as the answer to the nation's maritime problems. Thus at last the major segments of America's maritime trades came together in a concerted effort to gain aid--and perhaps survival--for the shipbuilders and ocean shippers through subsidies.

Trying to convince Congress of the wisdom of subsidies in the late 1880's was no easy task, particularly because Congress had been down that road not once, but twice, before. The mail subsidy (or subvention) attempts of 1847 to 1859 have been recounted. But notwithstanding their failure, Congress had been persuaded in 1864 to try again, this time with subsidized service to Brazil. Congress was convinced, by those persons most likely to gain, that such a subsidized line would increase trade with Brazil and all of South America, and passed a mail subsidy law calling for monthly service to that South American country. The government agreed to pay up to $150,000 per year, and Brazil agreed to pay another

201

$100,000, for the service. Only one bid was received, this from the
United States and Brazil Mail Steamship Company. The line, however,
did not prosper as had been prophesied, and the subsidy was withdrawn
in 1875.

A second interim attempt at mail subsidies ended not in economic
failure, but in political corruption. In February 1865, Congress
authorized up to $500,000 per year for monthly service to the Far East
via Hawaii. It was argued that this run would build trade with both
areas. The Pacific Mail Company, under subsidy from 1847 to 1859, was
awarded the contract and agreed to furnish twelve round-trip voyages to
China and Japan from the West Coast. Service was begun in 1867 and was
so successful, according to its patrons, that Congress was soon persuaded to vote another $500,000 to increase the service to a semi-monthly
basis. This subsidy grant was ended, however, by an act of abrogation
by Congress in 1875, when a Congressional investigation revealed that
the company had engaged in corrupt lobbying for the increased subsidy
and that some $335,000 in company funds could not be accounted for.

Thus the Pacific Mail Company subsidy and the Brazil subsidy were
withdrawn by an indignant Congress. Both Congress and the general public were left with a sour taste in their months regarding subsidies, although the Pacific Mail Company continued on again without subsidies
until well into the 20th century. Pacific Mail still had a virtual monopoly of the Far Eastern trade and could profitably operate with or without government help. The California, Oregon and Mexican Steamship
Company, established to carry the mails to Hawaii when Pacific Mail was
allowed to step out of this leg of the journey to establish faster,
direct service to the Far East, lasted only until 1874 (before its contract even expired), even though it received subsidies of $425,000 dur-
ing its brief life. None of these three lines resulted in the predicted
increase in trade. Another argument was added against all mail subsidies.

Congress had not been in a very receptive mood, either, when Congressman John Lynch of Maine tried in 1870 to get general bounties for
both shipbuilders and shipowners. His bill, which incurred the wrath
of the shipowners for not giving them enough, and of many Congressmen
for giving bounties to the already-protected coastal trades, failed on
two occasions to pass the House of Representatives. The most Congress
could be persuaded to do was to amend the tariff laws in 1872 to allow
free importation of materials for building and equipping wooden vessels
for the foreign trade or for the intercoastal trade between the Atlantic
and Pacific coasts--although such an intercoastal vessel could engage in
any other coastal trade for no more than two months each year. This concession had virtually no effect at all on the depressed shipbuilding industry, since those shippers who might take advantage of the concession
for a foreign-trade ship (even a wooden one) wanted more than a two-
month allowable time in the protected coastal trade if they were forced
into this second channel of trade in order to make money.

In 1884 Congress also agreed to a drawback (rebate) on tariffs paid
for materials used for building vessels in America if the vessels were

subsequently sold abroad (with the United States retaining 10 percent of the drawback). The McKinley Tariff of 1890 extended the free importation provision of 1872 to iron and steel ships, but with little effect because of the two-month rule on engaging in the coastal trade, which continued until 1909 when it was increased to six months. Only in 1912 was the coastal restriction removed completely. Thus it took Congress forty years before it allowed American shipbuilders some benefits by allowing them to buy foreign materials and technology without restriction.

The lack of clear and forceful commitment on the part of Congress during the second period of subsidies and in the liberalization of the tariff for the benefit of the merchant marine was also seen on the mail subsidy or subvention issue throughout the last years of the 19th century. Only in 1889 when James G. Blaine of Maine was re-appointed as Secretary of State under President Benjamin Harrison (having served for a short time under James A. Garfield) was any action taken at all. Blaine's favorite project was an increase in South American trade through the use of subsidies. The Secretary of State used the printed word and an inter-American conference held in Washington to hammer home his theme that better service was needed between the United States and its Latin American neighbors to build up trade between the two areas. He argued that an increase in trade could come to fruition only by subsidizing steamship lines. Blaine convinced President Harrison, who, in turn, carried the message to Congress.

The result was the Frye-Farquhar bounty bill of 1890, which provided for both bounties to builders and subsidies to shippers. Although the House refused to go along with giving bounties and reduced the amounts of the subsidies considerably, the idea of subsidies remained alive to be incorporated into the Postal Act of 1891, passed by Congress and signed into law by Harrison. By the terms of this bill, the postmaster general was allowed to enter into contracts with American citizens using American-built ships for the dispatch of mail to all countries of the world except Canada. The act specified four classes of vessels (the highest being of iron or steel construction of 8,000 tons or more capable of at least 20 knots of speed, down to the lowest, of metal or wood, of 1,500 tons and capable of 12 knots). Class I vessels would receive $4 per mile; Class II, $2 per mile; Class III, $1 per mile; and Class IV, 66 2/3¢ per mile. All vessels had to be built under the supervision of naval authorities and had to be capable of use as auxiliary cruisers in time of war. They also had to be officered by Americans and have a crew of whom at least one-half were Americans within three years of contract. Contracts were to run for five to ten years.

An exception to the "American-built" clause was granted in 1892 to the American Line, which received a Class I contract for mail service with England when it asked for permission to use two British-built vessels of the Inman Line, which had had its subsidy withdrawn by Britain when the line was purchased by Americans. The exception was granted only on the stipulation that the American Line would build two more vessels in America of the same size and quality as the British-built vessels. Accordingly, Wm. Cramp & Sons of Philadelphia turned out a

pair of excellent ships, the St. Louis and the St. Paul, in 1894 and
1895.

The postal subsidy bill of 1891 never accomplished what was expected of it and did little to build up the oceangoing merchant marine.
Considering the high cost of American-built ships and the absence of a
strong, stable American maritime policy regularly and properly adminis-
tered, it probably could not have worked. Much of the mail continued
to be carried by American and foreign ships on a non-contractual basis
because the bill created few new lines to sail the various routes of the
world. The Post Office Department invited proposals on a total of
fifty-three lines, but never more than eight were ever put into operation, and more than half of the $29.6 million paid out under the con-
tracts went to one line, the American Line sailing to Europe. Many of
the newly-created lines barely remained in operation, and the subventions resulted in no substantial expansion of shipbuilding or
foreign trade, the very reasons for their being created.

The Spanish-American War showed conclusively that the law had failed to create a merchant marine capable of supplying American needs in
time of war. This brief and very limited "splendid little war" of 1898
saw the United States forced to lease and otherwise obtain an additional
136,700 tons of foreign ships just to carry the armies to Cuba and the
Philippines and to supply them there.

The Republican leadership could do little about improving their
failing subsidy program after 1891. Since their policy basically con-
ferred economic benefits on a few favored companies and was obviously
motivated by a tender attachment to the needs of the shipbuilders, it
was not difficult for the opponents of the party and the program to
raise the cry of aid to monopolies at public expense, a popular partisan
issue at the turn of the century. Dominant as it might be in Congress,
there was no way the Republican party could convert its solicitude into
concrete aid in the face of widespread public distrust of big business
and government favoritism.

Yet when the Democrats, generally opposed to subsidies and bounties,
got their chance to aid the merchant marine, they could do no better.
They forced the Republicans to grant limited concessions by including in
the tariff bill of 1909 the provision that shipbuilding materials of any
type be included on the free list if the ships were to engage in foreign
trade or in the coastal trade less than six months out of the year. This
provision was of little value, so the Democrats secured an amendment to
the Panama Canal Bill of 1912 which allowed Americans to purchase foreign-
built ships--the "free ships" proposal rejected after the Civil War. But
the amendment limited the purchase of foreign ships to those not more
than five years old and excluded them from the coastal trade, although
they were eligible for mail contracts. Also, all shipbuilding materials
were admitted duty free, and ships thus constructed could engage in both
the foreign and coastal trades.

This mixed bag of benefits bore meager results. "Free ships" had
become law, but not a single ship was admitted to American registry as

a result of the act of 1912. Americans owning ships of foreign registry refused to place them under the American flag because of the higher operating costs, and the five-years-or-younger provision prevented American owners from investing in the potentially lucrative world tramp-steamer market. This market was based on the use of older ships, the chief source of supply for the rising merchant marines of Norway, Italy, and Japan, but Americans could not enter because they were not allowed to buy these time-worn vessels. Furthermore, these older vessels could not engage in the flourishing coastal trade, which limited their useful-ness. The Democrat solutions were no better than the Republican policy of subsidies.

Not until World War I with its rush to American flag by American-owned foreign companies did the "free ships" law bear fruit. Between August 1914, when the Ship Registry Act was passed allowing American registry to all foreign-built ships with no distinctions, and June 1918, 739,843 gross tons of shipping came under the American flag. This was a 70 percent increase in four years. Thus the effects of World War I in Europe, not American policy or foresight, finally resulted in the first significant revival of American shipping--and American merchant marine fortunes--since before the Civil War. The Maritime Commission estimated in 1935 that if American vessels had carried only one-half of the na-tion's world commerce from 1865 to 1914, it would have gained about $3 billion in revenues. Even if aid in the amount of $10 million per year had been granted to attain this share of its ocean commerce (for a fifty-year expense of $500 million), the income generated would have been 600 percent higher than the expense, and America would have main-tained a merchant marine suitable of its needs.

As the distinguished maritime historian Robert G. Albion summarized the situation so well in his Seaports South of Sahara:

> Decade after decade, as those maritime systems [of Britain and of Germany, now rising to industrial and commercial prom-inence] expanded in size and power, the American flag appear-ed less and less on the distant seas. The United States still kept a respectable total tonnage, protected from that foreign competition, in the coastal trade and on inland rivers and lakes, in steam as well as sail. For a while, too, in foreign trade, the tramp Down East square-riggers still carried on their losing struggle; but in steam, the handful of subsidized lines were woefully few. The government subsidy policy was too spasmodic and inadequate to accomplish much. Occasional acts from 1864 onward produced a temporary line to Brazil, the more important and longer-lived Pacific Mail service to the Far East, and the fairly successful American Line route on the transat-lantic main line, already well served by foreign-flag liners. Some shorter lines to the Caribbean completed the meager list. Even the comprehensive mail subsidy act of 1891 had rates too low for substantial results. When the nation eventually return-ed to the distant sea lanes in World War I, it had to start from scratch . . . . (p. 5)

A weaker oceangoing maritime situation could hardly be imagined as the United States moved boldly onto the world stage in the 20th century.

SUGGESTIONS FOR FURTHER READING

Albion, Robert G., with the collaboration of Jennie B. Pope. Seaports South of Sahara: The Achievements of an American Steamship Service. New York: Appleton-Century-Crofts, 1959.

Dalzell, George W. Flight from the Flag: The Continuing Effects of the Civil War upon the American Carrying Trade. Chapel Hill: University of North Carolina Press, 1940.

Hall, Henry. American Navigation, with some account of the Causes of Its Recent Decay and of the Means by which Its Prosperity may be Restored. Rev. & enlarged ed. New York: D. Appleton and Company, 1880.

Hutchins, John G. B. The American Maritime Industries and Public Policy, 1789-1914: An Economic History. Harvard Economic Studies, Vol. LXXI. Cambridge: Harvard University Press, 1941.

Johnson, Emory R., et al. History of Domestic and Foreign Commerce of the United States. Vol's I & II in one volume. Washington, D.C.: Carnegie Institution, 1915.

Marvin, Winthrop L. The American Merchant Marine: Its History and Romances from 1620 to 1902. New York: Charles Scribner's Sons, 1916.

McKee, Marguerite M. The Ship Subsidy Question in United States Politics. Smith College Studies in History, Vol. 8, No. 1. Northampton, Mass.: Smith College, 1922.

Spears, John R. The Story of the Merchant Marine. New York: The Macmillan Co., 1915.

Tyler, David B. Steam Conquers the Atlantic. New York: D. Appleton-Century Co., 1939.

_____. The American Clyde: A History of Iron and Steel Shipbuilding on the Delaware from 1840 to World War I. New York: Associated College Presses for the University of Delaware Press, 1958.

U.S. Dept. of Commerce. Government Aid to Merchant Shipping. Study of Subsidies, Subventions and Other Forms of State Aid in Principal Countries of the World. By Grosvenor M. Jones. Rev. ed., Aug. 1, 1923. Washington: Government Printing Office, 1925.

Zeis, Paul M. American Shipping Policy. Princeton: Princeton University Press, 1938.

CHAPTER XI.

ATTEMPTS AT MARITIME RECOVERY THROUGH LEGISLATION, 1915-1970

Although the American merchant marine, by the first years of the 20th century, had dwindled to almost nothing on the high seas, only a few shipowners and shipbuilders continued to warn of American maritime vulnerability. The nation rested secure in the belief that its commerce, prosperity, and well-being were hardly affected by its reliance on foreign bottoms to carry its exports and imports to and from their destinations. The outbreak of the First World War in the summer of 1914, after dilatory efforts to avoid a final solution to Europe's seething nationalism failed to prevent the conflict, finally revealed to America how it had become part of an international order and how vulnerable the nation had become when interruptions in the carriage of its goods and those of its allies became reality.

THE WORLD WAR I EMERGENCY. The summer of 1914 produced panic among American exporters as they found it impossible to move their goods across the ocean to their European customers. The long-predicted shipping crisis had arrived. The ships of the belligerent nations were tied up out of fear of capture or were being used in home waters and could not carry American goods; the small number of American ships available also hesitated to sail. Marine insurance companies were reluctant to underwrite ships and cargoes sailing into European waters because of the danger of loss. As a result, insurance rates began to skyrocket and were soon to the point of exorbitance. Faced with this crisis in marine insurance, in August 1914 the Treasury Department rushed to establish war-risk insurance coverage, but only for American vessels, and the crisis on the docks and in the warehouses persisted with too few ships to carry American goods.

The Wilson administration and Congress responded to the crisis with the Ship Registry Law within the same month. The law was an invitation to owners of ships under British or other foreign registry to prevent capture or destruction of their vessels by bringing them under the neutral American flag. The act repealed the five-years-or-younger provision of the Panama Canal Act of two years before by opening American registry to foreign ships of any age, young and old. The act also removed another barrier to the transfer of ships to American registry by giving the President the right to suspend navigation law requirements that all watch officers and crews by American citizens. Thus foreign-flag vessels could be transferred to American registry and continue to sail with the same personnel.

Unlike the Panama Canal Act, which tried half-heartedly to induce a return to American registry (to no avail), the Ship Registry Law with its liberal provisions--and the critical war situation for the allied powers--was very effective. By the end of 1914, more than one-half of all American-owned vessels operating under foreign flags had returned to the U.S. flag, and by 1917 some 650,000 tons or more had been transferred to American registry from foreign flags. As the American export trade to import-starved Europe climbed from $2.7 billion in June 1915 to more than $4.3 billion a year later, the newly-registered vessels with American war-risk insurance coverage played a large part in effecting the transfer of the goods, although rates were still considerably higher than before the war.

In the meantime, the forces of liberal Progressivism had claimed a victory regarding working conditions on American vessels. The Seamen's Act of 1915--often called the LaFollette Seamen's Bill after Robert M. LaFollette, Sr., the Wisconsin senator prominent in its passage--was the culmination of years of agitation by the International Seamen's Union. The act extended the principles established by previous, weaker bills in 1895 and 1898. It abolished imprisonment of seamen for desertion and also provided that the United States would not arrest deserters from foreign vessels in American ports. In addition, the act gave the seamen the right to receive one-half of the wages due them at every port and extended the same right to foreign seamen in American ports. Formerly a seaman had the right to his pay only when signing off after a completed voyage. The act also reflected the labor union bias of its sponsors; it mandated that 75 percent of the crew had to understand the language of their officers and required that within five years 65 percent of the crew had to be able seamen of nineteen years of age or older. "Able seamen" were those with at least three years of deck experience. These provisions were designed to eliminate Chinese crews and to assure berths for the able seamen-members of the unions. In the interest of safety, the act provided for a two-watch system for sailors and a three-watch system for critical firemen, oilers, and water-tenders. It also established space requirements for the crew's berths and liberalized the provisioning scale, as well as requiring more life-saving equipment on U.S.-flag vessels.

The Seamen's Act of 1915 was more than a mere reform measure passed during a time of reform enthusiasm; it laid the groundwork for all subsequent seamen legislation and provided at long last a clear guarantee that humane conditions would exist on American vessels. The days of the packet rats and their ill-fed and abused successors were at an end. The days of the maritime unions were beginning.

But social legislation to aid the American seamen did nothing to cure the problem of not having enough ships to carry American goods, so shipbuilding legislation was soon forthcoming. President Woodrow Wilson and Secretary of the Treasury William McAdoo were in fundamental agreement that private capital was inadequate to the task; both favored government ownership of the fleet. This would protect against avarice by private owners and would assure a merchant marine strong enough to be used as a lever in foreign trade negotiations. While by no means taking over the private merchant fleet as Wilson and McAdoo may have thought best, still the legislation drafted and pushed by these two influential executive powers reflected the thrust of their thinking.

The Shipping Act of 1916 provided for a Shipping Board, which was to create an Emergency Fleet Corporation--a public corporation--to purchase, construct, and operate government merchant ships in time of national need. The bill specified that such a corporation could exist for only five years after the end of the war--an assurance that a permanent public fleet would not become a reality--and $50 million was allocated to the project. The Emergency Fleet Corporation, then, was only "half a loaf" for Mr. Wilson's dream of a government fleet; but, as time would reveal, it was an important stepping stone to a more active part in shipbuilding and ownership by the government.

The Shipping Bill also gave the Shipping Board regulatory powers over foreign commerce, including the proviso that any shipping combinations, or conferences, had to file their shipping rates with the government to be reviewed for their essential fairness. The bill outlawed deferred rebates and any discrimination against American exporters for not using any particular shipping line. It also proscribed the use of "fighting ships," a device whereby ships would be utilized against a competing line by a shipping combination at rates so low that the competitor would be driven out of business. Tramp shipping was not included in the legislation; the bill was intended to cover liner shipping only. With the American farmer groups actively supporting this legislation to aid American shippers (now that they feared their grains could not reach their rich European markets without an American merchant fleet), the bill passed with little difficulty. However, the legislation was looked upon not as a signal to begin building a vast American fleet, but rather as a stand-by measure to assure adequate American commerce in a warring world. But within a year, America was in the war; and the building provisions took on new importance as the United States embarked on the largest crash program in shipbuilding it had ever witnessed.

The declaration of war by the United States on April 6, 1917, was followed by a series of laws giving emergency powers to the President. Those having to do with shipbuilding and operation were forthwith delegated by him to the Shipping Board and the Emergency Fleet Corporation. In June 1917, the sum of $750 million was allocated for the building or purchase of ships, and the President was given power to modify, cancel, or requisition all shipbuilding contracts, commandeer shipyards, and purchase outright any ships under construction. Subsequent laws increased the amount appropriated to $2.8 billion for construction, in addition to monies for ship purchasing and operation. The Shipping Board was given the duties of acquiring vessels, operating them, and regulating all shipping and shipbuilding.

The Emergency Fleet Corporation was given the task of constructing the ships, and later it took over the operation of the American fleet from the Shipping Board. By 1918 the program saw 186 shipbuilding and supply operations either under construction or delivering ships, up from only fifty shipyards before the war. Using standardized parts and practices and the mass requisitioning and allocations of materials, the

Corporation was supplying 898 shipways before the end of the war. By
the end of 1918 there was 300,000-plus shipbuilders and another 375,000
men in auxiliary industries laboring at the job of creating a merchant
fleet; and the Corporation, in order to care for its men and their
families during the giant undertaking, constructed or acquired 8,949
houses, 1,119 apartment buildings, and eight hotels for some 55,000
workers and their families. The total shipbuilding effort cost approximately $3.3 billion, and by the Armistice in November 1917, 107 steel
ships of 615,000 deadweight tons, plus 67 wooden and four composite
vessels, had been built at a cost of about $200 per ton. In carrying
out this building feat, the time required to build a 3,500-to-9,000-ton
ship was lowered from between nine and eighteen months to between
thirty and one-hundred-five days. At its peak, in October 1918, the
Corporation saw seventy-seven vessels of 398,000 total tons slide down
its shipways in that month alone.

Still, despite this prodigious effort, more than one-half of all
American troops carried to France during the war were ferried in foreign
vessels, especially in British cargo carriers. Many sailed on ex-German
passenger liners like the Leviathan which had been seized at the outbreak of the war. Nevertheless, by its building program of almost a
million vessel tons completed, augmented by 700,000 tons of German ships
confiscated, two million tons chartered from various countries, one-and-
a-half million tons taken over in American shipyards under contract for
foreign buyers, and 675 steel oceangoing cargo or passenger ships requisitioned for the war, the United States had built its "bridge of ships"
across the Atlantic. With the continued construction of ships under
contract, in addition to those built during the war, when the program
was concluded in May 1922, the nation again had a world oceangoing fleet.
It totaled 13.5 million gross tons--five times the pre-war U.S. flag
tonnage--and represented 22 percent of the world fleet. Questions had
already arisen as to how this great merchant fleet would be used after
the war.

ATTEMPTS AT POLICY IN THE 1920'S. Since the Shipping Act of 1916
said nothing about the conditions of the transfer of a government-owned
merchant marine fleet to private hands after the war or about the peacetime role of the merchant marine, these questions came to the fore in
the debate and discussion over the Merchant Marine Act of 1920. Unfortunately, the debate was short, although the need for forming a long-
range policy was critical, and the bill that emerged was long on hope
but lacking in clarity and substance. The act stated that the United
States must develop and maintain a merchant marine to carry the greater
part of its commerce and also to serve as a naval and military auxiliary
in time of war--a statement which has been the basis of American merchant
marine policy ever since. However, in their rush to adjourn, the congressmen gave little thought as to how this end could best be accomplished and instead only passed a series of provisions that appeared to contain great promise for restoring American maritime prowess.

The Merchant Marine Act of 1920 gave the Shipping Board the power
to determine which lines should be established to promote foreign and
coastwise commerce and allowed it to sell or charter the government ves-

sels needed to do so. It further stated that if private shipping interests could not or would not establish the necessary lines, the
government could do so through the Board. The act exempted marine insurance companies from the anti-trust laws and authorized the Shipping
Board to establish a construction loan fund of $25 million to aid
private construction for American shipping lines. The act also rein-
stated the traditional cabotage protection to American coastal shipping
by stating that no foreign-built vessels acquired by Americans after
February 1, 1920, could be used in the coastal trade, although those
foreign-built ships brought under the flag during the war were allowed
to remain. The aim of the act was clearly to establish new trade routes
and demonstrate that American ships could be profitable on them. The
government was to aid in this enterprise by operating the vessels temporarily, if necessary. By doing so, it was hoped the requisite private
expertise would be developed within industry personnel, and profitable
trades would be established so that the United States would henceforth
be a major power again after six decades of neglect.

The high hopes hurriedly written into the Merchant Marine Act of
1920 were soon cruelly squashed; only one year later the postwar shipping boom collapsed as the world's economies readjusted to peacetime
conditions and European fields and factories began production again.
Before 1921 had ended, 17 percent of the world's fleets was idled, and
the Shipping Board had no choice but to sell off its ships for which
there was no employment. They could only be operated at a terrible
loss, but they could only be sold at a terrible loss too. Ships built
for $200 to $250 per ton were sold in 1921 for $150 to $175 per ton,
and the next year they were selling for only $30 per ton. Disposing
of the surplus vessels at sacrifice prices seemed to be the only way
the Shipping Board could cut its mounting losses.

Many of the ships sold by the Board to private operators during the
boom years of 1919-21 had been sold for very small downpayments. With
the collapse in shipping, the private owners simply returned the ships
to the Board. Of the selling price of over $87 million for the ships
sold during the boom, the government received only about $8 million in
payments, giving the operators two years' use of the vessels at the
cost of only about $12 per ton. Those vessels not sold off were placed
under managing operators for the government, but their contracts were
written so that if a managing company made money, it was allowed to keep
its profits, but if it lost--which was usually the case--the losses were
absorbed by the Shipping Board. The government was in a foundering ship-
operating business in a time of shipping depression and could not get
out without great losses. Dreams of a great American merchant fleet
upon the seas of the world had quickly vanished.

In 1922 the Harding administration made an attempt to save the
fleet by pushing for subsidy legislation in Congress. The subsidy bill
passed the House, but never even got to a vote in the Senate. The ships
could not operate without a subsidy, and Congress showed itself unwilling to subsidize the fleet or otherwise commit itself to its salvation.
Furthermore, the private operators were adamantly opposed to continued
government possession of the war-built fleet because it held rates down

by the very threat of its being used, and also kept open the possibility of governmental operations in the passenger and cargo service. Besides, the private liner operators wanted to buy the best of the war-built vessels. They therefore argued that the government should sell the best, scrap the rest, and get out of the business altogether.

Faced with no alternatives, since it could only operate with subsidies that would not be forthcoming or else at a continuing loss, the Shipping Board disposed of an excess of 1,100 ships of 5.4 million deadweight tons between 1921 and 1928. For these it received only $90.6 million (or $17 to $18 per ton). The vessels sold included many of the finest afloat, all going at bargain rates. For example, the Dollar Line bought seven "President"-type ships for $3.8 million to use in its cargo-passenger business. The ships had cost the government $29 million to build. The Board justified its sales at such low prices as helping to establish routes where they could not operate otherwise.

The program of government-private cooperation on the world's sea lanes, which looked so promising in 1920, had become a dismal nightmare of overtonnage eight years later. Gradually those ships not sold off for shipping routes were sold for scrap, and the government-operated ships were withdrawn from service as America once again retreated from the commercial lanes of the world. Still, the American lines continuing to operate, although much reduced in number in the fact of foreign competition, could not be abandoned completely, and so another attempt was made to resurrect the maritime oceangoing fleet, at least in the liner trades.

Faced with the continued deterioration of America's share of the world ocean transit in freight as the 1920's progressed, Congress reluctantly took up the challenge late in the decade and turned once again to mail subsidies, or subventions, as a device to shore up the American maritime trades. The result was the Merchant Marine Act of 1928, also known as the "Mail Subsidy Law of 1928." According to the provisions of this act, the Shipping Board and the postmaster general were to decide which trade routes should be subsidized and what types of ships were to receive the aid. Since the law stated that the ships were to be of the "latest and most approved types," it was assumed that this provision would result in construction of new vessels to replace the aging fleet. Furthermore, to protect American shipbuilders, the subsidy legislation applied only to vessels built in American yards and remaining under American registry during the entire ten-year term of the mail contracts. All officers and at least one-half of the crews (gradually moving up to two-thirds on a time scale) had to be American too. The vessels' owners were to receive mail subventions from a low of $1.50 per nautical mile outbound to a high of $12 per nautical mile outbound, according to the size and speed of the vessel. Congress assumed that with competitive bidding the actual amounts of the subsidies would be well below the maximum. To aid in the replacement of the older vessels, the Merchant Marine Act of 1928 also established a construction loan fund of $250 million. The loans were allowable for up to twenty years and could be written for up to three-fourths of the construction cost of a ship. In theory, then, the federal government was providing an operating subsidy and an aid in the building of ships in trying to reclaim part of the oceans' commerce for American liner vessels.

The law failed miserably. Many of the mail routes established were over the identical trade routes already being used by American vessels and, in fact, were written by the Shipping Board and the Post Office to match the needs of the favored bidder. Usually there was only one bidder anyway, and the maximum subsidy rates were awarded to him. In addition, some contracts given to nominal foreign-trade carriers were actually used to underwrite that carrier's domestic coastal operations against unsubsidized domestic competitors. Somehow, too, vessels were mis-classified so that they received higher payments for the carrying of mail. Nor did the act result in the building of many new ships, as Congress had intended. Of the forty-three contracts written, only twenty required new construction for their fulfillment, and only five ships were eventually built. Forty of these forty-three contracts had only one bidder, and only six specified less than maximum rates.

Under these conditions, it is no wonder that costs climbed while service failed to improve. In 1929, the subsidy program cost $9 million. From 1930 to 1933, the figures climbed to $13 million, then $18 million, then $22 million, and finally $26 million. The subventions were finally cut in 1935 and 1936 under the impact of the depression and ended in 1937, when the whole program was replaced. But in the meantime the shipping lines under mail contracts made spectacular profits--often having purchased government surplus vessels at a fraction of their cost too--while the government paid the difference between their high expenses and their limited income. The death knell for the program came in 1935 when Postmaster General James Farley issued a report on the subsidy program to President Franklin D. Roosevelt. It was a scathing indictment of the whole subsidy scheme and of the lines' practices within it. Clearly the 1928 subsidy law had failed to perform. A heavily-subsidized liner fleet was still afloat, but only because it was wastefully supported by the government, and no basic improvements had been forthcoming. It was time for re-appraisal.

The basic problem in the industry since the 1914 decision to support the ocean trades for national welfare was that the whole situation had not been clearly thought out, and priorities had not been established. The government in 1916 had rushed in to support the maritime industry as crucial to national defense and national economic well-being, but had never really faced the full implications of its actions. Was the government going to continue to operate its vessels beyond the war emergency or was it going to withdraw and turn them back to private hands? If it was going to operate a merchant fleet, on what basis? Would it do so in order to control or in order to compete? If it was going to sell off after the emergency, to whom, at what price, and for what services in return?

There was a marked tendency to withdraw from the full implications of the government's actions then, and the tendency has continued since that time. Was the maritime industry, in fact, beyond private control and operation by the very interdependence of the international economy as it had developed? Was it beyond private control by the nature of the industry, which operated under the press of international competition, which could not be controlled by any nation's domestic legislation or by international agreements? Could the industry be left essentially in private hands and yet be supported out of necessity by the government in order to assure a wartime auxiliary and to avoid a complete dependence on foreign bottoms to serve American needs? If so, how could the nation be assured that subsidies would be used for improvement and replacement of the fleet instead of for short-term advantage? Was the merchant fleet in fact fit for either commerce or defense; if not, how could the nation assure that it would be? Was government ownership and management or private ownership and management preferable? If the answers lay somewhere between these two extremes, where were they? In essence, what did the nation want to do about its merchant marine, so crucial to its commerce and defense? Without really probing any of these questions and the ramifications of all possible answers, Congress came up with an answer, an answer destined to be the keystone of American merchant marine policy to this day.

THE MERCHANT MARINE ACT OF 1936. Before passing the Merchant Marine Act of 1936, also known as the Bland-Copeland Act after its chief sponsors, Congressman Schuyler Otis Bland of Virginia and Senator Royal S. Copeland of Maine, both from shipbuilding states, the Congress made no attempt to probe the deeper issues of the need for a merchant marine and, if one was necessary, the characteristics it should have. The bill was debated in a dilatory fashion for fifteen months and then rushed through the Senate one day before adjournment so that the solons could attend the 1936 presidential conventions. It received the same type of speedy treatment in the House, because its members also had conventions to attend. Basically, support for the measure was based on the principle of economic recovery and the consequent need for employment possibilities during the depression, not on principles of a well-thought-out maritime policy that would best serve the nation. It included the same nationalist and protectionist principles as had been espoused by the Merchant Marine Act of 1920, showing a solicitude for protecting domestic waterborne commerce completely and also assuring a "substantial portion" of foreign commerce for American carriers. It did, however, rid the nation of the discredited mail subsidy program. Interestingly, the debate on the bill saw the Democratic party completely reverse itself under the pressure of economic events and now espouse the principle of maritime subsidies, a position anethema to it since the days of the Civil War. Politics and expediency co-authored the bill.

The Merchant Marine Act of 1936 stated that the United States had to maintain an adequate U.S. flag fleet in foreign commerce for both national defense and commercial purposes. This objective would be made possible by both construction differential subsidies and operating differential subsidies. Furthermore, the government would aid in shipbuilding by constructing ships for sale, or charter if necessary, and would develop an ocean route system for American liners where they could effectively compete with foreign flags. All mail contracts were to be terminated by June 30, 1937. The law contained five basic provisions.

216

Construction differential subsidy (CDS) payments were based on the principle of parity with foreign ship-construction costs. They would be carried out through contracts entered into by the government with both the shipping companies and the shipyards for particular vessels. The law stated that the government would pay up to 33 percent of the cost of the construction price, thus equalizing the difference between building costs in American yards and in foreign yards. If four of the five members of the newly-created United States Maritime Commission agreed, the subsidy could go as high as 50 percent. In addition, the shipping companies could also receive a government loan of 3.5 percent per annum on their cost of construction of a vessel if they paid at least 25 percent down. The construction loans were to run for up to twenty years. The law also provided that a company could place funds in a capital reserve fund to finance ship construction, and that this money would not be subject to corporate income taxes until such time as it was spent. The government thus entered in to help owners buy American ships because they could not buy foreign vessels under existing law and could not "buy American" because of higher costs. The government made up the cost difference. The construction differential subsidy, however, was only for dry cargo and passenger service on liner routes. The law made no reference to construction subsidies for tankers, tramps, coastwise vessels, or sounds and Great Lakes vessels.

Operating differential subsidies (ODS) were also provided. These subsidies were to cover the difference between operating under the American flag with its higher manning, victualing, and repair costs and operating under a lower-cost foreign flag. Foreign costs were to be the basemarks of the system. The government would make up the difference between them and American-flag expenses. The exact amount of the ODS payments was left to the Maritime Commission. This task was almost impossible to carry out with great accuracy because of the wide variation of costs between "typical" vessels. The contracts were to run for a maximum of twenty years. Again, as with the construction differential subsidies, the operating subsidies were to be operative only on the foreign-trade routes, and the subsidized shipowners could not compete with the unsubsidized coastal or intercoastal vessels.

The Merchant Marine Act of 1936 mandated that on subsidized passenger vessels all officers and 90 percent of the crew had to be American, and that on cargo vessels the officers and crews had to be entirely American. On unsubsidized vessels all officers and 75 percent of the crews had to be American citizens. Minimum wages and manning scales were to be written into all subsidy contracts. Thus the maritime unions, as well as the shipbuilders, were well taken care of by this bill.

The act addressed itself to the question of national defense when it stated that the Navy had to approve all shipbuilding plans for all subsidized and government-built vessels to assure their suitability for national defense auxiliary purposes. The government, through the Maritime Commission, was to pay all costs of "national defense features," and the Commission was authorized to purchase all subsidized vessels as needed in an emergency at cost minus depreciation. The Commission was also given the power to requisition all private vessels in the event of a national emergency.

If construction and operating subsidies did not result in a sufficient merchant marine for national commercial purposes, the act specified that the government could build its own ships in private shipyards
or in Navy yards. These could be sold, or else leased to private operators on a bare-boat charter basis, thus increasing the number of
American vessels available for the oceangoing trades. The act also
provided construction, but not operating, aids for vessels intended to
be used in the coastal trades. These were in the form of construction
loans of up to 75 percent of the vessel cost at 2.75 to 3.5 percent
interest per annum.

The entire operation of the various provisions of this omnibus
maritime law was to be supervised and carried out by the United States
Maritime Commission, a five-member, bi-partisan board that received all
the powers of the old Shipping Board and the Emergency Fleet Corporation
now dissolved by this legislation. The members of the Maritime Commission were to serve staggered six-year terms. Curiously, while the
members were appointed by the President, they were primarily responsible
to Congress according to the law. Joseph P. Kennedy was the first
chairman of the Commission and served ten months between 1937 and 1938.
He was succeeded by Rear Admiral Emory Land, who guided the Commission
and the program through the crucial years of World War II until 1945.

These were the provisions of the widely-touted "scientific subsidy
law" of 1936. The act is significant not only because it marked the end
of the Democratic party's long-time opposition to subsidies under the
pressure of providing jobs--the party platform in 1932 had specifically
condemned them--but also because it revealed that the Congress and the
President were still not ready to abandon the principle of private ownership of the American commercial oceangoing fleet or to acquiesce in
its demise. It represented a compromise of expediency dictated more by
a need for additional employment of American men than by any long-term
analysis of whether or not the country needed a merchant marine and, if
so, the best and most efficacious means of maintaining it. Yet it was
undoubtedly all that could be expected under the circumstances.

Whatever the merits of the legislation, however, subsidies open
and clear, no longer disguised as aid to the carriage of mails, were now
the cornerstone of American maritime policy. Congress, the President,
the shipbuilders, the shipowners, and the maritime unions looked forward
to the day when the American flag became a power on the ocean waters
once again thanks to the provisions of the act. The Maritime Commission
soon called for a long-range building program of 500 new ships in ten
years and let out twelve subsidy contracts covering between 30 and 40
percent of American dry cargo liners. Whether these steps would have
resulted in a revitalized merchant marine can never be ascertained.
World events soon intruded upon domestic concerns, and the American
people and the American merchant marine faced an even greater challenge
in the form of World War II.

THE SECOND EMERGENCY AND ITS AFTERMATH. Just as the 1936 program was really getting started, the storm clouds of World War II were gathering and the nation soon found it necessary for a second time in the century to build a large fleet to carry its troops and supplies to foreign countries and to assure a continued supply of raw materials coming into the country so that it could become the "Arsenal of Democracy." The effort called for dozens of new shipyards and the training of thousands of new workers to take on the gigantic task of creating a wartime merchant marine equal to the tasks imposed on it. The Maritime Commission early turned its attention to increasing production by utilizing standardized ship designs, which would make mass production techniques possible. First the standardized although non-glamorous "Liberty Ships" powered by old-fashioned reciprocating engines were built in assembly-line fashion utilizing welding instead of riveting; later the same techniques were used for the faster turbine-driven "Victory Ships." Production records established in World War I were soon easily eclipsed as old and new shipyards turned to the task of creating both a Navy and a merchant marine in record time. Between 1942 and 1945 almost 6,000 vessels were constructed for the merchant marine. These included 2,701 Liberty ships, 414 Victory ships, 651 tankers, 417 standardized cargo vessels, and 1,409 other military or minor types of vessels.

Not only did the government build ships faster than ever before in order to carry out its world-wide responsibilities, but also it entered directly into the ship-operating aspect of the business by means of the War Shipping Administration created in February 1942. The Shipping Administration was headed by the chairman of the Maritime Commission and was given overall direction of ship operation for the merchant services. The Administration requisitioned both private domestic and foreign vessels, bought foreign ships, and seized enemy vessels caught in American ports. It recruited and trained thousands of seamen for the merchant marine and was so successful that, in cooperation with the Maritime Commission building new ships, it was able to boast that four-fifths of all war supplies were carried in American vessels, in addition to bringing into the country the raw materials so crucial to the war effort.

The end of the fighting in 1945 did not mean the end of the demands on the merchant marine. Troops (and a considerable number of war brides) had to be returned to American soil, and food, clothing, and machinery had to be shipped to Europe in tremendous amounts to aid in the recovery of that war-torn continent. Although the War Shipping Administration was dissolved in September 1946, the task of maintaining the fleet continued under the Maritime Commission as government-owned vessels were chartered by private companies to carry relief shipments to Europe. Yet by 1947 this period of high demand for shipping was coming to an end, and private vessels were being returned to their owners. The decline of the shipping boom was made obvious by the fact that 1,500 government vessels were under charter in mid-1946, but the number had slipped to less than 100 by mid-1950.

Although the Maritime Commission had announced in 1946 the completely unrealistic goal of having American vessels carry 62 percent of all liner freight business, the maintenance of the American merchant marine at the numbers attained during the war when there were extraordinary demands placed upon it, and when there was virtually no European competition, was clearly impossible. Excess tonnage of government-owned vessels brought in no revenues and represented actual or potential competition to private vessels, which, according to policy, were to make up the bulk of the American fleet. Consequently, the Merchant Ship Sales Act of 1946 was passed to provide for the disposal of most of the war-built fleet. The best of the vessels were subsequently bought for service under the American flag by private operators, and many of the Liberty ships were sold to foreign flags to carry out those countries' commitments to commercial recovery. By the time of the Ship Sales Act's expiration date in January 1951, almost 2,000 ships had been sold, with 843 going to American ownership and 1,113 to foreign buyers. The government had paid approximately $2 billion for these ships. The remainder of the government-owned vessels were placed in reserve fleet status at eight anchorages along the East and West coasts to be available in case of another shipping emergency. The American merchant fleet returned to its status as a privately-owned entity sustained with government aid.

Little was done regarding maritime matters in the years that followed the passage of the Ship Sales Act of 1946. In 1950, however, the President's Reorganization Plan 21 was promulgated. It replaced the United States Maritime Commission with the Federal Maritime Board, whose duty it was to carry out the function of regulation of the merchant fleet and its subsidies. Plan 21 also created a second maritime control agency, the United States Maritime Administration, under the Department of Commerce, to administer all merchant marine programs of a promotional nature. Plan 21 called for the chairman of the Federal Maritime Board to be also ex officio administrator of the Maritime Administration for greater coordination.

This reorganization plan did not work out well and was replaced in 1961 under the President's Reorganization Plan 7, which abolished the Federal Maritime Board and set up two independent bodies over maritime affairs: the Federal Maritime Commission (FMC) to handle all regulatory matters such as conferences and the establishment and enforcement of rate agreements, and the Maritime Administration (MARAD) under the Department of Commerce to oversee the building and subsidy programs. The dual-track system of control through FMC and MARAD is still in effect.

On the operational level, many changes also came about during these years. Between 1952 and 1956, important steps were taken to liberalize the government's promotional programs and thus build up the merchant fleet. In 1952 the Long Range Shipping Act allowed construction subsidies to bulk carriers and to non-liner services or tramps, thus giving aid to crucial types of shipping services not covered under the Merchant Marine Act of 1936. Between 1954 and 1956 the government extended loan guarantees on private construction to a maximum of 90 percent of the amount borrowed for construction of a ship; this included loans for all types of services, including tramps. The guarantees were subsequently raised to 100 percent of the loan amount. It was important also that these guarantees were payable in cash to the lender in case of default on loan payments, not in ten-year debentures as was formerly the case. This provision insured the lender immediate reimbursement for loss rather than forcing the lender to wait years until payment would be made.

During these years the federal government also instituted its "trade in and build" program, which allowed the Secretary of Commerce to buy up pre-World War II vessels if the owners could replace these ancient vessels with new ones from American shipyards. Furthermore, construction differential subsidy maximums were raised to 55 percent in the case of new vessels and 60 percent in the case of reconstruction or modernization. The government also changed its regulations to permit shipping companies to invest their tax-free reserve funds in common stocks rather than in government bonds. This form of investment would increase the yield on the funds and free the companies from financial limitations, which, they argued, were both unnecessary and counterproductive, with common stocks returning greater yields than government securities.

THE CARGO PREFERENCE ACT OF 1954. Probably the most important benefit granted to the merchant marine operators during these years in order to keep them in operation was the passage of the Cargo Preference Act of 1954. It was built on the principles embodied in the Military Transportation Act of 1904, which mandated that all military supplies be carried by U.S.-flag vessels unless the charges incurred would be excessive or unreasonable, and upon Public Resolution No. 17 of 1934, which stated it was the sense of Congress that exports financed by American loans be carried on U.S. flag vessels. The Cargo Preference Act mandated the terms of carriage for all goods bought with federal funds. In the case of goods bought by the U.S. government on its own account, on goods bought by the government on the account of a foreign nation with no reimbursement called for, or on goods for which the government had advanced any funds or credits, 50 percent of those cargoes by gross tonnage had to be carried by privately-owned U.S.-flag vessels. In other words, approximately one-half of all goods shipped out of the country purchased in any way with federal funds would have to be carried on American ships. This requirement included all military and foreign-aid cargoes of any type.

That the Cargo Preference Act of 1954 was particularly helpful to the American operators--it was, in effect, a guarantee of a percentage of cargoes--was revealed by the fact that by 1962 almost two-thirds of the total tonnage employed under the American flag outbound and 75 percent of all outbound cargoes were reserved to it by this law. This cargo preference law was especially important to tramp vessels, but subsidized and non-subsidized liners also became very heavily dependent on government cargoes, one-half of which was guaranteed to them. It has been estimated that this cargo preference act cost the American government and the American taxpayers between $3 billion and $5 billion between 1952 and 1972, the amount of dollar difference between shipping by the cheapest means possible and shipping at least one-half of all government or government-sponsored goods in American vessels. This amount was even greater than the operating differential subsidy and the construction differential subsidies, which drew so much attention and criticism. Whether or not cargo preference was an expeditious means of shoring up the merchant carriers and the shipbuilders behind them, it became a pillar of support and a vital part of the whole maritime system in the decades following its adoption as official policy in 1954.

THE MERCHANT MARINE ACT OF 1970. By 1969 the federal government had spent $1.8 billion on construction differentials and $3.6 billion on operating differentials, had mandated American-built vessels for U.S.-flag operations, had reserved all coastal and intercoastal trade to American ships, and had guaranteed one-half of all government-sponsored shipments to American bottoms by its various laws. Still, nothing seemed to make any difference. Between 1956 and 1970, only 182 new vessels came off the ways for American-flag registry, and American shipping and shipbuilding continued to fall far behind world shipping and shipbuilding operations because of the higher cost of buying and shipping in American vessels. For example, in 1969 non-liner merchant vessels carried only 4.4 percent of American imports and exports by volume; and in the burgeoning tanker trade, American tankers carried only 5.5 percent by volume.

No matter which measure was used, the plain fact was that the United States merchant marine was shrinking both absolutely and relatively. It was nowhere near providing for American national defense and commercial purposes. Fifty percent of American imports and exports in American bottoms, the goal of the Merchant Marine Act of 1936, seemed like a cruel delusion. So Congress again attacked the problem. It was determined to stem the decline and to build in greater efficiency in both the building and operating of American merchant vessels while setting as a goal the building of 300 new vessels in a ten-year period.

In order to assure greater efficiency in the building of subsidized ships, the construction differential subsidy formula was changed to encourage a long-range, standardized-design building program, which would bring important economies of scale. The law provided that a shipyard could apply directly to MARAD for funds rather than acting as an independent building contractor for the shipbuyer. It was hoped that the yards would thus be encouraged to devise plans and building programs suited to them and to assure them direct benefits by winning contracts that reflected their attempts to be more economical and efficient. MARAD would then sign contracts with the buyer for receipt and usage of the ships and would be in a position of exerting leverage both on the shipbuilder and the shipowner to cut costs. Furthermore, costs would hopefully be cut down, because all subsidy computations would be based on the actual local cost for building a vessel, as opposed to the projected local cost compared to foreign cost. In order to reverse the practice of having the government pay about half the cost of the vessel (the average subsidy had climbed to 53.6 percent by that time), the 1970 law set a statutory limit of 50 percent on the construction subsidy and also set up a descending scale of subsidy so that by 1976 the figure would be down to a maximum 35 percent. These financial pressures apparently worked, because by 1974 the average subsidy grant was down to

41 percent.

Very important too is the fact that the construction subsidy was changed to include non-liner vessels so as to encourage the building of bulk carriers for the U.S. fleet. It was obvious that this type of vessel would be very important in freight transportation in the future. The subsidy was also extended to Great Lakes and coastal vessels and proved very important to their continued existence and improvement. Non-ocean trades also were aided by the fact that the 1970 act replaced the earlier reserve fund with a new Capital Construction Fund (Title V) and opened it to all vessels in all trades. Thus non-ocean and non-liner owners could now enjoy the benefits of tax-deferred construction reserve funds. The mortgage insurance fund also was opened to all vessels in all trades and raised to the amount of $3 billion. The new CDS was designed to assure greater efficiency in building and to extend its benefits to all the maritime trades. The time had finally come when the government was willing to spend money with more discretion to get a more efficient merchant marine on all its waters. The cost was estimated at the time of passage to be between $2.7 and $6 billion over a ten-year period, but Congress hoped that as a result more and better ships would be built at lower cost to the shipowner and the subsidizing taxpayers.

The Merchant Marine Act of 1970 also included a new operating differential subsidy and granted it to all carriers, not only to liners. This resource was critical to the tramp vessels; they were rapidly declining to nothing in the maritime picture without financial help. The simple fact behind another key change was that operating subsidies were costing too much and were producing too little. Under the old formula, the government simply paid the difference between foreign wages and American wages--an open invitation to the maritime unions to push wages and benefits to the highest levels possible and to the companies employing the seamen to pass these inflated costs on to the government, which would absorb them with no question. By 1969 the averages on all routes showed that the government was paying 67.3 percent of all wage costs, 28.7 percent of all insurance costs, and 27.6 percent of all maintenance and repair charges. Thus 67¢ of every dollar paid to seamen came from the government and 84 percent of all operating subsidy costs went to wages.

The new formula embodied in the bill allowed the Maritime Administration to subsidize only the difference between the estimated wages of foreign seamen and the wages American seamen would receive if they were employed at the same skill level in other industries. The law set parameters at between 90 and 110 percent of the true wage costs between these two poles of measurement. It also provided that crew size was to be agreed upon before construction of any vessel. If the owner-union agreement on the number of men needed to man the vessel was above the number determined by MARAD to be subsidizable, the owner could either agree to bear the additional costs on his own or could cancel the building contract. High union demands for crewing levels after the ship was built were thus avoided, demands that would mean higher owner cost and ultimately higher taxpayer expenditures.

The ODS was extended also to U.S. bulk carriers in particular, instead of only to liner freight carriers, under the belief that the bulk carriers represented the wave of the future and should be encouraged by this subsidy. Interestingly, too, the law opened the door for the return of merchant vessels under foreign flags by making them eligible for U.S.-flag operations and operating subsidies if their owners agreed to cease their foreign operations by April 15, 1990. Foreign flag operators could still use their foreign vessels until the end of the life of those vessels and could also receive American subsidies on the U.S.-flag operations at the same time.

The 1970 act was significant whether or not the thirty ships per year were built because it placed new emphasis on efficiency and growth. Of equal importance, it brought both domestic and bulk operations under the umbrella of aid offered by the government to those who would cooperate with it in rebuilding the American maritime trades. Whether or not it would be effective would be determined by time and circumstances.

SHIPPING CONFERENCES. One practice that has been embodied in the maritime legislation in the 20th century and has remained almost unchanged is the recognition of shipping conferences as an integral part of the international shipping picture. A shipping conference essentially is a cartel-type agreement between shippers in one part of the trade to agree on certain freight rates to be charged to all users of their services. The Shipping Act of 1916 recognized the existence of conferences and American participation in them by specifically exempting them from American anti-trust legislation. Americans were not forbidden to join them despite their inherent practices in restraint of trade, but American operators were forbidden to engage in certain practices, and foreign operators could be penalized for engaging in the same practices. The 1916 act forbade the granting of deferred rebates and all preferential rates to any shippers, whether by direct or indirect means. The law also forbade the use of "fighting ships" in order to drive competitors out of the trade by artificially lowered rates. Finally, the act forbade retaliation or discrimination against any shipper who chose to use the services of another carrier.

These practices could not be enforced by the United States against foreign shippers directly (in the absence of international agreements on conferences), but indirect controls could be used. Thus the act gave the government the right to refuse a foreign vessel American port privileges if the owner was engaged in such illegal conference practices. Direct control over American conference members took the form of giving the government the right through the Federal Maritime Board to declare that an American shipper could not participate in a particular conference and to penalize him if he did so. The act specified that all such agreements had to be filed with the Federal Maritime Board, which had the right to cancel or disapprove all conference agreements to which American owners were a party. The Federal Maritime Commission now has this power and control.

The Merchant Marine Act of 1936 stated that conferences could not

224

discriminate against any American port that had been improved with federal funds--an attempt to aid the development of new port traffic in certain parts of the United States. A law passed in 1961 codifying the act of 1916 specified that all conference members had to give thirty-day notice before raising their rates and that such rates could be disapproved by the Federal Maritime Commission if they were adjudged unreasonable.

Shipping conferences have always been the subject of much controversy. On the one hand, if American companies are allowed to participate in the conferences, the result will be higher freight rates to their customers. On the other hand, if Americans are not allowed to participate and have to face the determined competition of foreign vessels on their routes, the result will undoubtedly be a lowering of rates by the owners to meet foreign competition and greater losses, or even the possibility of folding in the face of lower-cost competition. This would mean greater federal aid to the owners so as to allow them to survive such practices and keep their ships in the trade. American vessel owners cannot afford to participate in international rate wars because of their higher costs, and such rate wars could also lead to international economic and political bitterness between the United States and countries whose friendship and cooperation is important to its continued economic and political existence.

Shipping conferences do carry out one function important to an international economy. They allow the operators to work out their own adjustments of cost outside of any political considerations. Freight rates can thus be determined by economic factors, not by nationalistic factors, which may seriously distort or even cancel out economic gains. The supporters of the conferences argue that they prevent rate wars and are self-correcting because non-member liners and tramps can enter into conference fields to take away their trade if conference rates get too high, and members themselves can defect if greater gains can be made by cutting rates. The supporters also argue that the shipping conferences produce stability in a business always subject to violent fluctuations of rates caused by inconstant supplies and demands for their services. Conferences ensure regular, dependable service that could not be obtained in the open market and, their supporters urge, also protect ports and shippers against unfair discrimination by agreeing to serve all shippers in the same way. Their detractors point out that conference rates are too high and are arbitrarily fixed not by economic considerations but by agreement and coercion. Rates are raised when necessary or when expeditious; they are not lowered when they could be. Furthermore, by violating economic efficiency by pegging rates to high-cost, low-efficiency firms, the conferences in effect allow the high-cost operators to stay in business despite their inefficiencies.

Whatever the merit of the arguments, the United States has consistently taken the position that stability in international trade necessitates cooperation among the international community of ocean shippers. It thus accepts the existence of the conferences and allows American shippers to participate actively in them, subject to the guidance and regulation of the Federal Maritime Commission to assure that they are open and fair. American maritime law and practice thus lives with reality when it comes to shipping conferences, an increasingly important part of the 20th-century maritime world.

SUGGESTIONS FOR FURTHER READING

Gorter, Wytze. United States Shipping Policy. New York: Harper &
Bros., 1956.

Hohman, Elmo Paul. History of American Merchant Seamen. Hamden, Conn.:
Shoe String Press, 1956.

Jantscher, Gerald R. Bread upon the Waters: Federal Aids to the Maritime Industries. Washington, D.C.: The Brookings Institution, 1975.

Lane, Frederic C. Ships for Victory: A History of Shipbuilding Under
the U.S. Maritime Commission in World War II. Baltimore: Johns
Hopkins Press, 1951.

Lawrence, Samuel A. United States Merchant Shipping Policies and Politics. Washington, D.C.: The Brookings Institution, 1966.

Marx, Daniel, Jr. International Shipping Cartels: A Study of Industrial
Self-Regulation by Shipping Conferences. Princeton: Princeton
University Press, 1953.

Mattox, W. C. Building the Emergency Fleet. Cleveland: Penton Publishing Co., 1920; reprint ed., New York: Library Editions, Ltd., 1970.

Reese, Howard C., ed. Merchant Marine Policy: Proceedings of the Sympo-
sium of the Fifteenth Ocean Shipping Management Institute of the
American University's School of Business Administration. Cambridge,
Md.: Cornell Maritime Press, 1963.

Safford, Jeffrey J. "The American Merchant Marine as an Expression of
Foreign Policy: Woodrow Wilson and the Genesis of Modern Maritime
Diplomacy," Ch. 6 in Benjamin W. Labaree, ed., The Atlantic World
of Robert G. Albion. Middletown, Conn.: Wesleyan University Press,
1975, pp. 144-68.

U.S. Department of Commerce. Government Aid to Merchant Shipping. Study
of Subsidies, Subventions and Other Forms of State Aid in Principal
Countries of the World. By Gorsvenor M. Jones. Rev. ed., Aug. 1,
1923. Washington: Government Printing Office, 1925.

_____. Maritime Subsidy Policy. Washington: Government Print-
ing Office, 1954.

_____. Maritime Administration. A Statistical Analysis of the
World's Merchant Fleets Showing Age, Size, Speed & Draft by Fre-
quency Groupings as of December 31, 1974. Washington: Government
Printing Office, 1975.

Zeis, Paul M. American Shipping Policy. Princeton: Princeton University
Press, 1938.

CHAPTER XII. THE MODERN OCEANS FLEET

The World War I shipbuilding program and the shipping boom that continued after the end of the fighting propelled the American foreign fleet to the best position it had enjoyed since the 1850's. In 1920 approximately 50 percent of American imports by value and 34 percent of American exports were carried in American bottoms. Total foreign trade reached the sum of $12 billion that year and the shipping industry experienced an unaccustomed glow of prosperity. Yet artificially induced wartime demands for ships and commerce could not be sustained with the coming of peace and the resumption of normal commercial conditions, and before a year had passed, the oceangoing merchant marine was in a posture of decline once again.

OVERVIEW OF THE FLEET SINCE 1920. In the last six months of 1920, ocean-fleet operations showed a net operating gain of $25.6 million and an average tonnage employed of 8.1 million deadweight tons. Conversely, the first six months of 1921 showed a net operating loss of $38.1 million and average tonnage at only 5.8 million tons. On July 1, 1920 only eighty-eight vessels were tied up, representing less than 6 percent of the fleet, and eighty-two of these vessels were of wooden construction. By February 1, 1921 a total of 513 ships were inactive, a figure representing more than 30 percent of the fleet, and including over 90 percent of the wooden vessels and almost 18 percent of the steel ships. A drop from $8.6 million in exports down to $4.5 million, and a corresponding decline of imports from $5.7 million to $3.2 million, was in large part the reason for the decline in fleet utilization between 1920 and 1921.

At the same time, comparative costs for wages and food on American versus foreign vessels also revealed the continued presence of higher manning expenses as a factor in the nation's maritime decline. In 1920-21, for example, a typical 8,800-ton coal-burning vessel in the American fleet was crewed by forty-eight men at a monthly expense of $6,775. A British vessel of the same type needed forty-five men and cost $5,019 a month, and a Canadian vessel required only thirty-eight mean and an expense of $4,564 a month. Lowest of all were Japanese vessels of this type, which, while employing fifty-nine men, cost only $4,189 for crewing expenses each month. With typical British manning outlays being only 75 percent of American costs, and with Canadian costs standing at 67 percent and Japanese costs at 62 percent, it is no wonder that American shippers faced almost insurmountable odds when trying to compete in world commerce in these years of declining trade. The pattern of higher costs experienced during these years, so evident since the demise of sail, has persisted through the 20th century to the enormous disadvantage of the U.S. merchant fleet.

As we have seen, the World War I fleet was sold off or scrapped during the 1920's in the face of foreign competition, and the United States limped into the 1930's with only a fraction of the world's, or its own, commerce under its control. Not until the Merchant Marine Act of 1936, by which time the American share of its total foreign commerce by weight had slipped to approximately 40 percent of imports and 23 percent of exports, was anything done; and the action taken than was motivated more by a desire for higher employment during the depression than by any particular concern over the demise of the U.S. fleet. After completion of a survey of the situation, the United States Maritime Commission announced a building program of fifty ships per year to review the American fleet, but the program did not begin until January 1939. By the end of that year, there were 127 dry-cargo ships and twelve tankers under contract. The ominous sounds of war in 1940 forced the government to accelerate its building program and attempt to build 200 freighters by the end of the year. December 1940 saw sixty vessels ordered for sale to Britain, and the following month some 200 "ugly ducklings," later styled "Liberty Ships," were contracted for. By the time of American entry into the war in December 1941, approximately 6 million deadweight tons of ships had been ordered for the government.

During the war years of 1942 to 1945 more than 6,000 ships were delivered at a cost of $12 billion. Never before had the nation built ships at such a rapid rate in so short a time. Even the celebrated "Bridge of Ships" of World War I paled before this second great effort. By the time the shipbuilding program reached peak production, it was capable of matching the total prewar tonnage in a period of just sixteen weeks and the whole prewar world fleet in less than three years. Maritime Commission-authorized vessels between 1939 and 1945 exceeded 56 million deadweight tons and included 417 standard cargo vessels, 2,701 Liberty cargo vessels, 414 Victory ships, 651 tankers, and 1,400-plus minor and military types including 117 transports. A combination of private enterprise and government control and coordination of production build a fleet that became one of the important keys to Allied victory in World War II.

When the war was over, there were available some 4,500 vessels suitable for commercial use, and the Merchant Ship Sales Act of 1946 was an attempt to dispose of this valuable maritime asset--too important to squander, yet too large for normal commercial use. More than 4,000 of these vessels were offered for sale to U.S. citizens and to the nation's allies as one means of helping those countries rebuilt after the devastation of the war. By December 1949, U.S. operators had purchased more than 1,100 vessels, with 80 percent of the dry cargo and passenger vessels entering foreign trade. At least 1,400 of the war-built ships were placed in the National Defense Reserve Fleet in 1946, at eight anchorages along the coasts. The number of ships thus maintained by the government hovered near 2,000 vessels during the 1950's, then gradually declined without replacements in the 1960's, and finally dwindled to slightly fewer than 300 by 1976.

Yet despite this concerted shipbuilding effort during World War II and the various steps taken in the three decades thereafter, the American oceangoing merchant marine again declined both absolutely and relatively during the second half of the 20th century, as a few statistics make clear. In 1950 America's 27.5 million gross tons of vessels represented 32.5 percent of the world total of 84.5 million tons. By 1960, world tonnage had climbed to 129.7 million tons, but U.S. tonnage had slipped to 24.8 million tons, or 19.1 percent. By 1970, American tonnage had again slipped, this time to 18.4 million tons, or 8.1 percent of the world total of 227.5 million gross tons. In 1976, with world gross tonnage of 372 million gross tons, American tonnage was only 12.5 million tons, or 4.1 percent of the world tonnage.

In 1950--to look at it another way--American bottoms carried 43.7 percent of the 96.7 million short tons of waterborne imports and 32.5 percent of the 62.6 million short tons of exports. By 1970, imports had grown 309 percent to 299 million tons, but only 5.1 percent came in American bottoms. Exports had quadrupled to 239.7 million tons since 1950, but American vessels carried only 6.2 percent of the goods. By 1973, imports had climbed to 405 million tons, with America's share climbing only to 6.3 percent; exports stood at 226 million tons and U.S. vessels had upped their share only fractionally to 6.4 percent.

The amounts of freight considered by value show a somewhat better picture with America's share of its total ocean commerce being greater by value than by weight, but still the pattern of post-World War II decline is evident. After standing at approximately 30 percent in 1956, it slipped to 25.8 percent by 1964, to 18.9 percent in 1973, and to 17.5 percent in 1975. Had it not been for the cargo preference laws favoring the liner vessels and the growth of tanker tonnage, American tonnage by value would have been even smaller. America's active fleet in 1976 consisted of only 543 vessels, of 9.6 million gross tons and 14.2 million deadweight tons. America's flag merchant fleet represented approximately one-third of the tonnage owned by Americans under foreign flags, and only slightly more than 4 percent of the total world tonnage. America had become not a second-rage, but a third-rate, maritime power by the mid-1970's.

THE COST OF THE FLEET. The attempts made by the government to maintain an oceangoing fleet for commercial and national defense purposes have been expensive. While the costs can only be estimated, they prove to be interesting and perhaps instructive. Between the beginning of the construction differential subsidies (the Merchant Marine Act of 1936) and the year 1973, the total construction and reconstruction subsidy cost totaled $1.8 billion. The average subsidy rate in 1969 was 53.6 percent of the cost of the vessel, but the new provisions for contracting as outlined in the Merchant Marine Act of 1970 lowered the rate considerably, so that by 1973 contract subsidies were sometimes as low as 16.5 percent. Still, despite the reduction of the statutory limit, the declining percentages, and the effects of competitive bidding, the cost remains high.

Between 1936 and 1973, the operating subsidy cost $3.6 billion. The operating differential subsidy has become lower per ship since 1970 because the newer vessels being built are larger and faster, have a faster turnaround time with less manpower lost, have smaller crews, and

231

are affected by the "subsidizable wage cost" formula. Millions of dollars will be saved by crew reductions, but the subsidy will continue to be paid in the future on American flag ships unless there is a fundamental change in government policy.

Preference cargo laws as outlined in the Cargo Preference Law of 1954 to clarify previous practice and to guarantee government-aid cargoes to American bottoms have been effective. Between 1964 and 1969, cargo preference shipments climbed from 72.1 percent to 83.1 percent of all exports by weight carried in American ships. During those same years, they represented from 50.1 to 56.8 percent of total exports and imports carried on U.S. ships. The cargo preference laws may, indeed, be the only thing keeping the liner merchant marine alive. But the cost of this aid has not been inconsiderable. Between 1952 and 1973 it totaled almost $3.8 billion of imputed subsidy, i.e., the additional expense of shipping in American vessels, as opposed to shipping by the cheapest means available.

In addition to these costs, considerable money has been expanded in the shipment of dry cargo and petroleum products by the Military Sealift Command. Since 1952 more than 86 percent of all MSC dry cargo shipments by ton-mile have been either by payment for space aboard liner vessels or by chartering private vessels. Between 1952 and 1972, the percentage of petroleum shipped for MSC by private concerns increased from 36.6 percent to 81.7 percent. More than 80 percent of all Military Sealift Command ton-mileage has been by private vessels. The cost for this service shows that at least $4.6 billion in revenues have been paid to private shippers for space, and more than $4 billion for chartering vessels. Thus a price tag of $8.6 billion or more can be placed on the MSC over the twenty-year period.

Assuming that the $9 million loss in the year 1962 by deferment of taxes on deposits by shipowners in the reserve funds, established by law to encourage more building, represents a fair average for the twenty-year period, between 1952 and 1972 approximately $180 million in taxes were lost to the government by this deferment. Another $8 million per year can be calculated as the cost to the government for ship-construction credit aids, for an additional $160 million for the period. Finally, at an average cost of approximately $12 million per year for free medical care for merchant seamen and for the subsidized training for officers of the ships, another $240 million can be added for the period.

Thus for the period 1936 through 1972 on the construction and operating differential subsidy programs and for the period 1952 to 1972 on the others, the various programs to aid the merchant marine have cost the nation almost $18.4 billion, without taking into account approximately $15 million per year for administrative overhead costs to government and industry. With the costs averaging out to roughly $1 billion per year, the question must finally be asked as to whether or not the result is worth the price.

The price of $1 billion per year, or approximately .3 percent of the federal budget in a typical year, may indeed be a bargain if a merchant marine must be kept afloat for commercial and defense reasons. On the other hand, if the fleet is not vital, or if the costs are inflated because they represent unjustifiable bonuses to uneconomical shipbuilders and shipowners and to their employees, the government and the taxpayers may be throwing good money after bad. One thing is clear: whatever their cost, these various aids to American shipbuilders, shipowners, and maritime employees have become vital to the continuation of the industry. Without them the merchant marine could not survive in its present form, if at all.

THE SHIPS THAT SAIL. Although the American fleet is now small in size and declining in numbers, the ships themselves include some of the swiftest and most modern vessels in the world and are designed for high productivity. These factors account for the higher percentage of value carried, because the ships themselves are capable of carrying high-value cargoes with great efficiency. American tankers and intermodal vessels in particular are among the finest in the world.

In the late 1970's there are approximately 150 freighters in the U.S. active fleet. Of these, almost all are owned by private corporations. Only 85,000 gross tons of the total 1.6 million gross tons and less than 10 percent of the vessels are government-owned. These freighters of the American-flag merchant marine are the traditional break-bulk vessels carrying dry cargoes. They can handle almost any type of non-liquid cargo from packaged materials to tractors or various types of machinery. Although of lesser importance than in the glory days of the early 20th century when they dominated world trade, the freighters are still able to take advantage of their versatility to attract a fair amount of trade. The vessels, however, are rather slow compared to many others, averaging only 18 to 20 knots, and are also relatively small in size. Most can carry loads of only 10,000 to 15,000 deadweight tons. The development of other specialized types of vessels seriously jeopardizes these ships in world trade despite their ability to unload themselves and serve in many ways that such competitors as roll-on/roll-off vessels and container ships find impossible. The decline of these versatile freighters has particular significance to national defense needs. It has been suggested by some that the United States should continue to build these vessels (if necessary, for the reserve fleet) in order to assure adequate carriage in the event of war.

Only slightly larger in numbers than the almost-extinct American passenger-cargo ship segment of the American fleet (the nation in 1976 had only six passenger-cargo ships in the active fleet and only fifty-three in the government-owned inactive fleet) is the bulk-carrier segment. There are only seventeen active bulk carriers, and two on inactive status. The total tonnage of the nineteen vessels is only slightly over 300,000 gross tons. Only three of these vessels are modern in design, including two 80,000 deadweight ton ore/bulk/oil ships (OBO's), which are capable of maximum efficiency in carrying bulk commodities such as coal, cement, grain, bauxite, and oil. The remainder of the tiny fleet of bulkers is made up of converted World War II tankers and cargo ships of marginal efficiency. While this type of ship is very important in foreign trade, the lack of subsidies granted to construction of these vessels and the lack of preference cargoes available to them has discouraged any significant building of this type of vessel under the American flag. Building and operation of OBO's have increased for American owners because of the demands for their services in foreign trade, but the great majority of those built have been constructed outside the country and placed under flags of convenience.

The largest segment of the American fleet consists of tankers. Late in 1976 there were more than 250 tankers on active or inactive status comprising over 5.5 million gross tons and 10 million deadweight tons. Approximately 15 percent of the total private and government tanker fleet was inactive; the 85 percent active was a reflection of the increased dependence of the United States on foreign oil to maintain its industrial economy. These vessels have grown tremendously in size in recent decades. The typical World War II tanker was of 10,000 to 18,000 deadweight tons; by the early 1950's this figure had climbed to between 25,000 and 30,000 deadweight tons. The closing of the Suez Canal in 1967 increased the demand for tankers, and their size increased correspondingly. By 1971 the average size of new tankers had reached 183,000 tons. Today tankers are being built and launched of over 500,000 deadweight tons, and the end is not in sight. The only factor limiting greater size is the lack of off-shore terminals to serve the tankers because their size and draft are too much for domestic ports to handle. The Middle East, Europe, and the Far East have the giant off-shore facilities necessary for the loading and unloading of the giant vessels, but the United States, lagging far behind in facilities, cannot become the destination for these efficient carriers with their consequent savings in carriage costs.

Yet the United States is belatedly attempting to catch up to the world in tanker tonnage. The Merchant Marine Act of 1970 endeavored to expand the American tanker fleet from its earlier limited role of carrying petroleum products between Gulf of Mexico and Eastern coastal ports by making subsidies available for these ships. The fluctuating demand for these vessels has resulted in an inconstancy in shipbuilding contracts for them, and the lack of adequate American dockage facilities for giant tankers has meant that all American building of tankers of this size has been for use in foreign ports; nevertheless, some building goes on. In particular, American shipbuilders are constructing some VLCC's (Very Large Crude Carriers) and ULCC's (Ultra Large Crude Carriers) for American registry. These vessels range up to 500,000 deadweight tons and are over 900 feet in length; their superstructures are equal in height above the waterline to a ten-story building. These behemoths also include LNG's (Liquid Natural Gas carriers) capable of transporting at 260° below freezing 125,000 cubic meters of natural gas. This amount of liquified natural gas carried in a semi-frozen condition expands to 2.6 billion cubic feet of natural gas when returned to its natural state, thus making possible a tremendous savings to suppliers and consumers when delivered by the LNG's.

But the VLCC's and ULCC's being built for the American flag will be used in most cases to carry their cargoes from the Persian Gulf to northern Europe or to Japan. Only when the United States builds proper port-ing facilities will be economic advantages of these large vessels be possible for the country. The smaller tankers of the United States serve mainly to deliver lesser quantities of petroleum products to and from coastal ports. It can be foreseen that the day will come when the giant tankers will carry petroleum products into the United States to be redistributed by smaller tankers or by pipelines; but the American tanker fleet is incapable of doing so at this time. The uncertainties of foreign petroleum supplies in the future and the lack of clear long-range energy policies on the part of the American government make building and investing in tankers very problematical undertakings. These conditions will undoubtedly inhibit expansion of the tanker segment of the American merchant fleet.

Intermodal vessels constitute the final section of the American merchant fleet. There are only approximately 150 of these vessels registered under the flag, and most of the 2.8 million tons of these ships are kept on active status. Intermodal vessels would appear to be the wave of the future in non-bulk, non-petroleum shipments, although certain types of intermodal vessels can accommodate these types of shipments too. The most familiar type of intermodal vessel is the containership. The use of standard-sized containers (to be hauled as truck trailers when wheels are attached, and stacked in and on vessels when detached from the wheels), into which merchandise can be loaded and sealed at one end of a trans-world or trans-continental shipment and remain sealed until its final delivery at the other end, has set off a virtual revolution in product handling both domestically and in the international shipping world. Convenience, safety from damage and pilferage, and lower cost all argue to its greater use in the latter half of the century.

The use of containers began at the turn of the century when cartons began to be placed on the decks of ships, but it was not until the 1950's, when the nation's trucking companies and shipping companies began to cooperate seriously in the containerization of merchandise, that the movement really began. Since then containerization has grown rapidly. Unlike conventional freighter vessels, on container ships the cargo-handling gear has usually been excluded during construction because the containers are loaded and unloaded by shoreside cranes instead. At the request of the Navy, however, government subsidy contracts for container vessels specify sufficient main deck strength for both crane rails and a gantry crane so that with modification the vessels can help unload themselves if necessary under wartime conditions.

Containerships, like other modern vessels, have grown tremendously in size. Some are now 900-plus feet in length and can load more than a thousand containers of thirty-five or forty-five feet in length. In the hold they are often stacked six deep and ten wide for the greater length of the hold; in addition, three or more layers are stacked on the deck. Thus the amount of containerized freight capable of being carried on these ships reaches proportions undreamed of a few decades ago and, combined with rapid shoreside unloading, has brought large economies to both domestic and international trade; a vessel of this type can be unloaded, reloaded, and sent on its way in as little as twenty-four hours.

Another type of intermodal vessel is the RO/RO (roll-on/roll-off) ship. Essentially the RO/RO is a container vessel designed to handle wheeled containers such as trailers or trucks which are driven or towed on and off the vessel via ramps and ports in the ship's hull. Because it handles these wheeled vehicles, the vessel has internal elevators and ramps. It can also take other vehicles such as automobiles and can store almost any type of prepackaged cargo with forklifts. The RO/RO has considerable versatility and, like the containership, would appear to have a very prominent part to play in future marine shipping operations.

Equally of importance in the future will be the intermodal ships classified as barge carriers. These are the LASH vessel and the SEABEE. The first-named of these most recent additions to the world's commercial fleet, the LASH (Lighter Aboard Ship), is designed to carry fully-loaded barges of up to 500 tons, which it picks up at the stern by gantry crane, transfers them over the deck area, and then lowers them into holds in the body of the ship. LASH ships can also carry additional lighters on deck and can carry containers with ease if the situation arises. These giant vessels, often running to more than 800 feet in length, can carry up to seventy-six barges, up to 1,500 containers, or a combination of each.

The second type of barge carrier, the SEABEE (Sea Barge Ship), is similar to the LASH. A SEABEE, however, has an elevator in the stern which can lift two loaded barges out of the water and transfer them to one of three decks where they are rolled on wheeled dollies, or hydraulic transporters, to their proper positions for carriage. SEABEE's also can carry containers if the need arises. Fully loaded, they can transport as many as thirty-eight barges equal to 24,000 tons, up to 1,800 containers, or a mixture of the two.

The LASH and SEABEE vessels may represent as great a technological revolution as the container in the years ahead because it is possible for them to pick up and deliver at coastal ports barges which can be towed hundreds of miles inland by river vessels. For example, it is now possible for a barge to be loaded with containerized freight or bulk products as far inland as Minneapolis, towed down the Mississippi River to New Orleans, carried by SEABEE to a European port, and then be again towed inland for hundreds of miles for discharging ot its cargo. By this means, goods can move faster, safer, and at lower cost, since transfers have been minimized. Some 400,000 containers were moving in trade by the four types of intermodal vessels by the mid-1970's.

The ocean transportation industry is rapidly moving to these types of intermodal vessels, and they, along with tankers, will soon come to dominate international maritime trade. In mid-1976, eleven bulk carriers, thirty-six tankers, sixteen LNG's, four RO/RO's, and three container vessels were under contract for building in American shipyards. Ocean transportation is undergoing a long-range technological shift in its mode of handling freight, perhaps as great a revolution in its implications as the movement from sail to steam or from wood to iron in the mid-19th century. American shipbuilders and shipowners are attempting to take advantage of the changes as fast as circumstances allow. In this sense, America's diminishing fleet shows some vitality as it struggles to hold its own in a rapidly-changing maritime world. America's newer vessels, at least, represent an attempt to remain competitive. Only time will tell if the industry will succeed.

FLAGS OF CONVENIENCE. A flag-of-convenience vessel is one registered in a country other than that of its owner under conditions convenient and favorable to the person registering the vessel. Flag-of-convenience vessels are of particular concern to the American people, for considerable numbers of American shipowners have in recent years sought and acquired foreign registry for their ships to obtain benefits that cannot be secured under United States registry. But it is also charged that the ships thus registered under foreign flags are able to operate in sub-standard condition, which gives them advantages over American shipowners and makes them navigational and environmental dangers to other shipping and to coastal areas. When U.S. vessels can no longer pass Coast Guard inspection, they can "go foreign" and continue to run under flags of convenience.

Friends of flag-of-convenience practices often refer to them as "flags of necessity" and "flags of attraction" to emphasize their owners' inability to operate profitably under American registration. Enemies of flag-of-convenience practices refer to them as "runaway flags" and "pirate flags" to stress the harm they do to the American maritime industry. Whether such registration is convenient, necessary, attractive, or piratical, it appears clear that flags of convenience will be a permanent part of the American maritime world in the years ahead.

Contrary to popular opinion, the use of flags of convenience is not a 20th-century device. In the 16th century, English ships were placed under Spanish registration to allow them to trade freely in the West Indies; and in the 17th century, English fishermen at Newfoundland transferred their registrations to France in order to escape deportation by the Crown. The practice became more widespread in the late 19th century, when shipowners of various European and American vessels changed registration to escape the consequences of national policies. And early in the 20th century, many American investors, such as the International Mercantile Marine Company, built and owned vessels under foreign flags in order to operate outside of American restrictions. In the early 1920's, a few American oil companies began to operate under foreign flag to escape high crew costs, and the United American Line even placed two cruise ships under Panamanian registry to avoid sailing "dry" ships during prohibition. Between 1939 and 1942, the American government actively urged American shipowners, especially of tanker vessels, to register their ships in Panama in order to circumvent American neutrality laws and thus sail unmolested to war-torn Britain with needed petroleum.

It was after World War II, however, that the large-scale "flight from the flag" really began. By 1949, Panama had registered 462 vessels of over 3 million gross tons for shipowners from thirty-three countries, and other nations were also in the game. By the mid-1950's, Liberia had surged ahead with more than 1,000 ships registered, totaling an excess of 11 million tons by the end of the decade. Honduras and Costa Rica also had sizeable registrations. Much of this postwar surge came when Greek and Greek-American nationals began to use Panamanian registry for American war-surplus vessels. Americans were also heavily involved in the practice, as illustrated by the fact that 65 percent of all Panamanian tankers and 48 percent of all Liberian tankers in 1958 were under indirect American control. In that same year, American companies and their affiliates owned or controlled more than 400 foreign-flag ships registered in at least thirteen countries with a total tonnage of 5.2 million gross tons. The greater number were registered in Panama and Liberia, but numbers of American-owned ships were registered also in European countries, especially in Great Britain. By the early 1960's, the practice had been adopted to such an extent by American nationals that an estimated 45 to 50 percent of the world flag-of-convenience fleet was owned by Americans, with another 40 percent owned by Greeks, and the final 10 to 15 percent by citizens of other countries. The number of American ships under foreign flag has continued to increase since then.

The basic reason given for this registry under flags of convenience has always been to avoid the higher costs incurred under American registry. That such registrations do offer relief from higher costs and also give further benefits by allowing American companies to avoid American taxes on earnings--as well as other economic advantages--is evident. In 1957, for example, a representative of Gulf Oil Company argued that it cost at least 70 percent more to sail a tanker under American registry than under a flag of convenience. Part of the differential is caused by the high wage scale paid on American vessels, which, it is urged, constitutes 90 to 95 percent of the economic disadvantage. Simply put, the American provision that 75 percent of a crew has to be of American nationality and subject to American wage scales is responsible for the higher manning costs.

At the same time, countries that urge flag-of-convenience registration under their flags have very liberal incorporation and ship-registration laws, with little or no citizenship requirements for the owners of vessels. In Panama, for example, registration is almost a formality, with no residence requirements for officers of the registering company; stockholders of the company are even allowed to meet and conduct business from outside Panama. It is no wonder, then, that as early as 1955 there were already some 10,000 base companies, subsidiaries of American corporations, established in Panama. In almost all cases, the shares of these base companies were owned by the parent company in the United States.

Flag-of-convenience countries outside of Europe compete with one another in their liberality by means of low registration fees because, low as the fees may be by American standards, they represent considerable income for the national treasuries of these countries. It has been estimated that some one-seventh of the revenue of the Liberian government comes from ship-registry fees. Taxes on vessels in these countries are also very low. Both Panama and Liberia virtually exempt vessels from taxes as long as they are engaged in international trade. At the same time, the United States cannot tax the foreign-based subsidiaries, be-

cause they are separate foreign entities. Their profits can only be
taxed if they are distributed to the parent company as dividends. But
here the advantage is all with the subsidiary and its parent company
because they can leave the profits of the subsidiary in the foreign
country, use it for new investments there, or put the money into new
shipbuilding contracts with lower-cost non-American shipbuilders. Therefore, the companies gain newer ships at lower cost, and thus make more
money, which is again plowed back into more ships. The effect is cumu-
lative, and the subsidiaries continue to gain. In such a favorable economic situation, the American financial houses have been very willing
to lend capital to the subsidiaries, and the cycle has become even more
advantageous. Barring the unlikely development of the nationalizing of
their flag fleets by these foreign countries to rob the American companies and their subsidiaries of their vessels and assets, from an economic point of view the system is extremely advantageous and is a convenient way to survive in a highly competitive international maritime
world.

Use of flags of convenience also gives an economic advantage in
lower labor costs. It has been estimated that over 35,000 billets for
American seamen have been lost as American owners have either transferred their ships to, or else had ships built under, foreign flags, especially for PanLibHon (Panama, Liberia, and Honduras) registry. Shipboard wage scales on American flag vessels tell much of the story. In
1936 the average wage for an able-bodied seaman on an American vessel
was $50 to $60 per month. By the mid-1960's, it had climbed to $825
per month including fringe benefits. Nor was this increase the effect
of inconstant dollar values. Real purchasing power of seamen's wages
had increased seven times over. To take another example, in pre-World
War II days, American wages were approximately 50 percent higher than
European wages on board ship; by the mid-1960's, they were from three
to five times higher. In 1936 an able-bodied seaman earned less than a
typical industrial production worker. In 1947 the same seaman earned
50 percent more than such a worker while at sea. And since that year,
wages for seamen have gone up 50 percent faster than in manufacturing.
Part of the reason for this jump can be found in the 1951 decision of
the Wage Stabilization Board, which ruled that seamen were subject to
the standard 40-hour workweek; since that time they have earned overtime
on all hours worked over forty per week, and they receive extra pay for
Saturdays and Sundays at sea.

While the seamen may be indeed work for and "deserve" high wages,
the fact remains that American wage costs are very high and have been a
factor in impelling American companies to utilize flags of convenience.
The unions which represent the officers and seamen of the American merchant marine are aggressive and well-disciplined, in particular the
National Maritime Union and the Seafarers International Union. Whatever
the justice of their cause, they have become such a power in national
political circles that they are in many respects unchallengeable. Armed
with a decision of the federal government that seamen can be hired only
through union hiring halls, the unionized seamen have in effect become
employees of the union, not of the companies. The unions with their
seniority and training system are in a position to say who will sail for

which employer, and the shipowners are unable to retain or effectively discipline seamen working for them. The maritime unions have clearly been responsible for the high wages earned by American seamen; labor productivity has lagged far behind seamen's wages and other benefits. The unions have given them job security so desperately lacking under the system that existed in the 19th century, but they have also helped price the American shipowners out of the market and induced them to flee the flag.

When one adds in the cost of American ship reconstruction, which is so labor-intensive that it runs as high as two-and-a-half times that of foreign reconstruction, and when an American-built tanker or bulker may cost as much as twice that of a foreign-built vessel, the loss of American registry becomes more understandable. Adding the fact that a new dry-cargo replacement for a World War II vintage vessel may be five to seven times as high as the vessel replaced, plus the investment advantages granted by foreign countries which can be used for just this purpose, the attraction of a foreign-flag registration becomes even more obvious.

Flag-of-convenience operators have frequently been charged with utilizing foreign registration in order to avoid American safety and pollution controls. There is undoubtedly a basis for this charge, at least in some cases. The American safety and pollution standards mandated by Congress and rather rigidly enforced by the Coast Guard are the highest in the world. These impose added costs upon the owner and force him to follow practices in building and manning which he can avoid under foreign flags. Instance after instance has been made public of vessels under flags of convenience that have had improper or inoperative navigational equipment, are in critical disrepair, or have crews unable or unwilling to maintain emergency procedures and practices as required by American law. It is a sad commentary that vessels unable to pass Coast Guard standards can be registered under foreign flags and continue to sail wherever they might go, and even into American ports if tight vigilance is not maintained, or if their cargo is valuable and needed. Furthermore, in a celebrated case in 1962 the Supreme Court ruled that the National Labor Relations Board has no jurisdiction over working conditions or seamen on vessels under foreign flags, so there is no way that leverage can be applied on foreign-flag operators. Congress has made no move to alter this policy because of the obvious fact that if such restrictions are placed on vessels of countries with which the nation has agreements regarding the return of these vessels in case of emergency, the doctrine of so-called "effective control," their owners would simply shift to another registry and all control over these vessels would be lost. Thus some unsafe and improperly-crewed ships continue to sail the sea lanes of the world with virtual immunity from effective regulation, yet they do serve a vital and economically useful function for this nation.

It is impossible to determine with accuracy how many American-owned flag-of-convenience vessels are active today. In 1974 it was estimated that there were 678 vessels (of 25.2 million gross tons) owned by Americans or American corporations in the world fleet. Of these vessels, 321 were registered in Liberia, 122 in the United Kingdom, 102 in Panama, 25 in the Netherlands, and 9 in Honduras. By type, 485 were tankers of over 21 million gross tons total; 224 of these tankers were under Liberian registration with 11.7 million gross tons. There were also 84 freighters and 109 ore and bulk vessels. Yet despite the fact that this registration under flags of convenience shows that there are many more American vessels under foreign registration than under active U.S.-flag status, the flag-of-convenience totals may in fact be far short of the true count in both numbers and tonnage because MARAD lists of foreign flag vessels do not include ships owned by unlisted corporations, by individuals, or by corporations which are effectively owned by American companies that do not own a majority interest in them. The total number of flag-of-convenience vessels may run as high as 30 percent above the 678 vessel and 25.2 million gross tons cited. Whatever the true figure, all competent observers agree that the tonnages of American-owned ships under flags of convenience are continuing to grow and that foreign (and even some domestic) shipyards will continue to build flag-of-convenience vessels for American owners in the future. Whatever their effects on American commerce, shipbuilding, and maritime labor, flags of convenience are now a major part of the American maritime picture.

THE FLEET AS A DEFENSE AUXILIARY. All maritime legislation in the 20th century, and in particular the Merchant Marine Act of 1936, the foundation stone of modern American maritime policy, has stressed that the merchant fleet must be maintained for two distinct and clear purposes: for commercial reasons, and for aiding in national defense. Although this solemn declaration of purposes has been made time and again, and has been used as the rationale for continued shipbuilding and merchant marine operations, seldom have the full implications of the policy been considered. An even more neglected aspect is whether or not the merchant marine is fulfilling either objective of the policy at the present time. If it is true that the merchant marine should stand ready to aid the armed forces of the country by transporting the men, equipment, and supplies wherever they are needed with maximum efficiency, it still needs to be considered whether the twin goals of merchant marine policy are in the last analysis complementary under present conditions and whether the attaining of one is of greater importance than the attaining of the other.

Basically it would appear that the government and the private sector want at the same time the security of an adequate fleet for defense purposes and commercial efficiency. But maintenance of a high-cost merchant marine capable of adequately serving defense purposes may not be economically efficient. The result of trying to establish this essentially contradictory situation has been a maritime policy that assures neither security nor economic efficiency. The politicians and policy makers have tried to gain both "on the cheap" and have succeeded in gaining neither. The merchant fleet is not capable of providing for the transportational needs of the armed forces--to say nothing of the necessity of continuing to supply American war-related industries at the same time--nor is it transporting anywhere near the 50 percent of American commerce envisioned. While the American fleet continues to decline relatively while barely maintaining itself absolutely in the commercial realm, it may also be declining in defense efficiency because of technological advances.

Yet it would seem that if the private merchant marine must be supported for defense needs, neither cost, nor commercial efficiency, nor
free-enterprise competition can be overriding considerations. If the
United States must have an auxiliary fleet of a given size with certain
capabilities in order to serve the defense needs of the nation, it would
follow that such a fleet must be built and maintained. Questions of
cost, commercial efficiency, and competition must be secondary to that
basic need. If both defense and commercial features must be built into
commercial vessels as a workable compromise, defense needs must come
first. If both can be built in without harm to one or the other, nothing
is lost; but to prepare vessels for commercial use that are unsuitable
for defense purposes and then rely upon those vessels to perform national
defense needs for which they are inappropriate would appear to be self-
defeating. To rely on vessels not under American control for national
defense purposes would also appear to be foolhardy. Yet American national defense needs, in fact, are tied to vessels that may not be functional for defense purposes, and American planners rely--perhaps wish-
fully--on the return of flag-of-convenience vessels to carry out American
defense commitments.

America has learned from two major wars in the 20th century and from
a number of smaller conflagrations that any war involving American troops
or American allies can only be adequately supported by sea. Both World
War I and World War II vividly illustrated dependence on the sea. Both
times, "bridges of ships" had to be built in order to carry out the war
efforts. Involvements since 1945 have proved that the case is still the
same. And no matter which type of foreign war or engagement is visualiz-
ed in the next quarter-century--other than a cataclysmic nuclear war or
an overseas invasion of the United States--American defense establish-
ments will be in critical need of support across the oceans. Thus the
merchant fleet's defense role must be examined and projected.

The Department of Defense assumes that in case of war, approximately
one-half of the nation's needed shipping capability will come from American vessels under flags of convenience. These vessels are held to be
under "effective control" of the United States. The doctrine of effective
control is based on agreements with Panama, Liberia, and Honduras that
the American government has the right to recall these vessels during an
emergency and that the governments of those nations will comply. The
doctrine is also based on the fact that ships that have previously been
under the U.S. flag, when transferring to the registry of any of these
three countries, will have American recall rights written into their
titles and the owners will post a performance bond of between $25,000 and
$250,000 to assure that the ships will be returned if recalled.

Considering that the Department of Defense assumes that these American-owned vessels will be available and returned, the doctrine of "effective control" must be examined. In the first place, the agreements
between the United States and the PanLibHon countries are not in the form
of treaties enforceable under international law. They are only written
agreements. It has been argued that because none of the three countries

has a navy which could prevent the return of the vessels to American waters upon recall, and that because few of the vessels ever touch at ports of their flag nation, they will be beyond the control of their flag country to limit their actions anyway. This assumption regarding their voluntary return itself rests on two assumptions: that the enemy will allow these American-owned vessels to return if it can do anything about it, and that the crews of the vessels will be willing to return the vessel to American waters to carry out war duties as a belligerent. But if the ship acts as an American vessel either in returning upon recall to an American port or in carrying American war goods, it runs the considerable risk of being sunk. And few foreign crews would relish the thought of being sunk as a belligerent when a vessel under neutral flag could continue to sail the seas unmolested. How can the American government compel the physical return of a vessel as provided for in American law, considering that the United States Navy may or may not be in a position to apply the necessary force--not to mention protection?

In addition, it would appear that, any agreements to the contrary, the nation that has registered a vessel under its flag has final legal control over it. Legally speaking, a wholly American-owned vessel under Panamanian flag belongs to Panama, not to the United States, and Panama would have the legal right to refuse to allow the vessel's return. Even clearer from a legal point of view, where there are no agreements for return (i.e., with countries other than Panama, Liberia, and Hondurus), the United States has absolutely no right to recall under any circumstances. To the objection that none of the PanLibHon nations have a navy to prevent the return of the vessel to American control, the point might be made that their friends or allies might have such a navy to aid that country in its right to prevent "illegal seizure" of a vessel under its flag. Thus the doctrine of "effective control" is open to serious question from many points of view, yet still remains a major part of the Department of Defense's planning.

Taking all of this into consideration and assuming that the United States cannot afford to build a giant stand-by fleet for overseas operations but must rely on the commercial fleet for auxiliary aid, where does the nation stand in this regard? The United States in December 1976 had 543 merchant ships active and 296 inactive, for a total of 839 vessels of 12.5 million gross tons. These included 61 combination passenger-cargo ships, 342 freighters, 18 bulk carriers, 266 tankers, and 152 intermodals. Of these vessels, 261 were government-owned, including 247 in the National Defense Reserve Fleet. Seventy-one of these Reserve Fleet vessels were candidates for scrapping and the average age of the vessels in the government fleet was 30 years.

America also had at least 678 vessels of 25.2 million gross tons under foreign flags. They included 485 tankers, 84 freighters, and 109 bulk and ore ships; 432 of these ships were under PanLibHon registry and presumably under "effective control." This total of 1,271 vessels under U.S. flag or under "effective control," would appear to be a sizeable fleet for defense support services.

However, if American-flag bulkers are excluded from consideration

243

since they would be of little or no use in directly supporting military operations, the United States would have only 821 vessels available under its own flag, including 61 passenger-cargo ships, 342 freighters, 266 tankers, and 152 intermodals. Because the remaining 234 government-owned vessels in the Reserve Fleet are of questionable value (they are slow and are becoming older and more technologically outmoded every day), they can well be excluded from practical consideration--leaving a total of only 587 vessels in the American fleet.

Prudently excluding from consideration the vessels under foreign flags because of the possible real problems of return, the United States would have readily available and suitable for troop support only the 587 vessels of 10.4 million gross tons. These 587 vessels include 9 combination passenger-cargo vessels, 162 freighters, 266 tankers, and 150 intermodal vessels. For a limited emergency of shorter duration in which the first thirty days would be crucial to any operation, the United States would have to depend upon these 587 ships to do the job, and these ships, of course, might well be scattered along the coasts and across the oceans. Thus the United States finds itself in the mid-1970's with a merchant marine not only inadequate for commercial purposes, but inadequate also as logistical support for the nation's defense effort. Many of the ships cannot be depended upon because of age, foreign-flag registration, and inappropriate carrying capacity. There are no indications that the government, the military, or industry is seriously alarmed over the situation.

SUGGESTIONS FOR FURTHER READING

Boczek, Boleslaw A. Flags of Convenience: An International Legal Study. Cambridge: Harvard University Press, 1962.

Goldberg, Joseph P. The Maritime Story: A Study in Labor-Management Relations. Wertheim Publications in Industrial Relations. Cambridge: Harvard University Press, 1958.

Ferguson, Allen R., et al. The Economic Value of the United States Merchant Marine. Evanston, Ill.: The Transportation Center at Northwestern University, 1961.

Hall, Paul. "A Union Leader Looks at the Merchant Marine," United States Naval Institute Proceedings, 100, 855 (May 1974), 178-89.

Hohman, Elmo Paul. History of American Merchant Seamen. Hamden, Conn.: Shoe String Press, 1956.

Jantscher, Gerald R. Bread upon the Waters: Federal Aids to the Maritime Industries. Washington, D.C.: The Brookings Institution, 1975.

Lawrence, Samuel A. United States Merchant Shipping Policies and Politics. Washington, D.C.: The Brookings Institution, 1966.

Lunsford, Everett P., Jr. "Our Merchant Mariners and Their Unions," United States Naval Institute Proceedings, 101, 867 (May 1975), 66-85.

Mostert, Noël. Supership. New York: Alfred A. Knopf, 1974.

Naess, Erling D. The Great PanLibHon Controversy: The Fight over the Flags of Shipping. Epping, Essex: Gower Press, 1972.

Reese, Howard C., ed. Merchant Marine Policy: Proceedings of the Symposium of the Fifteenth Ocean Shipping Management Institute of the American University's School of Business Administration. Cambridge, Md.: Cornell Maritime Press, 1963.

Saunders, George D. "Land Bridge Comes of Age," United States Naval Institute Proceedings, 99, 12/850 (December 1973), 38-43.

U.S. Department of Commerce. Maritime Administration. A Statistical Analysis of the World's Merchant Fleets Showing Age, Size, Speed & Draft by Frequency Groupings as of December 31, 1974. Washington: Government Printing Office, 1975.

CHAPTER XIII

THE GREAT LAKES-ST. LAWRENCE SYSTEM: THE FOURTH SEACOAST

The Great Lakes water system of 96,000 square miles contains at least one-half of all the fresh water on the face of the earth and a shoreline of 8,390 miles. Beginning far to the north with Lake Superior of 31,280 square miles at an elevation of 602 feet, the largest and deepest of the lakes, and on down to the south via the 70-mile-long St. Marys River to the confluence of Lake Michigan in the west and Lake Huron in the east (both lakes at an elevation of 578.5 feet), the giant bodies of water of the upper lakes deposit their fill through the St. Clair River, Lake St. Clair, and Detroit River watercourse (dropping 6.5 feet over this 77-mile distance) to Lake Erie, the shallowest of all the lakes. From the eastern end of this body of water, 193 miles in length at an elevation of 572 feet, and dotted with industrial and commercial cities, the Great Lakes' waters drop 320 feet over the great Niagara Falls, while boat traffic eases its way down the escarpment by means of the Welland Canal, to reach the waters of Lake Ontario at 246 feet in elevation and flow out to the east into the mighty St. Lawrence River. By the conclusion of the 2,300 mile journey from the tip of Lake Superior to sea level at the mouth of the St. Lawrence, the waters and the vessels that ride them have dropped more than 600 feet. This great network of lakes and rivers, as developed and tamed by man and his technology, has become one of the most important water systems in the world. It has become the nation's Fourth Seacoast.

THE GREAT LAKES, 1860-1900. In the forty years after the Civil War, the Great Lakes region, having shown considerable vitality in its decades of economic infancy prior to the war, continued to surge to agricultural and industrial prominence. The pace of development felt throughout the Lakes region in earlier decades, with great quantities of copper, iron, grains, and lumber being sent to Midwestern cities or to the urban areas of the East, now quickened and set the area's major cities on the road to commercial and manufacturing success as well. The pre-Civil War era had seen the Lakes area come alive economically; now it settled down to develop its resources with enthusiasm. As before, the Lakes played a major role in its economic expansion.

Even though 1,700 miles of internal canals were abandoned in the post-Civil War period throughout the United States, and railroads came to carry all but the bulkiest of goods, the Great Lakes maritime world did not decline but thrived and expanded from new demands placed upon it. The iron and copper mines of the Lake Superior region expanded rapidly. The harvesting of thousands of square miles of lumber proceeded apace, more and more virgin land was cleared for conversion into fields of grain, manufacturing began to grow apace on the lower shores of Lake Michigan and Lake Erie, and raw materials, grains, and mer-

247

chandise moved throughout and to and from the region. The entire area prospered as never before with the Great Lakes waterways serving to expedite the many changes.

Prior to the 1880's, Chicago, connected by rail with the interior grain fields, had been the center of the Midwest grain traffic. But during the 1880's, production shifted to the northwest, and Minneapolis and Duluth began to emerge as the foremost milling and grain and flour shipping cities of the nation. Their advantage lay not only in their rail connections with the expanding grain-producing states, but also in their proximity to the advantages offered by water transit of grain and flour by way of Lake Superior. The movement of flour and wheat on the St. Marys Falls Canal and the Soo Locks clearly reflected the growing importance of the grain trade. In 1860, slightly more than 50,000 barrels of flour moved through the Soo; by 1899, it exceeded 7 million barrels. Likewise, wheat shipment, which had been non-existent in 1860, by 1870 showed almost 50,000 bushels moving through the locks; and by 1899 more than 58 million bushels of wheat moved down the waterway from Lake Superior to ports on the lower Lakes. By 1899 also, Minneapolis had emerged as the largest, most productive milling center in the world, having topped 15 million barrels processed each year; the Great Lakes ports of Duluth, Superior, Milwaukee, Chicago, and Toledo were each milling between 1 and 5 million barrels each year. The grain trade grew to such proportions that the United States and its grain-producing interior began to be recognized as a definite power on the world's grain markets. The Great Lakes waterways played a vital part in the movement of this grain to its domestic and foreign markets.

The waterways also served the coal and iron ore trade. Bituminous coal from Pennsylvania, West Virginia, and Ohio moved by rail to ports on the lower Lakes, there to be shipped to the Lake Superior region to be used for both commercial and domestic purposes. In return, the Great Lakes vessels brought from Lake Superior ports tremendous amounts of iron ore to feed the furnaces of the American steel industry, the most basic of all industries in America's half-century surge to industrial prominence. Almost all the iron ore mined in the Lake Superior region was carried by "lakers," special Great Lakes bulk carriers not found anywhere else in the world and designed especially for the needs of the Lakes trade. On these vessels, the ore was shipped to Lake Erie and Lake Michigan ports, there to be converted into pig and steel in the plants of Pennsylvania, Ohio, New York, and Illinois. A measure of the importance of the Lake Superior iron-ore trade to the nation can be found in the fact that by the end of the century at least two-thirds of all ore mined in the United States was shipped from the Lake Superior region; the actual tonnage had grown from 859,000 long tons in 1870 to 18 million-plus long tons by 1899. In addition to this expansion in iron-ore tonnage, the valuable copper deposits of Lake Superior were expanding during the same decades after the Civil War. Furthermore, building on the combination of almost endless tracts of virgin timber in the upper Midwest, and on the continued demand for lumber caused by the expansion of the nation, huge cargoes of lumber also moved upon the Lakes. By the end of the century, Michigan, Minnesota, and Wisconsin were the chief sources for the nation's lumber supply of 35 billion feet cut, and the Lakes vessels brought the valued product to the emerging cities of the Midwest.

This growing traffic in coal, iron ore, copper, grains, and lumber was reflected in the growth in number and size of the Lakes vessels. In 1870, there were almost 1,700 sailing vessels on the Lakes with a total tonnage of over 264,000 tons; there were also 642 steam vessels of almost 143,000 tons. By 1890 the number of sailing vessels had declined more than 400 vessels, but the total tonnage was up to 328,000 tons. Steam vessels by 1890 had climbed in number to more than 1,500 vessels of almost 653,000 tons. The number of vessels from two decades before was doubled, and their tonnage of 1870 was more than four times greater. Total tonnage on the Lakes, including canal and barge boats, climbed from 684,704 tons in 1870 to 1,063,063 tons just twenty years later.

One of the more interesting vessels ever to sail in these trades was a Lakes vessel known as the "whaleback" or "pig boat." The whaleback freighter had a flat bottom and semi-cylindrical upper sides. Built of iron or steel, its hull sides rounded over at the top to join one another. Equipped with watertight bulkheads, it was thus a watertight freight-carrying vessel. Since it was conical at bow and stern, its shape inspired its nickname "pig boat" from its resemblance to a pig's snout. Invented by Alexander McDougall of Duluth, Minnesota, the whaleback was very popular in the 1880's and 1890's, carrying ore, wheat, and flour over the Lakes. Some whalebacks were self-sustaining steamers; others were without propelling machinery and served as barges.

The distinctive whalebacks faded from use early in the 20th century as their size and shape made them impractical for the larger demands of trade. But they became part of the lore of the Lakes, especially the Christopher Columbus, a passenger whaleback built in 1892 for the Columbian Exposition of 1893, which carried more than 2.6 million passengers for short cruises in connection with the celebration.

The increased traffic on the Lakes and the necessarily larger vessels built to carry the expanding traffic soon put pressure on the capacity of the locks at Sault Ste. Marie. The original American two-step locks, providing a total lift of 21 feet in chambers measuring 350 feet by 70 feet by 13 feet, had been built by the State of Michigan in 1855; but by 1870, with traffic through the Soo running in excess of 690,000 tons a year, it was obvious that a replacement had to be provided. Michigan was unable to raise the necessary funds to improve the waterway, so Congress was petitioned for the money to replace the old locks and initiate construction of new, larger ones. Between 1876 and 1881, under the direction of the Army Corps of Engineers, a 160-foot-wide and 16-foot-deep channel was dug, and a new 515-by-60-foot lock of 17-foot draft was completed. At the conclusion of the construction, the facility was formally transferred to federal ownership. But even the new channel and enlarged lock were not sufficient to carry the expanding tonnage. By 1880, before the new lock was even completed, more than 1.75 million tons of freight were moving through the Soo every year; and only five years later, it had risen to 3.25 million tons. Out of sheer necessity, further construction was soon begun; between 1887 and 1896, a new Lock, the Poe Lock, was constructed, with dimensions of 704 feet by 95 feet with a 16.6-foot draft.

But in the meantime, the great Mesabi iron ore range had been opened. The Mesabi contained at least twice the iron ore deposits of all the other ore fields in the Lakes region, and its discovery set off a rush of ore commerce down from the western tip of Lake Superior to the lower Lakes ports. By 1894 the Soo Locks were moving 13 million-plus tons of freight--about double the amount of the more highly-acclaimed Suez Canal--and the capacity of the new locks was reached in 1900. In that year, 25.6 million tons of freight moved through the Soo including 16.4 million tons of iron ore, 4.4 million tons of coal, and 56.6 million bushels of grain. The St. Marys River and Soo Locks and the waters of the total five-lake configuration constituted a key transportational network in the nation because of the vital cargoes that moved upon them.

But the nation benefitted, too, from the lower rates forced by competition between the Lakes vessels and the railroads. In 1890, the cost of shipping wheat from Chicago to New York was $1.94 per ton by the Lakes and canal, $4.77 per ton by rail. This same competition held even those high rail charges from Chicago to New York to approximately half the prevailing general average for the whole country. The rail rates between the two cities would have been four times higher than the water rates had it not been for water competition. It was estimated in 1890 that the water route alternate via the Great Lakes saved the American people at least $10 million per year, and probably double that amount. The lesson was clear that water competition regulated rail rates and thus saved on consumer costs even when water transportation was not used for shipment; but the lesson was often forgotten.

THE GREAT LAKES IN THE 20TH CENTURY. The statistics of growth in tonnage on the Lakes in the second half of the 19th century, impressive as they are, pale considerably when compared to statistics from the 20th century. Iron-ore traffic on the Lakes moved from 20.7 million tons in 1900 to 65.5 million tons in 1920, and then to 98 million tons in 1974. Coal shipments went from 8.9 million tons in 1900, to 26.4 million tons in 1920, to 35 million tons in 1974. Grain traffic increased from 5.6 million tons to 1900 to 19.6 million tons in 1974. Stone shipments, mainly limestone for steel, chemical, and construction industries, rose from no tonnage in the first decade of the century to 7.8 million tons in 1920 and then to 43.1 million tons in 1974. Total shipments of bulk goods on the Lakes, excluding petroleum products, went from 35.3 million tons in 1900 to 106.5 million tons in 1920 to 145.2 million tons in 1940. Total tonnage reached an all-time high of 209.5 million tons in 1970. In addition to these tonnages of bulk products in 1970, there were also shipped on the Lakes 13.8 million tons of petroleum products. By the mid-1970's, the Great Lakes were handling approximately 15 percent of all tonnage in domestic waterborne commerce with more than 190 vessels of almost 1.6 million gross tons carrying this freight.

The 20th century also brought the Great Lakes ports into foreign commerce via the St. Lawrence route. In 1924, approximately 16 million tons of cargo were moved on the Great Lakes in foreign commerce, representing almost 16 percent of the total foreign commerce of the United States by tonnage. By 1950, the total had grown to 29.3 million tons, 17.3 percent of the nation's total foreign commerce. With the opening of the St. Lawrence Seaway in 1959, the figures climbed dramatically, reaching 36 million tons in 1960 and then rising dramatically to 62.3 million tons by 1970. However, the more rapid growth of other modes of foreign commerce during the period 1950-70 meant that the Great Lakes' share of foreign commerce dropped to slightly over 10.5 percent. Yet with its tremendous absolute growth in both foreign and domestic commerce, the Great Lakes system was clearly as important to the continued growth and prosperity of the nation in the 20th century as it had been in the 19th.

As the types of Great Lakes cargoes and the routes they followed during the 20th century reflected the cargoes and routes of the 19th, so too did the developments in Lakes ships reflect the distinct economic needs of their area over the decades. The giant, bulk-carrying "laker" of today is the direct descendant of the Onoko, the prototype of the Lakes freighter. Built in 1882, this iron-hulled vessel, 300 feet in length, was propeller driven, with the engine aft and the bridge well forward. Amidship was a giant hold designed to accommodate 3,000 tons of iron ore. So successful in design and execution was the Onoko that it soon became the standard bulk carrier on the Lakes, and the elongated vessels with the bridge fore and engines aft, separated by a tremendous hold for the precious bulk cargo, came to dominate the Lakes, where the absence of widely-spaced waves made such vessels of great length and flat hull both practical and safe. By the turn of the century, the typical bulk carrier was 500 feet in length and could carry some 8,000 long tons. By the 1930's, the vessels had grown to more than 600 feet in length and could accommodate a load of more than 12,000 tons. By the 1960's, the Lakes bulkers were in excess of 700 feet in length and could more than double the typical load of three decades before, with a payload of 25,000 tons.

With the opening of the new Poe Lock at Sault Ste. Marie in 1969, with a lock 1,200 by 110 feet, accommodating vessels with up to 55,000 tons of cargo--combined with federal construction subsidies now available with the passage of the Merchant Marine Act of 1970--a new era of even larger ships had dawned. With a useable ship capacity of 1,000 feet by 105 feet at the Poe, the vessels grew to meet these dimensions and the demands of bulk trade. The 1970's saw the typical new bulk carrier on the Lakes at between 800 and 1,000 feet in length and capable of carrying a load of 40,000 to 50,000 tons. In 1974 there were more than 160 bulkers working the Lakes; they dominated the Lakes fleet, accounting for 1.5 million of the 1.6 million gross tons accounted for by these great vessels. In addition to 193 American vessels of 1.6 million gross tons on the Lakes, Canada had more than 150 vessels of 1.5 million tons on the same waters. These vessels were answering the economic needs of the North American heartland, and both nations recognized their dependence on them.

At the same time the Lakes boats were enlarging in size and carry-

251

ing capacity, a revolution in loading and unloading was taking place. In the 1850's, for example, iron ore was loaded into the early vessels by means of men with wheelbarrows dumping the ore into the holds of schooners. This tedious process required four days to load 300 tons. An improvement was made when the ore was instead shoveled into elevated bins. The bins had a chute at the bottom, and the vessels could be loaded with ore more quickly this way. Finding improved methods of unloading called for greater ingenuity. Originally men would go down into the hold and shovel the ore onto a temporary staging and then reshovel it again onto the deck of the schooner. It would then be wheelbarrowed to dockside piles. This cumbersome method required a full week to unload a typical 300-ton schooner. Shoveling the ore into tubs which would then be lifted up by a rope and pulley drawn by a mule and then swung ashore was the first improvement in method. Some further advancement took place in the 1860's as steam engines replaced the mules for lifting power, but basically the processes of loading and unloading remained the same for two decades.

In the 1880's, three important innovations greatly facilitated the unloading of the boats. First, the "Tom Collins" came into use, a mechanism by which the tubs were transported by mechanical power over tramlines directly to the ore piles for dumping. The second innovation was the self-filling grab bucket, or "clam," attached to a steam crane which would drop the bucket directly into the hold of the laker for a "bite," then lift and swing it to the ore piles ashore where the clam would be "tripped" to discharge its load. The third innovation was the placing of the steam cranes directly onto the ships for unloading ease. These inventions greatly speeded the task of off-loading the giant vessels, while improved elevated bins and chuting were speeding the loading process.

In 1899, an important unloading innovation on the Lakes was the invention and adoption of the "Hulett." The Hulett is a giant self-filling grab bucket suspended from a massive crane on dockside rails. The bucket is completely maneuverable and can be turned inside the hold by the operator, who rides directly above the bucket. It can take fuller bites and thus minimize the work of the men in the hold who formerly had to shovel the ore (or other bulk material) to the center of the hold for the old-style clam. The Hulett soon became the standard unloading device for bulk materials on the Lakes docks. In the 1970's, Huletts with a capacity of twenty tons per bite can unload 10,000 tons of bulk material in only 4 1/2 hours.

Yet adaptation and invention have not ended by any means. The latest Lakes bulkers are self-unloading. Built into the holds of these giant vessels are a series of "endless buckets" or belts. The hoppers at the bottom on the holds are opened to permit the discharge of the cargo onto the moving belts, which move it to elevator belts at the end of the ship. At the top of the elevator belt it is dumped onto another belt that carries it dockside. This process permits the unloading of even the largest lakers to be carried out in a matter of hours. Thus the lakers can be reloaded and sent on their way with minimum turnaround time and minimum cost to all concerned. Loading and unloading that took days a century ago is carried out now in a matter of hours.

And perhaps in another respect progress has only begun. Lake carriers and shippers are watching carefully the performance of the Presque Isle, a combination tug-and-barge launched in 1973. It consists of a 153-foot tug and a 974-foot barge. The notched barge is designed to fit exactly the snout of the 7,420 horsepower tug which pushes it at speeds of sixteen miles per hour. The barge has twenty-seven hatches and is self-unloading with a 250-foot boom to dockside. The barge is designed to self-unload at the rate of 10,000 tons per hour. Furthermore, by using this tug-barge combination, the operator is able to crew with only fourteen men instead of the twenty-five to thirty-five required on a typical laker of the same capacity. Whether or not the tug-barge combination idea as embodied in the Presque Isle becomes the Lakes cargo vessel of the future, it would appear certain that the final chapter in technological innovation on the Great Lakes has not been written.

The third revolution that has taken place on the Great Lakes in the 20th century is in the change in iron-ore movement, iron ore accounting for more than half the cargo tonnage on the Lakes. Between 1920 and 1955, almost all of the iron ore came from Lake Superior ports, which sent 87-to-91 percent of the ore through their facilities. Most of the ore was received on Lake Erie ports, although lower Lake Michigan ports received more than 20 percent of the total. But from 1955 on, there was a noticeable decline in mining in the Lake Superior region as the high-grade ore there became exhausted. Shipments declined from 95 million tons in 1955 to 51 million tons in 1959, and it appeared that the days of Lake Superior iron ore mining were numbered.

Recovery soon came about, however, when a means of efficiently utilizing the lower-grade ore by processing it into taconite pellets was discovered. By 1970 shipments of ore from the Lake Superior ports had recovered, and almost 80 million tons per year were being shipped. In the 1950's the Labrador ore fields in eastern Canada were also opened to development. Labrador ore is shipped by rail 360 miles to Seven Islands on the St. Lawrence, where it is loaded on vessels to be sent up the St. Lawrence Seaway to inland ports. The opening of the Seaway in 1959 made this movement of ore possible. As a result of these changes, approximately 73 percent of the ore used in the industrial Midwest still comes from the Lake Superior region; slightly more than 10 percent comes from the Lake Michigan railheads, and almost 15 percent moves west by way of the Seaway. No longer, as a consequence, is Lake Erie the ore-receiving center of the North American heartland. Lake Ontario ports now receive a greater share for transshipment to industrial furnaces. Yet, all in all, iron ore from Labrador or from Lake Superior, now approximately 75 percent in the form of taconite pellets, still constitutes the greatest single most important valuable commodity moving on the Great Lakes. The economy of the Midwest and the nation depends on it.

Whether or not the Great Lakes ports ever become of notable importance in international shipping, the cargoes of the lakers in bulk

products are crucial to the nation's economy. The network is irre-
placeable because the nation's railroads lack the capacity to move the
vital minerals and chemicals at as low a cost and in such quantity as
is done by the lakers. An added savings comes in fuel costs, because
railroads can transport cargo at a fuel ratio of only 200 ton-miles
per gallon, whereas a typical laker can carry cargo at 495 ton-miles
per gallon. The newer vessels can transport at the rate of up to 647
ton-miles per gallon of fuel consumed.

In addition, further advancements of equal importance seem to promise ever greater use of the Lakes network in the years to come. Such
developments as the increased used of pelletized ore, which is not affected by cold weather, and of larger vessels (six lakers of over
1,000 feet in length are under construction); deeper channels in the
connecting rivers; improved navigational aids, including better radio
communications systems; the use of bubblers under the water at the locks
to prevent or delay freezing during the winter months; and improved ice-
mapping and ice-breaking techniques, which will extend the navigation
season to almost year-around sailing--all point to a continued solid
future for Great Lakes traffic.

Furthermore, the provisions of the Merchant Marine Act of 1970,
which extended operating subsidies to vessels in trade with Canada and
the inclusion of the lakers in the construction reserve funds, have
apparently broken the logjam on new construction of boats for the Lakes.
The construction of almost two dozen vessels since that time is a clear
indication that the Great Lakes operators with their 1,700 officers and
over 4,000 men who work the boats feel confident in their future and in
their ability to continue to serve as the vital transportational link
for the industrial prowess which the Midwest provides for the nation
and, increasingly, for the world.

THE MODERN WELLAND CANAL. The Niagara escarpment was first conquered for sailing vessels in 1829, as we have seen, with the opening
of the original Welland Canal. It had forty locks, each 110 feet in
length, and the first vessels to use it were towed through it and into
and out of the locks by means of horses, mules, and oxen. The original
winding route of the canal was altered by 1833 to provide a straight cut
through to Gravelly Bay--now renamed Port Colborne--at the southern end
of the new section of the canal on Lake Erie. The government of Upper
Canada bought out the private Welland Canal Company in 1841 and made
plans to enlarge the vital artery, replacing the wooden locks with
locks of cut stone; by 1845 the "second Welland Canal" was opened. It
had fewer but larger locks, twenty-seven in all, of 150 feet in the
system. A depth of ten feet was provided all through the cut. By 1870,
however, three-fourths of the Lakes vessels could not traverse the
waterway, so construction was begun again. The "third Welland Canal"
was completed in 1877. It had twenty-six locks, each 270 feet in
length, and the canal was fourteen feet in depth throughout.

This third canal served the Lakes traffic well until early in the
20th century. It was then recognized that rebuilding had to take place.
Accordingly, the Canadian government undertook the rebuilding process

again, and between 1913 and 1932 the "fourth Welland Canal" was built. It was 27 1/2 miles in length and made a total 326-foot lift by its locks. For this construction, a new entrance on Lake Ontario was constructed. It was called Port Weller. The entire existing canal was significantly widened and deepened. When completed, the new Welland Canal had seven locks, each 820 feet in length and 30 feet in depth. In addition, locks number 3, 4, and 5 were twinned for greater speed of vessel transit through the system. At Port Colborne on Lake Erie, a new guard lock 1,380 feet in length was constructed to complete the project. Thus by the time of the decision to build the St. Lawrence Seaway, the Welland Canal had been thoroughly modernized and was capable of carrying most oceangoing vessels into the Great Lakes interior. One of the chief obstacles to transit into the inner Lakes had been removed by a process of construction and reconstruction carried on over a full century.

The Welland Canal become a functioning part of the Seaway system when it opened in 1959. Yet improvements continued to make the waterway even more efficient. Between 1966 and 1973, a new channel was dug to by-pass the city of Welland. It was 8.3 miles in length, was 350 feet wide to ensure easy two-way transit, and had a thirty-foot depth throughout. Yet even at its moment of completion and its proud boast of transiting 67.1 million tons in 1974, plans were being considered for further enlargement. Transit on the vital waterway by ships of larger size to serve the economic needs of both Canada and its American neighbor demanded that additional improvements be made on the Welland Canal and on the entire Seaway to better serve the two countries.

THE ST. LAWRENCE SEAWAY OPPOSED. The idea of improving the great natural waterway which is the St. Lawrence River for the purpose of better navigation into the interior Great Lakes and to serve the major cities along the river and the Lakes goes back into the 19th century. In 1871 a Canadian royal commission issued a report urging such an improvement, but nothing came of it. Instead, the Canadian government took on the task of improving the existing Welland Canal in the 1880's and completed various minor projects during the years that followed. Between 1886 and 1895, for example, the government built a single-lock canal on the north side of the St. Marys River at Sault Ste. Marie. In the St. Lawrence in the 1890's, the Canadian government constructed a new Soulanges Canal between Lakes St. Louis and St. Francis, this on the north side of the St. Lawrence to replace the older Beauhornois Canal. By 1904 there existed a fourteen-foot channel from the Atlantic at the Gulf of St. Lawrence all the way to Lake Erie.

Considerable progress had been made, but the dream of a channel with locks deep enough to accommodate oceangoing vessels still remained. Indeed, the idea persisted on both sides of the border; some Americans, too, especially in the upper Midwest, could see the tremendous possibilities that an all-water route to their doors would bring. The project appeared to be relatively simple since most of the St. Lawrence would not have to be touched. With the Welland Canal upgraded and functioning, the canalization of the St. Lawrence at a handful of key spots would open dozens of interior ports to the commercial entrepôts of the world. Yet many decades were to pass before the dream would become reality, and even then, obstacles continued to be thrown up in the way of full utilization of the Seaway.

In 1895 the United States and Canada each appointed seaway commissions to look into a projected seaway. The inquiry set off a storm of opposition from those most likely to be injured by the project. Eastern railways in particular condemned the project as unnecessary and wasteful and found ready allies in prominent cargo transfer points such as Montreal, Quebec, Buffalo, and New York City, all of whom saw dire ruin to themselves as the assured result of the building of a seaway. Interestingly enough, these "natural enemies" of the seaway project found ready allies in the owners of Lakes vessels who feared competition from larger ships in their home waters. American "patriots," too, argued against construction of the waterway since it would mean "Canadian control of American commerce." Whether they were fully aware of it or not, the investigators of 1895 had flushed out the core of opposition which would impede the building of the seaway for another five decades.

In the years that followed, further engineering studies were undertaken, but with the Canadian decisions to improve and deepen the St. Lawrence through the Soulanges, Cornwall, and Lachine Canal projects, interest in the idea of a complete deep-draft seaway faded. Some glimmer of interest reappeared now and again during the years before World War I. With the tremendous expansion of wheat-growing in Canada's prairie provinces and the resulting periodic shortage of railroad cars and trains to take the precious grain to market, agitation sometimes turned to improving the Great Lakes-St. Lawrence system as a necessary means of relief from chronic transportational problems. Again, interest in controlling the St. Lawrence waters for hydroelectric purposes often led to the idea of canalizing the river for the purpose, especially among hydroelectric enthusiasts in nearby New York and Ontario.

Yet it was only in 1919 that a concerted drive for the St. Lawrence Seaway really began. In that year the Great Lakes-St. Lawrence Tidewater Association was formed under the dynamic leadership of Charles L. Craig. Craig, an attorney and investment banker from Duluth, was an avid devotee of St. Lawrence improvement for the betterment of all the states and provinces fronting the Great Lakes-St. Lawrence configuration. From 1919 to 1933, the devoted Craig served as executive director of the Tidewater Association; under his leadership a central office was set up in Washington, D.C., to direct research and propaganda. With twenty-one states backing him as members of the Association, Craig was able to build contacts with Congress, as well as with Ontario, the Canadian Government, and upstate New York public hydroelectric forces.

From 1919 to 1921 hearings were held by the International Joint Committee composed of representatives from both countries. The hearings were set off by a severe rail shortage in the United States. But the testimony before the committee soon revealed that the American West was generally in favor of a seaway, but the Eastern terminals allied to the railroads were still adamantly opposed. New York City in particular led the opposition. On the Canadian side, the committee found Ontario was in favor of a seaway, but the prairie provinces were now more interested in developing rail connections with Hudson Bay. The Province of Quebec, on the other hand, was interested in a Georgian Bay seaway between the St. Lawrence and Georgian Bay via the Ottawa River. With these basic disagreements compounded by various "all-Canadian" or "all-American" nationalistic arguments--the latter used by New York City as its "issue" throughout the 1920's as to why a seaway should not be built--there was little the committee could do other than recommend that the St. Lawrence be improved on a piecemeal basis, including the installation of hydroelectric plants.

Acting on this suggestion, and out of its own critical need for electric power, the State of New York in 1931 created a Power Authority to develop public power as part of a seaway system. The driving force behind the Authority and the legislation was Governor Franklin D. Roosevelt, who believed that power had to be created with state aid. If a navigable seaway was part of the system, that would be an added bonus, but hydroelectric power was the key to New York's decision, not inland navigation.

Buoyed up by this development in New York, and convinced that the day of the Seaway had come, representatives of Canada and the United States met and drew up the St. Lawrence Deep Waterway Treaty of 1932. Solidly backed by President Herbert Hoover, the treaty called for 27-foot depths from the head of the Great Lakes to Montreal, with a ten-member joint commission to govern the Seaway. Each country agreed to maintain the works of the Seaway in its own territory and to share equally all hydroelectric power. The United States agreed to provide $272.4 million toward the building of the Seaway, and Canada agreed to provide $270.0 million (less $128 million for its expense in building the Welland Canal section and $772,000 for improving the channel in the area of the Thousand Islands, for a net commitment of $142.2 million). But the treaty of 1932, far from assuring a seaway, was rejected by the United States Senate two years later.

The defeat of Herbert Hoover in the election of 1932 and the worsening economic situation in both countries made the time most inauspicious for pushing a major project such as the Seaway. The opposition again came mainly from the eastern states and the railroads, who chose to overlook the fact that the Seaway would make an excellent means of increasing employment opportunities during construction. Joined by the advocates of those states along the Mississippi River and the Gulf of Mexico who wanted a Lakes-to-the-Gulf waterway instead, the enemies of the project again labeled the Seaway as unnecessary, harmful to the railroads and to the Atlantic ports, and more favorable to Canada than to the United States. The Midwest was in favor of the project, although the effectiveness of its support was diminished somewhat by the Lakes carriers who opposed it because of fear of new competition.

When the treaty was finally defeated in the Senate (despite a majority vote but less than the necessary two-thirds) it was clear that two factors had been responsible. First, the fear of losses by Eastern and Mississippi interests was too strong. Twenty-five of the forty-two votes against the project came from senators from the Eastern seaboard.

Second, President Roosevelt, while working for the treaty, did not make it a test of loyalty to himself and did not try hard to convince enough Democrats that the measure was needed as an emergency job-creating program. And so the measure died because of regional interests and lack of executive leadership. It remained a dead issue for almost twenty years.

When the depression had run its course and World War II had come and gone, the Seaway project was revived again. This time, Canada not only took the lead but also announced in 1951 that it would go it alone if necessary. By that time Canadian railroad, utility, and eastern port opposition had melted away. Yet even as Canada again extended an invitation to the United States to join in the Seaway by means of another treaty, the sectional interests in the United States were too strong. The Senate rejected a St. Lawrence treaty for a second time in 1952, despite the fact that President Harry S. Truman and the two major Republican candidates for President, Dwight D. Eisenhower and Robert A. Taft, Sr., spoke in favor of it. Again the opposition of the East coast, the Gulf states, and the Mississippi Valley states doomed the treaty. Needless to say, the Association of American Railroads also played a major part in defeating it. But time was on the side of the advocates of the Seaway, and before seven years had passed the deep-channel St. Lawrence Seaway had become a reality.

THE ST. LAWRENCE SEAWAY BUILT. Sectional differences could not gainsay the importance of the Labrador iron-ore discoveries. Faced with declining supplies of high-grade ore, steel companies, iron-ore processors, and all related companies saw that only an improved Seaway would make it possible to carry the ore to midwestern mills. The Labrador ore discoveries seriously divided the opposition to the Seaway. The Lake Carriers' Association, because many of the vessels in the Lakes fleet were owned by major steel companies, now swung around in favor of improving the waterway. Adding support to the cause was the recognition by Quebec that the Seaway would now mean economic gains, not losses, to the province. Continued development of the steel industry in Ontario meant that that province also had to have Labrador ore. With American defense arguments centering on assuring a continued supply of iron ore for steel production, a safe passage for ships without fear of enemy submarines, and a lessening of dependence for ore supplies via the vulnerable Soo Locks, serious opposition melted away; the stage was set for joint agreement between the two countries to bring the Seaway to fruition.

The American assent to the joint building of the St. Lawrence Seaway took the form of the Wiley-Dondero Bill of May 1954. Sponsored by and named after Senator Alexander Wiley of Wisconsin and Representative George Dondero of Michigan--two states always in the forefront of support for a Seaway--the bill called for a joint building of the Seaway by the two countries. Its passage was assured not only because it embodied an idea whose time had come, but also because Canada's obvious determination to "go it alone" if necessary cut the ground out from under American opposition to the Seaway. Now the private power interests, the railroads, and the Atlantic and Gulf ports saw that whatever damage would be done to them was going to occur anyway. In the face of Canadian determination to build the Seaway, the best option for the United States was to salvage its pride and national security by agreeing to share the cost and control of the waterway. If Americans could not tolerate an all-Canadian seaway that would hold their Great Lakes' development hostage, they had no choice but to go along with the project and do their share so that they could claim some control over it.

For over four years the mammoth building project was carried out. Construction of the Seaway involved building forty-five miles of dikes and sixty-nine miles of new channel. At its peak of construction, the project involved employment of 22,000 men. Construction took place in five sections. Farthest to the east, Canada's thirty-one mile Lachine Section from Montreal upriver involved building ten bridges, channeling, constructing the first two locks in the system (the St. Lambert and Côte Ste. Catherine Locks), and dredging of the La Praire Basin Canal for eighteen miles. The next section, the Soulanges Section of sixteen miles, included the Beauharnois Canal and the Upper and Lower Beauharnois Locks. The third section, the twenty-nine mile Lake St. Francis Section, involved mostly dredging.

The fourth section, the International Rapids Section of forty-four miles, was a joint Canadian-American venture. This section, from Cornwall to Chimney Point, was the most difficult of all to build because it involved the construction of the two American locks, the Eisenhower Lock and the Snell Lock, and also the Canadian Iroquois Lock, the Iroquois Canal, the Moses Saunders Power Dam, the Long Sault and Cornwall Dams, and the ten-mile-long Wiley-Dondero Ship Canal around the power dams. The final section, the Thousand Islands Section, was sixty-eight miles in length but involved only channel improvements.

When the St. Lawrence Seaway was formally opened in June 1959 by President Eisenhower and Queen Elizabeth II, the two nations could bask in the pride of knowing that a 27-foot ship channel from the Atlantic to the Great Lakes was now in existence. It included fifteen locks to lift and lower vessels 572 feet from Lake Erie to the ocean. The construction had involved nine separate government agencies representing four different governments, including the Province of Ontario and the State of New York on the hydroelectric facilities on the International Rapids Section, as well as the Canadian and American federal governments. The system, including the Welland Canal, could handle four-fifths of the world's vessels, including general cargo vessels of 9,000 ton capacity and ore vessels of 25,000 ton capacity. It had a maximum usable draft of 25.5 feet throughout its 300 mile length from Lake Erie to Montreal.

Combined with the extensive Great Lakes waters valuable to both countries, one of the most extensive internal waterways systems in the world had been completed. Tonnage figures soon confirmed the dreams of those who had been working for the Seaway for decades. By 1973, more than 67 million net tons of freight moved through the Welland Canal Section, and more than 57 million net tons were moving through the section from Montreal to Lake Ontario every year. Tolls for the transit were being collected according to the agreements reached between the two countries with Canada receiving 73 percent of the tolls and the United States receiving 23 percent. Partial tolls were set at 15 percent of total tolls per lock. Both "salties" from the ocean routes and vessels specifically designed to fit the allowable lock dimensions were moving back and forth through the Seaway.

But as with other inland waterway systems utilizing man-made improvements, traffic demands soon pushed against the allowable limits of vessel size of 730 feet by 75 feet with 25 1/2 feet of draft. Within less than a decade of the completion of the Seaway, studies had been undertaken for possible enlargement of the waterway. One proposal called for locks of 1,200 feet in length by 110 feet in breadth and 33 feet of draft (the same size as the new Poe Lock at Sault Ste. Marie) to allow the giant lakers and other modernized vessels to use the Seaway. Other more ambitious proposals called for lock lengths of up to 1,600 feet and a clear channel of thirty-six feet draft to make the Seaway and its allied Great Lakes waters usable into the 21st century.

Whatever future building may be necessary to keep the St. Lawrence Seaway at maximum efficiency, the pattern was once again clear. The job would never end because increases in trade would lead to larger-size vessels and locks. This, in turn, would lead to greater economies of scale and, therefore, to increased trade. As increased trade would again lead to larger vessels and locks, the cycle would be repeated. Whatever compromises emerge regarding the improvement of the St. Lawrence, it is clear by the mid-1970's that the 2,342-mile Fourth Seacoast from Duluth to the Atlantic will continue to play an important part in the economic life of the nation.

SUGGESTIONS FOR FURTHER READING

Benford, Harry, and Kilgore, Ullmann. Great Lakes Transport: Technological Forecasts and Means of Achievement. Department of Naval Architecture and Marine Engineering, Publication 28. Ann Arbor: University of Michigan College of Engineering, 1969.

Burnham, Oliver T. "The Fourth Coast: Five Lakes and Five Rivers," United States Naval Institute Proceedings, 101, 867 (May 1975), 174-87.

Chevrier, Lionel. The St. Lawrence Seaway. New York: St. Martin's Press, 1959.

Clowes, Ernest S. Shipways to the Sea: Our Inland and Coastal Waterways. Baltimore: Williams & Williams Co., 1929.

Easton, James. Transportation of Freight in the Year 2000 with particular reference to Great Lakes Area. Detroit: Detroit Edison Co., 1970.

Hatcher, Harlan. The Great Lakes. New York and Toronto: Oxford University Press, 1944.

Havighurst, Walter. The Long Ships Passing: The Story of the Great Lakes. New York: Macmillan Co., 1942; rev. ed., 1975.

Hazard, John L. The Next Decade . . . 1969-1979, the St. Lawrence Seaway. Ann Arbor: [Great Lakes Commission,] 1969.

LesStrang, Jacques. Seaway: The Untold Story of North America's Fourth Seacoast. Seattle: Superior Publishing Co., 1976.

Mabee, Carlton. The Seaway Story. New York: Macmillan Co., 1961.

U.S. Maritime Administration. Domestic Waterborne Trade of the United States, 1965-1972. [Prepared by the Office of Domestic Shipping, Burton T. Kyle, Director.] Washington: Government Printing Office, 1973.

U.S. Treasury Department. Report on the Internal Commerce of the United States for the Year 1891; Part II of Commerce and Navigation: The Commerce of the Great Lakes, the Mississippi River, and its Tributaries, by S.G. Brock, Chief of the Bureau of Statistics, Treasury Department. Washington: Government Printing Office, 1892.

Willoughby, William R. The St. Lawrence Waterway: A Study in Politics and Diplomacy. Madison: University of Wisconsin Press, 1961.

261

CHAPTER XIV.   ON COASTAL AND INTERCOASTAL WATERS

Coastal shipping has persistently been one of the strongest branches of the American merchant marine. It was protected from foreign competition first by an act of Congress in 1789, which placed higher port duties on all foreign vessels, and then by a second act in 1817, which decreed that goods could be carried between domestic ports only in United States-owned vessels. This principle of "cabotage" was later extended to intercoastal passage between the Atlantic and Pacific coasts and to the noncontiguous territories of Alaska, Hawaii, Guam, the Philippines, and Puerto Rico. It has been steadfastly reiterated in maritime legislation. Under these legal protections, the American coastal and intercoastal trades continued as two of the merchant marine's stronger segments until challenged by more efficient forces in the 20th century and forced into a lesser, but still important, position in America's transportation network.

EARLY COASTAL TRADE. The coastal trade, as we have seen, was a very important part of the colonial economy. The major seaports along the Atlantic coast served as entrepôts of colonial trade both for the individual colonies trading in their own agricultural and manufactured commodities and in the distribution of goods from England and other European countries. Although seriously disrupted by the Revolution, the coastal trade was quickly revived out of sheer economic necessity after 1781, only to suffer a notable slowdown between 1793 and 1815 by being caught in the restrictions of the embargoes and finally by the second war with Britain. The importance of this trade network was testified to by the resistance to the embargoes by coastal shippers and by the willingness of many coaster captains to circumvent the law by trading with Nova Scotia, Spanish Florida, and the West Indies when opportunities presented themselves or could be created. Then the War of 1812 brought both legal and illegal trade along the coasts and to nearby foreign colonies to a virtual halt as the British blockade closed ports from Maine to Louisiana, and the new nation felt the impact of economic strangulation.

With the end of that unfortunate war, however, and the return to normal peacetime conditions, the coastal trade began a century-long surge of success in the distribution of domestic commodities and foreign manufactures. It soon came to match, then finally eclipse, foreign trade, both in the number of ships engaged and in the value of the products transported. In 1815, at the end of the war, the gross tonnage of vessels engaged in foreign trade was almost twice the gross tonnage in coastal and internal trade, but by 1831, the tonnage in the coastal trade alone surpassed that in foreign commerce for the first time, and coasters also carried a greater value in goods. The expansiveness of the coastal trade up and down the Atlantic coast and around to Gulf ports during the early decades of the 19th century was based on the movement of a wide variety of cargoes that could be carried expeditiously only by water. Cotton, as we have seen, was of crucial importance as New York City in particular distorted the normal trade pattern between Europe and the South by detouring both Southern cotton and European manufactures to its wharves to be transshipped through the city's dynamic commercial system. But large quantities of rice, tobacco, and naval stores were also carried in coastal vessels from southern Atlantic ports; sugar and molasses from Louisiana were other important items of the Southern coastal trade. New Orleans, the commercial center of the Gulf coast, shipped to ports on the Eastern seaboard the cotton, whisky, tobacco, corn, and wheat that had been gathered at its wharves via the remarkable internal channel of trade, the Mississippi River. In exchange for these Southern goods, the North sent a variety of foreign and domestic manufactures in large quantities to its valued customers in Southern ports.

New York was, of course, the emerging leader in this expanding coastal trade, but other ports also grew rich in serving the increasing demands of their customers up and down the Atlantic seaboard. Philadelphia not only shipped huge amounts of anthracite coal brought to it from Pennsylvania's mountainous interior by the canal networks, but also carried on extensive trade in other goods with both Atlantic and Gulf Coast cities. Baltimore's cotton and rolling mills brought it into direct commercial contact with Southern ports, which sent raw cotton to its factories in return. The mills tied Baltimore to other major port cities also; its finished products were distributed to waiting clothing and sheeting manufacturers in these ports. Boston, while declining from its dominant position as the leading center for both domestic and foreign trade during colonial days, nevertheless maintained very important coastal trading connections with other cities up and down the Atlantic coast and into the Caribbean.

The Southern ports of Charleston, Savannah, Wilmington, Norfolk, and Richmond existed as very important regional trade centers with their extensive imports and exports of cotton, grains, flour, and manufactures. New Orleans acted as a gathering point for goods to be shipped into the interior of the nation via the Mississippi system. The growth of the coastal trade to match and then surpass that of foreign trade by 1831 was built on the very firm foundation of commercial exchange.

The coastwise trade in the three decades from 1830 to 1860 was similar in nature and scope to the coastal trade of the earlier years of the century. But the difference was that there was an enormous increase in volume in coasting as the canal networks and then the railroads began the process of effectively draining the interior to bring a larger amount and variety of goods to the wharves of the oceanside cities. Only in the 1850's and 1860's did rail connections between the Mississippi Valley and the Atlantic seaboard and between North and South begin to cut into the trade monopoly enjoyed by the coasters in carrying bulk products between these regions.

But before the railroads became a major factor, increases in the coastal trade arose from the growing commercial requirements of the

264

nation, including the further expansion of both New Orleans and Mobile as major ports. These Southern cities served the expanding cotton interests in the Southwest and also exported abundant amounts of sugar, molasses, and lumber from the emerging South. The value of goods carried in the coastal trade in 1851 amounted to $2.6 million, a value six times that of American foreign trade.

The final decade before the Civil War saw much of the traffic that had formerly been held by the coasters being shifted to the railroads. Agricultural and mineral products of the Mississippi Valley and the Great Lakes areas began to move to their Eastern markets directly by rail. The old, circuitous route down the Mississippi to New Orleans and then along the nation's coasts to Eastern cities had been abandoned first in favor of canals, and then in the 1850's in favor of the faster railroad networks. Local traffic between Atlantic cities also began to shift to rails, and many long-haul cargoes were consigned to railroad flatcars and boxcars too.

Despite all this, the coastal trade remained healthy, and actually expanded during the decade. The cotton trade via coasters remained strong, and the distribution of imports and Northern manufactures continued to be carried out from Northern to Southern ports largely by the coastal vessels. The coal trade in the Middle Atlantic states doubled during the decade, and the waterborne New England ice trade and the Middle Atlantic food trade increased significantly. Tonnage enrolled in the Atlantic coastal trade increased from 1.4 million tons to 2.1 million tons during the 1850's, the largest increase in tonnage in a ten-year period ever seen. Majestic square-riggers for the longer journeys and swift schooners, brigs, and sloops for the shorter, continued to play a major part in the business of carrying America's agricultural and industrial wealth.

Steam came to the coastal trades as it had to the foreign trade networks. By 1852, there were seventeen steamers running regularly between New York and the Southern ports of Charleston, Mobile, New Orleans, Savannah, Jacksonville, Richmond, Petersburg, and Norfolk, in addition to numerous smaller lines between these ports. New England's steamship freight and passenger lines were by far the most highly developed and tied its cities together with one another and with New York to the south. Wherever there was freight along the coast, there the coastal sailers and steamers were ready to do the job with efficiency despite growing railroad competition.

The coastal vessels, cooperating with the sail and steam packets on the ocean trades, connected American goods and markets with the markets of the world and helped create a commercial system that easily challenged the existing European trade networks. The United States stood on the threshold of industrial and commercial greatness in the decade of the 1850's. It was the coastal trade, not alone but in company with and complementary to the canals, the Mississippi and Great Lakes water systems, the rapidly-spreading railroads, and the expanding and ambitious population, which moved the nation to a plateau of economic development from which it would soon climb to heights which even then seemed unattainable in one generation.

THE COASTAL TRADE, 1865-1914.   Although the foreign-trade merchant
marine went into steep decline in the fifty years after the Civil War,
the coastal trade continued to grow both in enrolled tonnage and in the
amount of cargo carried.   There were three distinct advantages that the
coasters enjoyed.   First, in the transporting of bulky items such as
ice, coal, lumber, steel, stone, and ores, the railroads could not compete with the coasters' lower costs.   Second, the coastal trade was still
securely protected against foreign competition by the maritime laws,
which demanded that vessels in the coastal trade be American-built and
that three-fourths of the crew members be American.   Third, much of the
traffic was of the tramp type, which could move freight effectively by
inexpensive wooden schooners.   Rail competition was severe in this era
marked by great strides in railroad building, especially east of the
Mississippi, and the coasters could not compete with the railroads in
non-bulky items for which the costs of higher-priced rail transportation
could easily be borne or passed on to the consumer.   But when it came
to heavy bulk items, particularly along the waters of the Atlantic
coast, the lower prices offered by the coastal vessels gave them the
edge.   Utilizing a rate structure actually lower than in the pre-Civil
War years and insignificant compared to railroad tariffs on bulk items,
the coasters showed a steady growth during the period.

Unlike certain areas of the foreign trade that were very slow to
recover after the Civil War, the coastal trade quickly revived, especially that of New York, but Boston, Philadelphia, Baltimore, and other port
cities also restored regular services to Southern ports within six
months of the end of the war.   By 1880, the Atlantic and Gulf coasters
alone showed more than 1.3 million tons of ships enrolled in the coastal
trade, more than the total U.S. tonnage registered in foreign trade.   By
1890, the figure had climbed to 1.7 million tons in the Atlantic and
Gulf trades, as opposed to less than 1 million in foreign service.   In
1900, more than 2.1 million tons were enrolled in the Atlantic and Gulf
trades alone, with a total of 6.6 million tons or more in the entire
coastal network.   By World War I, almost 90 percent of the oceangoing
merchant marine fleet was operating in the protected coastal and intercoastal trades, including trade with Alaska, Hawaii, Puerto Rico, and
the other non-contiguous American territories.

On the Atlantic and Gulf coast routes, New York retained its lead
over all competitors, with coal and lumber dominating its coastal services; but it also handled a large traffic in European imports and exports, cotton, sugar, tobacco, and rice.   Boston sent out large quantities of merchandise and manufactures, and its merchants received in return coal, lumber, cotton, and vegetables for local and regional use.
Baltimore's coastal trade in coal and fishing products and Philadelphia's
coal trade kept them very busy in the domestic trades.   The New England
ports and the Southern ports of Charleston, Savannah, Galveston, New
Orleans, and Mobile still depended heavily on the coastal trade to carry
goods to them to be distributed to their hinterlands via the expanding
railroads spreading into the interior.

Southern exports in the coastal trade continued to be dominated by the reviving cotton fiber with New Orleans returning to prominence in transporting that item of trade. Galveston found its place in the cotton trade too. The Southern ports also shipped out large amounts of hides, cotton seed, molasses, naval stores, lumber products, rice, and tobacco in return for Northern manufactures not available in the agrarian South. After 1885, there was considerable movement of pig iron to New York and Philadelphia on the coastal vessels from Savannah, Norfolk, and Newport News; and coal from West Virginia found its markets by rail to the seaboard and then by shipment to the Eastern cities, often in enormous 5- and 6-masted coal schooners, through the ports of Norfolk and Newport News in Virginia. The rise of bituminous over anthracite coal gave these Southern ports a bright future in an industrializing America.

The Pacific Coast trade rose to match the pace of the Atlantic and Gulf Coasts during the post-Civil War years. The Pacific coastal trade began after 1848, when San Francisco, San Diego, and Santa Barbara emerged as trading posts, and lumber began to move down from Humboldt Bay and from Washington and Oregon for use in the more southerly cities in both construction and shipbuilding. Flour, cattle, and other foodstuffs were also shipped by the Pacific coasters to San Francisco and other cities from the farms of Oregon; and coal from Puget Sound found its market in San Francisco. By 1860 there were already 37,000-plus tons of coastal and river tonnage enrolled on the coast, and the possibilities for increased trade were unlimited.

As California's ranches, farms, vineyards, and forests were developed in the years after the Civil War, and as Washington and Oregon became important lumbering and agricultural states during the same decades, the Pacific coastal trade quickened to meet the new demands in commerce, especially in handling bulky items more easily transportable by water than by the expanding Pacific rail networks. Early dominated by wooden schooners, but with a considerable number of barkentines and brigs appearing in the trade too, the Pacific coastal trade made an easy transition to steam craft in the 1880's because of the adaptability of the latter vessels to the carrying of lumber. These were the halcyon days of the Pacific lumbering industry. The coastal steamboats tied the forest products to their markets down the coast. Enrolled steamboat tonnage in 1870 was only 110,000 tons, but by 1900 it had climbed to 307,000 tons, and by 1914 it had more than doubled to 637,000 tons. Even the coming domination of the lumbering trade by railroads, visible by the turn of the century, hardly diminished the amounts of cargo carried by the Pacific steamers because the demand for the lumber was so great. Pacific coastal steamers made the conversion to steel hulls and continued to supply the Pacific cities with lumber, grain, coal, oil, cement, iron, salt, and other bulky items through the war years of 1917-18 and beyond.

SCHOONERS, STEAMERS, AND BARGES. In the Atlantic and Pacific coastal trades the wooden schooner enjoyed its days of greatest prominence as a vital part of the American merchant marine. Taking advantage of the rapid expansion of bulk carriage on both coasts, technical improvements built in by ship designers, low-cost wooden shipyard labor, and the corresponding high prices for steel-hulled vessels, the inexpensive, multi-masted, fore-and-aft-rigged schooner found its place in the nation's trade network as the lowest-cost bulk carrier in those segments of the system where speed was not essential. In the years after 1870, three-masted schooners with their sails sub-divided for easier handling could easily beat up and down the sounds, bays, and harbors of America's coasts with fewer crew members (using steam "donkey engines" on the decks of the vessels to mechanically raise sails and anchors with ease) and carry out their vital functions without serious competition from steamers or from land-based railroad competition. By the 1880's, four-masters had appeared with their larger payloads and lower costs to shippers; and the next decade saw even larger vessels with more masts emerge in the lucrative coastal trade. These vessels, up to 8,000 tons in size after the turn of the century, came to be constructed with steel hulls and two steel decks for expanded cargo carriage. In 1902, the one and only seven-masted schooner, the Thomas W. Lawson, took its place in the forefront of the schooner-based coastal trade.

Mainly because of their size and durability, the schooners continued to compete in the maritime trades despite the advent of steamships on the waters and the railroads on land. Schooners could easily and cheaply shuttle between ports as tramp vessels, picking up and discharging cargoes as demand dictated. Their most important item of cargo was coal. Sailing heavy-laden out of Norfolk, Newport News, Baltimore, Philadelphia, and New York, the coal schooners carried their bulky but vital mineral cargo into Boston, New Haven, and Providence, or into other New England or Southern and West Indian ports. Homes and industries depended on the coal schooners for their anthracite and bituminous coal cargoes for heat and light. Boston, for example, imported some 3.1 million tons of coal in 1894. In the carriage of coal, the steam vessels were simply less efficient and more expensive, so the wooden coal schooners continued to dominate the trade.

The schooners' lower freight charges for bulky items help explain its dominance in the ice trade. Ice, cut from Northern rivers and ponds, enjoyed a boom after 1875, with urban growth exceeding local supplies, and the ice schooner came to help fill the resulting demand. Maine, for example, was exporting an excess of three million tons of ice per year by the 1890's, and the hard-working schooners formed the transportational backbone of the valuable trade. As has been noted, the Pacific lumber trade was built on the availability and low cost of the wooden schooners, but the Atlantic lumber trade was also of great importance to the seaboard cities dependent on the vessels for their growing demands. Coastal schooners also carried sulphur from Texas and sugar from Cuba, Haiti, and Louisiana, as well as large amounts of granite, steel, gypsum, iron ore, bricks, and even steel rails for their major competitors, the railroads. Wherever there was a demand for low-cost carriage of bulky items, there the coastal schooners could be found, usually operating on charter, either singly-owned or as part of fleets of thirty to forty dependable sailers like the Palmer fleet.

The schooner reached its zenith in the first decade of the 20th

century, long after steam had driven other sail-driven vessels into re-
tirement. Six-masters of more than 3,000 tons were common; crews of
eight to thirty-three men, depending on the size of the vessel, were
still 25 to 50 percent less than on other vessels. The building peak
for schooners was reached between 1905 and 1909, when ninety-two vessels
of 169,000 total gross tons came off the building ways, compared to only
forty-six coastwise steamers of 156,000 tons being built during the same
years. Maine, Massachusetts, and Connecticut excelled in the building
of these sailing giants. The materials that went into their construction were often brought great distances--tall pines from Oregon and
hardwoods from Canada were commonly used. The New England builders of
the wooden schooners could be competitive in cost because the wages for
shipbuilders there were comparatively low because of the scarcity of
work.

There was also considerable building of schooners in Puget Sound
and Columbia River ports and in San Francisco, because of the availability of local lumber supplies and the demands of the Pacific coastal
trade. As even these giant Western schooners finally gave way to in-
creasingly-efficient steam vessels in the succeeding decades of the 20th
century, the Pacific Northwest came to claim the distinction of being
the last home of the old shipbuilding industry in America. The schooners
had managed to extend the life of wood and sail in America far beyond its
appointed hour by their work in the coastal trades, but time had its way,
and the once-mighty fleet of wooden schooners gradually disappeared from
the nation's waters.

But despite the persistence of the sailing schooner in the coastal
trades until well into the 20th century, the years after the Civil War
were really years of transition, because steam competition could not be
denied. The first sign appeared in the passenger traffic along the
coasts, which came to be dominated by steam vessels as early as the
1840's. The steamers first came to prominence on the waters of Long
Island Sound. They joined all major cities from New York out along the
Sound and around Cape Cod all the way to Boston, in direct competition
with the railroads. Perhaps the most famous of these lines was the Fall
River Line, which existed from 1847 to 1937, giving ninety years of outstanding service to hundreds of thousands of passengers between Boston
and New York via the Sound.

But steamer runs to the South also came into being in the 1840's.
By the end of the decade, they dominated the passenger and fine-freight
service from New York down the Atlantic coast. These steamers were soon
organized on a packet-line basis and easily won the patronage of discriminating travelers and shippers. Among famous Southern lines were the
Baltimore Steam Packet Company's Old Bay Line between Baltimore and the
Hampton Roads' ports; the Star Line from New York to New Orleans (organized in the 1860's); and the Old Dominion Steamship Company (begun
in the same decade), which sailed between New York and Virginia. The
1870's saw the equally famous Mallory Line from New York to Galveston
and the Morgan Line from New York to New Orleans take their places on the
Southern runs. The various lines gradually consolidated and became
larger and more efficient. They continued to serve up and down the

Atlantic and Gulf coasts until well into the 20th century.

The success of the steamboats lay partly in the continued improvements in service they offered. Coming off the ways in Philadelphia; Wilmington, Delaware; and New York, as well as being built in New England and in Virginia, the vessels became larger, safer, and more commodious as the century progressed. Electric lighting, the wireless, and the use of fuel oil in place of coal had become standard on the coastal steamers by the 20th century. Having first taken the passenger service away from the sailing vessels, the steamers then captured the fine-freight cargoes with their high revenues, and finally gained the long-distance, semi-bulky items too. Speed and dependability eventually won out over low cost, and the steamer on coastal waters spelled the doom of the sailers as the nation entered the 20th century. Then the coastal steamers in their turn fell victim to the railroads and finally to the automobile, as new roads and bridges made their way along the Atlantic, Pacific, and Gulf coastal shores. By the end of World War II, the coastal steamer had finally been vanquished by its land-based competitors, but not before adding to the history of coastal transportation one of its more memorable and interesting chapters.

A second competitor to the sailing vessels on coastal waters was able to challenge and then dominate in the last remaining area of sailing dominance, the carrying of bulky freight. This was the coastal barge. Barges had, of course, been used extensively in the canal networks for the carriage of coal for decades, but in the 1870's they began to make their appearance along the seaboard too. Their movement onto coastal waters was made possible by advances in towboat design and power. The combination of powerful, economic towboats and low-priced barges designed to carry several tons of freight was difficult to overcome. Appearing first in the 1870's in the Long Island Sound coal trade, by the 1880's, towboat-cargo combinations could be seen all along the Atlantic coast, sometimes in strings of up to fourteen barges. The barges included both the square-ended scow and 200-to-600-ton ship-shaped barge (usually with a little house astern for the barge captain and his family) used in exposed waters. The latter were towed in line ahead by the powerful towboats. Some "schooner barges" would be used, remodelled schooners cut down with short masts and sails for steadying or for use in emergencies, but which depended on a towboat for normal movement.

The 20th-century coastal barges averaged 1,000 tons in capacity and measured 200 feet by 35 feet by 20 feet deep. They sometimes included watertight bulkheads for load safety. By that time they were definitely replacing schooners in the bulk trades, having gained much of the coal transport, as well as considerable amounts of gypsum, lime, lumber, and petroleum products. The advantages presented by barges assured their dominance in the bulk trades. They were less expensive to build and subsequently required less upkeep and fewer repairs. A combination of towboat and barges required as few as one-third the crew as a schooner. And the barges were shallow-draft, so they could be fully loaded at the wharves. The towboats could drop off and pick up the barges with little time lost in the transfer, and no time was wasted in loading and unloading the barges--hardly a minor advantage. Barge lines could offer to bulk shippers regular and fast service not possible for vessels which required loading and unloading time. Barges, teamed up with steam vessels, finally brought an end to the sailing vessels along the coastal waters.

The shift in coastal vessels in response to economic and technological imperatives was clear by the time of World War I. Whereas in 1889 there were 6,227 sailing vessels working on the Atlantic and Gulf coasts, by 1916 the number had slipped to only 2,539. On the other hand, the number of steam vessels had climbed from 2,536 in 1889 to an astonishing 8,347 by 1916. Likewise, unrigged vessels, i.e., barges, showed an increase from 3,425 to 10,772 during the same period. Steam and barges conquered the coastal trades in the first four decades of the 20th century, but not before the coastal sailing vessels, led by the mighty schooners, had served the nation well for three centuries stretching back to the early settlements in the 17th century, which had quickly turned to the ocean coastal waters to assure their existence and economic growth in the New World.

Yet the conquest of the coastal waters by steam and barge vessels did not mean that their future, in turn, was assured, for during the very years of their final victory over their sail-driven forebears, the railroads were striving to work their advantages in every way possible to dominate the passenger and freight traffic moving along the coasts. Between the years 1865 and 1914, the railroads built over 133,000 miles of track, an average of 3,604 miles per year, and saw their ton-miles in freight rise from 300 million in 1969 to 76 billion in 1890 and on up to 288 billion ton-miles on the eve of World War I. This tremendous record of growth naturally tended to retard the expansion of the coastal trades, especially on short runs and in passenger and fine-freight cargoes.

At the same time, the railroads sought to hamper and control their water-based competitors by buying them up either directly or through holding companies. This control was also used to kill off competing water carriers. For example, in 1884 the Morgan Line was taken over by the Southern Pacific Railroad, and when the same railroad line in 1902 took control of the Cromwell Line, it had complete control of all coasting steamers on the New York to New Orleans routes. Between 1893 and 1900, the New York, New Haven, and Hartford Railroad bought up twenty-two of the twenty-nine short-run steam-packet lines in New England. By 1909, the railroads had control of more than 54 percent of all vessels working the Atlantic and Gulf coasts and 61 percent of the total steamship tonnage. By 1913, they had control of more than seventy-two steamships in the Atlantic, Gulf, and West Indian trades. Railroad control included ownership of the shorter lines, in addition to the long-distance systems. By this means, the coastal steamships became subservient to their railroad competition, although they were not wiped out. The railroads' practice of control by direct or indirect ownership and the subsequent widespread criticism of that practice resulted in a special provision being included in the Panama Canal Act of 1912, prohibiting the railroads from ownership or control of a steamship line with which they competed, or with which they might compete, unless such ownership or control was clearly in the public interest.

But even the divesting of the steamship lines by the railroads when the act became effective in 1914 did not mean that the railroads were willing to step back and allow the coastal steamships and barges to gain all the traffic they might. They still continued to use such practices as slashing of rail rates between points where they competed with water carriers and giving favored rates to shippers for using all-rail routings. The final effects of these efforts by the railroads to stymie the steamers in the post-Civil War years are debatable, for the steamships could undoubtedly not have been able to compete with the railroads in the carriage of passengers and fine freight under any circumstances. On the other hand, the coastal steam service using the low-cost barges easily out-bid the railroads for bulk goods where speed was not essential. But whatever the effects of railroad competition on the coastal services, the modernized coastal steamers and barges continued to play an important part in domestic trade until well into the 20th century.

THE MODERN COASTAL AND INTERCOASTAL TRADES. By making necessary shifts in cargo types and vessels, the American coastal trades have been able to maintain themselves and even achieve growth in the years since World War I. Between 1920 and 1939, from 60 to 70 percent of all ocean-going dry-cargo vessels under the American flag were engaged in the coastal and intercoastal trades, and in the latter years, 442 vessels of almost 3 million deadweight tons were engaged in the coastal, inter-coastal, and possessional trades. This was an even higher number than the 262 vessels of 2.26 million deadweight tons engaged in the foreign trades. The advantages of freedom from territorial tariffs, a wide diversity of products that could easily and cheaply be carried by the coastal vessels, lower line-haul costs than the railroads, and the building of better port and terminal facilities as coastal ports upgraded themselves to try to attract more business--all worked to the coasters' advantage. In addition, their continued protection against lower-cost foreign competition and the opening of the crucial Panama Canal by the United States in 1914 gave the coasters every economic reason to continue to expand their work.

World War I had few adverse effects on the coastal trades. A limited amount of tonnage was drafted for the war effort, and when such requisitioning occurred, the compensation was liberal. Many of the coastal lines continued in operation, carrying out their vital part in the war effort by acting as managers or operators under agreements with the United States Shipping Board. Many other coastal lines worked in the foreign fields during that time of unusually high demand. Like the foreign trades, the coastal trades felt the postwar slump, but recovered quickly because of continued demands for their services and usually showed profits during the 1920's. With the regular demands for bulk cargo augmented by sizeable amounts of excursion and long-distance passenger traffic, the lines normally showed profits. Freight revenues, for example, climbed from $34 million in 1921 to $50 million a year by the end of the decade.

272

The 1930's represented the same period of trial for the coastal lines as they did for the rest of the depression-ridden nation. The drop in revenues from passenger service was particularly severe, but freight revenues never dipped below three-fifths of their 1929 levels. Many lines completely abandoned passenger service, and short-run ferry services declined quickly as a result of the building of bridges, tunnels, and highways as part of the New Deal economic recovery program.

At the same time, many overseas lines were driven back to coastal waters as the entire Western world suffered the effects of the economic slump. The most notable of these returnees were such giants as Pan-Atlantic, Moore-McCormick, and Lykes Brothers. The coastal trades suffered, too, from increased railroad competition, because the Interstate Commerce Commission allowed the rail lines to charge lower freight rates, including even taking losses, between points where they were in competition with water carriers. The I.C.C. allowed the railroads to make up these losses over their noncompetitive routes. At the same time, the construction and completion of much of the Atlantic and Gulf intracoastal waterways for barges and tow carriers made the existence of the oceangoing coasters even more difficult. As a result of these forces, the coastal lines and tramps tended to decline, and private and exempt bulk carriers moved to carrying 93 percent of all the freight traffic along the Atlantic and Gulf coasts.

World War II was equally unkind to the coastal trades. During the war, almost all line vessels were taken over by the government. After the war, none of the 200 requisitioned vessels returned to the Atlantic-Gulf waters, mainly because even before the war some 94 percent of the vessels in this coastal service had been fifteen years of age or older (64 percent had been in service twenty years). In addition to losing almost all of their remaining line vessels, the coastal shippers saw their costs sky-rocket as the maritime unions made tremendous gains among the seamen.

The combined result of the railroads' having gained accounts during the war that never returned to coastal service and of higher investment costs for the replacement of aged vessels after the war was that the numbers of tankers and dry cargo vessels in the trade quickly declined. In 1939 there were 675 vessels of 5.8 million tons in the coastal and intercoastal trades; by 1953 the number of vessels was down to 371, and tonnage was down to 5.3 million tons. The largest drop came in dry-cargo vessels, whose numbers shrunk from 350 to 102 in the late 1940's and early 1950's because owners either did not return to dry-cargo carriage after the war or did not expand their fleets in view of the higher replacement costs and severe competition from other modes of freight-handling.

Total cargoes in the coastal and intercoastal trades made only a modest gain from 83 million long tons to 122 million long tons during the sixteen-year period from 1939 to 1953. Only in the tanker trade was expansion present as deadweight tonnage grew from 3.3 million tons to 4.2 million tons over these years. The number of tankers actually declined from 297 to 269, but their average size increased from 11,000 tons to almost 16,000 dead-weight tons.

The same critical years from 1939 to the mid-1950's saw the number of American flag vessels engaged in the coastal and intercoastal trade decline from the 1933-39 average of 54 percent of American flag vessels to the 1948-54 average of 35 percent. Although there were considerable increases in the movement of cargoes such as sulphur, phosphate fertilizer, and industrial chemicals, the largest gains came in the cartage of petroleum products, which doubled during the period, explaining the increase in the tonnage of tankers as opposed to dry-cargo vessels. But offsetting these bulk-cargo gains were the dramatic falling-off in the amounts of coal moved, as well as in the coastal and intercoastal shipment of processed foods, canned goods, manufactures, and general merchandise.

The coastal trades simply never recovered from the effects of World War II. Before the war, the number and tonnages of vessels in the coastal, intercoastal, and possessional trades always exceeded the number and tonnages in foreign trade. In 1940 there were 693 vessels of 5.9 million tons in the coastal, intercoastal, and noncontiguous trades, as opposed to only 425 vessels of 3.7 million tons in foreign trade. But in 1950 the figures revealed a reversed situation: 434 active vessels of 5.4 million tons in the domestic trades compared to 711 vessels of 8.3 million tons in foreign service. By 1960 the domestic trades' total was only 372 vessels of 5.9 million tons, while the foreign trades had slipped to 558 vessels of 6.5 million tons. Even with the more rapid decline of the foreign-service American vessels, by 1970 the coastal, intercoastal, and noncontiguous vessels still trailed with only 245 vessels of 5.3 million tons as compared to 386 vessels of 5.7 million tons in the foreign trades.

The types of vessels in domestic service clearly reveal the changes that have taken place within the trade. Active tanker tonnage between 1940 and 1970 remained rather consistently in the 3 to 4 million tons range, and topped off at 4.5 million tons by 1970. In 1940, tankers represented 55 percent of all tonnage in domestic trade; by 1950, the figure stood at 68 percent, by 1960, at 73 percent, and by 1970, at 84 percent. In cargo vessels, the figures were 41 percent of total tonnage in 1940, 31 percent in 1950, 27 percent in 1960, and 15 percent in 1970. In passenger-cargo combination vessels, the tonnages were 3 percent in 1940, .5 percent in 1950, and negligible thereafter, with only two combination vessels enrolled in 1970. The modern coastal, intercoastal, and possessional trade network was, unlike the foreign trade segment of the merchant marine, holding its own only on the basis of its tanker trade in petroleum and chemical products. By tonnage carried, the coastal and intercoastal trades still claimed a consistent 25 percent of all freight in domestic waterborne commerce and 15 percent of all foreign and domestic waterborne trade and, with the other branches of the maritime industries, continued to serve the nation well.

THE BUILDING OF THE PANAMA CANAL. The dream of a canal across the Isthmus of Panama dates from centuries past, but it was only in the second half of the 19th century that steps were taken to bring the vision

274

to reality. The first time Americans were involved in a canal project in Central America was to construct a channel across Guatemala. In 1826 a New York company received permission from the Guatemalan government to dig a canal in the vicinity of Lake Nicaragua, but no steps were ever taken to carry out the project.

The first significant move toward facilitating traffic between the Atlantic and Pacific oceans in Latin America came between 1829 and 1835, when a short-lived packet line ran from New York to Cartagena in Columbia and on to Panama, where passengers and freight could make their way through the isthmian jungle to try to catch a vessel sailing along the Pacific shores. During the 1830's, American diplomatic and naval officers commonly reached the East Coast by means of land transportation across Panama or Mexico to avoid the long journey around Cape Horn. Service was improved somewhat in 1840, when the British established their Pacific Steam Navigation Company along the Pacific coast of South America. Two years later they established the Royal Mail Steam Packet Company between England and the West Indies; in 1846 this service was extended to Panama, where travelers could journey by canoe and mule-line across the isthmus to connect with the doughty steamers of the Pacific Steam Navigation Company.

The United States shared an active interest in improving transportation across Panama, and in 1846 made a treaty with the Republic of New Granada for a right-of-way and the right of transit across the isthmus by any means in existence either at that time or in the future. Panama was then a state within New Granada. The following year the Secretary of the Navy authorized mail contracts between New York and the new Oregon Territory by way of Panama. In 1848 vessels were ready for the journeys between New York and Chagres and between Panama and Astoria. By 1849 twelve steamers ran regularly between Panama and San Francisco, heavy demand for them having been created by the discovery of gold in California.

The United States held the Panama route to be of great importance. In 1850 the Clayton-Bulwer Treaty between the United States and Great Britain was drawn up guaranteeing mutual protection of any canal to be cut across the isthmus. But the American government was not depending on a Panama route alone. The Gadsden Treaty of 1853 with Mexico included the right of transit across the Isthmus of Tehuantepec by means of a plank road and railroad. All of this revived interest was based on the success of the U.S. Mail Steamship Company in service to Panama on the Atlantic coast and of the Pacific Mail Steamship Company on the Pacific. These were proving that the Panamanian shortcut was a valuable addition to American commerce. With the completion of the 47 1/2-mile Panama Railroad in 1855 the system was complete. With the steamer services fully operative on each ocean, the time of transit from New York to San Francisco via the Panama Railroad was cut to between twenty-one and thirty days. This improved steam service, as we have noted, meant the rapid decline of the clippers on the long Cape Horn run to California.

This steamship-railroad-steamship Panama route proved to be very

important; it was by far the best means of communication between the
Atlantic and Pacific coasts, although a crossing via Nicaragua including
movement by steamer across Lake Nicaragua carried some passengers and
freight. The Panama route meant far greater speed and safety for passengers on the journey and extended the same advantages to mail, express
freight, and valuable specie shipments. It was the fastest means of
communication between the East and West coasts until the advent of the
telegraph. It has been estimated that in the twenty-year period 1848-
69, more than 442,000 persons made the trip from New York to San Francisco via the Central American routes, 372,000-plus going by way of Panama
and another 67,000 going by way of Nicaragua. Eastbound, the numbers
were somewhat less at 366,000 total passenger transits, with the Panama
route again being the favorite. Without the Panama and Nicaragua short-
cuts combined with steamship services on both oceans, America would have
had to depend almost entirely on the old three-months-or-more journeys
by sail around the Horn to carry its people, messages, mail, freight,
and specie between its rapidly-developing East and West coasts in its
mid-century surge to economic and political unity.

But this Panama route was almost wiped out by subsidized and favored rail competition after the completion of the transcontinentals after
1869. The loss of trade on the Panama route was almost immediate. The
value of trade items moving between New York and San Francisco via
Panama was $15.3 million in 1870, but only $2.6 million by 1880, although it slowly revived to $4.2 million by 1910. The eastbound traffic,
always much smaller, suffered a similar decline, going from $3.1 million
to $2.8 million within ten years. Between 1909 and 1911, by which time
the American railroad system had been essentially completed from coast
to coast, the amount of freight moving from the Atlantic to the Pacific
was 89.5 percent by rail and only 10.5 percent by water. From Pacific
to Atlantic the percentages were even higher, with 95 percent going by
rail and only 5 percent by water. As a result of this rapid shift of
freight and passengers to rails, the steamship lines soon languished,
with only a few remaining in the trade. Coastal lines up and down the
East and West coasts of the United States continued to do good business,
as did Gulf of Mexico lines and domestic lines to the noncontiguous territories of Hawaii, Puerto Rico, and Alaska, early in the 20th century,
but the dream of an all-water Panama route seemed dead in the face of
railroad competition.

Railroad-crazed Americans paid scant attention to the advantages of
a Panama canal during the second half of the 19th century. The enterprising French were more enthusiastic about it by far. In 1879, Ferdi-
nand deLesseps, the famed builder of the Suez Canal, with much fanfare
and publicity on behalf of his Compagnie Universelle, attracted considerable financial support for his dream of a second great canal for
modern times. He began to construct a sea-level canal across the Isthmus
of Panama.

The years 1881 to 1884 were the halcyon days for the French company;
but they were followed by three years of landslides, fever, death, and
flooding. The forbidding mountain ranges, the soil strata and forma-
tions, the tropical rains and flooding, especially from the Chagres River,

and always the thick jungle growths--these proved to be too much for the French. Probably because they lacked the needed technological developments in construction and not because they were inefficient, the French company failed in December 1888. Ironically, in the same year the reluctant decision had been made by the company to switch to a locked canal and abandon the more difficult sea-level canal. The Compagnie Universelle went into bankruptcy; charges of bribery and political intrigue were laid against it. DeLesseps' son, who had been associated with him in the project, went to prison; the father died a broken old man, his unfinished project a mass of rusting equipment presiding over the graves of hundreds of men in the steamy Panamanian jungle.

America had watched the French effort with some interest; it had even bestirred itself to carry out surveys of Darien, Tehuantepec, and Nicaragua between 1870 and 1875. But the economic difficulties of the time precluded any further steps, and nothing developed. The impetus for building a shortcut between the American coasts came not from any recognition of its commercial importance, but from its military necessity. In 1898, during the Spanish-American War, the battleship Oregon required sixty-eight days to steam from Bremerton Naval Base in Washington to join the Atlantic fleet in Key West. This fact was seen as a defense weakness to the expanding Navy and rekindled U.S. interest in a water shortcut across Central America.

By 1903, events favoring a canal across Panama had begun to move with breakneck speed. Volcanoes and earthquakes in Nicaragua the year before had effectively scuttled any idea of building an American canal there, and the United States and Great Britain had agreed to America's building a canal in Panama. The only obstacle was the government of Colombia, of which Panama was then a part, which insisted on a goodly payment for the right to build a canal across its territory. The French company had received money for its rights in Panama; Colombia also wanted to be paid off by the Americans for the privilege of building a canal across its land. These demands were cut short by a "spontaneous" revolt in Panama against Colombia in 1903, in which American naval aid was given the revolutionaries. American recognition of the new country was granted almost immediately, and was followed in short order by the Hay-Bunau-Varilla Treaty for a canal. The treaty specified that the United States was to be given a ten-mile-wide zone across Panama in perpetuity, with all rights and authority as if it were sovereign over the territory and to the exclusion of the same to Panama. America could now build its canal.

When the American civilian canal-building commission began its work in 1904, almost 40 percent of the sea-level canal had been completed by the French. One of the first steps taken was to eradicate disease, specifically yellow fever and malaria, which hit 80 percent of the work force assembled in Panama for the construction project. This preliminary task being completed, the commission, working with 40,000 men, moved 388 million tons of dirt on the sea-level canal before 1906, when Congress decided on a cheaper and faster lock canal instead. In 1907 the whole project was turned over to the Army Engineers, and the dynamic Gen. George Washington Goethals was put in charge of the building of the locked canal. Under his direction, a 100-foot dam was built across Gatun Lake to control the wild Chagres River and its regular flooding and to provide the considerable amounts of water needed to operate the locks; soil was removed to locations miles from the worksites by rail so that the problems of landfalls were solved; four electric locomotives were installed to tow vessels through the three sets of locks (a double flight of three on the Atlantic side and double flights of two and one on the Pacific side); and the grand ditch with its locks was completed in 1913. It was formally opened the following year, nine years after the project was begun.

With the opening of the fifty-one mile Panama Canal a dream of centuries had come true; determination, technology, and American aggressiveness had conquered the Isthmus of Panama for transoceanic commercial and naval traffic.

THE IMPORTANCE OF THE PANAMA CANAL. Since 1914 the Canal has been periodically widened, deepened, and straightened. All locks are now paired for two-way traffic. The three locks in flight on the Atlantic approach have lifts of eighty-five feet to the summit level of 164-square-mile Gatun Lake, and the two locks on the Pacific side lift vessels fifty-four feet. The 1,000-foot locks provide real vessel limits of 975 feet by 106.9 feet by 39.5 feet draft. These real limits are known as the "Panamax" measure. Intermediate gates within the great locks save time and money by making it possible to reduce the size of the locks to 600 feet or 400 feet for lifting or lowering smaller vessels. The lock gates total ninety-two in number, and each is seven feet thick and sixty-five feet wide. Their height varies from forty-seven to eighty two feet, and they weigh from 300 to 600 tons each. However, they are easily opened and closed mechanically because they are watertight, with airtight compartments built in to give them buoyancy for easier movement despite their tremendous weight. The electric locomotives, or "mules," which move the ships into and out of the locks ride on center rack rails and are positioned with two to each side of a ship moving through, two at the bow and two at the stern. Their towing hawsers are held taut automatically as the mules climb and descend 22° grades along the locks. The average transit time for a ship through the 50.5-mile canal from deepwater to deepwater is seventeen hours. Ships are charged tolls of $10,000 to $20,000 per transit.

The distances and time saved by intercoastal vessels in using the Panama Canal are tremendous. From New York to San Francisco via the Straits of Magellan is 13,122 nautical miles; by Panama the distance is 5,263 nautical miles for a savings of 7,859 miles. From New York to Seattle the savings is 7,860 nautical miles; from New Orleans to San Francisco it is 8,806 miles. Translated into time saved on intercoastal voyages, from New York to Seattle a ship travelling at 20 knots and making approximately 480 nautical miles per day would take about 29 days via the Straits of Magellan, but only about 12.6 days via Panama for a net savings of 16.4 days.

In international trade the savings in distance and time are correspondingly great. For example, a ship travelling from New York to Yokohama at 20 knots would travel 9,700 nautical miles and take 20.2 days via the Panama Canal. By the next shortest route, by way of the Suez Canal, the journey would be 13,026 miles and would take 6.9 days longer. By the Cape of Good Hope the distance between New York and Yokohama would be 15,269 miles and would take 11.6 additional days.

When these distances and times are converted into money saved in fuel, the importance of the Panama Canal becomes even more evident. For example, on a trip from New York to San Francisco, a 25,000 gross ton containership travelling at 20 knots uses 179.5 tons of fuel per day. The fuel costs approximately $48 per ton. If the ship were to go by way of the Straits of Magellan, the journey would be 13,122 nautical miles and would take 27.3 days. By way of the Panama Canal the trip takes approximately 11 days for the 5,263 miles covered. The Panama Canal route, then, means a savings of 16.3 days transit time. At 179.5 tons of fuel per day, 2,925 tons of fuel at $48 per ton is saved, resulting in a fuel savings of $140,440 on just one trip from coast to coast. The same ship journeying from New York to Yokohama at the same speed via the Panama Canal instead of the next shortest route, the Suez Canal, would save 6.9 days and $59,450.

The savings would vary according to the type of ship and the price of fuel oil, but the point is clear: the Panama Canal allows tremendous economies for shippers, and eventually their customers, worldwide. Considering that in 1974 over 14,000 passages were made through the Canal by commercial ocean vessels, simple calculations reveal that billions of dollars are saved annually by the use of the Panama Canal. It is also clear that with these fuel economies, to say nothing of savings in crew costs, insurance costs, etc., the assigned tolls of $10,000 to $20,000 per vessel for transit through the Canal are not onerous.

The statistics of transits through the Canal testify to its world-wide importance. In 1915, slightly more than 1,000 commercial ocean transits carrying 4.8 million tons of commercial cargo were made. By 1935, commercial ship transits totaled 5,180 with 25.3 million tons of cargo transported. In 1955, 7,997 ships used the Canal for commercial purposes, and 40.6 million tons of cargo were carried through the waterway. In 1974, the figures had climbed to 14,053 commercial ocean transits and 147.9 million tons of commercial cargo. Tolls received began at $4.3 million in 1915 and topped $121 million in 1974. The highest number of ships using the Panama Canal are general cargo ships, followed by bulk carriers, refrigerated cargo vessels, and then tankers. American vessels using the Canal on intercoastal voyages have dropped from 7.3 million long tons in 1950 to 4.4 million long tons in 1974, but the Canal is still vital to intercoastal trade. Furthermore, the tremendous jump in cargo from the East coast of the United States to Asia from 4.2 million tons in 1950 to 59 million tons in 1974 testifies to the importance of the Canal to this new avenue of trade for the United States. This 59 million tons between the East coast and Asia represents a 51-million-ton lead over any other route utilizing the Canal and constitutes approximately 40 percent of all traffic through the Panama waterway.

The distance, time, and money savings the Canal affords to all nations, plus the vital part it continues to play in the intercoastal trade and in the rapidly-expanding U.S.-Asiatic trade network, make it clear that the Panama Canal under any nation's sovereignty is of vital importance to America's, and the world's, commercial future.

SUGGESTIONS FOR FURTHER READING

Brown, Alexander C. Steam Packets on the Chesapeake: A History of the Old Bay Line Since 1840. Cambridge, Md.: Cornell Maritime Press, Inc., 1961.

Burgess, Robert H., ed. Coasting Captain: Journals of Captain Leonard S. Tawes Relating His Career in Atlantic Coastwise Sailing Craft from 1868 to 1922. Newport News, Va.: The Mariners Museum, 1967.

Cameron, Ian. The Impossible Dream: The Building of the Panama Canal. London: Hodder and Stoughton, 1971

Gorter, Wytze, and Hildebrand, George H. The Pacific Coast Shipping Industry, 1930-1948, Vol. I, An Economic Profile, Vol. II, An Analysis of Performance. Berkeley & Los Angeles: University of California Press, 1952, 1954.

Hammond, Rolt, and Lewin, C.J. The Panama Canal. London: Frederick Huller, 1966.

Hazard, John L. Crisis in Coastal Shipping: The Atlantic-Gulf Case. University of Texas Bureau of Business Research Monograph, No. 16. [Austin]: University of Texas, 1955.

Hutchins, John G.B. The American Maritime Industries and Public Policy, 1789-1914: An Economic History. Harvard Economic Studies, Vol. LXXI. Cambridge: Harvard University Press, 1941.

Kemble, John H. The Panama Route, 1848-1869. University of California Publications in History, Vol. XXIX. Berkeley & Los Angeles: University of California Press, 1943.

Mack, Gerstle. The Land Divided: A History of the Panama Canal and Other Isthmian Canal Projects. New York: Alfred A. Knopf, 1944.

McAdam, Roger Williams. The Old Fall River Line. New York: Stephen Daye Press, 1955.

Miller, Robert. The New York Coastwise Trade (1865-1915). New York: Library Editions, Ltd., 1970.

Nelson, Robert A. Water Transportation in the Pacific Northwest. Olympia, Wash.: Washington State Department of Commerce and Economic Development, Business and Economic Research Division, 1959.

Parker, W.J.Lewis. The Great Coal Schooners of New England, 1870-1909. [Mystic, Conn.]: Marine Historical Association, Inc., 1948.

Sansone, Wallace T. "Domestic Shipping and American Maritime Policy,"

United States Naval Institute Proceedings, 100, 855 (May 1974), 162-77.

U.S. Department of Commerce. Maritime Administration. A Review of the Coastwise and Intercoastal Shipping Trades. Washington: Government Printing Office, 1955.

CHAPTER XV.   ON INLAND AND INTRACOASTAL WATERS

In the years of the nation's emergence economically and politically during the pre-Civil War era, the Mississippi River waterway and its tributaries played a major part in America's development. Goods from the vast interior were brought downriver to New Orleans in ever-increasing quantities to seek their national and world markets through the facilities of the Crescent City. In 1830, the value of goods shipped out through the port stood at $22 million, but the amount grew to an astounding $185 million in 1860. Here, too, goods carried in the flourishing coastal trade found their entry into the interior of the country via the Mississippi and its penetrating tributaries far to the north and the west. The prosperity brought to New Orleans by the river commerce was also evident in such important river cities as St. Louis, Cincinnati, and Pittsburgh, as well as in hundreds of smaller cities and towns along the riverbanks. First by flatboat and keelboat, and then by majestic steamboats, the commerce dependent upon the rivers kept the interior regions in economic lockstep with the industrial and commercial growth of the nation, a growing colossus spreading from the Atlantic to the Pacific.

DECLINE OF THE RIVER SYSTEMS. The Civil War brought the commercial river traffic to a virtual standstill. As the contending armies passed along the rivers, hundreds of craft were burned at their wharves, never to be rebuilt when the fighting came to an end. Traffic patterns formed by the steamboats in their glorious days as the queens of interior travel were broken and scattered in disarray by the tides of war, never to be renewed when peace finally came. Perhaps the potential for rebuilding was present after 1865, and perhaps the inland system could have shared the recovery and renewal that occurred in the coastal trades, but the pressure of railroad competition was simply too great for such a commercial rebirth on the inland waters.

The half-century after the Civil War was the era of railroad dominance in America. Whereas in 1860 the nation boasted of 30,000 miles of railroad track, by 1890 the trackage had reached 167,000 miles, with 85,000 miles of track laid in just the twelve-year period from 1878 to 1890. But the railroad kings were not content merely to build track and purchase equipment to compete with the waterways on the basis of efficiency and cost. Their tactics went far beyond the laissez faire ideal.

The railroads bought up river steamboat lines and then used them at a loss to bleed other lines to death by cutting rates to starvation levels. Often, too, the railroads purchased steamboat lines only to allow the vessels to rot at their moorings and their trade patterns to languish so that the railroad cars could take their place in internal commerce. When not following these destructive practices, the railroads used rate cutting along commercial routes served by both riverboats and rails to drive their water competitors out of business. They discriminated against freight shipments that did not follow all-rail routings from point of shipment to destination. The railroads also carried out deliberate policies of monopolizing waterfronts, often for no other purpose than to prevent the expeditious handling of waterborne freight shipments.

That these railroad tactics against the steamboat operators were successful is revealed by shipping statistics compiled at riverfront cities all along the system. For example, in 1885-86, of the twelve leading commodities shipped from Cincinnati, more than 95 percent moved by rail and less than 5 percent by water. Further downriver at Louisville, the figures for shipment of leading commodities from 1880 to 1886 were almost the same, with 94 percent going by rail and 6 percent by water. Memphis, in 1884, shipped 81.8 percent of its leading commodities by rail and only 18.2 percent by water, despite its most favorable water location on the Mississippi. Other cities showed similar patterns of transportation preference throughout the growing interior regions of the country.

Yet not all of these gains made by the railroads at the expense of the water carriers can be explained by railroad practices alone. Perhaps, in the last analysis, railroad practices of unfair competition only hastened the decline of the waterways; the railroads' advantages and the steamboats' disadvantages clearly favored the overland system. The railroads were able to give frequent, fast, and reliable service to their freight customers with connections to everywhere in the nation, including to major seaport cities for goods destined for foreign customers. The railroads also took advantage of all types of technical improvements, ranging from their locomotives and rolling stock to the track and rail beds over which the trains moved. Very important were the greater size and efficiency in rail operations, which led to reduced rates for freight; the average receipts of $1.92 per ton-mile of freight by the railroads in 1867 dropped more than half to only 80¢ per ton-mile by 1897.

Steamboat service, on the other hand, was often slow, uncertain, and unreliable. River navigation was almost constantly plagued by seasonal and natural hindrances. For example, in eleven of the twenty-four years between 1871 and 1895, there were serious problems on the rivers with low water levels impeding traffic movement. The steamboat services were also small-scale and individual operations and offered little coordination of freight movement. There was no specialization by express service to compete with the railroads in the rapid movement of goods, and there were few technical improvements made on the riverboats. Then, too, the waterways operators could not leave their natural channels and geographical boundaries to reach inland for further service. Freight traffic had to come to the rivers, but rail traffic could be sought out and secured almost anywhere the potential seemed worthwhile. The lower freight rates offered by the riverboats could not overcome the natural and technological advantages offered by the railroad competitors; indeed, the waterborne operators actually depended upon the railroads to reach inland and bring cargo traffic to them.

This decline in the use of the rivers did not come about because the federal government was insensitive to the natural problems of the waterways operators and parsimonious with its aid. Federal expenditures on rivers and harbors actually climbed astronomically during the period. In 1867 the government appropriated $1.2 million for rivers and harbors; by 1875, the amount had climbed to $6.4 million. The years that followed witnessed increased outlays of money, until by 1895 the figure stood at $19.9 million; and by 1910 it reached $29.2 million appropriated.

Yet despite the continued work by the Corps of Engineers on the inland rivers, steamboat traffic continued to decline. Steamboat tonnage employed on the Upper Mississippi declined 80 percent between 1870 and 1910, and on the Lower Mississippi it declined almost as much (70 percent). On the crucial Ohio River, steamboat tonnage dropped 75 percent in the same forth-year period. By 1900, the railroads carried 593 million tons of freight, compared to 60 million tons on the Great Lakes and only 28 million tons on the Mississippi system. Considering that railroad and waterways tonnages carried were approximately equal in 1860, the decline of the Mississippi system in particular was clear to all concerned. Unlike the Great Lakes waterways operators, the inland river interests seemed to have no natural advantages they could exploit to regain their place in the nation's transportational system and to offer their particular benefit of lower cost to America's shippers and customers.

The only area in which the inland waterways operators could and did offer technological improvements with which to compete with the railroads was in the development and use of barges for bulk commodities. Barges were first introduced in the 1850's, having proved their worth in the transportation of coal elsewhere. During that decade, the size of barges increased until they were of 10,000- to 20,000-bushel capacity. Steamboats began by towing the barges at their sterns, sometimes with ten barges or more in a tow with 7,000 to 8,000 bushels of freight per barge. By 1859, approximately one-half of all the coal shipped from western Pennsylvania moved by barge, and the use of barges for bulk commodities had spread from the upper Ohio above the Falls all the way to New Orleans. Lashed together, the barge tows sometimes measured from 36 to 50 feet in width and from 100 to 180 feet in length.

In the post-Civil War decades, the use of barges on the inland waters slowly revived and then began to accelerate quickly as their advantages became obvious. In 1868, for example, the Ajax moved from Louisville to New Orleans with a tow of twenty-four barges measuring a total dimension of 250 feet by 750 feet and transporting within the lashed barges 16,000 tons of coal. In 1878, another steamer moved thirty-two barges to New Orleans with 22,000 tons of freight; and in 1902, the Sprague moved a tow of sixty barges measuring 312 feet by 925 feet with over 67,000 tons of coal. More typically, tows above the Falls of the Ohio were usually 4,000 to 10,000 tons in capacity, compared to 15,000 to 25,000 tons below the Falls. In 1891, there were 6,000-plus barges of 3.1 million tons capacity on the Mississippi system, with approximately 5,000 of those barges being used on the Ohio River.

The Upper Mississippi added its own technological innovation in the form of giant timber rafts (typically 275 feet by 600 feet in size and enclosing as much as 3,500 tons of logs). These easily moved to lumber mills downstream when water conditions were favorable. Yet despite these gains in the use of thousands of barges for bulky commodities and timber rafts for logs, further innovation was slow in coming, and the problems of slow speed on the rivers could not be overcome. The slowness was particularly attributable to natural obstructions, and the increasing presence of railroad bridges across the rivers served as constant hazards to effective navigation. Interestingly, too, the towing interests actually opposed the building of slack-water locks and dams for better navigation because, they argued, these would cause unnecessary delays. Even the river interests themselves had much to learn about the possibilities of their trade.

REBIRTH OF THE INLAND WATERWAYS SYSTEM. It was only after three decades of decline that the inland river system became a center of renewed interest, which eventually led to a rebirth of the system. The dynamic force for rebirth did not come from the rivermen themselves, but from Congress. The lawmakers were motivated not by any particular concern over the economic benefits made possible by waterways improvements, but by their anxiety over railroad abuses and the lack of competition in the nation's transportational networks, and later by their concern over the need for conservation measures.

This Congressional concern was expressed first in the Rivers and Harbors Appropriations Act of 1876, but was more clearly reflected in the Rivers and Harbors Appropriations Act of 1882. The latter act stated Congress' concern for unifying the country and facilitating commerce between its various sections. It also envisioned the waterways as an inexpensive alternative to the rapidly-expanding railroads with their almost monopolistic hold on the nation's commerce. That Congress was determined to improve the waterways to control the railroads by competition was demonstrated when the act was passed over the veto of President Chester A. Arthur. The act included a general prohibition on tolls on the inland waters too.

These were but preliminary signs of concern, for the 1890's emerged as a decade of renewed solicitude for America's waterways, based on the belief that water transportation was both cheaper and an effective regulator of railroad rates. By the turn of the century, concern had developed into enthusiasm for the waterways' possibilities, and the rail-freight congestion and "car famines" of 1906-07 even induced some railroad leaders (James J. Hill, for one) to endorse some waterways projects to improve the nation's transportation system. When conservationists such as Theodore Roosevelt and Gifford Pinchot also looked to the nation's waterways and their improvement for gains in the field of conservation, the movement took a giant step forward; in 1907 President Roosevelt appointed the Inland Waterways Commission to study the needs and possibilities of the inland waterways.

All of this interest and enthusiasm bore fruit in the Panama Canal

Act of 1912, the legislative keystone for the revival of inland transportation. The act decreed that railroads could not own, control, or
operate a water carrier. This was a partial declaration of independence
for the inland carriers, as well as for the coastal operators, who had
also felt the restraining force of railroad ownership. The law did not
demand complete divorce of the systems; it stated, rather, that unless
the carrier traversed the Panama Canal (i.e., engaged in intercoastal
commerce), the Interstate Commerce Commission could allow ownership or
control as long as it did not reduce, exclude, or prevent competition.
The obscurities present in this statement of principle were cleared up
in the years that followed by litigation that led to court rulings in
favor of the divorce of the competitors unless water service was clearly
auxiliary to rail service.

After World War I, the government entered more fully into waterways
promotion by creating the Inland and Coastwise Waterways Service in 1918
to bring government support to water carriers, including barge lines on
the Mississippi River and on the Warrior River from Birmingham to Mobile.
The Transportation Act of 1920 declared that it was the intent of Congress to promote, encourage, and develop water transportation in the
United States. This declaration of intent was given reality when Congress in 1924 created the Inland Waterways Corporation to demonstrate the
capabilities of the modern towboats (actually square-bowed push-boats)
and barges to serve the transportation needs of the nation. The Corporation included $5 million in capital stock investment held by the United
States government. Control of the enterprise was given over to the Army
Crops of Engineers. With this act the modern inland transportation network was reborn after seventy years of neglect and soon grew to play a
larger role in the carriage of goods for the nation.

THE MODERN INLAND WATERWAYS SYSTEM. The success of the active part-
nership between the federal government and the inland operators is clearly revealed in the tonnage statistics gathered since that time. In 1924,
slightly over 34 million short tons of freight were carried on the inland
waters (9.6 percent of all domestic waterborne commerce and 7.5 percent
of all foreign and domestic waterborne commerce). By 1940, 70.2 million
tons were being carried on the inland waters for 14.1 percent of the domestic waterborne commerce and 11.5 percent of all waterborne commerce.
In 1955, the figures for tonnage carried had more than tripled to 249.7
million tons, which was 33.5 percent of domestic waterborne and 24.5 percent of domestic and foreign waterborne commerce. Only fifteen years
later, in 1970, tonnage had almost doubled to 472.1 million tons--49.6
percent of all domestic waterborne commerce and 30.8 percent of foreign
and domestic waterborne commerce. Since 1924, tonnage had increased almost fourteen times over; and there had been a 40 percent increase in the
percentage of domestic waterborne tonnage carried and a 23.3 percent increase in the amount of foreign and domestic waterborne commerce borne by
the inland water carriers. In 1970, approximately 10 percent of all commerce carried on nationally by all modes of transportation was moved by
the inland waterways.

A review of the waterways developed by the Corps of Engineers since
1924 reveals how this tremendous growth in tonnages and percentages was

made possible, for the watercourses now improved extend far beyond the early channels of the Mississippi and its tributaries to interior regions far inland and into areas where improvements in water transportation were never dreamed of before the 20th century. In the entire Mississippi River system, there are 8,954 miles of improved waterways, including 5,465 miles of over nine feet in channel depth. On the Pacific Coast there are another 1,491 miles, including 264 miles of over nine feet in depth. In this entire system only the Lower Mississippi and the Missouri Rivers are not slack-water systems, that is, they are not improved by the installation of locks and dams for easier navigation. The dams, where erected, provide on the high side of a stable channel for navigation and calm water for a considerable distance until the descent of the river requires another dam to raise the water level. Many of the dams include hydroelectric components. Since 1959, the Corps has established standard lock dimensions, and all locks around the dams are either 66 feet by 400 or 600 feet; 84 feet by 600, 800, or 1,200 feet; or 110 feet by 600, 800, or 1,200 feet. It takes a towboat-barge combination an average of twenty to thirty minutes to pass through each lock; but if the tows are long and have to be unlashed and taken through in sections, the time required may be as much as an hour-and-a-half for this double lockage and reassembly of the tow.

The channelized and free-flowing Lower Mississippi River constitutes 1,174 miles of navigable waterway. The non-slack-water Missouri River from Sioux City to St. Louis (and juncture with the Mississippi) has 732 miles of navigation. The Ohio River, first canalized in 1929, since 1959 has been the scene for the installation of nineteen new high-lift locks, which are 110 feet by 1,200 feet in size. The Ohio, busiest river in all the system, is 981 miles in length from its beginning at the confluence of the Allegheny and Monongahela Rivers at Pittsburgh to its joining with the waters of the Mississippi at Cairo, Illinois. The Upper Mississippi is 663 miles in length and has twenty-seven dams and locks along its improved path from Minneapolis-St. Paul toward the lower river at the mouth of the Missouri. The Arkansas River's improved channel is 448 miles in length and extends from Catoosa, Oklahoma, to the Mississippi via the Verdigris River.

Other major improved channels in the Mississippi system are the Illinois Waterway, flowing 353 miles from Chicago to a point on the Mississippi just north to St. Louis; the Cumberland River flowing through southern Kentucky and northern Tennessee for a length of 380.8 miles; and the Tennessee River flowing through western and eastern Tennessee and northern Alabama for a length of 652 miles. Construction is under way for the improvement of the Red River across Louisiana into northeastern Texas. Along the Gulf to the east of the Mississippi is the Warrior-Tombigbee River system in Alabama, which ties the important cities of Birmingham and Tuscaloosa to the sea of Mobile. Extensions are planned to carry traffic between the Warrior and the Tennessee Rivers via northeastern Mississippi and along the Alabama River and its extensions all the way to Rome, Georgia. Another river reaching Gulf waters in the inland waterway system is the improved Chattahoochee along the Alabama-Georgia border and passing through the panhandle of Florida, the construction is planned on the Trinity River in Texas, which will connect Dallas-Ft. Worth to the sea by means of twenty-one locks and dams.

On the Pacific Coast, the major improved channels are the Columbia-Snake River system now developed for both navigational and hydroelectric purposes. It is 340 miles in navigable length and includes locks with lifts exceeding forty feet. This system carries 5.5 million tons of logs per year, as well as large tonnages of grain from the rich Northwestern interior. The other major Pacific improved channels are the Willamette River of 132 miles and the Sacramento River system of 245 miles, both of which open their interior territories to the savings of bulk carriage directly to the Pacific Ocean waters. The improved San Joaquin River channels add another 131 miles to the Pacific system.

TOWBOATS, BARGES, AND TRANSIT TIMES. Working all of these rivers and responsible for the tremendous tonnages moved on them are the towboats that move the barges to their destinations. Actually the name "towboat" is a misnomer; the barges are pushed, not towed, along the river systems at speeds of from three to twenty miles per hour. The towboats are from 117 to 160 feet in length and from 30 to 40 feet in width. They are virtually flat-bottomed and draw from 7.6 to 8.6 feet of water. They rise as high as forty feet above the water and give their pilots good visibility over their loads as they push the barges up and down the rivers. The towboats are from single to quadruple screwed with each propeller connected to a separate diesel engine. This gives the towboats from 1,000 to 6,000 horsepower, and the Kort nozzles that enclose the propellers and channel the water past the propellers give up to 25 percent more thrust to the drive mechanisms than could otherwise be obtained. The largest of the towboats, with 6,000 horsepower, can move up to 50,000 tons of cargo with little difficulty. Almost all the towboats are now diesel-powered and have electric steering controls, radio and radio-telephone units for constant communication, radar to give exact fixes on their location on the rivers, depth finders, and swing indicators to assure that the entire load is lined up properly.

The largest towboats can push up to forty barges at a time, a cargo equal in capacity to 650 railroad cars. The barges are lashed together side-by-side and back-to-front by steel cables and are also lashed to the towboat at its giant "towing knees" at the forward end of the blunt-bowed vessel. There are about 3,000 towboats working the inland and intracoastal waterways in the 1970's with ever-increasing power and ever-increasing efficiency.

The barges used in modern towing systems have a draft of from six to twelve feet and carry bulk loads of from 500 to 3,000 tons. Their cargo consists of anything from raw materials to petroleum products, chemicals, grains, coal, and large manufactured items. Barge tows can be "non-integrated," meaning that each barge is raked at both ends so that drag is created at the juncture of each barge with another in the tow. Tows can also be "fully integrated," meaning that the center barges have blunt ends with no rake, and the front barges in a tow have their single rake forward and the rear barges have their single rake in the stern. This combination reduces drag by effectively creating a tow with a smooth

289

bottom from front to rear, so greater efficiency is gained; but difficulties arise when the center (non-raked) barges are separated because
they are very unwieldy in that state. A compromise of this arrangement
is the "semi-integrated" tow, in which barges having one end raked and
the other flat are lashed with the barges' flat sterns together, giving
a raked bow and stern to the tow as it moves through the water, but
avoids utilizing non-raked barges. That such innovations and arrangements are very important is made evident by the fact that semi-integrated tows can carry 8 percent more load than non-integrated tows while
creating 18 percent less water resistance--with an increase of 25 percent more cargo carried per ton-mile-per-hour and therefore a considerable savings.

Barges are basically of four types. Most numerous are the hopper-
type barges, which are essentially double-skinned boxes which can carry
dry bulk cargoes in addition to vehicles and manufactures of various
types. Open hoppers run to lengths of 290 feet and can carry up to
3,000 tons. They usually carry raw materials for the steel and aluminum
industries plus sand, gravel, coal, limestone, lumber, fertilizer,
machinery, and many other bulk goods. Covered hoppers running up to 195
feet in length and carrying up to 1,500 tons of cargo have watertight
covers over their cargo holds, which either lift off or roll back during
loading and unloading. These commonly carry grains, coffee, paper and
paper products, cement, dry chemicals, lumber, and all types of packaged
goods. There are approximately 17,000 dry-cargo barges and scows, total-
ling more than 21 million tons capacity, in use on the inland waterways
system.

The second most numerous type of barge is the tank barge, which may
be up to 290 feet in length and 50 feet in width and has a capacity of
1,000 to 3,000 tons (or 300,000 to 900,000 gallons of fluid cargo). Some
are single-skinned, with bow and stern collision bulkheads, and others
are double-skinned with an inner and outer shell. A third model of tank
barge has independent cylindrical tanks fitted into a hopper-type barge
to permit expansion and contraction and can carry liquids under pressure.
There are at least 2,600 tank barges with 6.1 million tons total capacity
in use; they move more than 154 million tons of liquid products each
year, including various petroleum products, plus amonia, liquified sulphur, liquified methane, and liquid hydrogen.

The less numerous of the barge types include: the deck barges,
which have a box hull and heavy plated decks to which machinery and
equipment are lashed for shipment; carfloats which can carry ten to twenty
railroad cars from railhead to railhead or from railhead to shipside;
automobile haulers; square-ended scows, for general hauling; self-unloading barges, for cement and grain movement; and derrick and crane barges,
for special purposes. There are even cattle barges for the carrying of
livestock to market. The transportation of bulk commodities has clearly
come a long way since the pioneer days of flatboats and keelboats in the
early days of river traffic on the Mississippi and its tributaries.

Typical transit times for these giant towboat-barge combinations
would be a wonder to the early rivermen of a century ago. From Pitts-

burgh to New Orleans, a journey of 1,852 miles, now takes less than nine days downstream and only fourteen days upstream. From Minneapolis, at the head of Mississippi travel, to New Orleans on the Gulf takes but eight days for the 2,257 mile trip downstream, and about 13 1/2 days upstream. From St. Louis to New Orleans is a journey of over 1,000 miles, but modern towboat-barge combinations make the trip in a little over four days downstream and less than nine days upstream. Thus while inland barge service is slower than its rail or highway competitors, its combination of large bulk capacity moving night and day with modern navigational aids at speeds of up to twenty miles per hour is able to ensure delivery of its cargoes in reasonable times at a fraction of the cost of its speedier competitors.

For that reason, the inland waterways system has developed rapidly. In 1974 the total inland waterways system, including the intracoastal waterways, transported 119 million tons of bituminous coal and lignite, 70.4 million tons of sand, gravel, and crushed stone, 66 million tons of residual fuel oil, 40.9 million tons of distillate fuel oil, 30 million tons of gasoline, 28.9 million tons of grain and grain products, 19.5 million tons of rafted logs, 18 million tons of marine shells, and 13.4 million tons of basic chemicals of various types, as well as dozens of other bulk products, for a total movement of almost 600 million tons of cargo.

All of this cargo moved at an average cost of approximately three mills per ton-mile as compared to 15 mills (1 1/2¢) per ton-mile by railroads (although some special-unit train rates ran at the rate of 6-7 mills per ton-mile). Movement by truck costs an average 65 mills (6 1/2¢) per ton-mile, and air freight as much as 20¢ per ton-mile. Water carriage is still the least expensive means of transportation, and shippers of bulk cargoes are clearly moving to it.

Responding to the increased customer demand for their services, the inland waterways operators are expanding and improving their services. Unlike other areas of America's merchant marine, the inland waterways are using newer equipment, most of it having been obtained since World War II, and are increasing their technological efficiency. More than $1.65 billion has been invested in this mode of bulk transport, and the future appears bright for the 80,000 persons employed directly on the inland waterways and for an equal number employed in their ancillary shore-based operations. The inland waterways system has matured to become a basic transportational industry in the half-century since its rebirth in 1924.

THE GULF INTRACOASTAL WATERWAY. Very important to the economy of the states that front the Gulf of Mexico is the Gulf Intracoastal Waterway, built in the 20th century. It goes from St. Marks, Florida, south of Tallahasee on Apalachee Bay, to Brownsville, Texas, on the Mexican border 1,108 miles away. Approximately one-half of the total mileage is across existing lakes, bays, and sounds. An extension of the waterway is the Houston Ship Channel, which connects that city with the waterway and the Gulf of Mexico fifty-two miles away. A projected extension of the

Gulf Intracoastal Waterway is the deepening of the Trinity River to Dallas-Ft. Worth. Completion of the Cross-Florida Barge Canal in northern Florida would tie in the Gulf Intracoastal Waterway to the St. Johns River and the Atlantic Intracoastal Waterway, but this last project has been subjected to many delays in Congress.

The Gulf Intracoastal Waterway is one of the busier waterways in the nation. In 1974, 103 million tons of cargo representing 17 billion ton-miles moved along the main channel, with another 15 million net tons and 970 million ton-miles accounted for on its sixty-four-mile alternate routing between Morgan City and Port Allen, Louisiana, on the Mississippi across from Baton Rouge. Of this total of 118 million net tons of cargo, almost half was made up of petroleum products; 25.8 million tons were in processed fuel products, and another 25.1 million tons consisted of crude petroleum. In addition to this petroleum cargo, the busy waterway also moved large amounts of sand, gravel, crushed rock, industrial chemicals and minerals, iron and steel products, and some manufactured products.

What is particularly interesting about the Gulf Intracoastal Waterway is the fact that almost all of its cargo movement is directed to other points on the system rather than beyond the Gulf region. Approximately 80 percent of all dry products move to other points on the Waterway, and 65 percent of tanker cargoes also are destined for cities on the Gulf. Furthermore, 9 percent of the remaining 20 percent of dry cargo is shipped to points on the nearby Lower Mississippi; 24 percent of the remaining 35 percent of tank cargo is destined for Lower Mississippi ports. The other 11 percent of the tank cargo finds its destination on the Upper Mississippi and on the Ohio and its tributaries, with a fractional amount moving to Great Lakes points.

The importance of the Gulf Intracoastal Waterway is therefore chiefly in the benefits it gives to the Gulf states; but the ripple effects of this localized industrial carrier, which is helping to transform the Gulf coast into an industrial region, are nationwide. It is also interesting to note that a full 98 percent of all cargo movement on the Gulf Intracoastal is in barges. Here, as on the Mississippi, Ohio, and Pacific systems, the towboat and barge have scored an almost complete victory over other modes of water transportation.

THE ATLANTIC INTRACOASTAL WATERWAY. Canalization parallel to the seaboard for more efficient movement of goods was not a new idea in the states along the Atlantic, as we have seen, but it was only in the 20th century that an integrated system of protected passage along the Atlantic seacoast was achieved. Parts of the system, such as the Chesapeake and Delaware Canal between the bays, and the Albemarle and Chesapeake and Dismal Swamp Canals from Chesapeake Bay to the North Carolina sounds, had been in existence since the middle of the 19th century and before, but the enthusiasm for water systems that surfaced in the early 20th century was required to complete the system--with one notable "missing link"-- utilizing sounds, bays, bayous, and man-made channels from New England to the tip of the Florida peninsula.

292

Direct agitation in favor of such a protected waterway down the Atlantic coast began in the 1880's and resulted in Congressional approval of twelve projects during that decade. The 1890's saw thirteen additional projects begun. Between 1910 and 1919, another sixteen projected links were begun; and the 1920's and 1930's saw another twenty-nine authorized. Much of the impetus for this waterways improvement flowed out of the National Rivers and Harbors Congress, which met in 1901; and 1907 saw the formation of the very influential Atlantic Deeper Waterways Association, which carried on very effective agitation in favor of completing the system from Boston to Key West, utilizing natural water systems connected via short canals. By 1941, eleven of the twelve major links had been completed in the waterway, which stretches for 2,000 miles along the coast. The twelfth and final "missing link" was a ship channel across New Jersey. In the 1940's, another thirty-one minor projects to complete the waterway were carried out, and the Atlantic Intracoastal Waterway was essentially completed during that decade.

The Atlantic Intracoastal Waterway utilizes the natural water bodies of Massachusetts Bay, Long Island Sound, New York harbor and its connecting channels, the Delaware Bay and River, Chesapeake Bay, and the sounds of North Carolina--plus numerous smaller bodies of water to the south along the coast--to reach from Boston to southern Florida. These natural links are joined by the man-made channels of the Cape Cod Canal, the Delaware and Raritan Canal from New York harbor to the Delaware River, the Chesapeake and Delaware Canal from Delaware Bay to Chesapeake Bay, and the two alternate canals between Chesapeake Bay and the North Carolina Sounds. The most important of the man-made links are the Cape Cod Canal, the Chesapeake and Delaware Ship Canal, and the Albemarle and Chesapeake Canal.

The Cape Cod Canal, cutting through Cape Cod between Massachusetts Bay on the north and Buzzards Bay on the south, is a 7.5-mile man-made canal that follows an ancient Indian canoe portage route. It was designed to save ships and their crews the trip around the stormy tip of Cape Cod on their journeys between Boston and New York. Dreamed of first in the 17th century, the canal was privately built between 1909 and 1914 and was taken over by the federal government in 1925 after a payment of $11.5 million to its owners. Despite the hopes put forth for the more complete utilization of this sea-level canal, 100 feet wide and 25 feet deep at low water, the canal remains too narrow for modern shipping of either self-propelled or towed vessels.

The Chesapeake and Delaware Canal is a 55-mile, deep-water channel between the bays. As we have seen, the canal was first built in 1829 and was gradually improved and widened, but was still of limited use because of its relatively small vessel limitations. Then in 1919 the Chesapeake and Delaware was taken over by the federal government, although little was done to improve it. But in 1935, with the nation in the grip of the depression, Congress decided to convert the Chesapeake and Delaware into a full sea-level ship canal as a job-producing measure. The new channel was 250 feet wide and 25 feet deep along its entire length, a great boon to ships operating between Philadelphia and Baltimore. With the locks eliminated, so successful was the Chesapeake and Delaware as a ship canal that in 1962 the decision was made to improve it still further to keep pace with the larger ships operating in the coastal and international trade.

The new channel as now completed is 450 feet wide and 35 feet deep, large enough for moderate-sized ocean vessels as well as towboat-barge combinations to use the channel with little difficulty. It is estimated that a full 40 percent of all ships calling at Baltimore harbor make use of the Chesapeake and Delaware Ship Canal. The channel averages 20,000 vessel passages per year, even though it is limited to vessels of 650 feet or less in length. These vessels account for the 10 million-plus tons of shipping that pass through the valuable waterway each year. The canal is undoubtedly the most important link in the whole system in terms of ship and cargo tonnage because of its continued improvement and its location between two of the most vital water bodies on the East Coast.

The Albemarle and Chesapeake Canal, opened in 1859 in competition with the alternate Dismal Swamp Canal to the west and improved by the federal government after acquisition in 1912, is a third link in the Atlantic Intracoastal Waterway, although all the waterway south of Norfolk is limited by its comparatively shallow project depth of only twelve feet and by its confining width. The Albemarle and Chesapeake handles small towboat-barge combinations and a large number of pleasure craft making their way up and down the coast, but today's large oceangoing tow-barge combinations and coastal vessels cannot be accommodated on the limited waterway. This is most unfortunate because the Albemarle and Chesapeake takes advantage of many shallow natural bodies of water as it makes its way one hundred miles south from Norfolk to Beaufort, North Carolina. By utilizing the south branch of the Elizabeth River, the North Landing River, and Albemarle and Pamlico Sounds, a sea-level canal is created with no locks except for a tidal lock at its northern entrance, no tolls, and a twelve-foot minimum depth throughout. Yet to convert the Albemarle and Chesapeake Canal and the Intracoastal Waterway into an ocean ship channel would be such an expensive undertaking that it has never been seriously contemplated. Given the ever-increasing size of oceangoing and coastal vessels, a new waterway would probably be outmoded by the time it was built.

Often considered part of the Atlantic Intracoastal Waterway is the 353-mile New York State Barge Canal, owned and operated by the State of New York. The Barge Canal was designed to repace the Old Erie Canal and to recapture for New York some of the cargoes moving away from it along the St. Lawrence or lost to various railroads that touched the Atlantic seaboard at other points. The rebuilding of the Erie began in 1903 and was finally completed in 1918. It cost $155 million and was designed to take vessels of 1,000 tons when the reconstruction was completed. Connected in the east with the Hudson, it was to enlarge that river's barge traffic and tie it to the cargoes moving to the east from the Midwestern and western New York regions.

The Barge Canal basically followed the path of the old Erie Canal from Buffalo to the Oswego and Seneca Rivers, then across Oneida Lake to make connection with the Mohawk River and thence to the Hudson north of Troy, providing a considerable amount of slack-water navigation before reaching a remarkable flight of locks at Waterford. Three branches were tied into it, one of twenty-four miles to Oswego on Lake Ontario to tap the traffic there, a second of sixty-three miles to the north of Waterford to Lake Champlain (and continued to the north by Canada's Richelieu Canal to the St. Lawrence), and a third in the Finger Lakes region known as the Cayuga-Seneca Canal. The whole canal system has widths of 75 to 200 feet and a twelve-foot minimum depth. There are thirty-four main locks in the system, each lock 310 feet long, 45 feet wide, and 12 feet in depth over the sills.

Unfortunately for the backers of the project, the completed Barge Canal has always been limited by its small lock capacity. Reaching a high in tonnage carried of 5 million tons in the late 1930's, the Canal has slowly been declining ever since, and in 1974, it carried only 2.2 million tons of cargo. Like much of the Atlantic Intracoastal Waterway with which it is connected, the New York State Barge Canal has never lived up to its expectations and is limited to local traffic because of its size limitations.

The northeastern section of the Atlantic Intracoastal Waterway, whatever its backers' hopes, has evolved into a waterway important for local traffic only. While it carried more than 62.5 million tons of tanker cargo in 1972, 99 percent of this cargo was destined for area use. What is true of the northeastern section is true also for the Waterway's main section from Norfolk 1,200 miles south to Key West. In 1972, a full 100 percent of its 44.2 million tons of tanker traffic and its 18.3 million tons of dry cargo traffic was consigned to regional use. Thus the Atlantic Intracoastal Waterway, like the Gulf Intracoastal Waterway, is primarily a protected regional waterway system, and in this function it continues to have importance in the latter decades of the 20th century.

The entire inland waterways network including the dominating Mississippi River system, the Gulf Intracoastal Waterway, and the Atlantic and Pacific systems, continues to play a very important part in moving the bulk goods of the nation, and does so at relatively low cost. In 1975, there were almost 4,000 towboats and tugs in commercial use on the inland waters, and more than 25,000 barges of various sizes and descriptions carried their giant loads to meet the demands of commerce. Freight tonnages carried rose from 183.4 million tons in 1940 to 599.2 million tons in 1974, while net ton-miles rose in the same period from 22.4 billion to 247.4 billion ton-miles. Coal, sand, gravel, rock, crude oil, processed petroleum products, chemicals, and grain and grain products accounted for 436.5 million net tons of the total freight tonnage of 599.2 million tons--a full 73 percent of all tonnage. The 599.2 million tons carried by the inland vessels accounted for 39 percent of the total waterborne commerce of the United States. If the Atlantic Intracoastal Waterway and the New York State Barge Canal have never lived up to their promises in modern times, the same cannot be said for the Mississippi, Gulf, and Pacific systems. They are vital and expanding segments of America's bulk transportation network and a valued national asset.

295

SUGGESTIONS FOR FURTHER READING

American Waterways Operators, Inc. Big Load Afloat: U.S. Inland Water Transportation Resources. Washington, D.C.: American Waterways Operators, Inc., 1965.

_____. Inland Waterborne Commerce Statistics. Arlington, Va.: American Waterways Operators, Inc., annual publication, 1963--.

Baughn, William H. The Impact of World War II on the New Orleans Port-Mississippi River Transportation System. Baton Rouge: College of Commerce, Louisiana State University, 1950.

Clowes, Ernest S. Shipways to the Sea: Our Inland and Coastal Waterways. Baltimore: Williams & Williams Co., 1929.

Gray, Ralph D. The National Waterway: A History of the Chesapeake and Delaware Canal, 1769-1965. Urbana: University of Illinois Press, 1967.

Hunter, Louis C. Steamboats on the Western Rivers: An Economic and Technological History. Cambridge: Harvard University Press, 1949; reprint ed., New York: Octagon Books, 1969.

Lass, William E. A History of Steamboating on the Upper Missouri River. Lincoln: University of Nebraska Press, 1962.

Moulton, Harold G. Waterways versus Railways. Boston and New York: Houghton Mifflin Company, 1909.

U.S. Army. Corps of Engineers. The Intracoastal Waterway: Atlantic Section. Washington: Government Printing Office, 1961.

CHAPTER XVI. AMERICA'S MARITIME POSTURE, PRESENT AND FUTURE

A concern for America's future and for the various elements that
will ensure its continued vitality in the latter decades of the 20th
century requires a recognition and overview of its existing maritime
strengths and weaknesses, both on its inland waters and on the oceans.
The nation has developed into an industrial giant now dependent to a
substantial degree on the continued movement of its raw materials and
semi-finished and finished goods to and from various locations throughout the land and across the oceans of the world. The United States is
now an integral part of the industrial-agricultural complex of mutual
dependence that is coming to dominate the world economic scene. Its raw
materials and processed goods must move domestically at least in part by
water; its raw materials and other goods to and from foreign lands must
by necessity depend on water transportation almost entirely. Economic
isolation is as impossible for the United States today in the international commercial world as it is for the solitary citizen within the
complexities of the domestic economy. Politically and militarily, too,
the nation has an important stake in water transportation, a stake only
vaguely perceived--if at all--by the citizens of the nation. What
America will be in the future will depend to a considerable degree on
the decisions it makes regarding its maritime potential in the 1970's
and beyond.

THE CURRENT OCEANGOING FLEET. In December 1976, the United States
oceans fleet consisted of 531 active private vessels and 12 government-
owned vessels for a total of 543 active ships. There were also 47 inactive private and 249 inactive government vessels, bringing the totals
to 578 private vessels and 261 government vessels for a total potential
fleet complement of 839 merchant vessels. The active vessels included
6 private and 3 government passenger-cargo combination ships, 146 private and 7 government freighters, 16 private bulkers, 222 private and 2
government tankers, and 141 intermodal vessels. This total of 543
active private and government ships had an aggregate of 9.6 million gross
tons and 14.3 million deadweight tons. The 47 inactive private and 261
inactive government vessels represented 2.9 million gross tons and 4 million deadweight tons. Thus the overall total of 578 private and 261
government active and inactive vessels was 839 vessels of 12.5 million
gross tons and 18.3 million deadweight tons. The 543 active vessels of
9.6 million tons represented only 2.6 percent of the total gross world
tonnage of 372 million gross tons. If the 296 inactive vessels are included, the total U.S. flag fleet of 839 vessels and 12.5 million gross
tons raises its percentages of world gross tonnage to only 4.1 percent.

The 543 active American oceangoing vessels included 348 engaged in
foreign trade. Of these, 274 were involved in trade between the United

States and other countries; 16 vessels were in nearby foreign trade; 3 were in Great Lakes-St. Lawrence foreign trade; and 255 were in overseas foreign trade. The 274 vessels represented 6.7 million deadweight tons. Another 15 vessels of 1.12 million deadweight tons were engaged in trade between one foreign country and another, and 59 vessels of 1.15 million deadweight tons were in foreign trade under U.S. government agency charters. Compared to these 348 vessels of almost 9 million deadweight tons engaged in foreign trade, oceangoing flag vessels in domestic trade totaled 195 vessels of 5.23 million deadweight tons. These included 116 vessels in the coastwise trade, 25 vessels in the intercoastal trade, and 54 vessels in trade with the noncontiguous possessions.

The average age of the private vessels in the American merchant fleet is seventeen years; the average of the government vessels is thirty years. Together their average age is twenty-one years--the oldest fleet in the world.

If active tonnage alone is considered, the U.S. flag fleet of 9.6 million gross tons is the eleventh largest in the world. Leading in gross tonnage is Liberia with 73.4 million tons, followed by Japan with 41.6 million, the United Kingdom with 32.9 million, Norway with 27.9 million, Greece with 25 million, the U.S.S.R. with 20.6 million, Panama with 15.6 million, France with 112 million, Italy with 11.1 million, and then the United States with 9.6 million. If active and inactive tonnage is considered, the United States is eighth in the world.

As stated earlier, the United States fleet constitutes 2.6 percent of the world's fleet if only active vessels are considered; if active and inactive vessels are considered, the figure rises to 4.1 percent. If, however, the approximately 25.2 million gross tons of American-owned or American-controlled shipping under foreign flags is added to the totals, the foreign flag and active American fleet is 34.8 million tons or 9.3 percent of the world's fleet. The foreign flag plus active and inactive American fleet total is 37.7 million tons or 10.1 percent of the world's fleet. Either figure places the American fleet third in the world according to gross tonnage. By numbers of vessels active, the United States has 543 of the world total of approximately 22,500 for a percentage of 2.4; adding the inactive vessels brings the figure to 3.7 percent, but the gross tonnage of vessels is a much more accurage indication of maritime strength than mere numbers of vessels. Of the active vessels in the American fleet, 190 (all private) are subsidized in their operations by the federal government; this is 35.7 percent of all active vessels.

The size of the American fleet and its ability to carry necessary cargoes into and out of the country is extremely important to the future of the nation. Whether or not the American fleet is sufficient to meet all economic needs must be measured, in part, by its ability to bring into the country essential raw materials for the nation's industrial society. Whether delivered by American or by foreign vessels, the United States imports 100 percent of its tin, rubber, cobalt, and chro-

mite, 99 percent of its manganese ore, 88 percent of its nickel, 87 percent of its bauxite, 85 percent of its asbestos, 44 percent of its lead,
32 percent of its iron ore, and at least 40 percent of its petroleum.
These raw materials are absolutely essential to the American industrial
complex; without them the manufacturing processes would stop, and the
nation's industrial economy would fail. In addition to the 500 million
tons of these and other products imported, the United States exports
266 million tons of cargoes to foreign countries by means of water.

America must decide if its merchant fleet is adequate to these
tasks. Is it willing to see American bottoms carry only 6.4 percent of
its exports and 6.3 percent of its imports by weight and 17.5 percent of
its exports and imports by value? If it judges the oceangoing fleet to
be inadequate and the nation vulnerable, it must decide what it is going
to do about improving the merchant fleet.

THE MARITIME UNIONS. The nation must also decide what it will do
regarding the ships' crews, their working conditions, and their labor
unions. Since the 1920's the number of berths on American merchant ships
has been steadily decreasing. In 1929 there were 63,800 men employed on
U.S. merchant vessels, excluding the Great Lakes and inland waters. As
of 1970, there were only 37,600 berths. It is within the context of
this decline that the problems of crewing and unions must be considered.

Shipboard employment has been an area of contention between workers'
representatives and management since the formation of the first maritime
unions in the 1880's and 1890's. It is only since 1915 with the Seamen's
Act that the federal government has been brought into the picture in a
major way, but even there the government has been unable to approach the
situation with an even hand. In the 1920's the maritime unions were
broken by the shipping depression, but the industry did nothing to try
to improve working conditions for the seamen who remained in the industry. Management made no efforts to devise systems of job security
through continuous employment or any of the other devices utilized by
progressive land-based industries to assure worker loyalty and satisfac-
tion. This neglect explains, at least in part, the militancy of the
maritime unions as they experienced a resurgence in the 1930's. In
particular, it explains how the unions gained the right of exclusive hiring through union halls. The companies' hiring practices had given no
assurances of employment to the capable seaman however good his attitudes
and work. As a result of the strength gained by the unions during the
1930's, labor-management relations have evolved into mutual warfare with
little cooperation either way, but with the unions usually winning their
demands because of the government's rather myopic allegiance to the
unions' cause. The results of the constant struggle have been a poorer
class of seamen and shoddy job performance under poor working conditions.

The unions have negotiated contracts with no common expiration
dates and have employed "rolling barrage" tactics against the shipping
companies, with first one and then the other hitting the companies with
demands and strikes. The companies, on the other hand, rendered power-
less by the hiring hall system either to reward the good worker or to
punish the bad, have largely given up, because the seamen have become,

in effect, employees of the union, not of the companies, who merely contract for a number of workers through the unions. If an employee is fired for reasons either good or bad, he has to be returned to the union hall at company expense and is there usually hired out for another job. The companies have the right to choose only their captains and chief engineers; the rest of the crew is chosen by and is under the control of the unions.

All of these factors, combined with higher and higher wage rates, have driven many companies out of business and others to foreign flags. The combination of the unions and government support of their practices and demands has driven many companies to the wall. The government mediators only seem to want fast settlements of any disputes and are willing to utilize court injunctions in order to attain them. While the unions are gradually becoming less militant in the face of the merchant marine retrogression they have helped cause, they remain very powerful and hold a hammerlock on any long-range solutions to the problems of the American oceangoing merchant marine.

There are four principal maritime unions. These are the Seafarers' International Union of North America (SIU), made up primarily of the unlicensed crewmen on unsubsidized vessels; the National Maritime Union of America (NMU), representing principally the unlicensed crews of subsidized vessels; the International Organization of Masters, Mates, and Pilots (IOMMP), representing deck officers and captains; and the National Marine Engineers' Beneficial Association (MEBA), composed of all the engineers. These maritime unions control not only hiring through their halls, but also all questions of pensions, seniority, wages, and promotion. Again, other than captains and chief engineers, all other members of the crews in effect work for the union that hires them out to the shipowners.

Through the efforts of these unions, however, working and living conditions have greatly improved on American flag vessels. Modern vessels now include semi-private accommodations for the crew members, as well as more than adequate food, plus air-conditioning, linen service, and crew recreation rooms. Wages for a typical work year of seven months at sea now average about $6,800 for a utility man, $13,500 for an electrician, and $27,268 for a chief engineer, this in addition to approximately $1,200 per man in fringe benefits and no deductions for room, board, and living services while on board ship. The combined pay rates and other expenses assumed by the companies for their crews are approximately double that of crews on foreign-flag vessels. Consequently, American-flag operators can compete only by capital intensive operations; but here again the unions have been adamant in protecting the larger crews by less capital-intensive operations.

Faced with the labor-management problems of the industry, MARAD is now more inclined to back the idea of reducing crew sizes and costs in the industry, because American-flag shipping simply cannot continue under these expense pressures. Thus the Merchant Marine Act of 1970 calls for agreements on crew sizes before construction is even begun on a vessel that will operate under subsidy. But the unions are fighting

300

back through intensive lobbying and public protests. In the mid-1970's they have sought to protect American cargoes, and therefore the jobs of their members, by demanding a change in the law to mandate that a full 100 percent of all government cargoes--not the older 50 percent--and at least 30 percent of all oil and gas imports into the country be carried by U.S.-flag vessels. Despite the fact that this would raise the costs on these items significantly to pay for an even more heavily subsidized merchant marine program, and despite the fact that such legislation as been vetoed by Republican Presidents, the chances would appear to be good that passage of some type of guaranteed cargo law--with the enthusiastic support of the shipbuilders too--might well pass the Congress and receive a President's signature.

Other proposals, designed more to cut crew costs than to maintain or increase costs as demanded by the unions, have been tendered. One of these is to allow general-purpose crewing of a vessel with no craft union boundries to increase efficiency. These general-purpose crews would do many different jobs on board ship and would be company employees with all wages and benefits worked out between the companies and their crews, not with the unions. Advocates of the plan argue it would significantly cut crew costs, upgrade crew standards, and result in higher pay for the crew members. They point to its apparently successful adoption on some British flag vessels. Needless to say, the unions and their allies in government are adamantly opposed to general-purpose crewing. It has also been suggested that better crewing and work standards would result by taking on women as sailors and by providing accommodations for wives of the crew members on their extended voyages. Both of these suggestions have already been adopted by various foreign nations.

Whatever the answers to the problems of union control of maritime crews, company unwillingness to expend time and efforts on better labor relations, the high cost of American crewing, the flight from the flag by American-owned vessels to avoid these and other higher costs, the ability of American vessels to attract freight with or without cargo guarantees, and possible innovations in crewing arrangements, Congress must ultimately face up to the problems and adopt laws and policies that extend beyond its members' partisan and regional concerns. The politicians and all concerned might well examine carefully the working conditions and arrangements on America's inland waters, where a more open labor supply and better working conditions have been achieved under conditions of open competition with less interference from the deadening hand of federal bureaucracies.

SHIPBUILDING. If labor policies and practices are forcing the United States out of the world market in shipping, it can be argued that American shipbuilding practices are also making a significant contribution to the decline. During the heavy demand for shipping during World War II, fifty-seven shipyards built almost 6,000 ships in record time. This success was achieved by multiple production of standard designs, by a conversion from riveted to welded shipbuilding, and by the prefabrication of large sub-assemblies. These innovations were adopted by Japanese and European yards after the war, but American shipyards by and large returned to their more antiquated methods of construction. Because of the erosion in demand for American-built ships since 1965, the number of private shipyards has fallen from fifty-seven to only fifteen, while related employment has dropped 80 percent.

The less-efficient construction of vessels on a one-or-few-ships-at-a-time basis with its higher costs has been fostered by government policies. MARAD has parcelled out orders for vessels among various yards instead of consolidating the building of certain types of vessels in extended runs by one or a few shipyards. The result has been small numbers of vessels built by yards to individual specifications with modern mass production techniques impossible to obtain. The instability in ship orders caused by wide fluctuations in demand has forced the shipyards to adopt policies of risk aversion by avoiding extensive long-term investments in newer equipment and processes. The result, in turn, has been lower efficiency and a more labor-intensive mode of building, since costs can be cut more expeditiously through discharging men than through discharging debts for capital improvements. American shipbuilding, as a result, is very labor intensive, meaning it uses a very high number of men to carry out its processes rather than using machines to do the same things. The result, of course, is higher costs for the vessels built.

Like almost all American manufacturing industries, American shipbuilding is much more labor intensive than are its foreign competitors. Unlike other manufacturing industries, however, the amount of capital expenditures per employee in shipbuilding is decreasing while the amount spent in other manufacturing is rising. For example, in 1964, capital investment in all American manufacturing industries stood at $789 per employee. In motor vehicle manufacturing it amounted to $1,286. In shipbuilding it stood at only $269. The other industries showed an increase in capital investment per employee over the years; the shipbuilding industry had actually declined from $327 per employee in 1958. As a result of this lack of capital investment, cost-saving technological innovations are coming to the shipbuilding industry much more slowly than elsewhere. Simply put, American shipbuilders are not substituting capital for labor very speedily, with the result that costs are higher and productivity per man is lower.

Productivity in American shipbuilding is now approximately one-half the rate in Sweden and Japan because of these factors, while foreign wage rates stand at about one-third to one-half the current American rates in equal dollars. As a result, the United States cannot compete internationally in shipbuilding despite its industrial prowess, and the United States shipbuilding subsidy is a subsidy to industrial inefficiency as it is now being applied because it forces the American ship buyer to pay higher costs for ships of American make with the taxpayer making up the difference between foreign and American yard costs. Added to this shipbuilding inefficiency, the American taxpayer must also pay the higher expenditures for American-flag operation through the operating differential subsidy. The drop in the construction subsidy to amounts far below the old 50 percent rate under pressure from MARAD and the Merchant Marine

Act of 1970 is a hopeful sign that technological efficiency is being gained in shipbuilding despite the barriers thrown up against it by the system. But American shipbuilding still has a long way to go before it lowers its costs sufficiently to compete effectively in the world ship-building market with or without shipbuilding subsidies.

One suggestion that has been made calls for the federal government to play its effective role as the single buyer and controller of ship production through its naval building and commercial subsidy programs. It is argued that the federal government should assure orders of types of vessels large enough in quantity and spread out over a number of years to ensure a rational structure in the industry and the cost effectiveness of technological innovation. If the government would allow builders of naval and merchant vessels to bid on larger numbers of essentially the same type of vessels to assure a long-term building program at their yards, it would then be possible for them to invest in new machines and processes to assure technological efficiencies impossible on small quantity, special order contracts. This policy would allow the yards to specialize according to their present and future capabilities and to effect cost savings to all concerned. It would, of course, also mean that the government should not continue to sustain uneconomical shipyards that are unwilling or unable to produce naval and merchant ships effi-ciently. While this policy would result in some regional unemployment, the evidence of the high rate of turnover in American shipyards clearly shows that the unemployed shipyard workers could and would be re-employed in other industries with a minimum of adjustment. Such a buying and building program, it is estimated, would result in a savings of at least $90 million per year in shipbuilding costs if only a 5 percent price de-cline in vessel cost was achieved. Keeping a lesser number of yards ful-ly employed with maximum efficiency would also result in a more satisfac-tory core of productivity and skill for rapid expansion in case of na-tional necessity than would keeping fifteen yards of questionable effi-ciency alive as a potential nucleus.

Whether or not such basic changes in the shipbuilding industry will be made to assure greater efficiency at lower cost for an essentially stronger industry is problematical. It is a fact of life in America and in the entire field of shipbuilding that with heavy government involve-ment in the process--for good or ill--the inevitable result is policy de-cisions that are essentially political, not economic. Nevertheless, economic imperatives call out for serious consideration of the nation's alternatives in its shipbuilding industry. The public and the policy-makers must consider alternatives to programs that promise little hope of long-term success.

FLAGS OF CONVENIENCE. As is obvious from maritime statistics, high-er American shipbuilding and manning costs, whatever their justification or lack of justification, are forcing more and more American-owned ves-sels to flee the flag to foreign registry. In 1974, recorded ships of convenience (i.e., those owned by American companies or their foreign affiliates, but not including those owned directly by American citizens or by companies not direct affiliates of U.S. companies) totaled 678 in number of 25.2 million gross tons and 47.9 million deadweight tons. By

comparison, in 1976, there were 543 active ships of 9.6 million gross
tons under American registry. The 678 foreign-flag American vessels
included 485 tankers, 84 freighters, and 109 bulk and ore carriers. Of
these vessels, 321 were under Liberian registry, 102 were under Panamanian registry, and 9 were under Honduran registry. These 432 vessels
of 32.24 million deadweight tons were thus with countries with which the
United States has agreements for return in case of emergency, leaving
246 (36 percent) of the vessels of 15.6 million deadweight tons under
flags of countries with which the United States has no agreements and,
therefore, not under effective control. Besides the three PanLibHon
countries, American-owned vessels are also registered in the United
Kingdom (122), and the Netherlands (25), as well as in France, West
Germany, Argentine, Italy, and Norway. Being built for use under foreign
flags in 1974 were 123 vessels of 24.99 million deadweight tons, 94 of
which vessels (20.8 million deadweight tons) were for Liberian registry.
The American-owned flag-of-convenience fleet, then, is larger by number
and probably three times as great by capacity than the active American
flag oceangoing fleet, and is expanding rapidly.

Whether or not these flag-of-convenience vessels are available for
American use in time of need depends upon the interpretation of the doctrine of effective control. Under American law, the Secretary of Commerce has the right to requisition any vessels owned by American citizens
in case of a national emergency. In addition, as we have seen, when
transferring to a foreign flag, a shipowner signs contracts with MARAD
guaranteeing ultimate ownership of the vessels by Americans and a majority
of Americans on the board of directors of the company owning the vessel,
as well as contracts guaranteeing the availability of the vessel upon
national need, including the right of the United States Navy to take over
the vessel in such a case of emergency.

However, under international law it would appear that ultimately the
flag country has the complete right to control the movement and activities
of vessels under its flag. Furthermore, there is nothing in international
law on the right of requisition in time of war over a vessel owned by
citizens of one country but under the flag of another. Yet the United
States does have agreements with Panama, Liberia, and Honduras to the effect that the ships would be made available to the United States. But
these agreements are not by treaty, although the three nations would undoubtedly allow--or could not prevent--the return of the vessels to American registry.

Yet if this doctrine of effective control seems to give the edge toward America's regaining the PanLibHon vessels, it must be recalled that
the right of angary applies only in territorial waters; and that if a vessel is on the high seas, it can be taken only by the navy of the nation of
its registry. Therefore, the United States might be able to seize a flag-
of-convenience vessel under the right of angary only if it were in American territorial waters.

At the same time, it must be borne in mind that even if the United
States did requisition the vessels and they were returned, the vessels

304

under flags of convenience are primarily in the European and Japanese trades, so such confiscations would leave our probable allies economically vulnerable. The cost of such damage to their economies might be too great to make seizure feasible. Of course, the United States could always take the flag-of-convenience vessels on the reasoning that an enemy would consider them belligerent and destroy them anyway; but such a doctrine is questionable under international law.

All in all, whatever the complexities of American rights under international law, whether or not a vessel is returned to American registry in case of emergency may well boil down to its location, the circumstances in which it finds itself, and the attitudes and actions of the captain and crew. These latter may well not be Americans and may feel no compulsion to return their vessel to American waters and have their ship assume the more dangerous status of a belligerent vessel in time of war. The doctrine of effective control, taken in its best light, is at least questionable and has never been tested; at its worst, it may well represent but wishful thinking. But if the legal questions are finally settled by force as applied by the United States Navy, then, too, the Navy may well have a worldwide task rounding up the giant vessels for American use and shepherding them home.

One legal principle regarding flags of convenience, however, is very clear. In a unanimous decision in 1963, the United States Supreme Court ruled that the National Labor Relations Board has no jurisdiction over foreign-flag crews because the law of the flag state governs the internal affairs of a ship, and picketing such a ship in American waters is not allowable by law and is damageable in court. Thus there is no way the maritime unions can force their wage standards or working rules on foreign flag operators, and wage scales undoubtedly will continue to be lower than on American vessels.

It is largely on this question of wage scales that the American owners of foreign flag vessels argue to the necessity of their vessels' status. They assert that they have been forced from the American flag by the high costs of wages, and that if they did not utilize PanLibHon flags then they would be forced to register under European flags where the United States has no right of effective control. They further contend that adequate, cheap, and efficient transportation of raw materials is needed by the United States and the whole world, so they are serving a real economic need both for their own country and for the international economic order. They also justify their actions by pointing out that they represent a savings to the United States since they ask for and receive no subsidies from the taxpayers because of their more efficient method of doing business. They argue that while other traditional maritime nations continue to grow, it is only the United States, with its high costs, that sees its shipowners forced to use flags of convenience; if they did not, they assert, there would be even less American presence on the high sea lanes. They sum up their arguments by saying that their vessels will be available to the United States in case of emergency according to contract and the doctrine of effective control, but that they simply cannot operate under the United States flag with its inflated labor costs and its mandate to buy American-made vessels, which cost twice as much as vessels built in other countries, to say nothing of the costs and delays imposed by the increasing American maritime bureaucracy.

Opponents of flag-of-convenience practices counter with the argument that the real reason for operating under foreign flag is to continue to operate many older vessels that could not pass U.S. Coast Guard inspection. The result is vessels that are unsafe to their crews and, with their lower standards of building and maintenance, also contribute to such dangers as water pollution through oil spills and careless flushing and ballast procedures. They contend that the vessels are in fact not inspected with any care or diligence because the countries of registry do not care. The countries could not enforce higher standards anyway, as the ships seldom if ever visit the nations in which they are registered, but continue to sail all around the world. The American maritime unions are particularly opposed to the use of flags of convenience because they claim that it results in a serious loss of jobs both in manning and in the shipbuilding industry. The maritime unions would prefer to call the flags of convenience "runaway flags" or "pirate flags."

Whatever the legal status of flags of convenience in case of a national emergency when the doctrine of effective control would really be tested, whatever their necessity, and whatever their destructive effects on attempts to impose higher safety standards and control pollution through national legislation and the 1960 International Convention on Safety of Life at Sea ("SOLAS"), the fact remains that the fleet of over 600 vessels under flags of convenience is too important to American trade--especially in the importation of vital raw materials--to deny them across to American ports. The patterns of ship ownership and registry since World War II clearly point to the continued use and growth of the flag-of-convenience fleet and of America's dependence upon it to sustain itself economically. Whatever policies may be made in regard to the flags of convenience, they will have to reflect these basic realities.

SOVIET CHALLENGES. If the American merchant marine continues to maintain only a small part of world tonnage and to carry only a limited amount of goods in world trade, the same cannot be said for the merchant marine sponsored and controlled by the Soviet Union. Since 1953 the Russian merchant fleet has grown from 483 vessels to over 2,400 vessels of 20.6 million gross tons. Russia is one of the fastest-growing maritime powers in the world. Since the Soviet Union does not need the sea lanes for communication between the parts of its vast empire and is almost self-sufficient in both energy and raw materials, it must be assumed that the purpose for this build-up of maritime power must lie elsewhere. Some other reasons must explain why so much energy and money are being put into shipbuilding and the operation of a merchant marine. The reasons probably lie in the political-economic advantages that a merchant marine gives to the Soviet Union. Clearly, one reason for its rush to merchant marine power is to decrease the nation's pre-1960 dependence on Western charter vessels, which is both expensive and would be a potential weakness if these charters were withdrawn for any reason.

It would appear that the Russian merchant marine is being built up to enable its ships to carry more than one-half of Russia's foreign trade, to enable it to deliver without interference both economic and military aid to the nation's present or future client nations, to earn currency to offset the unfavorable Soviet balance of payments, and to supply Russia's own limited coastal needs. That the merchant marine could enable the Soviet Union to deliver goods to its client states was dramatically revealed in Angola in July 1975, when Soviet vessels delivered critical supplies to the rebel forces being supported in that country. The Russian merchant marine will also serve as a national defense auxiliary supporting its navy and armed forces in their areas of operation wherever they might be. It is important too that the merchant marine can serve as a visible presence of Soviet concern in areas where military presence might provoke an unfavorable response. An imposing merchant fleet can say as much as can naval vessels to people reading political signs and symbols.

Whatever the reasons for the Soviet merchant marine presence on the seas of the world, it is clearly growing. While the Soviet fleet may have few modern, cost-effective vessels at the present time, a huge building program for such ships is under way; and since 1965 the Soviet merchant marine has grown at the rate of approximately 600,000 tons a year. Western nations provide about 50 percent of the shipbuilding tonnage. Part of the Russian building program calls for increasing numbers of giant tankers for the use of emerging countries to allow them to break their dependence upon the West for transportation of their petroleum--and to make them dependent upon the Soviet fleet instead. Construction is beginning on tankers of 370,000 tons displacement and over 1,100 feet in length. In addition, the Russian fleet has about 125 containerships and a number of lesser-sized self-unloaders to be used in smaller countries and ports, perhaps to increase Soviet influence there. The Soviets are also making an effort to capture the international cruise market by building seventy new passenger ships, which will pay off in hard currency, prestige, and influence.

It seems clear from what can be understood about Soviet merchant marine policy that it is an extension of the Soviet design to surpass the West by economic means wherever possible. If the Soviet merchant fleet has a long way to go before it achieves major maritime status, it is apparently on the way to that goal and desires to utilize its maritime power effectively upon the world scene. Already cargoes usually carried by American vessels are being taken away by lower-rate Soviet vessels; more of the same can reasonably be expected given the discrepancies in cost between the two fleets and the support they enjoy from their respective nations.

If Soviet merchant vessels portend difficulties for the future, Soviet fishing vessels represent severe difficulties already for the United States. Since the Soviet Union depends on fish for about one-third of the protein requirements of its people, fishing is a crucial industry for that nation. Fishing is also used to build up commercial relations with other countries, one important way being the Soviet method of converting "trash fish" into protein concentrate, which is used as an additive for foods and is being exported by Russia as a form of aid to more than fifty countries.

The Soviet fishing fleets now operate in the Caribbean, the Indian Ocean, the Persian Gulf, and along both coasts of North and South America. Soviet fishing is carried out by flotillas that include processing and freezing vessels in addition to trawlers. The Soviet fishing fleet consists of more than 5,000 fishing and support vessels of 5 million-plus gross tons. After testing an area and being assured of an adequate catch, the flotilla of factory ships (800 feet in length and capable of processing 300 tons of fish per day), trawlers, oilers, and refrigerated transports moves in for the catch. The Soviets utilize helicopters and many other sophisticated fish-locating devices in their work. A flotilla may run to more than 100 ships and can cover an area fifteen by twenty miles at a time, taking virtually all available fish from the sea in that area. These flotillas first made their appearance in the Western Hemisphere in the 1950's off the coast of Newfoundland and Labrador. In the 1960's, they arrived with regularity off Cape Cod and on the east and west coasts of the United States and South America.

The fishing projects in various parts of the world, including the Near East and some African and Indian Ocean countries, are used as part of Russia's aid program to those countries and allows them to use port facilities in these strategic areas. Closer to the United States, Cuba has been built up as a base for Russian fishing in Latin American and Caribbean waters and has been maintained despite the low catches in these waters by Soviet fishing vessels. The total harvest from these waters is less than 1 percent of the total Soviet fishing catch. It is generally accepted in military and intelligence circles that these Soviet fishing flotillas also carry on very important intelligence-gathering missions including plotting radar installations, monitoring military radio messages, and gathering oceanographic data. The Soviet fishing fleets have even been known to trail and observe U.S. Navy fleet operations. Whatever their military value, the fishing fleets win for Russia about $100 million per year in foreign exchange. The Soviet fishing fleet is the second largest in the world, with an annual catch of almost 8 million metric tons; Japan is first with more than 10 million metric tons. The American fishing industry is a distant fifth behind these two leaders. It also trails Peru and Norway.

In contrast to the Soviet fishing efforts, and partly as a result of them, the United States fishing industry is in a state of regression. While the American catch of fish remains constant at less than 3 million metric tons per year, 70 percent of the fish products used in America are imported at a loss of approximately $1 billion to the country. As a matter of fact, some American companies regularly buy directly from Polish and Romanian companies via the French islands of St. Pierre and Miquelon off Newfoundland and from Canadian ports. New England in particular has been hard hit by the fishing decline, showing 46 percent less landings in the decade of the 1960's alone.

The American fleet is still mainly using fixed gear methods instead of trawling. The average age of the smaller boats making up the American fishing fleet is twenty-six years, and they are ill-equipped for modern fishing techniques. The American deepwater fisherman faces high insurance premiums in addition to being limited to buying and using higher-cost American-built vessels if he intends to land his catch in the United States. Despite his pleas for help, he is the victim of inadequate government aid in both the construction and the insuring of his vessels. Whether or not the 200-mile limit for commercial purposes unilaterally imposed by the United States for its ocean borders, which went into effect on March 1, 1977, will be able to be enforced adequately to assure American fishing grounds to American fleets remains to be seen. Whether this step, combined with possible Congressional limitations on imports of fish into the country, as has been constantly urged by fishing interests, will preserve America's once-plentiful supply of fish and lead to a resurgence of the fishing fleet will be watched with interest in the years ahead. While the American fishing interests in Chesapeake Bay, in the Gulf of Mexico, and in Alaskan waters have shown an increase since 1950, New England, Middle Atlantic, and Pacific Coast fishing has gone into precipitous decline because of Russian competition. Perhaps new American initiatives will reverse the trends in the American deep-sea fishing industry and will lead to a revival of a once-prominent American industry.

THE PANAMA CANAL. As has been pointed out in Chapter XIV, the American coastal and intercoastal maritime fleets have been in a state of decline. The once-predominant coastal trade network now consists primarily of tankers and towed barges owned or chartered by independent companies as the liner trades have disappeared. Oil, ore, and coal still move along coastal waters in significant amounts, with Gulf-to-Atlantic oil tanker traffic constituting the primary traffic pattern.

Intercoastal traffic, too, has declined in the face of high operating costs and rail competition. The land-bridge concept has developed in the United States, wherein special, fast rail units carry containers from Atlantic to Pacific ports for water shipment beyond, and from various ports of the country to the Gulf for further water movement. This constitutes a major challenge to the already-declining intercoastal water routes. Whether the shipments by trailer-on-flatcar or container-on-flatcar utilize the "Mini-Bridge" (shipments that begin or end in the United States) or the "Land-Bridge" (shipments that begin and end in a foreign country), the result is a faster method of container movement utilizing both rail and water facilities, that is rapidly growing in popularity. But whatever the fate of the remaining intercoastal vessels, the most vital link in both intercoastal American shipments and in international shipping in the Western Hemisphere, the Panama Canal, will remain crucial to American commerce and concern at least throughout the remainder of the 20th century.

Approximately 78 million tons of cargo, or more than 17 percent of America's 457 million tons of waterborne foreign commerce, utilize the Panama Canal to reach their destinations. By value, more than 35 percent of all cargoes in United States foreign trade pass through the Canal. An average of forty vessels per day traverse the waterway; transits total 14,000-plus per year. These vessels are all of necessity within the 975-by-106.9-by-39.5-foot "Panamax" limits and carry no more than 65,000 long tons. Approximately 80 percent of all ships of all flags passing through the Canal are going to or coming from the United States, and 90 percent of the shipments between some of the Latin American nations and the United States use the Canal. In addition, 40 percent of all commercial traffic through the Canal is made up of shipments from the East Coast of the United States to and from Asian ports.

The current rate of 14,000 transits per year will climb to approximately 16,000 or 17,000 by 1985, and the physical limit of 23,000 to 24,000 transits will be reached in about the year 2000. By that time the Canal will be handling about 515 million long tons of traffic, assuming continued national and international growth rates, the building of additional deep water ports, the increasing size of ships, and other factors. The estimated absolute maximum for the Canal will be 26,800 passages per year, a figure that should be reached by the year 2010. In the meantime the United States has been carrying on a number of short-run improvements to assure maximum use of the channel for the next twenty-five years. These include increased water supplies, improved navigational aids including radar, improved scheduling of transits, and shortened lockage time, including the installation of new and more effective electric mules. It is assumed that with these improvements the present canal can be kept functioning until past the year 2000, at which time it could still handle approximately 90 percent of the world's vessels.

In the long run, however, other alternatives have been examined. These include improving the present canal by installing a third-locks system to supplement the double locks. This third-lock system would cost about $950 million to $1.5 billion depending on the size of the new locks, but would increase capacity to 35,000 transits per year. Also under study has been a plan for construction of a sea-level canal elsewhere in Panama. Usually designated as Route #10, this would be a double-lane canal and could handle up to 38,000 transits a year without lockage delays. It would cost approximately $2.9 billion. An alternative to Route #10 would be a sea-level canal in the Canal Zone itself following one of two routes. Either of these Canal Zone sea-level canals would cost approximately $3 billion, but would permit transit of 39,000 vessels per year.

Other sea-level alternatives lie outside the immediate area of the present canal. They include a longer sea-level canal further northwest across southern Nicaragua and northern Costa Rica. It would cost $11 billion to build and would handle 35,000 vessels a year. Another plan would call for cutting a canal across eastern Panama from Darien to San Miguel Bay. This alternate route would handle 42,000 transits per year but would be very expensive, costing at least $3 billion if nuclear devices were used to excavate and much more by conventional digging. A fifth sea-level alternative would be to cut a new canal further to the east close to the South American mainland in northern Colombia from the Gulf of Uraba to Humboldt Bay. Studies show that this would be by far the most logical route from the tonnage point of view because this sea-level canal could handle approximately 65,000 vessels per year, more than double the absolute maximum of the present canal. Its cost would be $2.1

billion by nuclear excavation. Which alternative the United States--or some other nation or consortium of nations--will take is not clear and has not really been discussed at any length. The attention of the nation has been focused instead on the more immediate problems of maintaining the present canal until--of if ever--a new alternate route is opened and of continued American ownership of the Canal.

In the last thirty years there has been increasing pressure building up in Panama against American presence and ownership of the canal across Panamanian territory. Numerous changes have been made in the relationship between the two countries since the Hay-Bunau-Varilla Treaty of 1903 concerning the Canal, and annuities to Panama have been increased considerably. However, riots in the Canal Zone between 1958 and 1964 put greater pressure on the governments to adjust the situation, and talks began in 1964 to remove the causes of conflict over the Canal and the Canal Zone. These resulted in a treaty that included the element of increased Panamanian sovereignty over the Canal Zone. The new treaty was to run for sixty years, but was rejected both by the Congressional Committee on Merchant Marine and Fisheries and by Panama in 1967. Talks resumed in 1968 and draft treaties recognizing Panamanian ownership of the Canal and Zone by the year 2000 were signed in 1977.

However, despite Panamanian nationalistic determination to throw the Americans out and reclaim its national asset and an American determination to continue to control the militarily and commercially valuable Canal and the Canal Zone as long as possible, a treaty was agreed to and signed in 1978 which gradually shifts full sovereignty over the Canal and the Canal Zone to Panama by the year 2000. But whether under American control prior to that date or under Panamanian control afterwards, it is clear that the Panama Canal will continue to be vital to the United States and to all the shipping nations of the world until well into the 21st century.

THE GREAT LAKES-ST. LAWRENCE SYSTEM AND THE INLAND WATERWAYS. However events develop in regard to the oceangoing merchant marine--with its problems of the nation's increased dependence on foreign vessels and flags of convenience, its problems in shipbuilding and with maritime unions, its continued and fervid competition from the fleets of other nations including the Soviet Union, and its increasing dependence on the Panama Canal--domestic waterborne commerce will continue to grow and to loom large in any consideration of America's economic future.

Great Lakes' interests look to the future with considerable confidence. By 1974 the Lakes carried 146 million net tons of cargo and accounted for 1,128 billion ton-miles of cargo handled. This was 5.5 percent of the nation's domestic commerce. Between 1975 and 1982 there are fourteen self-unloading bulk carriers being built and due to be placed in service. Eleven of these lakers are 1,000 feet long with a beam of 105 feet, the maximum size allowed by the Poe Lock of 1968 at Sault Ste. Marie. They are designed for speeds of up to twenty miles per hour with a capacity of 59,000 tons of cargo.

These vessels are being built in expectation of new and increased traffic trends on the Lakes. Three-fourths of the iron ore shipped on the Lakes is now dehydrated into taconite pellets which make ideal cargo for the new self-unloaders as they result in a cargo which is uniform in shape and does not freeze. Self-unloaders are also used extensively for the continued high volume of coal, stone, and grain which moves along the Lakes. In recent years, too, more Western low-sulphur coal is being shipped from Lake Superior ports to ports on the lower Lakes in a reversal of the traditional coal traffic patterns on the Lakes. These increased coal shipments have resulted in major loading facilities being placed under construction as waterborne coal traffic is being complemented by long-haul unit trains moving to the coal ports from Western coal fields. The shippers also look to a regular ten-month shipping season to expand their trade networks, leaving only February and March as too cold to permit traffic movement. It is in new developments in ice-breaking and in the use of air bubblers at lock gates to prevent freezing that the shippers put their greatest hopes.

The only area that has not lived up to its early promise has been general cargo movement for overseas delivery. This phase of commerce has actually been declining since 1974. Containerization came to the Lakes in the late 1960's, but after several United States subsidized lines tried and gave up in the container business on the Lakes, almost all foreign container cargo has moved by moderate-sized foreign break-bulk vessels. The basic difficulty has been that the cost-effective modern container vessels are too large for transit through the St. Lawrence Seaway and require more concentration of shipping loads at key regional ports than the Lakes areas have been willing or able to develop. Still, some 95 percent of all the general merchandise moving on the Lakes is non-container, and the movement of heavy-lift, bulky manufactured items from the Lakes ports has been considerable.

A possibility being explored is the greater utilization of barges for Great Lakes foreign trade. These would either be towed down the Mississippi River to the Gulf or out to lower St. Lawrence ports for transshipment on the oceans either by LASH or SEABEE vessels, or by loading the containers from the barges onto giant container vessels at these locations. This freight-handling process is still in its infancy on the Lakes, but developments elsewhere indicate that it may become prominent in future decades unless the St. Lawrence Seaway is enlarged to take modern container vessels of considerable size, especially because railroad and truck overland competition to the developing Eastern ports has been severe, and the Great Lakes water shippers must find an economical way to compete.

The Great Lakes merchant marine has shown considerable rejuvenation since the passage of the Merchant Marine Act of 1970 and the inclusion of Lakes vessels in the benefits of the construction reserve fund. Building of new vessels and lengthening of older vessels are proceeding rapidly. Between 1960 and 1968, no ships were built for Lakes duty, and the average age of the Lakers was forty-five years. Between 1968 and 1974, twenty-three ships (twenty-one bulkers and two tankers) had either been built or had been contracted for. All are of the most modern designs available. This construction is a tangible sign of a renewed life on the Lakes based on increasing bulk traffic to meet the nation's industrial needs and the latest ships and handling methods to assure even greater economies in the movement of the crucial Lakes cargoes.

Equally successful in bulk operations and expecting to see a continued growth of this trade rather than in general cargoes has been the St. Lawrence Seaway. Tonnages on the waterway from its opening to traffic in 1959 climbed to almost 50 million tons by 1966 and then leveled off. Most of this tonnage is in grain, iron ore, and various tanker products. A full 85 percent of it is carried on Canadian flag vessels moving from the Eastern Canadian frontier into the industrial mid-continent. The physical capacity of the Seaway is approximately 70 million tons, so the waterway is not working to capacity at 50 million tons per year, although normal economic growth should push it to its limit by the end of the century.

The problems associated with increased use of the Seaway, other than a lack of full utilization because of railroad competition for freight cargoes between the Midwest and the East Coast, lie in the size of the present locks and in the time required to move vessels through the lockage facilities. Accordingly, studies have been done to determine the feasibility of a canal and lock system north and east of Niagara Falls in New York State as an alternative to the Welland Canal because a "permanent jam-up" has been predicted at the Canadian waterway by 1990. The all-American canal, approximately thirty miles long, would run from Buffalo north around Grand Island and then overland to Lake Ontario. It would be 600 feet wide to permit two-way passage and would have a draft of thirty feet. Four giant locks of eighty-foot lift would be built; each would be 1,200 feet by 110 feet in dimension and thus could take the larger lakers as well as oceangoing vessels of moderate draft. The cost for the new canal would approach $2.3 billion dollars.

Another suggested improvement on the Seaway is double-locking all the existing Seaway locks for greater vessel transit through the system. The second locks to be built alongside the existing 730-foot locks would be 1,200 feet by 110 feet in dimension to accommodate modern vessels. These dimensions, incidentally, were suggested in the 1950's as being necessary to the future commerce of the Seaway and were rejected as unrealistic. Canada is currently investigating the possibility of doubling the locks on the Welland Canal and improving the whole system by installing two sets of 1,220-foot tandem locks of 180-foot lift each to replace the seven existing locks which are at the St. Lawrence dimension of 730 feet.

It seems clear that if the St. Lawrence is to grow and function, especially in the increased movement of bulk goods by giant freighters, and if its growth in container traffic is to be achieved by making the channel usable by larger container vessels (which will surely dominate international transoceanic freight movement in the future), improvements in the St. Lawrence Seaway will have to be considered by both Canada and the United States for the continued economic health of the continent's heartland.

If real and potential traffic growth on the Great Lakes and on the St. Lawrence calls for continued work to upgrade the systems to make it possible for them to serve the nation adequately in the decades to come, the inland waterway system also demands continued improvement and encouragement because of its growing bulk carriage of goods at the lowest freight-revenue rates possible in domestic transportation. In 1914 the inland waterways carried 599 million net tons of freight for 15.1 percent of total freight carriage in domestic commerce. This amounted to 247 billion ton-miles or 12.8 percent of total ton-miles. In comparison, rails carried 44.1 percent of the aggregate ton-miles, trucks carried 11.3 percent, and pipelines 26.2 percent. Only pipelines have a freight rate per ton-miles comparable to that of water transportation. Moderate projections of freight traffic patterns indicate the waterways will carry 447 billion ton-miles by 1980, and 900 billion ton-miles by the year 2000, each figure representing 17 percent of intercity freight movement.

In revenues gained by carriers under federal regulation, water carriers claim only approximately 1.5 percent of revenues, whereas rails claim 41.3 percent, trucks tally 50.7 percent, and pipelines take 2.5 percent of total revenues. Consequently, the inland waterways carry approximately 15 percent of all net tonnage and 12.8 percent of the cargo ton-miles for less than 2 percent of the revenues expanded for domestic carriage--mute testimony to the lower waterways rate of only three mills per ton-mile and an important argument for continued improvement of the inland waterways system.

Water cost is always less than half that of any other means of domestic transportation of goods with the exception of pipelines. Waterways transit, furthermore, forces savings on the railroads by its competitive position. The result is a savings for shippers and consumers. For example, rail rates on grain to Atlantic, Pacific, and Gulf ports are determined by barge rates for grain to New Orleans. A curtailment of the vital work by the Corps of Engineers of upgrading the Mississippi River system in particular and also forcing waterways operators to pay tolls for lockage are, nevertheless, being seriously considered by Congress. Either move could only mean more bulk freight business for the less efficient and more costly railroads and could only result in higher carriage rates on bulk goods, along the river channels and also throughout the nation, with water competition curtailed.

Unless strangled by federal policy, the inland waterways should continue to expand in the years to come. Particularly helpful would be the development of a deepwater port in the Gulf region; existence of such a port would lead to expansion of bulk imports and exports such as grain, ore, coal, and petroleum products. Access to the interior for these products can easily be assured by an already-functioning barge system, which will bring the efficiencies of this type of bulk transportation into the interior of the country. LASH and SEABEE barge-carriers will be complemented by the barge system, which will bring their cargoes to them from deep in the interior and, in turn, will deliver their incoming car-

goes in the same way. LASH lighters, squared in shape and loading as
much as 400 tons, and SEABEE barges, which can be fitted easily into a
typical Mississippi River tow, are becoming common on the inland waters.
Approximately 4,000 LASH and SEABEE barges are in operation or on order
for Mississippi-system service, and about 25 percent of all barges on
the Mississippi-Ohio system are presently of this type.

There is no longer a question as to the ability of the inland waterways to connect the interior of America to the markets of the world in
bulk cargoes, containerized merchandise, and manufactures. The interior
of the United States is being tied economically to the interiors of European and Far Eastern countries through the combination of barges and
LASH and SEABEE vessels and perhaps by container barges from the Great
Lakes. The wave of the future for cargo handling seems to point to continued importance for the inland waterways, the Great Lakes, and the St.
Lawrence Seaway as critical conduits of trade for the United States.
Local bulk traffic and interregional and international cargoes of all
types are increasingly moving to this lower-cost system. But local and
regional myopia and competitors' lobbying efforts could seriously impede
further development of the inland waterways system to the detriment of
the entire country if they are allowed to dominate maritime policy.

THE MERCHANT MARINE AND NATIONAL DEFENSE. The American merchant
marine is clearly of critical importance to the nation's economic health.
Twentieth-century maritime legislation has reflected the vital part the
merchant marine must play in the commercial life of the nation, and the
various programs of subsidy and other aids are a reflection of this concern over its health and continued existence. However, maritime legislation has also been predicated on another need that the oceangoing merchant marine in particular must fulfill for the good of the nation. This
second function of aid to the merchant fleet is its crucial function as
a national defense auxiliary. Stated simply, if United States military
forces are deployed anywhere in the world to carry out operations, there
must be a merchant marine to provide them with logistical support wherever they require it. Only a merchant marine can move the necessary
goods and supplies across the oceans to the point they are needed for
sustained American military operations. The United States did not possess
that capability during the early parts of both World War I and World War
II in this century, a situation that provided not only the impetus for
this justification, but also obvious testimony as to the foolishness of
formulating a maritime policy without adequate consideration of national
defense needs.

Stated another way, airplanes can put land forces virtually anywhere
on the fact of the earth overnight--where they will starve to death at
the end of the pipeline if an adequate merchant marine is not available
to supply them with their continuing operational needs. In the long
Vietnam war, when 95 percent of all war supplies went to that land by sea
and 400 dry-cargo ships had to be pulled out of the Reserve Fleet to keep
the supply lines open, that fact became obvious. Again, 75 percent of
American support to Israel in the short Yom Kippur War of 1973 went by
sea. The movement of goods by sea is vital to national defense efforts;

the merchant marine must always be prepared to play that role.

However, when that much is granted, a strange paradox becomes clear in American maritime policy, and penetrating questions must be asked. If a private merchant marine has to be supported for national defense needs, it would follow that neither cost nor commercial efficiency should be of overriding consideration. In other words, if the United States must have a merchant marine to serve the armed forces adequately in the interest of national survival, should this need not take precedence? And should not any aid given and any conditions demanded of operators who receive the aid reflect this primary goal of maritime legislation? If ships built with subsidies serve commerce but are not able to serve the military, should they even be built with federal funds? What if these commercial vessels are not suitable for defense needs but there are no other ships available in case of overseas operations? Should more, or a different type of, aid be given to assure that commercial ships will serve both commercial and military needs? This question would seem to imply the logical answer, but neither government nor the maritime industry wants to face the logic of conditions now imposed on the merchant marine by time and circumstance. Both government and industry have wanted and have demanded both defense security and commercial efficiency from their merchant marine. Congress in particular has wanted to maintain the merchant marine "on the cheap," with the result that perhaps the oceangoing merchant marine is now attaining neither goal. There are surely problems in its ability to carry out its national defense functions.

The first problems the nation has in regard to its fleet in a national defense role are those of numbers and availability. As we have seen in Chapter XII, according to statistics published by MARAD at the end of 1976, the United States had 543 ships active, of 9.6 million gross tons. Another 296 ships, of 2.9 million gross tons, were inactive, for a total active and inactive fleet of 839 vessels, of 12.5 million gross tons. Within this total were 261 government-owned vessels, including 247 ships in the National Reserve Fleet locations. These reserve vessels averaged thirty years of age, and 71 were candidates for scrapping. The total 839 vessels active and inactive consisted of 61 combination passenger-cargo ships, 342 break-bulk freighters, 18 bulk carriers, 266 tankers, and 152 intermodal vessels. In addition to these, of the estimated total of 678 American-owned or American-controlled vessels of 25.2 million gross tons registered under all foreign flags, 485 are tankers, 84 are freighters, and 109 are bulk and ore carriers. Of these, the United States has approximately 432 ships under effective control under registry with Panama, Liberia, and Honduras. Thus the United States had in 1976 a fleet of 1,271 vessels of various types either under American flag or under agreement to return upon demand of the government as its hypothetical national defense fleet.

However, if bulkers must be removed from consideration because of their general inappropriateness for military cargoes, only 821 vessels are left. These include 61 combinations, 342 freighters, 266 tankers, and 152 intermodals, all clearly of national defense capabilities. Yet if the remaining 234 Reserve Fleet vessels, which are of questionable value considering their age, are prudently not included in these calculations, only 587 vessels remain. Practical considerations of obtaining the effective and speedy return of the 84 flag-of-convenience freighters and the 485 flag-of-convenience tankers make these of questionable reliability in case of national conflict. The nation remains, then, with only 587 vessels of approximately 10.4 million gross tons to serve its national defense needs. This effective national defense fleet includes 9 combination vessels, 153 active and 9 inactive freighters, 224 active and 42 inactive tankers, and 141 active and 9 inactive intermodal vessels. This is hardly sufficient to carry out any type of sustained military operation on foreign soil.

A further problem that concerns military planners regarding their logistical support by the American merchant marine is the composition of the American fleet and its vulnerability. A highly productive fleet of larger vessels with greater tonnage capacity is very vulnerable. During World War II, Germany's submarines were few in number and Allied ships were many, yet for a period of time both North Atlantic and Caribbean shipping were nearly cut off by these submarines. Assuming that a future war might pit the Allies against the Soviet Union, the fact exists that Russia could employ ten times the amount of commerce raiders against only one-tenth the number of American ships. Losses in number would necessarily be high, and a far larger quantity of goods would be lost with each sinking. Also, unlike World War II and its use of comparatively small freighters, today's large intermodal vessels cannot be used effectively if they have to await convoying such as was finally employed in World War II to get the supplies through. They are designed for fast speed and maximum carriage of goods. At the same time, their effectiveness would be seriously curtailed if no terminal unloading facilities were available to them, an item obviously not overlooked by any potential enemy.

It is true that today's ships are faster to avoid submarines, but today's submarines are faster too and have far more sophisticated attack apparatus. Even if smaller and faster convoys were utilized, defense planners are aware that in the event of war there would be few naval ships and few attack submarines available for fast antisubmarine warfare tactics because of the declining relative strength of American naval surface and sub-surface fleets. The larger commercial ships with their greater capacity might indeed be more vulnerable than their World War II counterparts. Their commercial efficiency might be of little aid to them when faced by both submarine menace and the absence of unloading facilities in a foreign port.

Aware that logistical support for the first five to ten days of an operation until facilities could be established would be a considerable problem and could spell the success or failure of a mission, military planners have looked to sea-based unloading sources as the only alternative during this first, critical part of an operation. Experiments have been carried out using heavy-lift helicopters to transfer containers either directly ashore or to amphibious craft. Another concept under consideration is ELF (Merchant Ship Expeditionary Logistic Facility). ELF calls for the use of LASH vessels with pre-existing gantry cranes to be

317

used in support of an operation by the installation of revolving cranes above the gantries. These improved LASH ships would be able to unload their own cargoes and that of other ships to landing craft or directly to shore as the situation demanded. The problem with the concept is that it assumes quiet waters and safe conditions and that the cranes would be built and stored for use when military demands dictated such a move. However, this arrangement does not answer either to the time lost in the adding of cranes, or to the proper storage of the cranes at critical points, for the commercial vessels to which they would be attached might be anywhere in the world and would have to be dispatched to some suitable harbor for conversion. How much time would be lost in such a situation? ELF fails to consider also that less than two dozen American-flag LASH vessels exist, nor the damage done to commercial transportation by the removal of these critical vessels, nor the cost of modification to existing vessels (which will run between $14.5 and $18.6 million per vessel).

Almost all container vessels, unlike LASH and SEABEE ships, cannot unload themselves. Essential containerized supplies might be moved to shore by helicopter, but each ship would still require mobile gantry cranes to bring the containers to the "flight deck;" and container vessels would have to be constructed so that helicopters could land and take off from them. Newer existing container vessels have strengthened decks for support of a gantry or revolving crane; but here again, installation of cranes at time of mobilization assumes that the unloading devices are ready and stockpiled at a convenient location. They are not. Furthermore, installation of gantry cranes on vessels would mean significantly higher costs and approximately a 15 percent loss in cargo space. The cranes would have little use in normal commercial operations. Other problems with the concept of crane-equipped container vessels include that of motion between the ship and the lighter or barge receiving the containers. This kind of transfer could probably be accomplished only in sheltered waters or in a dead calm.

A possible solution to the problem of off-loading of intermodal vessels lies in converting older tankers or ore ships into crane vessels to unload other vessels where shore-based facilities are not available. These could be moved into a field of operations with reasonable dispatch under their own power. Use of large barges for the same purpose would be possible. These could be carried by SEABEE vessels or could be towed to their desired location. Practical as these solutions might seem, to date they exist only as studies; no cranes for containers and no special crane vessels are in existence.

On the positive side, RO/RO vessels with minor modifications could be effectively utilized for the carrying of vehicles, especially in armored and mechanized Army divisions, but it must be borne in mind that the United States has only a handful of these vessels either in service or being built at the present time. SEABEE and LASH vessels, discharging cargo in lighters or barges, have been used successfully in moving military equipment to foreign ports in recent years, including the movement of helicopters to inland locations in Europe and tanks to Greece and Turkey. However, would these lighters and barges be as effective where they could not be put alongside a pier or wharf for unloading using a pre-existing crane? One answer might be to design and stockpile lighters and barges with bow ramps for direct unloading on shore; but where would such lighters and barges be stockpiled for military use and how would they be moved to shore without a sizeable number of tugs or towboats available at the scene? Furthermore, how many of the approximately two dozen existing LASH and SEABEE vessels would be available for foreign military needs when they would also be in critical demand for moving supplies to home industry in support of the war and might well be scattered on the world's oceans at the time they were most needed?

A third general area of difficulty lies in the area of policy and priorities. The United States fleet is limited in size, must meet commercial demands, and must be usable for limited war. Modifications for military use involve a loss of cargo capacity and effectiveness in commercial operations, and such modifications also involve higher construction and operation costs. The situation would seem to demand a modification in CDS and ODS provisions to cover the modifications and their consequent costs to the shipowner and operator. Perhaps formulae for the extra cost or lost revenues from these modifications--which would take into consideration loss of speed, the installation of excess generating capacity, the storage of equipment necessary to the vessel to be prepared to be involved in military operations, the loss of cargo space, and the amount of charter cost if the vessel is requisitioned for military duty-- could be devised and built into MARAD contracts.

Yet this solution assumes that very close coordination would have to exist among military planners, representatives of the shipbuilding and shipping industries, and MARAD. Such coordination is not now taking place, despite its obvious urgency, and no authority exists for any agency to mandate all necessary changes and modifications in shipbuilding and ship operations, such as would be necessary for maintaining an effective maritime defense auxiliary. Such a coordinating authority might also consider the limitations of the National Defense Reserve Fleet, which is being rapidly outmoded; the lack of ships in the Military Sealift Command, which maintains no reserve for wartime service while operating at full capacity in peacetime; and the possibility of replacing the outmoded Reserve Fleet vessels with newer conventional freighters (which are being supplanted by the container revolution on the high seas) because the Reserve Fleet must be constantly upgraded or will fall further into obsolescence as a defense auxiliary. A central maritime authority would also have to consider how much of the commercial fleet could be utilized for defense purposes without strangling the necessary industrial production at home to support military operations of either the United States or its allies.

If America were ever again called upon to become the "arsenal of democracy," the need for ships to transport vital imports of raw materials and energy resources would be just as critical as it was during World War II. In this respect, bulkers, tankers, and LNG's would be critical, especially the flag-of-convenience vessels of this type, but the approximate needs in ships and men must be determined before the fact, not after.

319

The luxury of having months and years to create a wartime merchant fleet, which the United States enjoyed in both World War I and World War II, has vanished. Modern, high-productivity ships suitable for a limited or unlimited war cannot be built in thirty days as in the case of the Liberties and Victories. The necessary shipping capacity for both military and industrial use must be available and be readily adaptable to its proper function. Only if the Army, the Navy, the shipbuilders, the maritime industry, and the government agencies--particularly the Maritime Administration, which controls all civilian shipbuilding--can be brought into effective coordination can an American commercial fleet suitable for both peacetime and wartime needs be created and sustained.

The modern American merchant marine working on the oceans, the Lakes, and the inland waterways systems remains as vital to the continued existence and well-being of the nation as it has ever been. In its wartime functions, as well as in its peacetime functions, its maintenance and improvement cannot be ignored in the 20th century. The future of the United States cannot be built in part on a waterborne transportation base that cannot sustain it economically and militarily in an ever-more-competitive world.

SUGGESTIONS FOR FURTHER READING

Ackley, Richard T. "The Soviet Merchant Fleet," United States Naval Institute Proceedings, 102, 2/876 (February 1976), 27-37.

Atlantic-Pacific Interoceanic Canal Study Commission. Interoceanic Canal Studies, 1970. Washington: Government Printing Office, 1970.

Beazer, William F., Cox, William A., Harvey, Curtis A., and Watkins, Nancy. U.S. Shipbuilding in the 1970's. Lexington, Mass.: D.C. Heath & Co., 1972.

Chase, John D. "U.S. Merchant Marine--For Commerce and Defense," United States Naval Institute Proceedings, 102, 879 (May 1976), 131-45.

Christy, F.T., Jr., et al., eds. The Law of the Seas: Caracas and Beyond. Proceedings of the Ninth Annual Conference of the Law of the Sea Institute, University of Rhode Island. Cambridge, Mass.: Ballinger Publishing Company, 1975.

Kendall, Lane. "A Merchant Marine Auxiliary," United States Naval Institute Proceedings, 100, 5/854 (April 1974), 84-91.

Kiss, Ronald K and Coffman, Eugene L. "Ships of the U.S. Merchant Marine," Naval Engineers Journal, 88, 5 (October 1976), 15-33.

Klette, Immanuel J. From Atlantic to Pacific: A New Interocean Canal. New York and Evanston: Harper and Row, Publishers, 1967.

Lunsford, Everett P., Jr. "Our Merchant Mariners and Their Unions," United States Naval Institute Proceedings, 101, 867 (May 1975), 66-85.

Mayer, Harold M. The Great Lakes: Internal and External Shipping. Contribution No. 125, Center for Great Lakes Studies, The University of Wisconsin-Milwaukee. Milwaukee: University of Wisconsin-Milwaukee, 1975.

Miller, George H. "The New Soviet Maritime Strategy--And the Lack of An Effective U.S. Counter-Strategy," Sea Power, 19, 5 (May 1976), 17-20.

_____ and McLean, Max C. "The U.S. Shipping Emergency of the Seventies," United States Naval Institute Proceedings, 98, 831 (May 1972), 142-57.

Padelford, Norman J. and Gibbs, Stephen R. Maritime Commerce and the Future of the Panama Canal. Cambridge, Md.: Cornell Maritime Press, 1975.

Sansone, Wallace T. "Domestic Shipping and American Maritime Policy,"

United States Naval Institute Proceedings, 100, 855 (May 1974), 162-77.

Saunders, George D. "Land Bridge Comes of Age," United States Naval Institute Proceedings, 99, 12/850 (December 1973), 38-43.

Transportation Institute. Analysis of the Direct Impact of the Merchant Marine on National Security. Washington, D.C.: Transportation Institute, 1976.

U.S. Department of Commerce. Maritime Administration. U.S. Merchant Marine Data Sheet. Washington: Maritime Administration, monthly issue, 1975-76.